MELINA —

DON'T FALL OUT OF
THE SWING WHEN YOU
ARE READING THIS!

DON SNEMECER

THE BLACKHORSE IN VIETNAM

THE BLACKHORSE IN VIETNAM

The 11th Armored Cavalry Regiment in Vietnam
and Cambodia, 1966–1972

DONALD SNEDEKER

CASEMATE
Philadelphia & Oxford

AN AUSA BOOK
Association of the United States Army
2425 Wilson Boulevard, Arlington, Virginia, 22201, USA

Published in the United States of America and Great Britain in 2020 by
CASEMATE PUBLISHERS
1950 Lawrence Road, Havertown, PA 19083, USA
and
The Old Music Hall, 106–108 Cowley Road, Oxford OX4 1JE, UK

Hardback Edition: ISBN 978-1-61200-846-2
Digital Edition: ISBN 978-1-61200-847-9

A CIP record for this book is available from the British Library

Printed and bound in the United States of America

Typeset in India for Casemate Publishing Services. www.casematepublishingservices.com

For a complete list of Casemate titles, please contact:

CASEMATE PUBLISHERS (US)
Telephone (610) 853-9131
Fax (610) 853-9146
Email: casemate@casematepublishers.com
www.casematepublishers.com

CASEMATE PUBLISHERS (UK)
Telephone (01865) 241249
Email: casemate-uk@casematepublishers.co.uk
www.casematepublishers.co.uk

Contents

Foreword

When men and women from across America become members of our armed forces and take an oath to protect and defend our constitution, with their lives should that be necessary, there is an implied and sacred trust that we will be there for them when they come home and that we will be there for the families of our fallen. In fulfillment of that trust, as a nation and as individual Americans, we cannot say or do too much to honor and respect those who serve and especially those who in President Abraham Lincoln's immortal words "gave the last full measure of devotion" and their families who endure the pain of their loss forever.

That trust was fractured during and after the war in Vietnam. Since that time and more recently with the 50-year commemoration of Vietnam service, our national leadership and our people have made large strides to honor those veterans and families and to rebuild that trust incurred so long ago.

If we want to know why that trust is so special and sacred, then we should read histories of what our fellow citizens endured and accomplished. They answered our nation's call, went and did what was asked of them with skill, fierce devotion to one another, extraordinary courage, intense teamwork, and sacrifice. They won battlefield victories equal to any generation in our nation's history. Such performance of duty was characteristic of our Vietnam generation who my friend, historian Dr. Lewis (Bob) Sorley, calls a generation that is "also great."

I was privileged to be one of the over 25,000 of my fellow Americans to serve in Vietnam with the 11th Armored Cavalry Regiment. There have been many accounts written of this distinguished Regiment in Vietnam, distinguished by honors earned by the selfless devotion and skill of those in the ranks in the fierce crucible that is armored land combat—and particularly armored land combat in the close terrain of Southeast Asia. Now is a need for a definitive history.

The best military histories tell those individual stories of that skill, intrepid courage, and devotion to each other of the cavalry troopers and their small unit commissioned and noncommissioned officer leadership. They also set those actions in the broader tactical, operational, military and political strategic contexts, in a factual way, devoid of the usual and tiresome points of view of those who were neither there, nor barely knew anyone who fought there.

Don Snedeker has written such a definitive history of this distinguished 11th Armored Cavalry Regiment in this splendid book, *The Blackhorse in Vietnam.*

Any combat veteran of any war will tell you battles and engagements in that tough crucible of land combat are won on the ground by the skill, teamwork, toughness, leadership and sacrifice of those in the small combat units—the squads, platoons, companies, and troops engaged in direct fire fight with the enemy. Those victories are enabled by those giving supporting fire from the air, indirect fires from mortars and artillery, as well as the efforts of those supplying them and providing them life-saving medical care, often at the risk of their own lives. Their senior commanders, in our case in the squadrons and the Regiment, orchestrate all that so the entire formation is a coordinated all-arms team or, as World War II General George Patton Jr. would call them, "Musicians of Mars." The generals in higher command make sure that the heroism and sacrifice of those they ordered into those direct *contacts* with the enemy, and who gain those victories in that crucible, lead to victory on the battlefield and ultimately at the political level to seal those victories. Those who do that tough fighting, those wounded, and the fallen and their families, trust the senior military and political leadership will make that happen.

In Vietnam in the 11th Armored Cavalry Regiment, the famous Blackhorse, those battle victories were won again and again, from the first actions after the regiment arrived in 1966 to the Regiment's rapid movement and actions in Tet 1968 to Michelin Plantation battles to Montana Raider to the invasion of Cambodia to the last in 1972. In this uniquely organized all-arms cavalry Regiment they were won by the tightly knit combat family in those small units and the supporting team of arms and leaders right to regimental commanders and regimental sergeant majors. I was honored to serve in the ranks of the Second Squadron of the Blackhorse, commanded by Lieutenant Colonel Grail Brookshire, as great a combat leader as I have ever known, and was personal witness to all that in the time I served in 1969–1970, under the great regimental command of Colonel Jimmie Leach and Colonel Donn Starry.

Twenty-one years later during *Desert Storm* in 1991, I was privileged to command VII Corps, 146,000 US and British soldiers, in our 89-hour mounted all-arms armored attack, in the largest tank battle in US Army history that, as part of the multinational coalition, liberated Kuwait. Many of our senior commanders and noncommissioned officers were Blackhorse Vietnam veterans. The lineage of that 1991 battlefield victory runs directly to Vietnam, and to my and their service many years before. There was not a day that I did not remember and think about those I was honored to serve with in the Blackhorse in Vietnam. Those were inspiring and motivating memories, and there were lessons learned about fighting combined arms battles and engagements: about finding the enemy then hitting them with a closed fist of synchronized and all available overwhelming combat power; then about making sure this conflict turned out differently for those soldiers who fought, those who lost their lives or were seriously wounded, and their families than did our earlier experience so many years before.

Some years later I was honored, indeed humbled, to offer a few remarks at the reunion of the 11th Armored Cavalry Veterans of Vietnam and Cambodia, founded and run by those who achieved those small unit victories in the Blackhorse from 1966–1972 and so precisely recorded by that organization's historian Don Snedeker in this book. That organization contacted almost everyone who had served in our valorous Regiment and many were there. I offer parts of those remarks in tribute and honor of those who served in our Regiment in Vietnam, especially the 730 who gave "the last full measure of devotion," and their families who still cherish the memory of their loved ones' lives and sacrifices.

"There was not a day in *Desert Storm* commanding VII Corps that I did not remember Vietnam and the Blackhorse. It was a powerful force. I remembered those lessons of combat to be sure. Many I learned right there in the second squadron. But I remembered more than that. I remembered the names and the faces. I remembered the sacrifice and the pain. I remembered the pride and the intense teamwork. I remembered the tight combat family of the cavalry in the Blackhorse. I remembered Valley Forge Army Hospital and my fellow amputees there. I remembered a generation who went and did what our country asked. Who did their duty and did it with such skill and courage, and at such sacrifice. Who got no thanks. No parades. No days of remembrance. We remembered. The Blackhorse patch earned in combat was on my right shoulder (underneath my chemical overgarment) as it was for my VII Corps chief of staff, three brigade commanders, countless platoon sergeants, and sergeants major. My Corps Command Sergeant Major and I had served together in the Blackhorse in the early 1960s. That memory was a constant force. It was a hot blue flame for me. 'Find the bastards and pile on,' Regimental Commander Colonel George Patton said in Vietnam. We found Saddam Hussein's Iraqi Republican Guards who chose to defend. We piled on with five armored divisions day and night, and our soldiers as part of the global coalition won a great victory and liberated Kuwait.

"I guarantee you I remembered. I remembered small unit NCO leaders from my three tours of duty in the Blackhorse one in Vietnam, two in Germany in the Cold War: Ponds, Humber, Lyerly, Means, Vinson, Huff, Hayes, Pfannenstein, Chittick, Hawthorne, Bolan, Johnson, Easter, Krivek, Christian, Jones, Burkett, Lindberg, McVey, Williams, Cotton, Hutton, Alston. I remembered my troop commander from the early 1960s in 3rd Squadron in the Blackhorse in Germany, Captain Jim Moore, killed in action in Vietnam. I remembered there were sons and daughters of Vietnam and Blackhorse veterans in VII Corps. I remembered Fire Support Bases with names of Marge, Ruth, Eunice, Deb, and Ft Defiance on Hill 95 in War Zone C. I remembered combat around An Loc, Loc Ninh, Bu Dop, War Zone C, and Snoul, Cambodia; the red clay dirt, the rubber plantations, the triple canopy jungle, the battles day after day. I remembered Valley Forge Hospital. Every time I strapped on my leg I remembered. I remembered Germany and OP Alpha, Fulda, alerts in early morning darkness, Rotz border camp, Grafenwohr, Hohenfels. It was all there. I could not forget. I would not forget. It inspired all of us. It drove me and my sense of duty and my sense of what we had and what we owed all of you.

"The lineage of that victory was long and stretched from your courage on the battlefields of Vietnam and Cambodia to the rebuilding of our army in the 70s and 80s to the readiness and sharp-edged vigilance of the Border Legions to the desert sands of Iraq and Kuwait. This one was different because of that connection. That was for sure.

"I was often asked after *Desert Storm* to compare the Vietnam soldiers with the *Desert Storm* soldiers. I never did that. The reason was simple. They are the same. I said the generation of soldiers who I was privileged to serve with in Vietnam in the Blackhorse went and did what our nation asked with great skill and courage and at great sacrifice. The generation who fought in the sands of Iraq and Kuwait did the same.

"After the parade following *Desert Storm*, held in Washington, DC in June 1991, there was one place my wife Denise and I wanted to go. The quiet place. The Vietnam Veterans Memorial. The names of friends, relatives, fellow soldiers; gone but never forgotten, never far away. This one was for you, too. The silence there. Yes, the memories of heroes who went and did what our country asked. Who served with pride, sacrifice, and great courage and who forever should be proud of answering our nation's call so well."

Our heroes are all around us in our Veteran community who answered our nation's call and to whom we owe that bond of trust when they come home. Many of my own heroes are in this Blackhorse family whose history and intrepid courage and sacrifice are told so well in this splendid book, *The Blackhorse in Vietnam*.

Frederick M. Franks Jr.
General US Army (retired)

Introduction

Private Jack Wachtel joined the 11th Cavalry—already at that time known Army-wide as the Blackhorse Regiment—at Camp L.J. Hearn, California in 1929, located just 12 miles outside San Diego and near the border with Mexico. Forty years later, almost to the minute from the time of his original enlistment, Jack reported back into the Blackhorse—this time as a guest of the Regimental Commander, Colonel George Patton, and Regimental Sergeant Major, Paul Squires. This time the Regiment was located at Blackhorse Base Camp in South Vietnam.

Trooper Jack[1] compared the actions of the Regiment on the day in early 1969 when he visited—"a day of heavy engagement in widely scattered locations"—to what the first sergeant had him and two other new recruits doing in the Mexican border heat. "It was a far cry from the routine of 1929 Platoon drill, horse exercise, and stable fatigue … and a trooper's main concern was how much of his $21 pay he'd draw at the end of the month after satisfying his several creditors."

Briefings and equipment orientation filled trooper Jack's day with the Regiment in 1969, rather than mounted drill and mucking the stable. He met and talked with a number of the new troopers, including the newest recruit in Bravo Troop,[2] Private First Class Ronald Robertson, who told Jack: "The 11th is home for me now. My buddy from Fort Knox is sitting over on the next tank and we like this service. We're going to stay with it." Clearly trooper Jack understood what he meant; he had felt the same way four decades earlier.

At the end of the day, trooper Jack thought back on what he had seen and learned and decided that he still recognized *his* Regiment.

> You enlist in a regiment of cavalry—some 690 horses and men, a few mules and maybe a half dozen of these newfangled motor trucks … You come back to it three wars and forty years later and what do you find? Nearly 5,000 officers and men, a thousand vehicles of all types and 50 command and combat helicopters …
>
> Viewed from a distance of 40 years, morale in the 11th Cavalry is as high as it ever was. Weapons and means of movement have changed but the spirit of the men is the same, and the principle of closing with the enemy and destroying him—"Find the bastards, then pile on"[3]—continues as a basic military precept. And one more thing hasn't changed. The heat and dust of the Mexican border, 1929, has its exact counterpart in Chau Thanh province north and east of Saigon, 1969.

When the 11th Armored Cavalry Regiment came ashore at Vung Tau, South Vietnam, in September 1966, it faced a number of challenges. The enemy—Viet Cong (VC) and North Vietnamese Army (NVA)—was, of course, the most critical challenge. But the terrain and weather were also factors that could adversely affect the employment of both armored vehicles and helicopters alike. The dearth of doctrine and tactics for the employment of armored cavalry in a counterinsurgency was equally challenging—especially during the pre-deployment training and initial combat operations.

But just as importantly, there was an institutional bias within the Army that an insurgency was an *infantryman's* war, that there was no role for armor—except maybe to protect fire bases and convoys.

The Army's skepticism was clear in a statement published within two weeks of the Regiment's arrival in country. The Associated Press reported: "Pentagon sources reported Tuesday [20 September] the number of US tanks in the war theater has grown to 450 and may grow higher pending performance studies. However, they foresee no classic armored operations involving formations of tanks advancing through jungled areas that abound in the country." A high-ranking but unnamed officer was quoted in the same article as saying: "Hunting Viet Cong with tanks is like chasing a fox with a tractor."

This notion was based in part on the less than stellar record of French armored forces in the first Indo-China War. Many military professionals had read Bernard Fall's accounts of the death of *Groupe Mobile 100* in the Central Highlands in 1954, coming away convinced that there was no place for armor in Vietnam. Period.

Arguments that antiquated equipment and poor tactics contributed to this fail-ure did not persuade the non-believers.[4] The British achieved remarkable success against Malaysian Communist guerrillas (1948–60) without any armor, so why did we need tanks against Vietnamese Communist guerrillas? The success of South Vietnam's Army of the Republic of Vietnam (ARVN) armored cavalry units con-ducting convoy security and rapid reaction missions country-wide notwithstanding, the Army leadership remained obstinately convinced that armor was not suitable for operations in Vietnam.

One of the most important things that the infantry leaders failed to recognize was, as George Patton said to a reporter from the *New York Times* in 1968, "Armor just doesn't mean steel and tanks … Armor is a way of thinking …"

Despite enemy mines and rocket-propelled grenades (RPGs), despite the thick jungle and monsoonal rains, despite the lack of doctrinal guidance, and despite the best efforts of the "Infantry Mafia" that ran the Army in the 1960s, Blackhorse leaders found a way to overcome the obstacles and accomplish the mission.

Prior to the arrival of the Regiment in Vietnam, there were just four armor, armored cavalry, or air cavalry battalion-sized units in country.[5] By the end of 1967, that number had tripled. With the Regiment's arrival, the total number of tanks and armored personnel carriers (APCs) in South Vietnam was raised to 450 (including 150 belonging to the Marine Corps) and 600 respectively. Over a third of them belonged to the Blackhorse Regiment.

The mission initially assigned to the 11th Cavalry was to clear the major lines of communication—Highways 1, 2, and 20—in Long Khanh Province east of Saigon so that military and civilian traffic could use them on a routine basis. The mission was based on the premise that the armored vehicles would be primarily road bound.

The Blackhorse leadership understood that this mission could not be accomplished simply by driving up and down the roads; to do so would leave the initiative of when and where to attack wholly in the hands of the enemy. Getting off the roads to find VC base camps and to disrupt ambush preparations was one key to success. Implicitly, Colonel Bill Cobb (the regimental commander) and his fellow armor officers also understood that the 11th Cavalry needed to demonstrate its ability to fight in any terrain and under any conditions. Only in this manner were the infantrymen running the war likely to accept that armored vehicles could contribute to battlefield victories.

Within a year of their arrival in Vietnam, Blackhorse troopers overcame ambushes that featured volleys of anti-tank weapons (recoilless rifles and RPGs), multitudes of mines, and coordinated assaults by reinforced enemy regiments against troop-sized positions. They defeated an entire enemy division (VC 5th Division) twice their size. Most importantly, the 11th Cavalry successfully demonstrated the ability to operate on and *off* the roads, in the jungle, and during both the wet and dry seasons.

By the spring of 1967, Army leaders were beginning to realize the value of armored forces in Vietnam. With the Blackhorse Regiment leading the way, armor was considered an essential part of the combat team. Army Chief of Staff General Harold Johnson, long a proponent for the use of armor in South Vietnam, told the Senate Appropriations and Armed Services subcommittees: "… tanks have been used in the area northwest of Saigon very successfully. The 11th Armd Cav Regt that went out in late summer … operated east and southeast of Saigon very successfully with a combination of tanks and armored personnel carriers."

The Regiment's first year in country had been used to sharpen combat skills, to gain experience fighting the enemy, to get acquainted with the terrain and weather, and to establish a foundation for expanding the missions and contributions that Blackhorse troopers could accomplish.

Both the 1st Squadron, 4th Cavalry (1st Infantry Division) and 3rd Squadron, 4th Cavalry (25th Infantry Division) were deployed well before the 11th Cavalry was.[6] They did yeoman service in establishing the credibility of armored forces in Vietnam. They were the first and deserve tremendous credit for setting the standard for all who followed. Through trial and error, they developed "new techniques" (such as the herringbone formation in reaction to ambushes) that served as *de facto* doctrine in lieu of waiting for the Armor Center to publish new field manuals.

There was no other unit in country, however, that had the capabilities of an armored cavalry regiment. Also, the modified M113 armored personnel carrier—transformed with the addition of more weapons and armored protection into an armored cavalry assault vehicle (ACAV) by the 11th Cavalry during its pre-deployment training—was unique to the Blackhorse. So, in many respects, the Regiment was on its own.

The Regiment used the time between February 1966 and February 1968 to develop the tactics and doctrine that would make it one of the most effective units in Vietnam. Tactics and techniques developed during the late 1966 ambushes (21 November and 2 December), the two mid-1967 ambushes (21 May and 21 July), the battle for Slope 30 (19 June 67), and the pacification of Long Khanh Province, long an uncontested VC safe area, honed the combined-arms team into an incredible fighting machine.

Beginning in 1968, *Find the bastards, and pile on!* was the Regiment's motto and the tactic was a wholly Blackhorse design. It meant sending ground and aerial scouts out to locate enemy forces and, once found, to reinforce with as many additional forces (ground and air) and firepower (artillery, gunships and bombers) as quickly as possible.

It wasn't until after Tet '68 that the Regiment could begin to employ—with devastating effectiveness—the tactics of "find the bastards and pile on." It was only at this point that the Blackhorse wrested the initiative from the enemy on a wide scale, leaving security of the base camps more and more frequently to less mobile forces. It was only at this point—midway through the Vietnam War and a full year and a half after the Regiment arrived in-country—that General Abrams and his staff gave the green light to Colonels Patton, Starry, Leach, Gerrity, and Nutting, allowing—no, *enabling*—the Blackhorse to work its magic. Working in tandem with (rather than in support of) the 1st and 25th Infantry Divisions and especially the 1st Cavalry Division, the Regiment moved north to and eventually across the Cambodian border, finding the "bastards," piling on and sending them packing—minus large numbers of their comrades, tons of rice, hundreds of weapons and, most importantly of all, the battlefield initiative.

In the early months after its arrival, the 11th Cavalry was not called upon to react to contacts by other units, which is what many had expected and wanted—a chance to demonstrate the Blackhorse's mobility, firepower, and shock effect. Major Warner Stanley (the regimental personnel officer) remembers a time in mid-May 1967 when the 199th Light Infantry Brigade had a pretty substantial contact near the Vietnamese Armor School. The Regiment's 1st Squadron was at Lai Khe, preparing for an operation with the 1st Infantry Division, and 3rd Squadron was at the base camp south of Xuan Loc conducting local security operations. In other words, hundreds of ACAVs, tanks, and self-propelled artillery pieces were close by, available to swoop down on the enemy force responsible for overrunning an ARVN outpost.

The call never came. Maybe because the leadership didn't want a repeat of *Groupe Mobile 100* in the Mang Yang Pass. Or maybe it was something else.

Stanley continues: "We weren't called in. I can recall all day long the Regiment sitting there waiting to go … But because of the management of AOs [areas of operation] almost as baronial fiefdoms at times, the Regiment was not committed as a mobile reaction force." Heaven forbid that an infantry commander should admit that he couldn't handle a few VC by himself. The combined US-South Vietnamese airmobile infantry assault and pursuit over two days accounted for a mere dozen enemy dead. They simply weren't fast or powerful enough to catch and destroy the enemy.

What the senior commanders and staff officers failed to realize was that the combination of ACAVs, tanks, artillery, engineers, and helicopters found in the Blackhorse Regiment could quickly move, shoot, and communicate anywhere they were sent and accomplish a wide variety of missions against the best fighters the VC and NVA could field.

Regardless of when or where the enemy struck, Blackhorse troopers had the armor protection to survive the initial assault, the weapons to quickly achieve fire superiority and the three-dimensional mobility to fix the enemy in place and destroy him. All of these capabilities were under the single command and control of the regimental commander; he didn't have to go to anyone else to receive immediate support. It was these capabilities that made the 11th Cavalry *the* most effective unit in the counterinsurgency war.

The enemy recognized it—even before some in the US chain of command. An NVA lieutenant was captured by the Regiment in early 1969. After several long debriefing sessions, the lieutenant requested permission to ask a question. Pointing to the subdued Blackhorse patch on his interrogator's shoulder, the NVA officer asked if that was the same as the red and white patch painted on the dreaded helicopters that had made his life so miserable.

The lieutenant described what happened on the day he was captured: "The men in the tanks just kept coming, they weren't afraid of anything; they killed most of the men in my company." The NVA lieutenant went on to say that this was not just his opinion. He had heard from comrades that the Blackhorse was the "fiercest" unit in the whole Army.

Service in the Blackhorse Regiment in Vietnam and Cambodia influenced 20,000-plus young American men (and their families) in a mostly positive way. The Vietnam War—and the social upheaval that occurred along with it—changed the course of American history and impacted a generation of Americans. The "Sixties" (1964–1974) are inexorably linked with the Vietnam War; those who served in the 11th Cavalry in combat in the middle of this decade are forever connected with those events and with each other. They came home from the war, hid their uniforms and memories away, and got on with their lives.

Due to space limitations, not every battle fought by Blackhorse troopers between September 1966 and March 1972 is recounted in the following narrative. Although they are not specifically identified in every case, almost every platoon-level fight included a medic and a mechanic. Recovery specialists, cooks, and other "non-combatant" troopers were found in almost every night defensive position. Squadron fire bases under mortar and rocket fire invariably included clerk-typists, truck drivers, chaplain's assistants, and even a mailman.

So, yes, they too were there. And although they may not be mentioned by name, they too earned citations for bravery and Purple Hearts. Their combined efforts earned the troops, companies, batteries, and squadrons the Valorous and Presidential Unit Citations and the Vietnamese Crosses of Gallantry. They too are Blackhorse troopers.

In his Organizational Day message to the troopers of the Blackhorse Regiment in 1967, Colonel Bill Cobb put their efforts in context: "The Regiment's travels," he said,

> ... have been many and varied. Ranging from the jungles and mountains of the Philippines, the parched plains of northern Mexico, the rivers and forests of Europe during World War II, the hills of the Iron Curtain country during the Cold War to the jungles and savannahs of South Vietnam where we fight today so that a young country can build a democracy for the future. On this auspicious day we should not only take time to reflect on the Regiment's past deeds and await with eager anticipation for its future successes but consider our many brothers-in-arms who have given their lives for the ideals [for] which our country stands. Let us all in our own way pay homage to those gallant men and what they stood for.

Thirty-four years later, Tom White passed a similar message on to the Blackhorse troopers. At the time, he was serving as the 18th Secretary of the Army. He had many responsibilities in this position but, when asked, he made time to help commemorate the centennial of the founding of the 11th United States Cavalry Regiment—1901 to 2001. In his speech to the assembled troopers—both active and veterans—and their families, he quoted the famous line from Shakespeare's *The Life of King Henry V* about "we few, we happy few, we Band of Brothers." Tom was remembering his own experience as a platoon leader in 1969–70:

> Inspired by those simple yet powerful words, King Henry's men went on to win that famous battle, just as the Blackhorse have shed blood together for 100 years as a "Band of Brothers," a happy few, unique among our fellow citizens, prevailing in battle after battle in the dust, dark, rain, and mud of faraway places—noble by our sacrifice, magnificent by our performance, and respected by all.

It is these gallant men, this Band of over 25,000 Blackhorse troopers, to whom this history is dedicated.

Preparing for War: Southeast Germany to Southeast United States to Southeast Asia, 1964 to 1966

There is no field manual for the type of combat we may encounter in the near future ... Nobody at Fort Knox is busily writing those doctrines of employment. They must be developed here and each of us will participate in their formulation.

BILL COBB, COMMANDER, 11TH CAVALRY, 1966–67

In the Fall of 1965, I was drafted into the U.S. Army. This was not how I'd planned to spend the next two years but my Dad, Brother, Uncles and cousins had served in the military, so I felt it was the honorable thing to do.

BILL LEWELLEN, JR., KILO TROOP, 3/11 ACR

What did I know? I thought the cavalry was John Wayne, the Lone Ranger and the Old West. I soon found out what armored cav was really all about ...

LARRY HAWORTH, HEADQUARTERS AND HEADQUARTERS TROOP, 3/11 ACR

The intelligence report came in to the regimental headquarters in the afternoon. Local security forces had engaged a group of about 200 insurgents near a village 15 miles to the south. The staff reported the news to the commander, who ordered the formation of a task force for the mission. Six troops were available; they were reinforced by some heavy weapons and a supply train. The troopers were told to make sure they had enough rations for three days. The regimental commander directed one of his reliable majors—Robert Howze—to assume command of the provisional squadron. His mission was to find and attack the insurgents.

The Cavalrymen used the cover of darkness to move south toward where the enemy had last been seen. It was, one of the troopers remembered later, an unusually dark night. Their map reading skills were good though and they arrived at the village around midnight. The local security forces told Major Howze that they had fought "desperately" all day long—not counting the hour-long break both sides took for luncheon. Both sides had retired from the battlefield at nightfall. There were no apparent casualties on either side. The insurgents had returned to their base camp an unknown distance from the village. The local security forces were in for the night; they weren't going anywhere after dark.

The major asked the allies for guides but they refused. The combination of imbibing the locally-produced "joy juice" and distaste for further action made them unwilling to help. There were, however, a couple of the villagers who knew the way to the insurgents' base camp and volunteered to act as guides. All this took time, so they didn't leave the village until three hours later. They rode hard and arrived at the outer edge of the enemy base camp right at dawn.

Before leaving the village, Major Howze gave his orders to the troop commanders. In accordance with standard operating procedure (SOP), the approach would be in a column. The lead troop would form the center of the attack formation. On order, the follow-on troops would peel off alternately to the right and left and come on line for the attack.

Arriving at dawn, the lead troop penetrated into the heart of the enemy's base camp, while the other troops maneuvered left and right. A lieutenant who was there said that "the rapid deployment of the troops from column made a very pretty sight." A small number of the insurgents remained to defend the camp, pouring heavy but inaccurate fire at the troopers as they charged. The remaining enemy took off to the southwest with five troops of cavalry in hot pursuit. One troop remained behind to clear the base camp.

They chased the bad guys for several miles then rallied back to Major Howze at the base camp. Some of the insurgents escaped by melting into the local population; the rest scattered into the surrounding landscape. The action was over two hours after it began.

Troopers found a small cache of weapons in the few structures inside the camp. They also found a lieutenant and four soldiers from the local security force who had been captured the previous day. The insurgents were about to execute them when the cavalry barged in. One of the freed prisoners volunteered to execute the captured insurgents if someone would only lend him a weapon; the offer was declined.

There were no friendly casualties; 44 of the insurgents died on the battlefield. It was, in the words of one of the lead scouts, a "Damfine fight."[1]

The Philippines in 1902? Cuba in 1907? Vietnam in 1968? Iraq in 2004?

No—Ojos Azules, Mexico, 5 May 1916, during Black Jack Pershing's punitive expedition to hunt down Pancho Villa.[2]

This is the heritage of the 11th United States Cavalry.

Transitioning from Cold War to Hot War: Mid-1960s

Under President John Kennedy in 1960, the Pentagon initiated a major review of the national security strategy of the United States and ultimately came up with "Flexible Response," a graduated series of responses that reflected the lessons learned during the Cold War. Nuclear retaliation remained at the heart of the Nation's military power but flexible response recognized that even tactical nuclear weapons were an unlikely course of action in cases such as the emerging Communist-sponsored wars of national liberation. There had to be other levels of military and non-military response for lower-level threats.

The US Army's contribution to implementing this strategy involved increased emphasis on special operations forces and airmobility. At Fort Knox, the "Home of Armor," while war planning focused on conventional warfare, the assistant commandant commissioned a study on armor's possible contributions to flexible response below the conventional warfare threshold. Brigadier General Frederick Boye, Jr., had just returned from a tour with the Military Assistance Advisory Group (MAAG) in Vietnam and understood the need to get ahead of the coming storm. He was a member of the so-called Howze Board (1962) that set the groundwork for the development of airmobility.[3] He wanted to ensure there was a role for armor and cavalry in the coming transformation of the force. The resulting study, published in 1962, had the propitious title: "The Role of Armored Cavalry in Counterinsurgency Operations."[4]

This study was ground-breaking, but initially attracted little attention. It addressed doctrinal, organizational, and equipment issues, making insightful recommendations in each area. The study debunked the myth that armor had no role to play in counterinsurgency operations, stating explicitly that armored cavalry could—and should—be employed in counterinsurgency operations, such as the ongoing fight in Southeast Asia. The study concluded that the French experience in Indochina was not a valid guide to the employment of armored forces in future conflicts—due primarily to improvements in equipment and employment concepts. But to make a contribution, then-current armored cavalry units needed to be reorganized.

Specifically, the study suggested that the aviation company (organized and equipped for command and control and liaison) of the armored cavalry regiment be replaced by an air cavalry troop (organized and equipped for reconnaissance and security). The light wheeled vehicles (1/4-ton jeeps) in the reconnaissance troops (ideal for border patrols along the Iron Curtain in Germany) also needed to be upgraded to armor-protected, tracked vehicles with plenty of firepower.

In the fall of 1963, as part of a drive to cut the defense budget by at least two percent, the Pentagon focused on Europe, particularly the forces sent to West Germany as a result of the 1961 Berlin crisis. The 3rd Armored Cavalry Regiment (Brave Rifles) was regarded as the prime candidate for redeployment back to Fort Meade, where it had been stationed prior to the crisis. But the Bonn government objected, believing that it was the wrong signal to send to Moscow at the time. So, the redeployment plans were delayed for six months. By the time the decision was implemented the following spring, the 11th Armored Cavalry Regiment (Blackhorse) was selected to be stationed at Fort Meade, not the 3rd. In other circumstances, the Brave Rifles Regiment would have been the one deployed to Vietnam two years later, not the Blackhorse Regiment.

Consequently, in the summer of 1964, about 2,800 11th Cavalry troopers and their families boarded ships in Bremerhaven, Germany and steamed for Baltimore, Maryland. Many of the troopers were near the end of their enlistments, so the Regiment's strength quickly dwindled to less than 2,000. Over the next 18 months, the 11th Cavalry's numbers continued to dwindle. Personnel levies came in for higher priority units located overseas. Worst of all, a substantial number of experienced non-commissioned officers (NCOs) were needed elsewhere to train the influx of new recruits resulting from increased draft calls for the growing war in Vietnam. By the end of the year, almost everyone was a replacement and new to the Regiment.

The Blackhorse was under the command of Colonel Don Boyer when it moved from Germany in 1964. Boyer was the real thing—a hero of the battle of the Bulge who had spent four months in a prisoner of war camp in Germany. It was under his guidance that the initial build-up for Vietnam began. In October 1965, Boyer turned the 11th Cavalry over to Colonel Bill Cobb, the man who would forge the Blackhorse Regiment into a battle stallion of unequaled stature.

In the spring of 1965, General William Westmoreland requested a substantial increase in US forces in South Vietnam, in line with his plan to escalate the conflict from scattered firefights with Viet Cong (VC) guerrilla bands to prolonged campaigns against conventional North Vietnamese Army (NVA) force units. The Military Assistance Command Vietnam (MACV) request included an armored cavalry regiment (ACR) "for route security for National Route 1, with base at Xuan Loc" as part of the 1966 buildup.

Almost immediately, MACV started to backtrack, eventually expressing a preference for a mechanized infantry brigade over an armored cavalry regiment. In a leap of logic that does not appear to be supported by any Army doctrine or in-country lessons learned, the MACV history concludes that "mechanized infantry units, by reason of equipment and training, were better suited than the ACR then programmed for the mission of LOC [Lines of Communications] security."

Lieutenant Colonel Ray Battreall was the most senior armor officer in Vietnam in 1965–66. He remembers that he was called to MACV headquarters one day early in 1966. He was then serving as the senior advisor to the South Vietnamese Armor Command and Westy's staff wanted to hear his opinion on an ongoing force development issue that involved armor.

> I was … asked if tanks could operate in the III Corps area surrounding Saigon. I said they could and was then advised that we were considering bringing either another mechanized brigade … or an Armored Cavalry Regiment to Viet Nam. GEN [General] Westmoreland's deputy, Lt. Gen. Heintges, favored the mech brigade, but I was able to persuade … Maj Gen DePuy [MACV's operations officer], that he would get more bang for the buck from the ACR … I also suggested removing the tanks from the Reconnaissance troops while retaining them in each squadron's tank company.

Back in the Pentagon, the Army Chief of Staff (General Harold Johnson) directed his staff to compare the capabilities of the two unit types and to make a recommendation.

Lieutenant Colonel George Patton (later to command the Regiment) was assigned as the study lead. His conclusions are not surprising. The staff study favored the armored cavalry regiment over a mechanized infantry brigade due to a higher density of automatic weapons (771 versus 662), decentralized artillery organizations (the three organic self-propelled howitzer batteries) and the availability of tanks (the three organic tank companies). Most importantly, an armored cavalry regiment was organized and trained to do the mission laid out by MACV.

The record does not show what convinced Harold Johnson to agree with this recommendation but he did, overruling Westmoreland. Westy reluctantly agreed but only if the tanks were withdrawn from the recon platoons. The stage was set for the Blackhorse Regiment to go to war.

Organization for War: December 1965 to September 1966

Before proceeding, a brief discussion of the organization and capabilities of the 11th Armored Cavalry Regiment is in order. The following describes the Regiment "on an average day" because the organization was modified on almost a continual basis between 1965 (when the 11th Cavalry began to ramp up for war) and 1972 (when it came home). This snapshot captures the major elements of the Regiment, along with the units that were habitually attached or under the operational control of the regimental commander (Blackhorse 6).[5]

From the mid-1960s to mid-1970s, the 11th Cavalry consisted of three squadrons (1st Squadron or 1/11, 2nd Squadron or 2/11, and 3rd Squadron or 3/11), a headquarters and headquarters troop and an air cavalry troop. Each squadron was organized similarly, with a headquarters and headquarters troop, three reconnaissance (recon) troops, a tank company, and a howitzer battery. Each of the three squadrons averaged about 50 officers, 6 warrant officers, and 1,100 enlisted men between 1966 and 1972. Thus, the 11th Armored Cavalry Regiment totaled about 3,600 officers, warrant officers, and enlisted.

These numbers only reflect the *assigned* elements of the Blackhorse, however. Seven other units deployed with the 11th Cavalry in 1966 and remained *attached* until 1971. These included (in numerical order): the Air Force's 11th Tactical Air Control Party (TACP), 17th Public Information Detachment (PID), 28th Military History Detachment (MHD), 37th Medical Company, 409th Radio Research Detachment (RRD), 541st Military Intelligence Detachment (MID), and 919th Engineer Company (Armored). Numerous other units were temporarily attached or placed under the operational control of the Regiment, providing invaluable combat and combat service support over the years. When combined, these units brought the strength of the Blackhorse to over 4,500 men.

It was the 11th Cavalry's ability to move, shoot, and communicate under one commander that made it such a unique unit. It was a combined-arms force unlike any other in Vietnam. Everybody wore the same unit crest and patch; they all worked

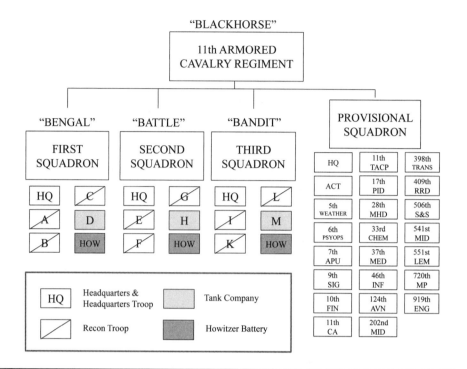

PROVISIONAL SQUADRON

Air Cavalry Troop; Team 1, 5th Weather Squadron, 1st Weather Group (USAF); 5th Field Team, Company B, 6th Psychological Operations Battalion; 7th Army Postal Unit; 9th Signal Detachment (Avionics Maintenance); 10th Finance Disbursing Section; 11th AA Platoon, 2nd Civil Affairs Company; 11th Tactical Air Control Party (USAF); 17th Public Information Detachment; 28th Military History Detachment; 33rd Chemical Detachment; 37th Medical Company; 46th Infantry Platoon (Scout Dog); 124th Aviation Detachment (Avionics); 202nd Military Intelligence Detachment; 398th Transportation Detachment (Aviation Maintenance); 409th Radio Research Detachment; 506th Supply and Service Company (Support); 541st Military Intelligence Detachment; 55th Light Equipment Maintenance Company (Support); 1st Detachment, Company B, 720th Military Police Battalion; 919th Engineer Company (Armored)

---

for the same man. Blackhorse 6 was in charge and all the troopers followed his orders—scouts, tankers, artillerymen, engineers, pilots, intelligence analysts, truck drivers, supply clerks, medics, and cooks alike—and they all had a ride.

The unit was 100 percent mobile with its own organic equipment. This is a critical factor. The regimental commander did not have to beg, borrow or steal trucks,

Major Equipment	
M113 Armored Cavalry Assault Vehicles	Approx. 300
M48 Patton Tanks	54
M551 Sheridans	81 (1969>)
M106 and M125 Mortars	27
M108 and M109 Howitzers	18
M60 AVLB Bridges	9
M132 Flame thrower (Zippos)	9
M577 Command Post Vehicles	36
M728 Combat Engineer Vehicles	2
M578 and M88 Recovery Vehicles	22
UH-1B/C Huey Hog and AH-1G Cobra Gunships	9
OH-23 Raven and OH-6A Cayuse Scouts/C&C	17
UH-1D/H Huey Lift/C&C	22

helicopters or armored vehicles to get his troopers from one place to another. He had everything he needed under his own command. No other brigade-sized unit in Vietnam could make the same claim. In addition, all of the combat vehicles had radios, allowing rapid and effective communications to quickly consolidate all that firepower at the right place at the right time.

And what an array of equipment it was! More than 400 armored vehicles and almost 50 helicopters—all bristling with weapons—crewed by Blackhorse troopers who knew how to use them. No other unit in Vietnam was as well equipped to find the enemy as the 11th Cavalry; and no other unit could pile on with an armor-protected, combined-arms team possessing enough firepower to overwhelm anything the enemy could muster.

But before the Blackhorse could prove this boast, the troopers had to be organized and trained to use that equipment.

Assembly: Late 1965 to Early 1966

Thrust into world-power status by the Spanish-American War, the United States Department of War determined that five new cavalry regiments (11th through 15th) would be required to garrison America's still-rebellious overseas territories—including Cuba and the Philippines. Following congressional approval, Colonel Francis Moore was directed to form the 11th United States Cavalry on 2 February 1901 at Fort Myer, Virginia. The new troopers were, for the most part, raw recruits just out of civilian life, with only a smattering of veterans from the Spanish-American War within their ranks. Most of the NCOs and officers had fought in Cuba or the

Philippines; some were even old Indian fighters. The leadership focused training on marksmanship and other basic soldier skills. Most of all, the men in the new regiment had to become part of a cohesive fighting unit in less than a year; one ready for combat in the Philippines.

As the commanding officer of 1st Squadron famously wrote in the spring of 1901: "I have four hundred horses that have never seen a soldier, four hundred recruits that have never seen a horse, and four second lieutenants that have never seen either a soldier or a horse."

These events were replicated just over six decades later.

***

When the Department of the Army identified the 11th Armored Cavalry Regiment at Fort Meade for eventual deployment to Vietnam, it was a skeleton of the unit it would become in less than a year. The order came in October 1965. The overall strength of the Regiment was at less than 50 percent (1,207 personnel present for duty out of 3,049 authorized). One squadron was in caretaker status, and training was limited to basic soldier skills for everyone else. When Lieutenant John Casterman arrived in 3rd Squadron's M (Mike) Company[6] in late October, he found he was in command of a platoon sergeant, a staff sergeant, and four enlisted troopers—two of whom were soon leaving the Army. The "rest of the Platoon showed up fresh out of Basic [Training] at 1900 [hours] one night [in early 1966]," John remembers, "and that became the 1st Platoon of Mike Company."

Among the most significant personnel shortages were at the squad and section leader levels—the heart and soul of the small-unit building blocks of a well-trained organization. Considering that the Regiment would deploy to combat less than nine months later, the shortfall in staff sergeant scouts (43 assigned of 176 authorized) and tankers (46 of 130 authorized) in early 1966 were especially grievous—since those were the personnel most needed to accomplish its combat missions. Gene Johnson recalls that he and Bob Merriman were the first two infantryman assigned to the Aero Rifle Platoon—Gene from Germany and Bob from Korea. They were both privates first class; because of the personnel shortages, they were immediately promoted to specialist 4 and became mentors for the group of basic training graduates who arrived shortly thereafter. "We had no leadership experience, but we had plenty to do until some NCOs arrived," Gene remembers.

Between January and February 1966, almost 2,000 new personnel, mostly brand-new basic training graduates with just eight weeks in the Army, were assigned to the 11th Cavalry. They arrived in the midst of rumors about where the Regiment was going after training was completed. There was only one hot war going on and most didn't need a crystal ball to know that their destination started with "Viet" and ended with "Nam."

It wasn't until 16 May that Colonel Cobb (Blackhorse 6) received authorization to inform his unit that the rumors were true—the Regiment was, once again, headed off to war in Asia. But security considerations meant that civilians—the family members, for example—could not be informed. As it always does, the word got out and families began the process of getting ready to move—some for the first time, some for the umpteenth time.

Paraphrasing that earlier 11th Cavalry leader, John Landry recalled 47 years later that the Blackhorse had "1,000 recruits who have never seen a second lieutenant, 100 second lieutenants who have never seen a recruit, and 200 NCOs who wanted to trade the lieutenants in for 200 horses."

Drill Call: Spring 1966

Somehow, the leaders assigned to the 11th Armored Cavalry Regiment made it work. They didn't have the experienced junior leaders (corporals and sergeants) assigned, so they picked the most promising of the newly-assigned recruits and made them acting-corporals and acting-sergeants.[7] They didn't have the requisite training areas at Fort Meade to qualify armored crewmen, so they moved the entire Regiment to Camps A.P. Hill and Pickett—over 100 miles away in Virginia—to prepare for combat. Department of the Army kept changing the Regiment's organization and equipment (e.g., removing the tanks from the recon troops at Westy's request and replacing the M114 armored reconnaissance vehicle with the M113 armored personnel carrier), but Colonel Cobb and his subordinate commanders quickly adjusted and kept moving forward.

Because of the short amount of time available, the commanders concluded that they should emphasize making small units proficient in their combat missions rather than spending a lot of time training individuals on their military occupational skills. The 3rd Squadron commander, Lieutenant Colonel (LTC) Palmer Peterson, explains the rationale. "Since time was the critical factor, the training program followed by the squadron was based on platoon training ... It was and is my opinion that if the platoons could learn to function effectively as independent units in training, the transition to combat would be easier since platoon independent engagements and missions were to be expected in Vietnam."

The crews learned by doing—hands-on training took precedence over classroom instruction in this modified "get-ready-for-war" program. The young troopers drove in endless convoys, reacted to countless ambushes and set up innumerable night defensive positions. They were blindfolded and told to locate a weapon on board their vehicles, to turn on the radios, or to start the engine (so they could do so at night while being shot at). They disassembled, cleaned, and reassembled their weapons over and over and over again—and then once more for good measure. About 20 percent of the training was conducted during the hours of darkness, with special emphasis on patrolling and ambush techniques. Fortunately, there was plenty of ammo available allowing tasks to be repeated when necessary.[8]

It is difficult enough to take a bunch of new recruits and mold them into a cohesive, battle-ready unit under the best of conditions. It is even more difficult if your first-line leaders are missing. But it is exceptionally difficult if you are not even sure what equipment you will fight with, what your exact mission will be, or how you are expected to accomplish your mission with the equipment you have.

Having studied the available lessons learned by armored cavalry units already in Vietnam, the officers and senior NCOs assigned to the Blackhorse recognized that the M113 armored personnel carrier, configured at the time as a "battlefield taxi," was not a fighting vehicle. Even if the Regiment was to be employed primarily on the roads, these World War II and Korea combat veterans recognized that they would need something more than the M113's single .50-caliber machine gun to accomplish their mission. That "something" included both more firepower and more crew protection. It was the collective efforts of the Blackhorse Regiment that came up with the addition of two M60 machine guns with gunshields mounted on each side of the M113 and a gunshield and armor around the track commander's[9] .50-caliber machine gun. This is what would become known as an Armored Cavalry Assault Vehicle—an ACAV.[10]

LTC Peterson remembers how the concept of an ACAV evolved. He had personally seen what South Vietnamese units did with their M113s, so he had a head start on the process. Between Cobb, Peterson, Howell and several veteran NCOs, they came up with a great solution.

> The ACAV was designed and developed by the 11th ACR ... based on my [Peterson] observations and experiences with ACTIV in SVN [Army Concepts Team in Viet Nam in South Vietnam] during 1964 ... My experience in SVN (1964) indicated it was desirable to fight mounted in the vast majority of the engagements ... [The two] additional machine guns increased the fire power of each vehicle, which would have the effect of reducing casualties among the crew members.

LTC Kibbey Horne, the 2nd Squadron commander, tells why this was so important: "The ACAV allowed us to fight from the vehicle ... [getting] us out of the armored infantry role and back into cavalry tactics."

The 11th Cavalry was on its own in virtually every aspect of its pre-deployment preparations. All of the personnel and equipment changes meant that doctrine and tactics had to be reviewed—and possibly modified. As Colonel Cobb noted:

> There is no field manual [FM] for the type of combat we may encounter in the near future. This does not mean that the principles of employment of Armor as stated in FM 17-1 [*Armor Operations*] and other manuals are not valid. The principles are sound and form the basis for action under all conditions. They will, however, require adaptation ... The change in the organization of the Reconnaissance Troops is in itself reason for the need to develop new ways, new formations and new battle drills. It is impossible to find any field manual that discusses the employment of the M113 as a fighting vehicle ... Nobody at Fort Knox is busily writing these doctrines of employment. They must be developed here and each of us will participate in their formulation.

While changes in structure and equipment in the ground elements were substantial, of any part of the 11th Cavalry it was the aviation elements that were probably the most affected by the reorganization and pre-combat build-up.

Air Cavalry Troop was the youngest of the units organic to the Blackhorse, barely six years old as the Regiment prepared to go to war. Activated as Aviation Company in May, 1960 in Germany, the company's mission when it was formed was mostly to enhance command and control over a unit that was habitually spread over a considerable area of real estate. There was no mention of reconnaissance or engaging the enemy from the air. At the time of its formation, the company had both helicopters and fixed-wing aircraft sitting in the hangers, used primarily for command and control, artillery spotting, and liaison missions. Not one of these aircraft was armed.

When the Army decided to deploy the Regiment to Vietnam, all fixed-wing aircraft were withdrawn, and the OH-13 Sioux liaison helicopters were replaced by the more modern OH-23 Raven. Brand new UH-1D "Hueys" took over for the obsolete "flying bananas" (CH-21 Shawnee), both as transportation for the new Aero Rifle Platoon and as command and control (C&C) platforms. The Aviation Company was redesignated Air Cavalry Troop and organized using the lessons learned from a year of fighting by the 1st Cavalry Division in the central highlands of South Vietnam. Aviation sections—with both observation and gunship helicopters—were formed in the regimental headquarters and in each squadron.[11]

Somehow, it all came together. Somehow, despite all of the organizational and equipment changes, all of the personnel shortfalls, and the doctrinal voids, the 11th Cavalry passed all its tests. The Regiment was declared "combat ready" at the end of an Annual General Inspection conducted just two weeks before the ships carrying the Blackhorse to Vietnam left the West Coast in mid-August. Colonel Cobb summed it up: "In war the test is simple and infallible. You win or lose. There are no prizes for second place. And remember this, there can be no second place for the Blackhorse Regiment."

General Creighton Abrams, Jr., the Vice Chief of Staff of the Army—and the senior Armor officer in the Army—came to Fort Meade as the inspection was ending. He wanted to make sure the troopers understood the importance of the mission upon which they were embarking. He congratulated everyone on a job well done and spoke of the fearsome combat they would probably see. Then he spoke with the heart of the old horse cavalryman that he was. "In his brief but pointed speech he … emphasized the tremendous responsibility the 11th Armored Cavalry Regiment had as the first major Armor command employed in Vietnam."

Golf Troop's first sergeant, Jim Embrey, sums up the raucous six months that preceded deployment.

> Ninety percent of the soldiers we received were fresh out of Basic Training needing Advanced Individual Training and Unit Training … At first, our troop had only two officers and a few NCOs to guide this wild assembly of new recruits. Three hours sleep a night was common.

Thankfully before long we began to fill up with Officers and NCO's ... [Five] officers and 86 Enlisted men thrown together at record pace went on short leave with orders to assemble later in California for deployment. Mercy! Wonder how many would show up? Every d**n one! Thumbing their noses and various other body parts to peace-sign-waving hippies along the way.

Boots and Saddles: August to September 1966

On 18 August, 3,000-plus troopers, carrying their duffel bags and individual weapons, started boarding charter aircraft at Baltimore's Friendship Airport bound for California. Three days later, the Regiment reassembled at Oakland Army Terminal. Like many of their fathers, uncles and older brothers, they walked up the gangway to board troopships for a trans-oceanic cruise.

San Francisco was a happenin' place in the summer of 1966. Icons of rock 'n' roll were jammin' from the Fillmore to the Cow Palace. Big Brother and the Holding Company (with Janis Joplin still wailing on leads), the Mothers of Invention, Grateful Dead, Beach Boys, Rolling Stones, Four Tops, and Beatles all performed in town that summer. LSD was still legal, pot was plentiful, and free love was flowing at the corner of Haight and Ashbury. John Casterman remembers that music, drugs, and hippies were not the only forms of entertainment in town. The ship that was to take him to war, the US Naval Ship (USNS) *Barrett*, remained tied up to the pier for a couple of days because of a boiler in need of repair.

> We were stuck on the ship, but I noticed the Merchant Marine sailors leaving the ship each night. So I borrowed some scruffy civilian clothes from one of the crew and went over the side with them at night. I called a buddy of mine in San Francisco and we went down to the Tenderloin District. I just had to see Carol Doda.[12] I told my friend: "Just make sure I am back on that ship before dawn." We did that several nights. I had a nightmare of getting back to the dock and finding the ship had left without me.

The late summer of 1966 was not the first time that troopers had to wait to go to war because of boiler problems.

The 1st Squadron arrived by train in San Francisco in mid-December 1901. They were en route from Jefferson Barracks, outside St. Louis, to the Philippines. The Regiment was headed for war. But their transport ship, the US Army Transport (USAT) *Sheridan*, had been delayed in Japan due to a typhoon and a faulty boiler and would not arrive until the end of the year. The troopers—mostly new recruits who joined the Regiment after its formation just ten months earlier—went into temporary camp at the Presidio of San Francisco. It being the holiday season, most were given passes. As was usually the case outside a military post in the early 1900s, a large number of saloons (not unlike the Tenderloin District in the 1960s) had grown up within a mile of the front gate of the Presidio; the troopers headed straight for them.

Dave Tarpey's was one of those "hell holes" (thus described by the Post Commander) where troopers getting ready to go off to war could drown their fear and loneliness in overpriced beer and watered-down liquor. Allegedly, on Christmas night, an 11th Cavalry corporal might have picked a fight with another trooper. The bartender, an off-duty artilleryman intervened (inadvisably); the corporal came back later and stabbed the bartender with a knife. The rumor spread to the bartender's artillery regiment that one of their own had been killed (not true) by a member of the 11th Cavalry Regiment. A huge street fight broke out.

Over two days, about a thousand soldiers rioted in the area immediately outside the Presidio gates. They ransacked saloons, stole liquor, attacked and severely injured policemen and ran civilians off the streets. Squads of baton-wielding policemen, reinforced by mounted and dismounted soldiers, waded into the drunken rioters and eventually restored order. Nearly a hundred soldiers were put into the local jail or the post guardhouse. The commander of the Presidio locked the post down, no passes to anyone. Within 24 hours, the rioters had been convicted and sentenced to three months in lock-up. Except, that is, for the troopers of the 11th Cavalry, who were sentenced to join their unit aboard the USAT *Sheridan* and to go to war.

***

The 3,000-plus troopers who boarded the US Naval Ships *Daniel L. Sultan* (1/11 and Provisional Squadron), *William P. Upshur* (2/11 and 28th Military History Detachment), and *Charles D. Barrett* (3/11) in mid-August 1966 proudly call themselves the "Boat People." These were the men who had trained together and were now headed off to war together. In their capable hands was the reputation of not only the Blackhorse Regiment, but also Armor as a branch in the United States Army. That challenge lay on the horizon they sailed into every day. But first they had to endure three weeks at sea.

The troopers who went up the gangways were, for the most part, Baby Boomers. Their fathers (and some of their mothers) fought the Second World War, came home, and got on with their lives. The Boomers were raised on a diet of Dr. Spock, TV dinners, and WWII movies. It was inevitable that virtually everyone who saw their troop transports for the first time was reminded of some black-and-white film starring Van Johnson or Robert Mitchum. The hero is standing on the pier saying goodbye to his sweetheart as his fellow GIs are seen streaming aboard in the fuzzy background. Stirring music plays for that "one last kiss."

There were no sweethearts on the dock or stirring music as the 11th Cavalry set sail for Vietnam in August 1966.

For the officers and senior NCOs, life on board was boring but tolerable. They bunked in cabins with two or three others of similar rank. Lieutenant Jim Abel recalls: "For the officers, living conditions on board were pretty good. The three Platoon Leaders of E Troop bunked in a cabin above the main deck. We ate in a dining hall with waiters serving. The food was good ..." Bravo Troop platoon leader

Bernie Carpenter likened his trip aboard the *Sultan* as "uneventful … like a cruise without your girlfriend or wife."

On the other hand, when asked four decades later to describe the living conditions for the enlisted troopers in the hold of the *Barrett*, Rick Organ replied: "This I can do <u>vividly</u>! Our bunks, more like stiff hammocks—mine was inches off the deck. I could half-extend my arm and touch a soldier laying on top, extend my feet [and] touch a head, reach over my head [and] touch feet, extend arms to both sides, two more troopers. Plus, each of us had a stuffed duffel bag. Plus, most of us did not take a shower the 20 days aboard the ship."

CHAPTER 2

The Blackhorse Enters Combat: September 1966 to May 1967

The American cavalryman, trained to maneuver and fight with equal facility on foot and on horseback, is the best type of soldier for general purposes now to be found in the world.
THEODORE ROOSEVELT, PRESIDENT, 1901

A few days before our arrival, we were issued ammunition for our M16s. I knew it was for real then. Until that time, it all seemed like a training exercise that would end soon. I knew there was no turning back or getting out of there any time soon. I was very apprehensive that last night aboard the *Barrett*, listening to the sounds and seeing flashes inland. I thought to myself, "Momma, come get me."
LARRY BURWICK, INDIA TROOP, 3/11TH CAVALRY

I couldn't see the VC from my side at first, but when the bullets started coming my way, I saw Charlie and let him have it.
WALTER FLICK, GOLF TROOP, 2/11 CAVALRY

Less than one year after its formation in February 1901, the 11th Cavalry Regiment made its first deployment overseas to the Philippines. The American Army had made great strides in quelling the rebellion there, but some serious fighting remained. Major General Adna Chaffee, the Military Governor of the Philippines (and a fellow cavalryman), reported that "the prolongation of guerrilla warfare is due to the physical character of the country and to the nature of the warfare carried on by the insurgents who in the same hour pose as friends and act as enemies ... and to the fear of assassination on the part of those natives who are friendly disposed towards the Americans should they give the latter information concerning the movements or whereabouts of the insurgents."

Similar words were spoken 64 years later when the Blackhorse Regiment returned to Asia.

For two years, 11th Cavalry troopers fought mounted and dismounted against the so-called Filipino *insurectos*, conducting small unit reconnaissance operations in the jungle, seeking out weapons and food caches, cordoning and searching *pueblos* and *barrios* and clearing and securing highways. They repaired roads and schools, dug wells, provided medical care to civilians, and helped local governments "pacify" the provinces in which they were stationed. Searching for and engaging *insurectos* was a small-unit war, with junior officers and sergeants forced to make on-the-ground decisions on a daily basis. Outside the villages, the troopers encountered mountainous jungles with no signs of civilization.

Back at home, activists condemned the American "baby killers" (while ignoring the enemy's own brutal atrocities). Newspapers published tales of the indiscriminate burning of villages and the torture of captured *insurectos*. Members of Congress introduced bills condemning the actions of the military, especially on Samar and in Batangas.

Half a century later, President Johnson might just as easily have repeated what Teddy Roosevelt said 60-plus years earlier when he asked Congress in 1965 to bring the 11th Armored Cavalry Regiment to full wartime strength and send them off to counter another insurgency in Asia. These modern-day cavalrymen were still the best men for the job. They were flexible in thought and action. They had the organic mobility and firepower to accomplish any mission. They were well trained and well led, able to fight in three dimensions across all types of terrain.

The Evolving War in Vietnam: Fall 1966

In the year that it took the Regiment to go from virtual caretaker status to fully combat-ready, the war in Vietnam had changed dramatically. By the fall of 1965, the war had cost the lives of approximately 1,500 American soldiers, sailors, airmen, and marines. Battles involving GIs were still infrequent enough to warrant front-page coverage in most newspapers. The award of a Medal of Honor or Distinguished Service Cross (DSC) was still "big news" and garnered plenty of attention—13 Medals of Honor were awarded in 1965, as well as 31 DSCs (all Services). One year later, as the Regiment was boarding ships for its second tour in an Asian war zone, the situation was considerably different. US killed in action were approaching the 6,000 mark. By the end of 1966, Medal of Honor recipients had more than doubled (28), and four times as many DSCs (129) had been awarded as in the previous year.

The military campaign in III Corps Tactical Zone (III CTZ, about the size of New Hampshire)[1] where the 11th Cavalry was stationed had a different character than elsewhere in South Vietnam. Because of the location of the capital of Saigon, military operations focused on the key terrain and the friendly population, rather than just the destruction of enemy forces. This region-specific strategy was repeatedly vindicated, since between 1966 and 1969 the enemy focused his own efforts on these same targets—the economic and population centers in III CTZ, the roads entering and exiting those areas, and the key government installations scattered across the region.

As Blackhorse troopers arrived in Vietnam, officials were optimistic about the progress of the war. In a memo to the Secretary of Defense, the Chairman of the Joint Chiefs of Staff (General Earle Wheeler) wrote in October 1966 that the military

Map of the Corps Tactical Zones in Vietnam in 1967 (patch shows location of Blackhorse Base Camp). (basic map, US Army)

situation in South Vietnam had improved "substantially" in the past 12 months. General Wheeler concluded that the Communists could not win *militarily* at their current level of effort.

About the same time as General Wheeler and the other Service Chiefs were drawing this conclusion, their counterparts in Hanoi and the jungles of South Vietnam were drawing their own conclusions. They determined that the military buildup had been insufficient in the military region around Saigon. They assessed that only half of their enlarged and well-equipped main force had proven effective in combat situations. In addition to enhancing the training of main-force units, Hanoi ordered the 7th (NVA) Division to reinforce the 5th (VC) and 9th (VC) Divisions already threatening Saigon.[2]

The Communist leadership gave specific instructions to the new units to focus on attacking the road network in and around Saigon—the so-called lines of communication. Confrontation with the newly-arrived 11th Cavalry, whose initial mission was to open and secure those lines of communication, became a foregone conclusion in the fall of 1966.

The Communists believed, however, that the coming months could be decisive in the outcome of the war. Their strategy would be to isolate and strangle Saigon into submission by closing the major roads that fed (literally and figuratively) the population and preventing essential supplies (e.g., food and raw rubber) from getting into Saigon. They would tax or steal from the peasants and demonstrate that the South Vietnamese "generals-turned-politicians" were unable to prevent VC attacks and terrorism. Achieving this goal would require strengthening every element of insurgent forces throughout the province. The Viet Cong and their North Vietnamese Army comrades would keep up the pressure and wait out the enemy. The war, they were convinced, would be won in Washington.

The US Army's official history for the period concluded: "The importance of III Corps to the enemy could not be underestimated." As in its initial combat service so long ago in the Philippines, the Blackhorse Regiment in Vietnam was going where the action was expected to be heaviest—and most important.

The 11th Armored Cavalry Regiment Comes Ashore: September 1966

Back in The World,[3] the Beatles' "Yellow Submarine" had risen to number four on the pop music charts. The psychedelic world portrayed in those lyrics was about as far from the reality of being off the coast of Vietnam as one could get. But after an eight-hour trans-continental plane ride and a 21-day trans-Pacific voyage, that is precisely where 3,000-plus Blackhorse troopers found themselves. This was it, the Big Time, the Majors. No more training, no more second chances. Mike Company's John Casterman recalls:

The night before we were due to arrive off Vietnam, the Squadron Commander—Lieutenant Colonel Palmer Peterson, a tough little professional soldier that was well respected by his troopers—gathered us all together on deck and said: "This is serious stuff, so shut up and listen." We did. He said: "Look to your left and look to your right. One of the three of you won't be going home." That's when it struck home that this was serious business.

The USNS *Sultan* (1/11 and Provisional Squadron) arrived first on the night of 6 September and started off-loading the next morning. The USNS *Upshur* (2/11) was next, arriving a day later. The boiler- and cyclone-hindered USNS *Barrett* (3/11) finally limped into its anchorage on 11 September—the same day the Rolling Stones performed on the Ed Sullivan Show.[4]

Black-and-white clips flashed through many troopers' minds as they boarded the landing craft to get to shore. Would this be like World War II, an amphibious assault under fire? Private First Class Joe Hogan sums it up. "Then we off-load into an assault craft for the ride to the beach. Just like WWII movies. Weapons, steel pots [helmets], full packs headed towards the beach—all of us wondering what was waiting for us."

Private Al Noetzel went through a whole scenario in his head.

I'm packed in among 150 other soldiers like canned sardines. It's getting hot as the morning sun starts to beat down ... After ten minutes the craft comes to a jolting halt and the ramp comes down, I hear the command, "Move ... Move ... Move ... This is a beach assault. What are you waiting for?" I jumped into the water which was up to my chest. Then it hits me. What will I do when I arrive on the beach? I know, I'll take out that right flank machine gun that is certain to be there. Step by step my boots dig into the solid, sand bottom ... When ankle high in the water I'm able to run. This is it! ... Do or die! ... Wait a minute! Where are all the bombs, machine gun fire and grenade explosions? ... "Over here ... Come on ... We don't have all day," yelled a fat sergeant. I climbed aboard the first bus ...

What awaited the Blackhorse Regiment came as a big surprise to most. Instead of machine guns, there were classes of Vietnamese school girls in their white *ao dais* handing out flower leis. Instead of mortars, there were round-eyed Red Cross Donut Dollies handing out coffee and donuts—and hundreds of dignitaries. Banners welcoming them to Vietnam stretched across the beach. A small black horse stood by placidly to greet the troopers of the Blackhorse Regiment.[5]

This wasn't Normandy or Iwo Jima and their fathers' war anymore; this was Vietnam and their war. And what a peculiar start to a peculiar year in a peculiar war it was.

The next stop was the Long Binh Staging Area, where the 200-trooper strong regimental advanced party (including virtually all of the 919th Engineer Company) had already set up tents and other facilities.[6] Their job had been made even more difficult due to the time of year—the height of the rainy season. Attempting to mark unit areas, set up tents, and build mess halls in the wind, rain, and mud was no fun. The unbearable heat in the day and "cold" and wet at night made it even worse. Sergeant (SGT) Frank Gowrie was a member of the advanced party. He recalls: "It was the rainy season, so there was close to a foot of water, or mud inside the tents we were sleeping in." Lieutenant Ron Kelly was never so cold, wet, and miserable in all his life as during those first few days in country. "It was raining four times a day—once at each meal and all night ... It got so damn cold there at night, when you're wet ..."

The Regiment's equipment began arriving by ship within a week. Drivers and track commanders (TCs) went to the docks in Saigon and drove their vehicles back to the staging area. Crews reconditioned them after the long ocean voyage. ACAV kits and weapons were mounted, tools and auxiliary equipment was inventoried, and weapons were bore sighted or zeroed at nearby ranges.

Not everything went according to plan, however. Platoon leader John Casterman describes one case of "oops."

> We left Long Binh and went down to the dock to pick up our tanks—two men per tank to drive them back to the staging area ... We stood on the dock and watched as the stevedores lifted the first tank off the ship and placed it on a barge to bring it ashore. The barge was big enough for about four tanks, so they put that first one in one corner of the barge. As soon as they let go the lines from the crane, the barge tilted over and the tank slid off into the muddy harbor waters. Damned if they didn't do the same thing with the next tank—with the same results. I'm standing there thinking: "There goes my Platoon into Saigon Harbor." So, they finally got it right and we drove home that day with just three instead of five tanks.

As it turned out, those tanks did not end up as artificial reefs in Saigon harbor. Both tanks were successfully recovered.

The 11th Armored Cavalry Regiment's first year in Vietnam was an action-packed one. Within the first four months, troopers were involved in four major combat actions; three more followed before the start of the 1967 rainy season. By the one-year mark, the Regiment had proven to even the most skeptical observer that there was indeed a major role for armor in Vietnam. Getting to that point, however, was fraught with many bloody lessons learned.

Initiating Combat Operations: October to December 1966

General Westmoreland gave straightforward guidance to his subordinate commanders for 1966 in his Military Assistance Command Vietnam Campaign Plan.

> The basic objectives of the campaign for 1966 [are] to clear, secure, and assist in the economic development of the heavily populated areas around Saigon, in the Mekong Delta, and in selected portions of the coastal plain. Along with the basic objectives, the defense of significant outlying political centers [is] to be achieved by undertaking search and destroy operations in the surrounding areas against major VC/NVN [Viet Cong/North Vietnam] forces ... All friendly forces [are] to conduct operations against VC forces in heretofore "safe haven" areas and bases.

From these objectives, Colonel Bill Cobb took his mission. He told the squadron commanders that the 11th Cavalry was to "assist in the economic development of the heavily populated areas around Saigon" by opening and securing (for both military

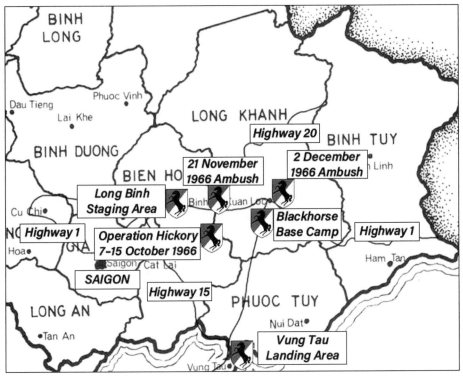

Map of 11th Armored Cavalry Regiment operations in 1966. (basic map, US Army)

and civilian traffic) National Highway 1 between Long Binh and the II–III Corps boundary, Highway 2 from Xuan Loc to the province border, and Highway 20 to where it met Lam Dong Province. Conducting search and destroy operations to clear the VC from eastern and southern Long Khanh Province enabled the people to get their rice and other products to market and contributed to this primary mission for the Regiment.

Additional missions included establishing and securing the new base camp and its surrounding area, clearing the enemy's previously "safe haven" areas and bases in the Hat Dich and May Tao areas south and east of the base camp, and being prepared to reinforce installations in the Long Binh-Bien Hoa area. The Regiment was also expected to help train and conduct combined operations with South Vietnamese forces in the province.

While in the staging area, troopers were eased into the combat environment by being assigned a wide variety of routine missions. For example, 1/11 conducted the Regiment's first operational mission just three weeks after arriving at Vung Tau, escorting heavy engineer equipment from Long Binh to Xuan Loc. Recon troops were tasked to provide perimeter guards in the base camp of the 173rd Airborne Brigade (Skysoldiers), secure the sprawling Long Binh ammo dump, the Ho Nai railway station, a sensitive communications site, and a rock quarry. Eventually, they were given more tactical missions under the code name Operation *Uniontown*, including convoy escorts and search and destroy sweeps with 173rd Skysoldiers.

Weather continued to be a significant issue for the troopers of the Blackhorse, as the Southwest Monsoon reigned over the southern half of South Vietnam well into October. The prevailing winds, coming from the southwest, brought with them the moisture gathered from both the Indian Ocean and the Gulf of Siam. Energy-sucking mud, disease-carrying mosquitoes, and pervasive jungle rot greeted the troopers as they struggled to establish the staging area. By the time work began on the new base camp, the Southwest Monsoon had passed, only to be replaced by the choking dust and stifling heat of the Northeast Monsoon.

Operation *Hickory* (7–15 October 1966) was the first week-long squadron-sized operation conducted by the 11th Cavalry in Vietnam. Although contact was generally light, the Regiment suffered its first fatality during the operation. Given the terrain and inexperienced crews, it was fortunate that most Viet Cong had left the area. The 3rd Squadron commander (Lieutenant Colonel Palmer Peterson) noted that: "The chance to evaluate our operating techniques and smooth out normal internal problems before operating against a hard-core VC Force will no doubt prove invaluable."

Valuable lessons were learned from Operation *Hickory*, lessons that would resonate across the five and a half years of the Regiment's service in Vietnam and Cambodia. Tactics developed during stateside training were tested, refined or dropped entirely. Operational techniques were learned, often the hard way. As Peterson recorded them:

> Major problems encountered during the first day were difficulties in land navigation; lack of adequate road nets in the area and impassable terrain. Some of the problems with the terrain resulted from inexperience with the area and inability to adequately judge the trafficability of the ground … Occasional thunder showers during the day added to the problems of extracting mired vehicles. The Squadron began making its own roads with bulldozers, tanks, and ACAVs to increase its access to certain areas.

Colonel Cobb's first priority was finding a permanent home for his Regiment in a location that was accessible during the dry and wet seasons and close to the roads coming into Saigon from the north, east, and south, thus facilitating mission accomplishment. Cobb recalls how he picked the base camp's location (near the Courtney Rubber Plantation).

> General William Westmoreland's staff had selected an area southeast of Xuan Loc, about where Highway 1 turned east from Route 2 to Gia Ray. I reconnoitered by air and could see water glistening through the growth. It was apparent to me that this was no place for us with our tracked vehicles … I was [eventually] told [by Westmoreland's staff] to select my own area, as long as it was in the Xuan Loc vicinity and in a position to control Route 2 to the south … After several air and map reconnaissance missions … we selected an area 10 miles south of Xuan Loc, on Route 2 at Long Giao.

Operation *Atlanta* (20 October–8 December 1966) moved the Regiment from the Long Binh Staging Area into its new home—Blackhorse Base Camp. First Squadron started out from Long Binh in the middle of the night, hoping to catch the local VC by surprise. Sergeant John Monaghan recalls seeing the area designated for the new base camp after daylight: "The only thing there was elephant grass and the Viet Cong."

The regimental psychological operations section developed several leaflets (a half million were scattered by air drops) addressed to two different audiences. One leaflet was to the "friendly" civilians, the other to the enemy. The message in both was the same: the 11th Cavalry is here to stay. This was no short-term operation. Long Giao is our new home.

> The 11th Armored Cavalry has arrived in Vietnam. They have mighty tanks that will seek out and destroy the Viet Cong. When not fighting the Viet Cong bandits who rebel against their own people, the U.S. 11th Armored Cavalry will be helping to build schools, treat the sick and injured and distribute food to the people of Vietnam. But, they can only help you if you help them. When you see the American soldiers wearing the big black horse on their shoulder, remember, we are your friends.

There was one little problem. At the time, the Regiment was not authorized to have its own patch. The solution—do it yourself. Local tailors started making unauthorized Blackhorse patches.[7]

***

Throughout the first month after arriving at Long Giao, there were repeated—almost daily—probes by individuals and small groups of enemy soldiers, as well as attacks by indirect and direct fire to test reaction times and fire discipline. Aggressive day and night patrolling resulted in numerous minor encounters with local VC, with small numbers of casualties on both sides.[8]

Enemy confrontation with the 11th Cavalry, whose initial mission was to open and secure lines of communication, became a foregone conclusion in the fall of 1966. The Viet Cong had long had a free hand in their "liberated" area, one that was rich in rice. The many roads, crowded with trucks headed to Saigon with lumber, charcoal, and fresh vegetables were great money-makers for VC tax collectors. Hitting the newly arrived Blackhorse Regiment would send a signal to the local population that they (the VC) were still in charge.

The enemy was, in fact, already feeling the effects of the Regiment's presence. The history of the D440 (VC) Battalion tells the story in unusually straightforward terms.

> In September 1966, the Americans brought in the 11th Armored Cavalry Brigade (equivalent to a regiment) with hundreds of tanks and armoured vehicles, and stationed the formation at the Long Giao base on Route 2 in the Xuan Loc-Long Khanh area. This force launched unrelenting sweeping operations into the Province's liberated areas ... that threatened our supply routes and the base area region ... and blocked access into many important areas ... and important communication routes such as Route 1 and Route 15.

The "feeling out" period ended with a bang on 21 November 1966.

On 8 November, 1st Squadron was siphoned off on short notice to conduct route and area security and act as a ready reaction force for the 1st Infantry Division (Big Red One) on Operation *Attleboro* (see below). They spent the next 11 days with no enemy contact and lots of convoy-escort miles on their vehicles. Colonel Cobb's persistent request for the return of his squadron finally paid off; 1/11 was released on the 19th. The Howitzer Battery, escorted by Alpha Troop, went directly home to the new base camp, while the rest of the squadron escorted the 173rd Airborne Brigade back to Long Binh. They closed into the staging area on the 20th in the midst of a rain storm.

The daily convoys to Blackhorse Base Camp carried in the mail as well as things like food, beer and spare parts, so their arrival was eagerly anticipated. The convoy on 21 November, consisting of 51 wheeled vehicles, was escorted by nine Armored Cavalry Assault Vehicles (ACAVs) (four each from Bravo Troop's 1st and 2nd platoons, as well as one from Alpha Troop). They departed the staging area at 0933 hours, destined for the base camp. In accordance with regimental standard operating procedure (SOP), Lieutenant (LT) Neil Keltner, the convoy commander, was monitoring and reporting check points on the 1/11 command radio net. Also, in accordance with SOP, there was a forward air controller (FAC) overhead; the sole operational gunship from the squadron's aviation section was there too.

The enemy had watched the pattern of daily resupply convoys and determined that this would be their target. On the afternoon of 20 November, two convoys had travelled the same route between Long Binh and Blackhorse Base Camp. They were neither ambushed nor did they notice anything "out of the ordinary" that might have been a tip off on the impending ambush.

Unbeknownst to the 11th Cavalry, the enemy began isolating the battlefield early that morning. A train headed toward Saigon struck a mine just south of Ap Hung Nghia, derailing the engine and two cars. As a result, this relatively high-speed avenue of approach for reaction forces coming from the east was blocked. Three-quarters of an hour later, a South Vietnamese (ARVN) infantry patrol got into a firefight with an enemy unit about a kilometer southwest of Highway 1. The western approach to the ambush site was now also blocked. Neither of these reports made it to the Blackhorse Tactical Operations Center (TOC) before the ambush. It seems that the telephone line between the South Vietnamese and US operations center was out of order that day.

The Blackhorse's 409th Radio Research Detachment, whose mission it was to intercept enemy communications, had an unofficial motto: "In God we trust. Everybody else we intercept." The Regiment was very thankful that the 409th troopers practiced what they preached that day. The radio direction finding specialists picked up an increase in Vietnamese-language radio traffic emanating from near the highway. It was road watchers reporting the convoy's movement. About the same time, a US Air Force airborne collection and direction-finding aircraft intercepted a radio

message that sounded like an enemy unit getting ready to spring an ambush. It was
the 274th (VC) Regiment, set up on the south side of Highway 1, just short of Ap
Hung Nghia. The aircraft crew relayed the heads-up to the 409th—the regimental
intelligence officer had it in less than a minute.

Captain (CPT) Larry Gunderman, on duty in the 1/11 tactical operations center,
called to warn the convoy. "I was in the TOC, and we got a spot report about an
intercept from a VC regiment. I got on the horn [radio] to Keltner, to let him
know about it and I could already hear the guns firing … The next call was a net
call informing ground troops of the ambush. CPT Bob Garrott [C Troop com-
mander] and the rest of Charlie Troop were on the road in a flash, with the rest of
the squadron close behind."

Specialist 4 (SP4) Steve Page was on an ACAV, part of the Bravo Troop convoy
escort. "We had a bunch of reefer trucks, JP-4 trucks, fuel for the aircraft, mail,
a pretty good convoy … It was like a regular day. It was awful quiet. In the fields

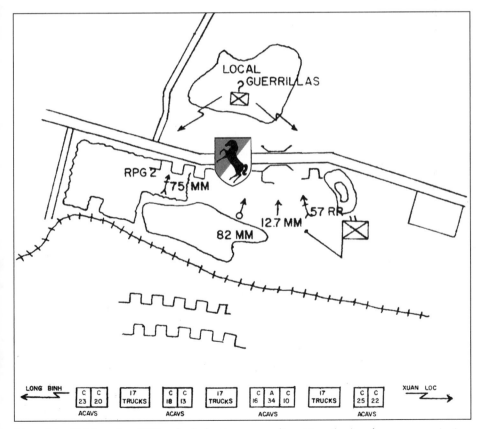

Map of the 21 November 1966 ambush showing enemy dispositions (top) and convoy organization
(bottom) (reproduced from the regimental after-action report). (basic map, US Army)

was a lot of women and children, working in the fields. Which I thought was kind of odd [no men]."

Two reinforced battalions of the 274th (VC) Regiment (about 600 men) occupied their 2.5-kilometer-long ambush positions on the south side of Highway 1 after darkness on 20 November. Stoically, the VC soldiers sat through the long, rainy night. The enemy commander placed his recoilless rifles—three 75mm and at least six 57mm—near the ends of the intended killing zone. He had a .51-caliber (cal.) heavy machine gun in the middle, and three 82mm mortars off-set not far behind the line of riflemen. A local VC guerrilla unit was set up on the north side of the road; they were armed only with rifles. Perhaps it was their discomfort from the rain, or that they had never seen ACAVs before. Or maybe they just were not very well trained or disciplined. But when the "open fire" order was given by the VC commander, only a few scattered riflemen responded.

The lead two ACAVs and the lead section of 17 trucks were just inside the killing zone when the firing started. They were able to avoid substantial damage and, per SOP, continued—at high speed—down the road toward Blackhorse Base Camp.[9] The next ACAVs—C-16 (LT Keltner), C-10, and A-34[10]—came under more concentrated fire, but were still able to get out of the killing zone. Short of Ap Hung Nghia village, Keltner told A-34 to serve as the rear guard for the rump convoy and then turned around (with C-10) to return to the fight.

The next two ACAVs in the convoy were stuck in the heart of the killing zone, and they took the brunt of the enemy fire. C-13 was hit by four recoilless rifle rounds and three mortar rounds in less than a minute, as well as rifle and machine gun fire. One trooper was killed and the rest of the crew was wounded, but the driver managed to extract the burning vehicle from the killing zone, going about a mile before the engine quit. C-18 was not so lucky; it was struck by five recoilless rifle rounds and one mortar round and ground to a halt. The crew evacuated the vehicle, which eventually burned down to the road wheels. Four of the 17 trucks caught in the killing zone were hit by enemy fire and burned in place on the road. A small civilian bus was also caught in the cross-fire; the driver, a female passenger and a young child were killed.

Neil Keltner's bravery and leadership saved the day for the convoy on 21 November. Driving at top speed (35–40 mph), C-16 became a virtual war wagon, spewing machine gun fire to both sides of the road.[11] A direct hit by a 57 mm round knocked out the vehicle's radios but did not stop Keltner and his crew from scattering the VC infantrymen intent on overrunning the damaged trucks and killing or capturing the drivers huddled in the roadside ditch. At least five VC were felled by Keltner's .50-cal. machine gun (quite a feat, considering he was wounded and the vehicle was moving so fast on a pot-holed road surface); the rest fled back into the jungle. In all, Keltner made five gun runs through the killing zone, picking up and evacuating wounded, coordinating for a helicopter evacuation of the wounded (dustoff), organizing local defenses and providing cool leadership under fire. Those who knew him were not surprised. Army SP4-turned FBI Agent Judson Ray said five decades later: "He was the soldier's soldier. I can't imagine wanting to be like anybody else ... He was loved by everybody in that unit ... He saved the day, that day."

Almost immediately after the enemy initiated the ambush, the Blackhorse kicked back—hard. Captain Tony Nelson, from the 1/11 aviation section, was flying convoy escort in his Huey gunship when the ambush was sprung. From the middle of the killing zone, John Albright watched as Nelson did "a most incredible feat right as the ambush began." Instead of making a gun run, he came to a hover in the middle of Highway 1, dipped his nose in the direction of the enemy, and commenced firing—despite the ferocious return fire. Nelson then flew around, making four conventional gun runs (i.e., parallel to the road), engaging enemy soldiers who were within 20 meters of the convoy vehicles. A light fire team (LFT) of two gunships arrived next, followed within mere minutes by F100 jets from near-by Bien Hoa Air Base.

Imagine, if you will, being a member of the hapless 274th (VC) Regiment. Your commander, probably to the great disappointment of his Chinese advisor, has missed a one-time opportunity by letting the first part of a relatively lightly-defended truck convoy pass through the killing zone.[12] He then compounds his error by initiating the ambush with the bulk of the remaining trucks not yet in the killing zone. And where did these fire-spitting green dragons come from? The political officer was wrong; this was not a lightly-protected truck convoy after all!

You and many of your fellow riflemen are virtually unprotected, as your unit moved into position too late to properly dig in. Out of nowhere, you start receiving concentrated fire from the ground and the air. Fortunately, the flying dragons are coming one at a time and you are able to duck each time. You hope that the comrades on the anti-aircraft guns rid the skies of these pesky beasts.

To the contrary. You glance to your right and see not one, but three of those deadly dragons, breathing smoke and fire, headed your way, just 50 feet in the air. Twelve 7.62mm miniguns, swerving left and right, pumping out hundreds of rounds each. Six M60 machine guns with daredevil gunners standing on the skids, leaning out of the helicopter attached only by their monkey straps and firing constantly. Six pods spewing pairs of high-explosive rockets, salvos just two seconds apart. And they are all aimed at YOU! This wasn't part of the plan briefed by the political officer. Do you hit the ground or run back into the jungle? You think of your mother and father, your ancestors as the rounds get closer ...

There was a pre-planned airstrike called by the 10th (Army of the Republic of Vietnam—ARVN) Infantry Division that morning. One of the USAF forward air controllers was in the air and saw the smoke from the ambush. He called Major Mario Stefanelli, the 11th Cavalry FAC (radio call sign "Nile") and said: "Look,

I've got this pre-planned [bombing mission] about to take off from Bien Hoa and you need it more than we do." Major Stefanelli said: "Oh hell yes!"

But the real reason the FAC was in the air and the two F100s were on scene within 14 minutes of the start of the ambush was because the advisor team at Xuan Loc had run out of beer. According to Blackhorse historian John Albright, "he was on his way to Bien Hoa to stock up on beer, to put three or four cases in the back seat of the O-1 [aircraft] … It was a beer run. And the reason we got an air strike so quickly was because the 10th ARVN [American advisor] guys had run out of beer."

Thirty minutes after the ambush was sprung, ground reinforcements began to arrive from Long Binh. By shortly after noon—about three and a half hours after the fight began—the final ACAVs arrived from the new base camp and the battlefield was sealed off.

After all was said and done, the 21 November action was successful on several levels. First, the mobility, firepower and tactics of the armored cavalry-air cavalry team were proven to be more than capable of countering enemy infantry in an ambush. Air support (no artillery was initially in range) proved to be critical to success, as did rapid reinforcement on the ground.

Second, the leadership—from squadron commander down to individual track commander and gunship pilot—showed professionalism, flexibility and courage in the face of a determined foe. The FACs and helicopter crews could not talk directly with LT Keltner; they had to go through a radio relay station. Keltner could not reach all of his escorts or any of the trucks. Despite this disadvantage, each of these elements—helicopter gunships from three different aviation sections and three clusters of ACAVs from three different platoons and two troops (but all wearing the Blackhorse insignia)—not only survived, they meshed into a cohesive counter-ambush force that overwhelmed a numerically superior enemy. The individual crews performed magnificently under harrowing conditions. The value of months of stateside training together was demonstrated in spades.[13]

Most importantly, the supply convoy was protected. Forty-five combat troopers, outnumbered 13 to 1, soundly defeated the VC.[14] Despite the loss of four trucks and two ACAVs, the bulk of the supplies and personnel arrived at the base camp in good shape. There were no future large-scale attacks on the Long Binh-Blackhorse Base Camp supply convoys—ever. Jack Burns, in a letter home, highlighted the important point. "We messed up that VC battalion pretty bad. It will be a long time before they will think about messing with us again. A little note, the only truck that made it through the ambush without being stopped or hit was the beer truck."

The ACAVs proved equal to the mission—essentially, four ACAVs took on two VC battalions and came out on top. But the vehicles were shown to be vulnerable to concentrated anti-tank fire. The risk to the ACAV crews—especially since the vehicles still had gasoline engines—was vividly demonstrated on that stretch of

Highway 1. Ron Adams arrived on the scene after the major fighting was over. He didn't expect to see what he did.

> I will never forget coming around a bend in Highway 1 … I was shocked by what I saw. I expected to see bodies; I expected to see some burning "thin-skinned" vehicles [trucks]. What I wasn't prepared for was the smoldering mass in the middle of the road. It took me a moment to realize that what I saw was the burning road wheels and the keel of an ACAV; an entire Armored Cavalry Assault Vehicle that was totally destroyed … I can distinctly remember afterwards, all of us wondering, "What the hell have they got that can do that to our ACAVs?" We were not prepared for the intensity of the enemy's fire power … We learned very quickly that the way to respond to enemy contact was with massive use of our own fire power. We started putting tanks in every formation … From that point on, tanks and artillery [and helicopters] were routinely integrated into every operation that we conducted.

The cost of Westmoreland's mistaken insistence that the tanks be withdrawn from the recon platoons before deploying to Vietnam was vividly revealed on 21 November. Virtually all future convoy escorts included one or more tanks cross-attached from the squadrons' tank companies. Eleven days later, another regiment of the 5th (VC) Division ambushed a small convoy (seven vehicles) near the Gia Ray rock quarry. The convoy escort in this case was even more heavily outnumbered than on 21 November. On December 2, however, there were two Delta Company tanks present. As the official after-action report of that ambush recounts: "So violent was the execution of the counter-ambush that, within 70 minutes, the Squadron had rendered the 275th VC Regiment ineffective as a fighting force without the loss of a single trooper."

Bravo and Charlie Troops were awarded a Presidential Unit Citation (PUC) for their actions on 21 November and 2 December 1966. In the larger context, the award of the PUC to elements of the Blackhorse Regiment was doubly significant. First, it was proof that armored forces could make a valuable contribution to the counterinsurgency fight—even when outnumbered. Second, it was validation that the combination of training together and excellent leadership produced a combat-ready unit capable of success on any battlefield. Insofar as the success or failure of 11th Cavalry—representing Armor Branch—was being closely scrutinized, the PUC was a highly desirable vindication.

The Big Three—*Attleboro, Cedar Falls,* and *Junction City*: November 1966 to April 1967

Three multi-battalion operations highlighted the Military Assistance Command Vietnam's (MACV) 1966–67 dry season campaign around Saigon. Operations *Attleboro* (November 1966), *Cedar Falls* (January 1967) and *Junction City* (March–April 1967) were General Westmoreland's attempt to seize the initiative and "win" the war. The 11th Armored Cavalry Regiment participated in all three operations.

That participation was not distinguished by any dramatic battlefield actions. It was, however, particularly noteworthy for the evolution of the role the Blackhorse played within the overall scheme of MACV's plans and operations.

By late 1966 and early 1967, the ground war in South Vietnam had entered a new phase. Sufficient numbers of GIs were in the field to take the fight to the enemy threatening Saigon. GIs from the 1st and 25th Infantry Divisions were conducting aggressive battalion-sized search and destroy missions into areas between Saigon and the Cambodian border where the Communists had unchallenged control—in some cases since the 1930s. The enemy, for his part, had stepped back from the large-scale fights of 1965 and 1966.

Map showing 11th Armored Cavalry Regiment participation in Operations *Attleboro*, *Cedar Falls*, and *Junction City* in 1966 and 1967. (basic map, US Army)

By early 1967, the enemy's main force units had gone to ground in base areas deep in the jungle, hidden from the prying eyes of the ubiquitous helicopters and generally impervious to artillery and bombs. They were assessing the lessons learned from their initial encounters with the Americans, while reequipping and retraining their forces.

General Westmoreland was not content to allow the enemy to just fade away. If they would not leave their bunkers to attack us, then we would go and dig them out of those bunkers. In the six months between October 1966 and March 1967, Westy directed a campaign designed to take the fight to the enemy. Each operation was successively larger and more ambitious than the last. These operations were significant for the 11th Cavalry; they gave the Blackhorse troopers the opportunity to demonstrate the multiple layers of capability they brought to the battlefield, astride their ACAVs, tanks, howitzers and helicopters. The Regiment was finally assigned "normal" missions (i.e. not just convoy escort and road clearing), working alongside all of the other major units in the area.

Operation *Attleboro* started as a chance encounter in the jungles of War Zone C. The 196th Light Infantry Brigade (Chargers) was floundering around the area east of Tay Ninh, when they happened upon several large supply caches containing, among other things, about 1,000 tons of rice—stockpiled by the 9th (VC) Division in anticipation of the start of the Winter-Spring offensive later that month. When the 9th pushed back and two battalions of the 196th became decisively engaged in separate combat actions, the brigade commander seemed unable to mount an effective response. Major General (MG) Fred Weyand, the acting II Field Force commander, stepped in and ordered MG Bill DePuy's Big Red One to pile on. In typical DePuy fashion, they did so quickly and effectively, using both bold maneuver and massive firepower. Eleven infantry battalions eventually became involved in the operation.[15]

As first the 1st Infantry Division and then the 25th Infantry Division (Tropic Lightning), 173rd Airborne and two South Vietnamese Ranger battalions, replaced the 196th Light Infantry Brigade, Weyand became concerned that the enemy commander would hit the supply convoys to relieve pressure on his five regiments under attack. Blackhorse 6 was directed to send a squadron to provide convoy and route security on the road to Dau Tieng and on Highway 13. The 1st Squadron troopers dutifully accomplished their mission, simultaneously trying to convince the infantry colonels and generals that they could do so much more. Their pleas went unheard—for the moment.

Attleboro was a test drive (albeit an unintentional one) for multi-brigade search and destroy missions which became the hallmark of Westmoreland's command in Vietnam. It also demonstrated that mechanized forces could effectively operate in War Zone C, setting the stage for the employment of the 11th Cavalry in a leading, not just a supporting, role in the new year. Former skeptic DePuy became a champion of armor's role in the war; he was impressed by how quickly 1/11 reacted to his call for help and he noted that both ACAVs and tanks could operate freely on and off the roads.[16]

Even the enemy recognized the qualitative change in the war represented by the armored forces. In their official history of the war, the Communists wrote: "However, the soldiers and civilians of Tay Ninh faced an urgent problem that did not yet have a solution: the appearance of U.S. "heavy tanks" at a time when this theater of operations had few anti-tank weapons and when provincial forces had virtually no such weapons … [T]he U.S. tanks … had run rampant, penetrating into many important base areas."

Operation *Attleboro* was also a test drive for the troopers of 1/11. They moved from Gia Ray to Lai Khe, a distance of more than 150 kilometers, with over 140 vehicles in seven hours—without the loss of a single vehicle.[17] They then had the opportunity to practice and refine some of the tactics they had trained so hard on before deploying to Vietnam.

Westy's next multi-division operation was aimed at clearing the Iron Triangle, a 300-square kilometer area of thick jungle located just two-days' march north of Saigon. In early 1967, military intelligence placed a number of main force VC units inside the Iron Triangle (dubbed "steel earth" by the Communists), as well as the headquarters for VC Military Region 4, responsible for the entire Saigon area. Repeated attempts by South Vietnamese units had proven unsuccessful in ridding the area of its unwanted inhabitants. As long as the enemy could use the triangle with impunity, Saigon itself would be vulnerable. Operation *Cedar Falls* was ginned up to take care of this problem once and for all.

In many respects, *Cedar Falls* represented a classic World War II operation—not surprising, considering that most of the senior leaders had cut their professional teeth on the battlefields of Europe. The ground assault was preceded by eight days of concentrated B-52 strikes and massed artillery barrages, which "rattled the windows of Saigon."

The scheme of maneuver was to cordon off the battlefield, using the Saigon and Thi Thin Rivers that marked two sides of the triangle to establish an anvil. On the morning of 8 January, 1967, six infantry battalions were helicoptered into blocking positions across the top of the triangle. Just hours later, mobile forces (the hammer), including two squadrons of the 11th Cavalry under the operational control of the 173rd Airborne, in the words of a reporter, "swoop[ed] down upon the jungle." Subsequently, and by design, *Cedar Falls* assumed the "plodding, unspectacular characteristics" of a conventional war operation. The only problem was that the enemy was not fighting a conventional war and successfully evaded the hammer by withdrawing to areas outside the triangle.

Cedar Falls was significant for the Blackhorse as it represented the first time that planners integrated the Regiment into a major operation from the get-go. The mission assigned to the 11th Cavalry was to attack west from Ben Cat to cut the Iron Triangle in two. The Regiment then linked-up with the 173rd Airborne and conducted combined-arms search and clear missions with the Skysoldiers. Noteworthy here is that all of these operations were off the roads, moving cross-country through the jungle, rubber plantations, and savannah grass—something that had been considered "impossible" just six months earlier. The mounted troopers provided the jungle-busting, mobile firepower needed to root out the entrenched VC, demonstrating to leaders up and down the chain of command that armored units could operate pretty much anywhere.

Cedar Falls was important to the 11th Cavalry for another reason. As noted above, enemy commanders had recognized their own shortcoming in anti-tank weapons. Their solution was to use mines. Shortly after crossing Phase Line Orange, Platoon Sergeant Willie Morrison's ACAV hit the first mine. No one was injured, and the troop commander (CPT Dick Miller) told them to continue toward the objective. A Hotel Company tank further back in the column was the next to detonate a mine a short time later—again, the crew emerged unscathed.

Lieutenant (LT) Bruce Johnson's ACAV made it another 20 feet before "the world blew up. A deafening explosion consumed our ACAV." The mine blew the right-side track off, as well as one road wheel. One trooper had been peppered with small pieces of shrapnel, but did not require evacuation. At that point, CPT Miller sent dismounted mine sweepers forward and the assault continued, albeit at a much slower pace. They found four more mines by the end of the day.

Two Blackhorse ACAVs and one M48 tank were declared combat losses during *Cedar Falls*, and another 16 tracked and wheeled vehicles were damaged, almost exclusively from mines.

Cedar Falls was followed on 22 February by the largest US-led operation of the war. Located inside the 2,500-square kilometer *Junction City* area of operations were fortified installations housing the Communist headquarters and its propaganda organ, Liberation Radio—about 10,000 personnel combined. The Viet Minh began digging the elaborate underground bases early in their struggle against the French. They recognized that the heavy jungles and sparse population in the region provided optimal locations for both command and control and logistical forces. They were close enough to Saigon to threaten the capital, but far enough away and well enough hidden to preclude a surprise attack. Over the decades, the fortifications were reinforced (some with concrete) and made more livable. Defenses were built in layers with interconnecting tunnels, inter-locking fields of fire, and bunkers that were impervious to direct hits by even the largest bombs.

In the end, the operation involved more than ten percent of all US Army troops in Vietnam—about 35,000 on the ground and in support—deployed into an area about the size of Rhode Island.[18] Major General Weyand told his subordinate commanders that the goal of *Junction City* was to "clear (western) War Zone C of enemy forces and installations. The primary objective was the destruction of COSVN [the enemy headquarters]." The concept of the operation was a repeat of *Cedar Falls*;

create a horseshoe along the western, northern and eastern edges of the target area. Blocking positions were occupied by airmobile and airborne assaults along the edges, in preparation for an attack by mechanized forces along multiple axes through the open end of the horseshoe. Sixteen battalions from the US 1st and 25th Infantry Divisions, the 173rd Airborne Brigade and 196th Light Infantry Brigade established the horseshoe, into which two Blackhorse squadrons and a brigade of the Tropic Lightning Division attacked.

If *Cedar Falls* was the birth of the 11th Cavalry's jungle-bustin' capability, then *Junction City* brought it to fully-fledged maturity. As in the previous operation, contact with the enemy was sporadic (with one major exception) but mines were a daily challenge. On par with that challenge, however, was the jungle itself—much thicker than in the Iron Triangle. Larry Gunderman recalls that the War Zone C jungle "was everything it was cracked up to be. It was tough stuff." The heat and humidity didn't make the task any easier, either.

The enemy's infrastructure was a primary target for *Junction City* and War Zone C was a target-rich environment—albeit a well-camouflaged one. On the second day of the operation, a Bravo Troop ACAV started to throw a track.[19] But the crew noticed it before the track came all the way off. The track commander (TC) jumped down to guide the driver in an attempt to "jump" it back on the sprocket. LT Bernie Carpenter relates what happened. "The TC moved his foot and realized there was cement under the dirt." The crew dismounted and used C-4 explosives to blow a hole in the cement and climbed inside. "As we get down, we started finding bodies, commo wire ... If he'd not done that [started to throw a track], we probably would have just driven over it."

The 1st Squadron came the closest of any of the 31 maneuver battalions involved in *Junction City* to making contact with elements of the enemy headquarters. On 11–12 March, 1/11 fought its way through dense jungle and the defenses of a company from the 70th Guards Regiment (the Communists' "palace guard") and elements of the 271st Regiment, 9th (VC) Division, into a base camp that contained, among other things, three concrete bunkers belonging to the enemy's propaganda center.

Colonel Cobb wrote an assessment of the Regiment's performance at the end of *Junction City*. It serves as a worthy evaluation of what the 11th Cavalry had accomplished since its arrival in September.

> The unique dual combat capability of the Blackhorse Regiment ... the ability to move fast and the capability to conduct detailed search and destroy operations—was clearly demonstrated during the operation ... The success achieved by the squadrons in the search and destroy phase of the operation is shown by their discovery of large numbers of enemy base camps, medical facilities and fortified positions. The value of armor protection of fighting personnel was strikingly shown during the heavy and close-in fighting one squadron [1/11] experienced as it fought its way into a tenaciously defended VC Base Camp.

Even the Infantry leaders were beginning to take notice. Well, some of them, anyway.

During the last phase of *Junction City*, the Regiment was once again relegated to securing the lines of communication, clearing Highway 13 of mines and ambushes and escorting supply convoys. But there was also something else going on. Because of its one-of-a-kind status and growing reputation for getting the job done well, senior commanders were anxious to get their hands on some of the Regiment's firepower and mobility. In one eight-day stretch, the 2nd Squadron commander (Lieutenant Colonel Ben Harmon) reported to, in sequence, the commanders of the 2nd Brigade, 1st Infantry Division, the 173rd Airborne, back to the 2nd Brigade, then the 1st Brigade, 9th Infantry Division and on day eight back to the 173rd Airborne. Three days later, 2/11 returned to Regimental control.

The operative concept in each of these command and control relationships was that the Regiment was working for infantry commanders, many of whom had little to no experience working with armored cavalry. Echo Troop platoon leader Jim Abel recalls an incident during *Junction City*. "[W]e were under the command of infantry officers who did not understand or appreciate the capabilities and limitations of armor. For example, the order came down one evening that every man would dig a foxhole, not understanding that we carried our foxholes with us. To them, we were just another infantry outfit with some fancy troop carriers."

Civilian and military leaders in Saigon and Washington declared *Attleboro, Cedar Falls* and *Junction City* as significant victories. Despite the expenditure of tremendous resources and not inconsiderable losses, the Communists did not seem ready to change their operational strategy, however. The enemy was able to replenish his units with both men (from North Vietnam via the Ho Chi Minh Trail) and materiel (from the Soviet Union and China via the Cambodian port of Sihanoukville) by the start of the 1967 rainy season. As one newspaper analysis put it at the end of May: "The preponderance of American field victories in two years has tended to slow the Communists down rather than destroy them. There is still no real indication that the series of drastic defeats inflicted on enemy units in 18 months have sapped their morale. In fact, recent fighting indicates that the Communists are as eager and as well equipped, for battle as at any time in the past."

By the end of its first year in Vietnam, the Blackhorse would discover the validity of this analysis.

Major Changes for the 11th ACR: Late 1966 to Early 1967

Arrival of Air Cav Troop

When the Regiment arrived in Vietnam in September 1966, only a limited number of helicopters and crews came ashore with it. While the squadron aviation sections were mostly complete, the entire Air Cavalry Troop had been left behind. Army-wide aircraft and pilot shortages meant that the unit would not be completely equipped and trained until late in the year.

With the arrival of their equipment at Vung Tau in January 1967, the 11th Cavalry's Air Cavalry Troop—Thunderhorse—became operational and began to establish an enviable combat record. The Regiment was finally complete, with all of the elements available that the designers of the organization had intended. With aerial scouts, gunships, and an airmobile platoon of infantrymen, the Blackhorse now had a formation that could not only find the enemy and initiate a battle, but could also help determine the outcome of that battle.[20] Possessing mobility unfettered by the dense vegetation that could slow down the ground troops, Blackhorse 6 now had an asset under his direct command to bypass difficult terrain, envelop the enemy vertically, and supplement the tremendous firepower of the ACAVs, tanks, mortars, and howitzers.

Using the light fire team—two UH-1C Huey gunships—as the basic fighting force, the troop provided convoy escorts, surveillance in conjunction with the recon troops, immediately-responsive close air support, emergency ammo resupply in the middle of firefights, evacuation of wounded troopers, aerial delivery of propaganda leaflets and riot control gas canisters, and command and control (C&C). The value of these capabilities being immediately responsive to the regimental commander and his squadron commanders cannot be overstressed. Blackhorse 6 did not have to wrangle with other colonels or generals to get the support he needed; Thunderhorse worked for him, not some higher-up or adjacent headquarters. Aviation support in the form of far-reaching eyes, immediately responsive guns, and sneak-and-peak ground recon was at his fingertips, and starting with Colonel Cobb, successive commanders used these capabilities to their full extent.

New missions

Following Operations *Attleboro*, *Cedar Falls*, and *Junction City*, the II Field Force commander's conclusion was that the US and South Vietnamese divisions could concentrate their forces on major operations, while other units conducted economy of force operations to keep local VC units in place. This conclusion would have far-reaching effects on the 11th Cavalry; with its armored protection, mobility, and firepower, it became the premier economy of force unit in the corps area.

As a result of the demonstration of the versatility of its organization and equipment and the flexibility of its leaders, units of the Blackhorse were suddenly in high demand. The 1st and 25th Infantry Divisions were, starting in mid-1967 and with increasing frequency thereafter, reinforced with a Blackhorse squadron for economy of force missions. However, the squadron commanders were generally not content to just sit idly by as the infantry did all the hard work. It was an uphill battle convincing graduates of the Infantry School that parceling out small numbers of ACAVs and tanks to protect fire bases and convoys was not the most optimal use of these assets. Their true value came when they were employed *en masse*. Change did not come either quickly or easily. But it did come. The professionalism, bravery, and hard work of all troopers—from Blackhorse 6 on down—made it happen.

Infusion program

The Army's personnel policy during the Vietnam War was that officers, NCOs, and enlisted men (volunteers and draftees) alike served but one year in the war zone. For those who landed at Vung Tau in early September 1966, the 365-day calendar started on the day they boarded the ships in Oakland.

The personnel managers at US Army Vietnam recognized that this would mean there would be a virtual 100 percent turnover (other than casualties and those who voluntarily extended their tours) in Blackhorse personnel in early August 1967. Everyone would DEROS (Date Eligible to Return from Overseas) at the same time. The resulting loss in experience would be devastating to any unit. The solution was an infusion program, whereby a percentage of Blackhorse troopers would be transferred each month to other units in country in exchange for an equal number of personnel with either an earlier or later DEROS.

The uniqueness of the 11th Cavalry aggravated an already bad situation. There were no other armored cavalry regiments in country. In the area around Saigon, there were only a small number of units with the same military occupational specialties (MOS) as in the Blackhorse. Thus, the pool of MOS-qualified personnel (especially Armor officers, tankers, cavalry scouts, and armored vehicle mechanics) was very limited. Although the Blackhorse leadership had recognized in late 1966 that something had to be done to avoid the rotational hump that would come at the end of their first year in country, that "something" didn't happen in sufficient numbers to avoid the dramatic loss of experience that came when personnel began to go home.

This was especially true in the leadership positions, as commanders were reluctant to let their best leaders leave, to be replaced by unknown or untested officers and NCOs from other units or new in country. In some cases, there was a substantial lag between when a trooper went home and his replacement arrived—sometimes due to in-country shortages, but also because of Army-wide shortfalls. Third Squadron's Howitzer Battery commander, Captain Leo Deege, recalls that "as we were losing officers and no replacement came in, our operational capability became degraded … I must say we were spread very thin." Combined, these issues led to a substantial loss of experience in the Regiment starting in the early summer of 1967—leading to disastrous consequences on 21 July.

To make matters even worse, Westy needed a fire brigade up near the DMZ, and 2nd Squadron was tapped to be part of it.

Diversion up North: April to October 1967

General Giap in Hanoi was worried. Between *Attleboro, Cedar Falls,* and *Junction City,* his forces around Saigon were taking a beating. The men and supplies he could replace; but the base camps, cache sites and training areas would take considerable time to restore. They would probably have to be moved to Cambodia. His opposite number in Saigon (Westmoreland) did not appear to be willing to give him that time. Giap had to come up with a way to relieve the pressure.

Hanoi initiated offensive actions in the early spring of 1967; they got Westy's attention. He curtailed the large-scale operations north of Saigon after *Junction City* and sent a division's worth of Army forces northward, allowing the Marines to marshal their combat strength and deal with the enemy threat. In early April 1967, General Westmoreland initiated Contingency Plan North Carolina. Task Force (TF) Oregon, a division-sized ad hoc formation, was created with the mission of taking over the Chu Lai area south of the Demilitarized Zone. This allowed the Marines to concentrate forces nearer the border with North Vietnam being threatened by General Giap.[21]

The 11th Cavalry's 2nd Squadron was selected to be one of the Army forces making the northward trek.

Captain (CPT) Bill Abbey was the 2/11 aviation section leader at the time. He remembers the pressure to get everything ready in a hurry: "[S]even days before, [we had] been deep in War Zone C on Operation *Junction City* west of Quan Loi. With little warning, the Squadron had disengaged, road marched back to base camp, packed duffel and embarked by sea." The departure of 2/11 meant that the Regiment would operate for six months minus one-third of its ground combat power. No one asked Blackhorse 6 if he thought this was a good idea.

In March 1967 in an article entitled "GIs' 'Most Troublesome' Province," *Washington Post* Foreign Correspondent Ward Just characterized the area near Chu Lai as "probably the worst province in South Vietnam ... where outposts are overrun almost nightly, where North Vietnamese regulars can amass more than a division of men without difficulty, where a three-day battle can rage barely 10 miles from the [provincial] capital."

Although the original intent had been for 2/11 to serve as the *de facto* divisional armored cavalry squadron for TF Oregon as a whole, it remained under the operational control of the 196th Light Infantry Brigade the entire time it was deployed. The 2/11 troopers faced primarily first-line North Vietnamese Army units while operating as part of TF Oregon. These were not village VC, farmers by day, amateur soldiers by night. These were well-trained, well-led professionals; hard-core NVA with a mission.

Troopers soon fell into a daily routine of clearing Highway 1, protecting Marine and Army engineer work parties fixing the road, and conducting recons-in-force (RIFs) in the area around Chu Lai. Troops and platoons were placed under the

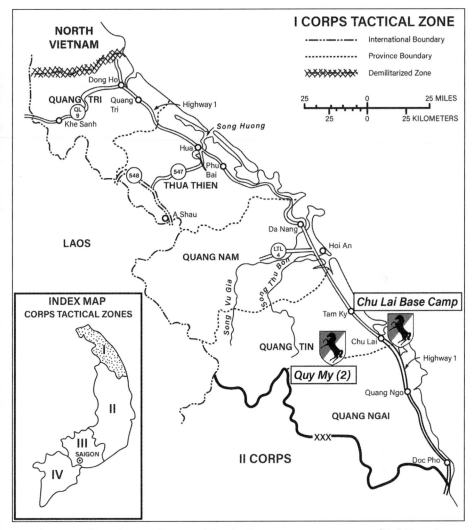

Map showing 2nd Squadron, 11th Armored Cavalry Regiment operations as part of Task Force Oregon in I Corps Tactical Zone in 1967. (basic map, US Army)

operational control of infantry battalions and companies, mostly to provide mobile firepower. In some cases, the armored vehicles ended up being virtual stationary pillboxes as the notoriously under-gunned Marines were grateful for any help they could get.

However, it wasn't until near the end of the squadron's deployment up north that 2nd Squadron had a direct confrontation with the 2nd (NVA) Division. It didn't go well for the NVA. During the battle of Quy My (2) hamlet on 24 September 1967, Fox Troop found the 3rd Company of the 3rd (NVA) Regiment in Quy My

(2) west of Chu Lai. Golf Troop, Howitzer Battery and the 2/11 aviation section piled on. The NVA company had been sent to the village as the advanced element in preparation for a regimental-sized attack against the Blackhorse troopers.

The fighting between the well-armed (rifles, light machine guns, rocket-propelled grenades (RPGs), recoilless rifles and mortars) NVA company and the Blackhorse ACAVs, howitzers, and gunships was fierce. The courageous NVA soldiers defended virtually every stone hut in the hamlet, but they were out-gunned and eventually overwhelmed.[22]

Of the estimated 60 NVA soldiers who comprised the enemy force in Quy My (2) on 24 September, 48 were killed—80 percent casualties, not including any wounded who managed to escape.

***

Mathematically, the departure of 2/11 had cut the Regiment's combat strength by one-third. In fact, it was even more debilitating. Although Blackhorse 6 rarely had all three squadrons under his operational control anyway (less than 30 days total in 12 months), now he only had two squadrons to start with. Operation *Kittyhawk* (the defense of the base camp and key installations in eastern Long Khanh Province) meant that one squadron was not available for other missions—leaving but one squadron and Air Troop to conduct offensive operations. As a result, from April to October 1967, the 11th Cavalry was significantly limited in the number and types of operations it could execute.

CHAPTER 3

The Fight Intensifies: May to July 1967

The war in South Viet-Nam is entering a violent phase.
GENERAL NGUYEN CHI THANH,[1] NORTH VIETNAMESE ARMY

Anti-tank weapons are organic to VC and NVA units company size and larger; the enemy prefers to use these weapons at 400 meters or less.
"VIETNAM BATTLE TIPS," 3/11 CAVALRY

We were veterans now. No one had to tell us how important it was to be ready to wheel into battle at a moment's notice.
RODNEY GEORGE, HOWITZER BATTERY, 3/11 CAVALRY

The situation for the 5th (VC) Division was getting desperate. Since the arrival of the 11th Cavalry in September 1966, eastern Long Khanh and western Binh Tuy Provinces had ceased to be hospitable places for their tax collectors, recruiting teams and base camps. The division was being (not so gently) shoved out of its traditional base areas and away from the rice growing and population centers.

The 1967 rainy season started on schedule in late May–early June. By this time, the 11th Armored Cavalry Regiment (minus 2/11 deployed with TF Oregon) had returned from the area north and west of Saigon to its assigned tactical area of operations near Xuan Loc. During the period that the bulk of the Blackhorse had been gone, the 5th (VC) Division had replenished its losses from the 21 November and 2 December ambushes. Replacements from North Vietnam made their way down the Ho Chi Minh Trail and infiltrated into the division's jungle hide-aways in the Hat Dich and May Tao Secret Zones and southern War Zone D.

Communist commanders and political officers alike pored over the lessons learned from their first combat engagements with the "steel ponies." The division's two regiments (274th and 275th) were strengthened with large quantities of RPG2s, the latest shoulder-fired rocket-propelled grenades provided by the Soviet Union and China. Unit commanders at all levels—platoon through regiment—applied the lessons learned, training the old hands and new recruits alike in ambush and assault techniques. RPGs should be fired in volleys they learned, concentrating multiple rounds on individual vehicles. Combined arms—anti-tank weapons, mortars, machine guns, and rifles—were to be used in heavy volume at all times. Hit-and-run techniques, with well-planned and rehearsed escape routes, were vital to success. Models of ACAVs, tanks and gunships were constructed. Gunners were repeatedly trained on their vulnerable points and engagement techniques, including how to lead a moving target.

Above all, detailed knowledge of the opposing force and intelligence preparation of the battlefield could ensure success. Not allowing major elements of a convoy to leave the killing zone—as had happened on 21 November—was stressed. Not allowing the elements in the killing zone to gain fire superiority—as had happened on 2 December—was emphasized over and over again.

By May 1967, the commander of the 5th (VC) Division was ready to strike against the Blackhorse Regiment again.

Pacification of Long Khanh Province: 21 May and 21 July Combat Actions

Back in The World in May and June of 1967, there were momentous events aplenty. Elvis married Priscilla in Las Vegas, as women around the world shed tears and men breathed a deep sigh of relief. At the Indianapolis 500 on Memorial Day, Al Unser, Sr., drove his white Lola Ford #5 over 164 miles per hour, but still came in second to A.J. Foyt. Al's #5 was emblazoned with the Blackhorse insignia during the race.[2]

Not long after that, the summer of love went into "high" gear in San Francisco. Dozens of flower children gathered in Golden Gate Park, chanting and meditating in time to tunes provided by The Grateful Dead and Big Brother and the Holding Company. Others greeted the summer solstice grooving to the sounds of the just-released *Sgt. Pepper's Lonely Hearts Club Band* (*Lucy in the Sky with Diamonds*, indeed). Fans were linin' and tokin' up at the Fillmore to hear Jefferson Airplane and the Jimi Hendrix Experience. Elsewhere, hate kicked into overdrive as race riots struck cities from Tampa to Buffalo. Israelis and Arabs were in open conflict, as the Six Day War saw Holy Land real estate change hands once again. Not to be left out, Hollywood created a make-believe war with the release of *The Dirty Dozen*. Those Blackhorse troopers who faced real bullets and explosives in mid-1967 could only shake their heads at the difference between war, Hollywood-style and war, VC-style. But few back at home were interested in what was happening in that far-off jungle. After all, how could you get excited about a few VC fireworks when Jimi Hendrix was setting his guitar on fire and Jim Brown was killing all those Nazis?

During early to mid-1967, the enemy made a concentrated effort to push the Blackhorse out of Long Khanh Province. Between the end of March and the end

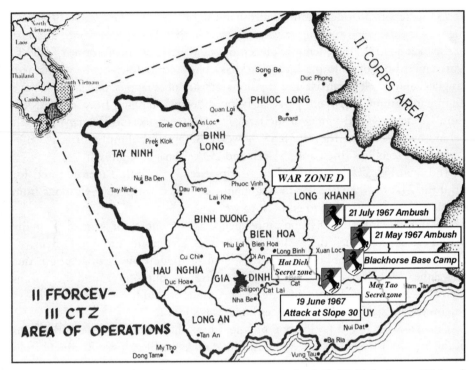

Map showing 11th Armored Cavalry Regiment operations in the first half of 1967. (basic map, US Army)

of July, the 5th (VC) Division, along with some VC Local Force and Main Force units, hit the cantonments (a claymore and grenade attack on the Long Binh Convoy Staging Area in mid-April and a mortar attack against Blackhorse Base Camp on the night of 3–4 April), as well as two significant convoy ambushes (on 21 May and 21 July) and a major attack against 3/11's Command Post (CP) on 19 June. These attacks were supplemented by well over a hundred mining incidents, small arms, and hit-and-run attacks against patrols, convoys, and helicopters.

With the sole exception of the 21 May ambush of a Kilo Troop convoy, the Blackhorse soundly defeated the VC forces, forcing the 5th (VC) Division to relocate deep into the jungles of War Zone D—far away from Saigon and the population- and resource-rich areas from which they had sustained their revolutionary efforts prior to the arrival of the 11th Cavalry.

21 May ambush

In late February 1967, the regimental intelligence officer received a report that two VC battalions had moved into the area northwest of the Gia Ray rock quarry (used by the engineers for road building and guarded by Blackhorse units). A follow-up report was received in early April indicating that the two battalions were still in the area. This report provided more details than the earlier one. The VC, according to the new report, were stopping travelers in the Gia Ray Forest area (south and east of the rock quarry). The enemy soldiers propagandized those they stopped. The VC wore a mixed-bag of uniforms, including khaki, blue, green, stolen South Vietnamese fatigues, and black pajamas. The division's arsenal of weapons was a logistician's nightmare (ammo and spare parts all being different), ranging from new AK47s from China to WWII-vintage American, French, German, and Russian rifles left behind by the French. They did have, however, 82mm and 60mm mortars, 75mm and 57mm recoilless rifles, and .51-cal. and .30-cal. machine guns.

The reported VC battalions then "disappeared," remaining unaccounted for until the 21st of May. The 274th Regiment, reinforced with heavy weapons from divisional units, was ready to go back to work.

The US 9th Infantry Division's intelligence assessment at the start of the rainy season forecast that the 5th (VC) Division would "step up its 'monsoon offensive', taking advantage of the hoped-for curtailment of friendly aircraft operations due to weather. Probable targets include those government outposts around the periphery of their May Tao Mountain base of operations ... [and] convoys along Hwys [highways] 1, 2, 15, and 20." That estimate was spot-on.

Unbeknownst to the 1st Platoon of Kilo Troop, they were to be the initial focus of the 5th (VC) Division's renewed push to dislodge the Blackhorse Regiment from the province.

Third Squadron assumed responsibility for security at the Blackhorse Base Camp and Gia Ray rock quarry, as well as the daily logistical convoys, on 12 May 1967. Kilo Troop was tasked with the mission of protecting the quarry, including the engineer and resupply convoys between there and the base camp. These missions had become strictly routine. Since the ambush on 2 December, the only action along this stretch of road came from the so-called "Suoi Cat sniper."

This VC rifleman fired at the convoys every day but never hit anything. After a while, the troopers even stopped shooting back—afraid that they might hit the sniper, who could be replaced with someone who was a better shot. There was, however, plenty of discussion about why the sniper could never hit anything.

The 1st Battalion, 274th (VC) Regiment bivouacked about 300 meters to the west of its chosen ambush site, then occupied their positions during the night of 20–21 May. Contrary to SOP, they did not dig in (other than a few spider holes); most soldiers just camouflaged themselves in the 30-inch tall grass and small bushes along Highway 1 just outside the village of Suoi Cat. The commander sited his one 75 mm recoilless rifle (RR) at one end, and his remaining six 57 mm RRs, four .51-caliber heavy machine guns, and numerous RPG2s on both sides of the road along the two kilometer-long killing zone. The RPG2s were the Communists' answer to the increased number of American armored vehicles entering the war. They had been issued to the 274th during its recent stand-down.

The 600-man strong 1st Battalion of the 274th was a mixed command, including new recruits just arrived from the north and experienced local guerrillas. They weren't parade ground material, but they could fight. Some sported red and blue checkered scarves. The commander had those wearing South Vietnamese uniforms stand out in the open by the side of the road in an attempt to make things look "normal."

The VC told the residents of Suoi Cat that their overnight assembly area was off limits to all civilians. Further, they ordered the woodcutters and farmers to not run away and hide like they usually did when a fight was coming. Their absence might be noticed, thus warning the oncoming convoy. Instead, the VC instructed them to stay in the fields until the shooting started and then to lie down. With all the preparations completed, the battalion settled in to await the ARVN convoy that was scheduled to pass that morning.

The plan was to attack the South Vietnamese Army truck convoy, then wait for the small American armored force to react from Gia Ray. The battalion would then take pre-arranged routes out of the area before more tanks could arrive from Blackhorse Base Camp.

The stretch of Highway 1 chosen by the VC for this ambush was well-acquainted with war. While Army engineers had turned parts of the national highway into an interstate-quality road around Saigon and Bien Hoa, the portion of the "highway"

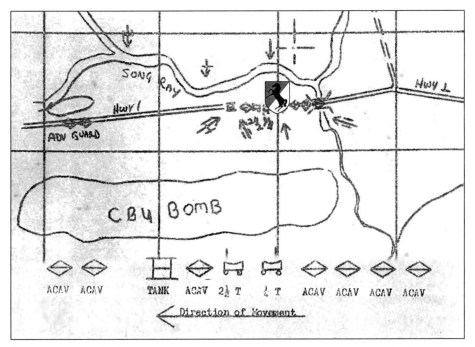

Map of the 21 May 1967 ambush showing enemy dispositions (top) and convoy organization (bottom) (reproduced from the regimental after-action report). (basic map, US Army)

that ran east out of Xuan Loc toward the coast was described by one Blackhorse trooper as "a pot holed and decrepit back country roadway that runs through a desolate jungle countryside." The uneven surface made mine-laying easier. The VC liked it that way, and the Saigon government was not able to do anything about it yet. That's why the Blackhorse had been sent to pacify this part of Long Khanh Province. But it still wasn't quite pacified.

The 1st Platoon of Kilo Troop passed through the ambush site twice that day, remembered by some as a beautiful Sunday morning. The VC were well camouflaged and none of the usual signs of trouble were evident. The farmers were in the fields, the kids in Suoi Cat waved and begged for candy, and there was civilian traffic on the road. When they passed through the second time headed east to west—just ahead of the ARVN truck convoy—the enemy commander apparently became concerned that he had been discovered and sprung the ambush.

Armored Cavalry Assault Vehicle K-10 was the first to be hit when the VC sprang the ambush at 0850 hours that morning. Together with K-11, the two vehicles were the advanced guard, traveling 600–700 meters in front of the main body. The tactic was intended to allow them to trip any ambushes before the main body entered the killing zone. In effect, the two lead tracks were the sacrificial lambs, hoping to force the enemy to prematurely trigger an ambush, allowing the main body to avoid the killing zone and maneuver against the flank of the ambushers. Recon scouts knew and accepted such risks. It was part of the job. But this time, the tactic did not work.

When the 75 mm recoilless rifle round slammed into his ACAV, Staff Sergeant (SSG) Homer Pittman immediately broadcast on the platoon radio net: "Ambush! Ambush! Ambush!" Within seconds, the VC opened up from both sides of the road with volleys of anti-tank rounds, light and heavy machine guns, rifles, and mortars. The seven ACAVs, one tank, one 2½-ton truck, and one ¼-ton jeep were all caught in the kilometer-long killing zone—K-10 and K-11 (the advanced guard) out front, followed by the lone tank (M-34), the platoon leader (K-16), the mess truck, engineer jeep, and the last four ACAVs (K-14, -13, -17, and -18). Every vehicle was hit by at least one anti-tank round in the initial fusillade. The enemy fire was not only heavy, it was accurate. Over the course of the half-hour-long ambush, each of the seven ACAVs was struck by an average of ten anti-tank rounds.

Private First Class (PFC) Tony Puglisi, a side-gunner on K-10, who had just celebrated his birthday the night before, remembers those first desperate moments.

> As we rode up to the ambush site, I was nervous because I saw a lot of soldiers dressed in what looked like ARVN (South Vietnamese) uniforms. There could have been about 30 or more. After the first RPG hit, they dispersed to the trees to our right … We took the first volleys of RPGs and we had to abandon the track, it was ablaze. [Anthony] Royball and myself jumped on to the first track that came along (K-11) … I looked to the rear and saw 2 uniformed soldiers aim their rifles at us. I knew we were goners but a mortar dropped right on top of them and when the smoke cleared there was only a smoking boot on the road (their own friendly fire). The ACAV continued down the road and we cleared the ambush site only to find a huge

ARVN unit truck convoy … That was when our Lieutenant said, "we have to go back—there are wounded that need help." So, we went back into the ambush to save our buddies.

The ARVN trucks—full of infantrymen—did not follow.

M-34, the lone tank in the column, was recognized as the biggest threat. Fourteen anti-tank rounds penetrated its armor, and many more left gouges where they glanced off the turret and hull (30 hits in all). The driver and loader were seriously wounded within the first few minutes; both machine guns, the main gun sight, range finder, and radios were all knocked out. The tank was immobile in a ditch. Despite this punishment and their own wounds, the surviving track commander (SSG David Wright) and gunner (PFC Kerry Nelson) continued to fight the tank until the relief force arrived.[3]

Nelson was hit by the third round that penetrated the turret, temporarily blinding him. Wright, too, was wounded in the initial barrage, but he poked his head out of the turret despite the danger. What he saw surprised and scared him, as the VC were "walking around the vehicles like it was an everyday occurrence to them and carrying their wounded." Some of the guerrillas were as close as 15 feet away from his tank.

At that point, Wright's and Nelson's training, instinct, and courage took over. Wright spotted where the rounds aimed at his tank were coming from—a recoilless rifle crew set up about 100 meters away. He tried using his pistol first, but—not surprisingly—missed. Nelson, who still couldn't see but had moved to the loader's position, fired his .45-caliber grease gun from the loader's hatch. He, too, missed. So Wright tried to fire the main gun, not expecting it to work. It did.

Firing a combination of white phosphorous and canister rounds (in effect, 90 mm shotgun rounds loaded with steel ball bearings), they killed the three-man RR crew and destroyed their weapon. Even though he couldn't see, Nelson slammed round after round into the chamber, while Wright fired from his exposed position. Wright would fire a round then traverse the turret slightly. Nelson, remembering his own training and using his hands as his eyes, would reload. Wright would then fire again. When the VC attempted to overrun the tank, Wright told Nelson where they were, and the still sightless gunner-turned-loader hurled hand grenades from the open loader's hatch. Because the .50-cal. machine gun had been damaged by one of the RPGs, David Wright resorted to firing his .45-caliber pistol to keep the VC at bay.[4]

The lesson learned after the 21 November ambush to include at least one tank in all convoys paid huge dividends on that fire-swept stretch of Highway 1 on 21 May 1967.

Further back in the column, the last four ACAVs were taking a beating. K-17 and K-18, the last two vehicles in the convoy, had just crossed the small bridge over the Suoi Rai Creek when they heard Pittman's call. They started firing. They did not, however, follow the SOP to herringbone[5] left and right; instead, the two ACAVs attempted to move forward through the killing zone. K-18 was the first to grind to a halt after multiple hits. The ammo and gas tank caught fire and the ACAV burned down to the road wheels, killing all aboard. The fire was so intense that the vehicle commander's body (SSG Walter Simpson) could not be identified.[6] It wasn't much longer before K-17 also came to a stop after being pummeled by anti-tank rounds. Only two of the crew survived, including the platoon medic, Jimmy Force. His actions in the midst of the hellacious enemy fire saved the lives of 24 of the 25 Troopers who were not killed in the ambush (Pittman was the sole unwounded trooper in the entire platoon).

K-13, just ahead of K-17, was hit multiple times in rapid sequence. PFC Ed Miller, a side-gunner, was the only crewmember to survive. "After moving about 50 yards or so," Ed recalls, "our ACAV was jolted by a recoilless round that struck the driver's compartment and disabled the engine. A second round struck the TC [track commander] turret and knocked out the .50-cal. machine gun with it. A third round hit the left side M60 (machine gun) and carried through hitting my M60 on the right side." All of the vehicle's weapons were "blown apart," so Miller picked up an M16 rifle, and then started heaving grenades at "the attackers that were moving in my direction." The VC retaliated with their own grenades.

> The blast knocked me down. I stood back up and they threw a second one at me. That one did knock me out. How much time went by, I don't know. I was starting to come to. My arms were out behind me and I was being dragged away by the VC. Again, some time has passed. The sound of the [relief force] choppers and tracks could be heard coming along with increased gun bursts. The VC dropped my arms, leaving me there. That is the last thing I remember of the ambush.

Fifteen minutes into the ambush, 1st Platoon, Kilo Troop, had ceased to exist as an organized military unit. As one trooper wrote later: "At this moment, all concerted action as a Platoon ceased. The Platoon Leader had no communications and the acting Platoon Sergeant had no vehicle or no radio. With the ambush only moments old, the fight had degenerated on the American side into a series of undirected and desperate actions on the part of single vehicles and individuals."

Homer Pittman was the acting platoon sergeant of Kilo Troop's 1st Platoon. He was one of the old timers who had been in country for nine months. Even though they had been over this road a hundred times or more, he wanted to be up front—not so much to navigate but to be where the action was likely to be if there was to be any action. He was single-handedly responsible for holding the platoon together. Extraordinary bravery was on display on board every one of the column's vehicles that morning, but Pittman stood out—literally and figuratively—amongst them all. His Distinguished Service Cross citation tells what happened from the start.

> Jumping from the vehicle, he immediately began grenading enemy soldiers to provide cover for his men. Seeing another vehicle nearby, Sergeant Pittman took command of it and fought through intense fire to evacuate the friendly wounded. This vehicle was also disabled and set afire by an enemy rocket ... Once on the ground he exposed himself to the enemy fire time after time to carry the ammunition to the perimeter he had set up. For twenty minutes Sergeant Pittman directed

the fire of his men to repel the assaults by the numerically superior and determined insurgents. His courage in the face of grave danger was responsible for saving the lives of many of his men.

The citation glosses over some important details from that morning. Sighting the initial group of VC about 25 meters from the side of the road, Pittman used his best baseball arm to toss grenades into their midst. Bodies went flying as he repeatedly hit the bull's eye. But this first group was not the only threat to his crew. "Bullets were flying everywhere," he later recalled. It was, in the vernacular, a target-rich environment. He saw three more VC on the side of the road, and two others on the road itself, apparently intent on pilfering the burning ACAVs. He tossed a couple of grenades in both directions. Enemy soldiers fell left and right.

About this time, K-11 and K-16 arrived at the head of the column. Pittman boarded K-11 and told the driver to head back into the maelstrom. He was sure there were troopers still alive in the killing zone and it was his responsibility to help them survive. As they drove, VC gunners took aim with all their weapons. Two RPGs hit (one through the back door) in quick succession, along with sheets of small arms fire, killing Specialist 4 (SP4) Anthony Royball and PFC Rodolfo Saenz. Then, as they passed M-34, a brave (but foolish) VC stepped out into the middle of the road and fired an RPG directly into K-11's engine compartment.

SP4 Dennis Christenson gunned the engine (which miraculously continued to work) and ran the enemy gunner over. The next RPG, however, struck the ACAV's transmission and K-11 slowly ground to a halt. But Homer Pittman had been able to contact the radio relay station atop Gia Ray Mountain and made sure the outside world knew his platoon needed help—pronto!

With K-11 now a sitting duck, Pittman, Smead Edwards, William Moline, Tony Puglisi, and Billy Brush dismounted, throwing weapons and boxes of ammo to the ground. They ran to a wood pile along the side of the road, prepared to make their last stand.[7] They were surrounded by burning vehicles, dead and dying troopers, and, of course, VC still trying to kill them.

Pittman organized his six-man defensive perimeter—one M60 machine gun on the right, one on the left, and four riflemen in between. For 20 minutes they fought back, concentrating their combined fire on targets as they emerged. Every time a VC rose to take a shot, he became a silhouette target for at least one M60 machine gun and four M16s. Somehow, they survived until help—in the form of Air Cav Troop gunships followed by the rest of Kilo Troop—arrived.

Tony Puglisi remembers those final moments.

> Homer Pittman acted in a military manner, he rose to the occasion and shouted out orders and took charge ... I fired over 1000–2000 [M60] rounds in the direction rounds came from that killed Saenz & Royball and it was a good thing that I did, an enemy soldier (NVA) approached me from a spider hole and he flung a satchel charge into the PC [personnel carrier] to my right with the ramp down. It went off and more than likely killed the soldier still sitting in the driver's seat ... At that point I did not know if we would live or die but I used all my

> training and I was determined to live ... Once the Gun Ships got there I was so happy to see them ... I knew then that I was now safe along with my Friends.

The ARVN convoy, loaded with armed infantrymen, that was apparently the intended target of the ambush, stopped short of the ambush site and did not even attempt to come to the rescue of the American platoon. They sat at a safe distance and watched and listened as Blackhorse troopers died. It is a tribute to the 45 brave troopers of Kilo Troop's 1st Platoon (and the three accompanying engineers)—and especially to Homer Pittman—that only 18 were killed. The major lesson learned was that no missions should be considered "routine."

Less than a month later, the 274th (VC) Regiment struck again—this time against the command post of the 3rd Squadron. In this case, the squadron commander (LTC Frank Cochran) meticulously followed both SOPs and lessons learned. The commander of the 274th, on the other hand, did not. The attack in the so-called "Slope 30" area south of Blackhorse Base Camp, featured an anti-armor heavy Viet Cong force against an outnumbered, but well-prepared, 11th Cavalry night defensive position.

Colonel Roy Farley, the new Blackhorse 6, who had been in command of the Regiment about a month when the Slope 30 attack occurred, believed that the action was significant. "For the first time," he wrote in the official after-action report, "the enemy chose to engage armored cavalry forces of the 3rd Squadron in a night attack." The attack, which was "successfully defended," proved that "armor protection, despite massive fires from enemy mortars, recoilless rifles, RPG-2's, and heavy machine guns" was decisive. Major Dave Doyle, the 3/11 operations officer who was inside the perimeter during the attack, was even more succinct: "The VC had tailored their regiment into an antitank heavy force in hopes of gaining a short, dramatic victory over a US Armor unit; a feat not accomplished to date ... A reinforced [Cavalry] troop had dealt a far superior force a stunning defeat."

The stage was now set for the final act in the 5th (VC) Division's attempts to retain control over eastern Long Khanh Province.

Highway 20 ambush

In early July, Colonel Farley was alerted to begin planning for a new operation. In January, Westy had informed senior US embassy officials that he considered Highway 20 between Saigon and Da Lat to be critical to the economic health of South Vietnam. He intended to upgrade the highway during the dry season. The senior civilians, from the ambassador on down, wholeheartedly endorsed this view. Operation *Emporia* was designed to fulfill this goal.

However, it was well into the rainy season when operations began on 21 July 1967. Since most of the work was expected to take place on or near the road, the higher-ups deemed the timing to be acceptable and the mounted 11th Cavalry to be the right force for the job. Third Squadron was assigned the lead role (2/11 was still up north and 1/11 was just back from Operation *Paddington* with the Australians). The squadron's mission was to "provide security for the engineer land clearing teams and to conduct local reconnaissance operations" along Highway 20.

Like many other roads in Vietnam at the time, Highway 20 was not well-maintained. Once paved, the neglected surface had washed out in many places, making travel an adventure. The idea behind Operation *Emporia* was to clear the road of VC, have the engineers repair it so that civilian and military traffic could drive unimpeded and more expeditiously to and from Da Lat, and to establish long-term security by improving the militia outposts along the highway.

Highway 20 was one of the more important roads for the economic viability of the South Vietnamese government. It was the main artery between the political capital of Saigon and the produce-growing capital of Da Lat. However, the road was not "secure"; throughout 1966 and well into 1967, it could not be traversed, even by military convoys, without the constant threat of ambush. The VC used the highway during the hours of darkness to transport rockets from secure base areas in the Central Highlands to launching sites surrounding Saigon. Troops from the 5th (VC) Division routinely ambushed military convoys, while local guerrillas extorted heavy taxes from the civilians who sought to get their vegetables to the hungry citizens of Saigon. As Tom Wicker wrote in the *New York Times* in early 1967: "Over the Dalat highway comes a large part of the vegetables to feed the 2.2 million people of Saigon. Yet the Viet Cong highway tax must first be paid on every head of lettuce, every bunch of carrots, before they reach the capital."

In the early morning hours of 20 July, two enemy battalions attacked a South Vietnamese infantry battalion south of Blackhorse Base Camp. A man who said he was a private from the 1st Battalion, 275th (VC) Regiment surrendered after the battle. He knew a lot more than most privates. Among the tidbits he shared with his interrogators was that the remaining two battalions of the 275th Regiment were located north of the Dong Nai River. As it turned out, that was not true. Those two battalions had crossed the river and were settling into their ambush positions along Highway 20, even as "Private" Nguyen Van Minh was telling his tall tale.

Given the notoriously leaky operational security in Saigon, it is safe to assume that sometime between January and July the enemy was informed that clearing and upgrading Highway 20 was a priority mission for the Americans. The commander of the 275th (VC) Regiment planned an ambush in advance and waited for the word that the 11th Cavalry was coming. He got that word from a reliable source.

In many cases, lax operational security amongst GIs gave the local VC warning about upcoming operations. Careless words spoken on the radio, maps lost out an open helicopter door, or casual conversation with the local barber were often the first hints of a new offensive. Increases in "routine" radio transmissions, helicopter overflights, and stockpiling of supplies at the base camp provided additional hints to the enemy about scale, location, and timing.[8]

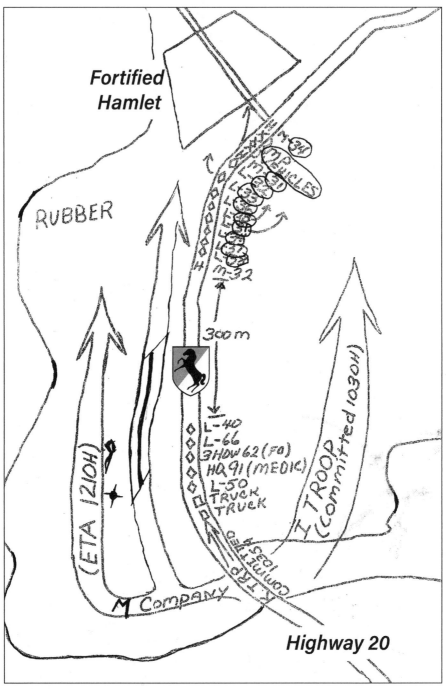

Map of the 21 July 1967 ambush showing initial and follow-on dispositions of 3rd Squadron units (reproduced from the regimental after-action report). (basic map, US Army)

In this case, however, the enemy commander didn't have to rely on conjecture or deductive reasoning. And, it was a good thing, for the 275th was not Hanoi's best. In fact, it had a pretty bad reputation, even among its own soldiers. Based on battlefield performance, prisoner of war interrogations, and captured documents, the 275th was seen as "somewhat of a stumblebum outfit."

But if you know when, where, and in what force your adversary will be coming, even the most unskilled—or unlucky—unit can achieve success. That was the case on 21 July 1967. The commander of the 275th (VC) Regiment had an insider to tell him all the details of the upcoming operation. *Dai Uy* (Captain) Trang was an officer in the Army of the Republic of Vietnam. Because of his English-language skills, he was assigned as an interpreter for the 11th Cavalry. As such, he had virtually unfettered access to the Long Giao base camp. Well before Operation *Emporia* was to begin, the local VC kidnapped *Dai Uy* Trang's two daughters. They said he would never see them alive again if he didn't tell them the details of the upcoming operation.

Dai Uy Trang did what most fathers would do.

Thus forewarned, the enemy commander knew where and when elements of the Regiment were coming. His was not to be a "hasty ambush." He planned a diversionary attack. He developed and implemented a multi-faceted deception plan. He moved two reinforced battalions into position at least two days before the day of the ambush. The operation was meticulously planned and flawlessly executed.[9]

This was not the first time that the Communists had ambushed a convoy on this stretch of road. The Viet Minh ambushed a French Army convoy on the La Nga River Bridge on 1 March 1948.[10] Then, as in July 1967, the VC were trying to cut lines of communication and deny the Saigon government control of the population. In both cases, the enemy inflicted significant casualties on those in the convoy.

The more things change, the more they stay the same.

The enemy plan was complex, but with an expert eye for detail. The site chosen for the ambush was ideal, with a ditch on one side of the road and a berm on the other side that offered protection for the ambushers and an obstacle for the armored vehicles to get off the exposed roadway. An abandoned South Vietnamese compound offered both cover and concealment for the anti-tank gunners tasked with halting the lead vehicles. The bend in the road ensured that the two elements of the convoy (separated by 300 meters) could not provide mutual support to each other. The rubber trees that came up to the edge of the road offered concealment for the ambushers as they lay in wait, as well as for their escape. Because they were planted diagonally to the road, the mature rubber trees hindered the advance of reinforcements as they tried to roll up the flanks of the ambush.

The enemy commander planned and executed supporting attacks against South Vietnamese militia installations to the north of the ambush, diverting attention and assets away from his main effort. Air Cav Troop and local militia troops responded to an attack on an outpost in the early morning hours of the 21st. That fight was barely over when elements of the D800 Dong Nai (VC) Battalion attacked another outpost further north on Highway 20. A militia company, mounted in armored cars, was ambushed by the same VC battalion as they rushed to the relief of their compatriots. This action occurred less than an hour before the lead elements of the 3/11 convoy entered the killing zone.

Moreover, the 5th (VC) Division implemented a deception plan that diverted attention away from the ambush site onto other parts of Long Khanh Province. Knowing that they were unlikely to completely conceal their pre-combat activities, the VC spread rumors to the local farmers that the division's objective was to attack Australian troops further to the south. An attack near the village of Cam My (south of Blackhorse Base Camp) in the early morning hours of 20 July was another piece of the deception plan. "Private" Minh's defection and confession was the final piece.

The deception plan was a smashing success. Two weeks before the ambush, the intelligence analysts at US Army Vietnam concluded that the 5th (VC) Division had deployed to attack the Australian units. One week before the 21 July ambush, the same analysts were convinced that the threat had shifted southwards into the zone of the 1st Australian Task Force and posed little to no threat to the 11th Cavalry.

A detachment of the 615th Military Police (MP) Company (720th MP Battalion) accompanied the convoy as it left Blackhorse Base Camp on the morning of 21 July 1967. The 15 enlisted MPs and one officer were mounted in armored gun jeeps (with M60 machine guns on pedestal mounts, "rat patrol" style) and a new V100 Commando armored car with twin .30-cal. machine guns. They were all near the head of the convoy with the mission of providing traffic control. Some of the MPs noticed, however, that there was virtually no civilian traffic once they turned from Highway 1 onto Highway 20.

Along the initial 50-plus kilometers, the MPs and a Mike Company tank (the repaired M-34 from the 21 May ambush) alternated leading the convoy. When the coast looked clear, an armored MP jeep led; when something just didn't look right, the MPs motioned for the tank to take the lead.

To Staff Sergeant (SSG) Bill Everett from 3rd Squadron's Howitzer Battery, things didn't look right. "We all knew that this was a big mission and were on our toes so to speak. The strange part of it was as we were going through the small village just before the ambush, that there were no children and hardly any people in town. But one thing did stand out; over on my left side was a French Priest, collar and all, giving us the sign of the cross and blessing us as we went by." In hindsight, Everett realizes that should have been a tip-off of what was to come.

Lieutenant (LT) John Miller was the track commander (TC) of M-34, the point of the 3/11 spear as it thrust into the enemy's stronghold of southern War Zone D. He had been in the Army about a year and in country just two months, but he already knew that the VC liked to ambush convoys on the highway. So he divided his time between land navigation and watching for signs of trouble. He recognized the abandoned South Vietnamese compound as the proposed temporary base camp for the 86th Engineers, so his map reading chore was just about complete. It was then that the MPs signaled for him to take the lead and clear an obstacle of felled trees across the roadway.

It's hard to miss a 50-plus ton tank clanking down a road in broad daylight, so the soldiers of the 275th (VC) Regiment hidden inside and around the abandoned compound saw M-34 before Miller saw them. As was typical, the VC targeted the lead vehicle with both recoilless rifle (RR) and rocket-propelled grenade (RPG) fire when they initiated the ambush. Sitting exposed in the TC's hatch, Miller and his equally exposed loader were also the targets of numerous rifles and light machine guns. Two RPGs hit the tank—one in the turret that knocked out the radios and the other in the track, immobilizing M-34 where it stood. Despite the onslaught of so much enemy firepower, John Miller coolly issued his fire commands. The crew of M-34 laced the ambushers with both canister and machine gun rounds. But the relentless volume of enemy fire eventually caused serious damage to their vehicle. The crew dismounted and sought shelter with their individual weapons in the roadside ditch.

LT George Powers was the leader of Lima Troop's 3rd Platoon, the squadron's advanced guard. He had his entire platoon of eight ACAVs, along with three tanks (M-34 and M-31 in the lead and M-32 further back). Powers was in the eighth vehicle in the column. They had departed the base camp main gate on time at 0700 hours and were now just under three hours into the mission.

When the ambush was sprung, Powers' platoon immediately executed the SOP-standard herringbone in order to engage the enemy forces on both sides of the road. He'd been in country almost six months, and this was not his first rodeo. But the six-foot deep ditch on one side and high berm with trees growing on top on the other side prevented the vehicles in the killing zone from getting off the road. Unable to maneuver his platoon, Powers attempted to gain fire superiority. Unusually, the Blackhorse troopers were out-gunned by the VC, and a number of vehicles were quickly knocked out of action.

Private First Class (PFC) Gary McLennan was driving one of the lead ACAVs when the shooting started. He had just over 70 days in country, but he made up for a lack of experience with plenty of courage. He did as he had been trained to do, immediately turning his track into the herringbone formation so that the vehicle commander and side gunners could engage the VC. But McLennan didn't just sit idly by in his driver's hatch. Looking in the direction of the enemy, he spotted several VC who were furiously firing their weapons into the killing zone. Gary mashed on the accelerator and ran over the enemy position. As he was backing up, his ACAV was struck by a recoilless rifle round and McLennan was mortally wounded.

Several of the vehicles attempted to assault what seemed to be the main source of enemy fire, the abandoned South Vietnamese compound. There was a dirt berm on four sides of the compound and a six to ten-foot deep moat in front of the berm. Numerous enemy gunners hid in the moat or behind the berm. The ACAVs that could maneuvered into the tall grass growing between the road and the old fort. ACAV L-33 made it as far as the moat before being stopped by enemy fire. The crew had to fight the VC hand-to-hand in order to evacuate their burning vehicle. RPG teams, low-crawling through the grass, assaulted the ACAVs at point-blank range, causing significant damage and many casualties. Their initial counter-assault was not successful, but the embattled Lima troopers gave at least as much as they took.[11]

A forward air controller (FAC), light fire team (two Huey gunships), and the 3/11 command and control (C&C) aircraft (with the squadron commander, Lieutenant Colonel (LTC) Hillman Dickinson, aboard) were all in the air when the ambush was sprung. While the C&C bird was further back (near the junction of Highways 1 and 20), the gunships were close to the ambush site. Thunderhorse 26—a UH-1C gunship flown by Captain (CPT) Galen Rosher and Chief Warrant Officer 2 (CW2) Melvin Strickland—immediately began making firing passes on the dug-in enemy on the eastern side of the road. Return fire was heavy and their Huey was hit numerous times. They were the first Blackhorse helicopter shot down by the enemy in Vietnam—but the crew of four all survived.

The airborne FAC quickly contacted the fast movers and, because of their close proximity to Bien Hoa, the first pair of F105s delivered their payload of 500-pound, 750-pound, and cluster bombs on the ambushers less than 30 minutes after the first shots were fired. They made additional passes to spray the ground with 20 mm cannon fire. Because of the short distances between the enemy and the friendly elements on the road (and the fact that the first call for fire contained erroneous coordinates), artillery was initially used sparingly in response to the ambush.

The wall and ditch along the road limited options, but also saved lives. As the crews abandoned their burning ACAVs, they gathered in the ditch to treat the wounded and continue the battle. Ron Kast was the commander of ACAV L-34. He was the platoon's scout section sergeant, responsible for his own ACAV and three others. His vehicle was hit multiple times in the first moments of the ambush. Gathering his crew, some of whom were badly wounded, he led them from the burning vehicle to the relative safety of the ditch. Several other troopers were already there. As the VC rose up from their ambush positions on both sides of the road in an attempt to overrun the vehicles and kill the men on the ground, Kast organized a 360-degree defense. Realizing that they needed more ammo, he ran through the withering fire to one of the abandoned ACAVs, returning with both bullets and grenades. His Silver Star citation relates what happened next.

> Despite the fact that Sergeant Kast and his men were surrounded, he successfully maintained order and discipline and rallied his men to repel the aggressors … Seeing that the insurgents

were within hand grenade range, Sergeant Kast stood up amidst the heavy fire and killed two enemy and dispersed the others. He then noticed a group of five Viet Cong attempting to capture the weapons aboard one of the vehicles. Sergeant Kast leaped from the ditch and charged the bewildered insurgents. He cut all of the aggressors down with accurate fire.

Specialist 5 (SP5) Mike Seigler was one of the Lima Troop medics helping to treat casualties. After pulling several wounded crewmen from one of the burning vehicles, he helped them to the ditch where he set about stopping the bleeding. Once they were stabilized, he returned to the chaos of the killing zone, twice entering disabled vehicles to help evacuate stricken troopers. Seigler realized that unless he could get the wounded out of the killing zone, they would likely all die. So he jumped into one of the MP escort jeeps, fired it up, and drove to his makeshift aid station. In full view of the enemy, he loaded several wounded on board and then drove through the length of the ambush—hundreds of meters through a veritable curtain of rifle, machine gun, grenade, and anti-tank fire—until he reached a spot where a helicopter could land. He told a reporter later: "I saw one RPG2 cross two feet in front of my face. I guess Charlie was so surprised at seeing a jeep barreling down the road he forgot to aim."

Mike Seigler saved the lives of 11 men that day.

The enemy commander had obviously given his soldiers an order to strip the vehicles of weapons whenever they could. Almost as soon as the wounded crewmembers reached the ditch—and in some cases while the crews were still on board—VC left their ambush positions and climbed up on the ACAVs. SSG Doyle Lucas (who had been in country less than one month) and his gunner, SP4 Mike Pasceri (who had ten months in-country), on tank M-32 at the back of the first group of vehicles, saw what was happening and decided to put an end to this battlefield thievery. Lucas on his .50-cal. and Pasceri using his coaxially-mounted 7.62 mm machine gun, raked the vehicles further up the road.[12] Under this hail of accurate fire, the VC scurried back into their spider holes—well, those that lived, anyway.

About 300 meters behind the lead element, the multiple antennas on ACAV L-66 (the troop commander's vehicle) and HOW-92 (the Howitzer Battery's forward observer vehicle) drew lead like magnets. The troop commander, CPT Bill Abernethy, was a 1962 graduate of The Citadel; he was a professional soldier. He had been in Vietnam since December 1966 and had been awarded a Silver Star at the Slope 30 fight on 19 June. He'd taken command of Lima Troop just two days before the ambush. He reported receiving "light small arms fire" just before the first RPG slammed into the lead tank.

On HOW-92, the driver and two side gunners were killed less than a minute into the ambush. SSG Bill Everett, the TC, was blown from the cupola by one of the RPG blasts. He recalls: "We took a RPG in the driver side and the ACAV stopped and on fire, [PFC John] Campa was hit very bad, [PFC George] Forster was KIA [killed in action], [PFC James] Bean was hit.[13] Everyone in and around the tanks and ACAVs were screaming and hollering rounds flying all over the place, we took another RPG hit that blew me off the cupola and into a ditch."

Everett was dazed from his unexpected dismount, which might explain what happened next. He joined a group of four or five wounded troopers in the ditch and started throwing grenades. "The VC kept coming at us and it was plain to see that we were going to get over run, I had about 2 grenades and 6 M79 [grenade launcher] rounds on my flak jacket and was throwing them at the VC. One of the men said, "Hey, you're throwing M79 [rounds] at them. I said, 'They don't know they are not grenades.'""[14]

CPT Abernethy was trying to accomplish multiple tasks—get Lima Troop in position to react to the ambush, report to his boss, call for artillery, and fire the left-side M60 machine gun. He was frantically trying to alert LTC Dickinson of what was happening (his radio signals were not going out, probably because the antennas had been swept away in the deluge of enemy bullets and RPGs) when the forward observer track behind him burst into flames. Directing his driver to place L-66 between the burning ACAV and the enemy so the crew could escape, he continued to engage the VC with his machine gun. That's when a barrage of anti-tank rounds struck his vehicle and mortally wounded the new troop commander.

SP4 John Effinger, the driver on ACAV L-31, describes the fate of the L-66 crew.

> PFC Clarence South was driving L-66 during the ambush. He was struck in the head by a homemade claymore and had a brass shell casing embedded in his forehead. Knocked unconscious, and slumped in the driver's seat with his head covered in blood, I suspect he appeared dead to the VC who later overran the track … I recall that Larry Dawson was the TC … Frank Leal would have been on the right side 60 [machine gun] and Captain Abernethy would have manned the left gun which was closest to the radios. There was also an ARVN interpreter assigned to L-66 who was killed … All crew members had survivable wounds but were shot once in the forehead and executed by the VC. It appears the crew were unable to defend themselves while being overrun …

L-66's right side gunner, Danny Leal, had written home the previous day: "Tomorrow morning we are going up north about 20 miles from here. We are going to support Vietnamese while they set up a new village." He and his crewmates never made it to that new village.

And so it went, all up and down the length of the convoy caught in the killing zone. The better part of an enemy regiment, reinforced with local VC—probably about 1,500 soldiers—in prepared positions and with plenty of anti-tank weapons and machine guns, against an armored cavalry troop, a tank platoon, and an MP platoon, stretched out single file along a kilometer and a half of exposed roadway. Under constant fire for almost two hours. Most on the ground, chased from their gasoline- and ammo-fueled blazing vehicles. With no radio contact and no idea if someone was coming to rescue them.

With great difficulty because of how the rubber trees were planted, India Troop got off Highway 20 and moved parallel to the road on the east (right) side. Mike

Company moved on a parallel track on the west (left) side. The going off-road was so slow that it took India Troop almost an hour to reach a point parallel with the head of the convoy, just over one kilometer from where they started. Kilo Troop moved straight up the highway and into the heart of the killing zone.

CPT Ron Hofmann (Kilo Troop commander) was the most experienced commander in the squadron. He had almost three years in country by this time and had never seen an enemy unit remain in contact this long. He was sure that the enemy "was long gone by now" and that his troop would simply be mopping up.

He was wrong.

What Kilo troopers found as they roared into the killing zone was the sight of enemy soldiers swarming over burning ACAVs. They were looking for weapons, ammo, radios, and the prized C-rations that might supplement their boringly-repetitive rice and *nuoc mam* (fish sauce) diet. Other VC remained in their ambush positions behind the berm on the left side of the road, hidden by the dirt and masked by the rubber trees. RPG gunners were as close as 15 meters away from their targets when Kilo Troop came up the road. They could hardly miss. In short order, numerous Kilo Troop ACAVs were hit and the crews knocked out of action. CPT Hofmann, one of his platoon leaders, and several TCs were either dead or seriously wounded.

Despite the desperateness of the fight, Kilo Troop's arrival tipped the balance. Slowly but surely the ACAVs gained fire superiority over the exceptionally determined VC. Within about 45 minutes of Kilo's arrival, return fire slackened noticeably. The survivors of the 275th (VC) Regiment broke contact and slipped away. Their rear guard kept up desultory fire until just after 1300 hours, while Mike Company and India Troop pursued the stragglers.

Mike Company's assault up the west side of the highway caught the VC just as they were breaking contact. Out in the open and exposed to the cross-fire between Mike's M48 tanks and Kilo's ACAVs, the VC suffered heavy casualties. At least nine VC were killed within the first few minutes of the tanks' arrival. Air strikes on the suspected routes of escape added to the death and destruction on the west, while artillery and India Troop worked the enemy over on the east.

Post-ambush estimates were that dozens of 75 mm recoilless rifle and RPG2 rounds were fired, along with tens of thousands of rifle and machine gun rounds. By this time, the few vehicles in the initial killing zone that were still operational were running out of their basic load of ammo of 20,000 machine gun rounds. The crews that had to dismount were in even worse shape. The gunships that responded to the ambush expended 72,000 rounds of minigun ammunition, 262 rockets, and 600 rounds of 40 mm grenades.

Unusually, the enemy did not employ mortars or mines during the ambush. Just as unusually, the enemy did not break contact after the initial barrage, or even after an hour's worth of fighting. The fact that the commander of the 275th (VC) Regiment was killed during the ambush (as were the commander and deputy commander of the attached Dong Nai Battalion) may have had something to do with these two abnormal tactics by the enemy. According to one of the VC battalion's assistant political officers (Captain Tran Van Tieng, captured in 1969): "On 20 July 67, the entire [275th] regiment left the base camp to go on an operation. On 21 July 67, the regiment ambushed an American armored column on Highway No. 20 north of Tuc Trung Strategic Hamlet. As a result of the action there were approx 30 vehicles left burning on the highway (sic). In the action the [275th] regiment sustained over 100 casualties, including both KIA and WIA [wounded in action]."

Much of the 11th Cavalry chain of command at all levels was new on 21 July 1967, as was the 3/11 staff. Colonel Roy Farley had taken over the Regiment in May. LTC Dickinson had been in command of 3/11 for 19 days; CPT Abernethy just two days. In fact, all of the troop/company commanders, except Ron Hofmann, had only recently taken command of their units. The squadron operations officer was new to the squadron, and the intelligence officer was new in country. LTC Dickinson estimated there was an "80 percent turnover of personnel in a six-week period in July and August 1967."

CPT Terry Wallace (the 3/11 personnel officer) recalls that with just two months in the squadron, he was considered "one of the old guys ... There were new people all over the place ... The infusion program didn't work very well."

Although the personnel and equipment losses were relatively high as a result of the 21 July ambush, the enemy suffered even more. As noted above, the commander of the 275th was killed during the ambush, as were two battalion commanders. Because of the significant number of killed and wounded and the loss of a substantial number of weapons, the 2nd and 3rd Battalions of the 275th (VC) Regiment and the Dong Nai Battalion were forced to retreat into their base areas hidden deep in the jungles of southern War Zone D.

India Troop's LT Charlie Locklin, recalls that there were other enemy casualties as well. After spending two days clearing the battlefield, 3/11 continued Operation *Emporia*. "It was during this time that we confirmed Chinese were advising and assisting the VC as we uncovered buried Chinese which we believed were casualties from the ambush on HWY 20 the 21st of July."

The Blackhorse Regiment held the battlefield, and, in cooperation with the 52nd (ARVN) Ranger Battalion, cleared Highway 20 all the way to the II Corps boundary. An operation that higher headquarters had estimated would take 45 to 60 days was completed in 27.

As Colonel Farley noted, it was a win-win proposition. "The population will be able to transport their goods to market freely [including not having to pay VC taxes] and allied forces will be able to react quickly to the movements of VC units in the province."

The 11th ACR had, at a substantial cost, accomplished its mission. Third Squadron was awarded a Valorous Unit Citation for its actions throughout June and July.

As the 11th Armored Cavalry approached its one-year anniversary in South Vietnam, a guiding principle took effect that distinguished the Blackhorse from all other units in country. It wasn't until a year later that Colonel George Patton put it into a catch phrase that became the motto of the Blackhorse troopers. But "find the bastards, then pile on!" was how the 11th Cavalry operated from this point forward.

The idea was simple. Send out multiple scouts on the ground and in the air. Once they found something, marshal overwhelming force to defeat whatever enemy force had been found. There was nothing new in that concept; it was tactics 101.

But what was different was the ability of the 11th Armored Cavalry Regiment to do it *all by itself.* No other single brigade-sized unit commander in Vietnam had the organic mobility, firepower, and agility to both find and pile on effectively. It was more than just a motto—it was what made the Blackhorse unique.

CHAPTER 4

The Blackhorse Makes Its Reputation: Late 1967 to Late 1968

> It is the consensus of responsible commanders that 1968 will be the pivotal year. The war may go on beyond 1968 but it is unlikely that the situation will return to the pre-TET condition.
>
> EARLE WHEELER, CHAIRMAN OF THE JOINT CHIEFS OF STAFF

> This province [Long Khanh], which little over a year ago was completely Viet Cong dominated, is now relatively safe.
>
> ROY FARLEY, BLACKHORSE 6, 1967

> Mobility and firepower were utilized to protect and reinforce threatened areas.
>
> *MACV COMMAND HISTORY 1968*

Back in The World, the transition from 1967 to 1968 brought a rise in both inflation and hemlines; the cost of living doubled, and the miniskirt length halved. Free love, hippies, and hallucinogenic drugs competed with race riots, Arab-Israeli warfare, and the Prague Spring for headlines. The youth of the world took to the streets to make their voices heard; gunshots that took the lives of Martin Luther King and Robert Kennedy were just as loud as those voices. On 21 November, Americans learned that there were now 200 million of their "fellow citizens."

Meanwhile, action in Vietnam reached a Clausewitzian culminating point.

***

The period from late 1967 to the end of 1968 saw a series of punches and counter-punches as both sides attempted to settle the war on the battlefields of South Vietnam. The assault on Loc Ninh in November 1967 was countered with a massive sweep of the border area in December-January by two divisions and the 11th Cavalry. The February and May Tet/mini-Tet offensives were each followed by multi-division counter-offensives involving over 100,000 allied troops. The enemy's feeble mid-August to mid-September "third offensive" was swept aside by increasingly effective clear-and-hold operations under the leadership of Westy's replacement, General Creighton Abrams.

At the end of the year, American and South Vietnamese forces held the battlefield, left to them by VC and NVA units hounded into Cambodia. But the battlefields were not the only things ceded to the allies; so, too, was the military initiative. The Politburo in Hanoi determined that the key to victory now lay in Paris and Washington, not in Saigon; in political, not military solutions.

For the 11th Cavalry, these developments meant gradually moving toward the border into new areas of operation, greater attention to cleaning out the village-level VC, and increased emphasis on working with South Vietnamese forces. Those would all come in 1969; until then, there was plenty of old fashioned, toe-to-toe fighting—fighting that resulted in recognition of the tremendous mobility and firepower of the 11th United States Cavalry. The year was one of decision on the battlefield. It was also a year of cementing the reputation of the Blackhorse Regiment.

In the fall of 1967, the Regiment was attached to the 9th Infantry Division, but was receiving its operational guidance directly from the commanding general of II Field Force Vietnam. The campaign plan for 1967 directed the Regiment to "conduct search and destroy operations within Long Khanh Province, to coordinate with the CG [commanding general], 18th Infantry Division (ARVN) to secure highways within the province and to hinder Viet Cong tax collection along these highways." The Blackhorse also had a "be prepared to" mission as the rapid reaction force for Long Binh, Bien Hoa, and Vung Tau.

For the Blackhorse troopers, this meant engaging in (as the Regiment's annual report stated) "extensive road and jungle clearing, penetrations into known or suspected base camps and staging areas, search and destroy operations aimed at preventing VC infiltration of populated areas and extensive night operations to interdict VC movements. Particular emphasis was placed on road and bridge repair and jungle clearing operations along major routes and near population centers."[1]

The Regiment had done a thorough job in pacifying Long Khanh and Binh Tuy Provinces. The ambushes along the major roads east of Saigon virtually stopped after July 1967, as did attacks on civilian and military targets in the provinces through which these roads passed. By the fall of 1967, the security situation in the provinces and along Highway 1 between Blackhorse Base Camp and Long Binh had stabilized to the point that convoys were being conducted primarily at night (when it was cooler and there was less civilian traffic), escorted only by MPs in machine gun jeeps. The night no longer belonged to Charlie in Long Khanh and Binh Tuy Provinces.

The enemy was reeling from the sustained assaults in the area south of Xuan Loc. Operations by the 11th Cavalry, a brigade of the 9th Infantry Division, the 1st Australian Task Force, and the 18th (ARVN) Infantry Division against the Hat Dich and May Tao Secret Zones disrupted the VC's ability to contribute to the Spring-Summer Campaign (Tet), allowed the local population to get their products to market, and ensured voters could cast their ballots in the September election. The combined US-Australian-South Vietnamese operations left the enemy on the verge of collapse in the area east of Saigon. The enemy realized that there was a new sheriff in town, and he rode a black horse.

A captured document from October 1967 revealed the depth of the enemy's problems.

> The enemy [allied] attacks and raids had caused us to suffer from quite a great deal of trouble in the task of supplying the front [i.e., the combat units]; we are having to face great difficulties in regard to food supplies. At the present time, our troops in the district and province are encountering many difficulties which greatly affect our fighting task ... Our people in the base and deep areas ... are living in an upsetful situation ... due to too much bombings ... [and] are suffering from all sorts of shortages. The constant attacks ... have greatly affected the people's mind ... The reason is that the enemy [allies] has strongly attacked and harassed us [the VC] and caused our troops to be constantly in a state of alert.

The Blackhorse had demonstrated the firepower and mobility of an armored cavalry regiment so well that General Westmoreland and his staff had been converted into at least partial believers. The Army Chief of Staff was already a believer when he convinced Westy to accept the Regiment in 1966. But, as General Johnson told Colonel Roy Farley during a visit in August 1967, despite the fact that "initially there had been doubts concerning the ability of armor to function in Vietnam," the "fine record of the 11th Armored Cavalry Regiment had eliminated these doubts." Even "Airborne Westy" was beginning to believe.

The record of the Blackhorse Regiment in, this, its most challenging period to date, speaks for itself. The troopers, from door gunners to engineers, from cooks to tunnel rats, from track commanders to first sergeants, from platoon leaders to Blackhorse 6 himself, got it right. They all wrote a new, brilliant chapter in the Regiment's history.

But some senior commanders still retained the ingrained conviction that Vietnam was not "armor country." All that changed in 1968.

Prelude to Tet: November 1967 to January 1968

By the end of 1967, Blackhorse troopers were facing an enemy that was qualitatively different from the enemy around Xuan Loc when they first arrived in country. In November 1967, the CIA—with input from Military Assistance Command Vietnam in Saigon—concluded that significant battlefield losses and recruitment difficulties had decimated local guerrilla forces. Heavy infiltration from the north had replaced the VC guerrillas with NVA regulars in most main force units. Thus, even the so-called VC regiments were, by mid- to late-1967, mostly led by and filled with officers and soldiers who had been trained and equipped in the north.

However, that same intelligence analysis concluded that major efforts would be required to maintain the status quo. "To do so will require both a level of infiltration much higher than observed [thus far] in 1967 and intensive VC recruitment as well.

Considering all the relevant factors, however, we believe there is a fairly good chance that the overall strength and effectiveness of the military forces and the political infrastructure will continue to decline."[2] Based on this estimate of the strength of the enemy forces, the analysis concluded that "Communist strategy is to sustain a protracted war of attrition ..."

This conclusion was wrong—very wrong.

This estimate, agreed upon by the representatives of the major intelligence agencies, contributed to the lack of strategic warning about the upcoming Tet offensive. There was a general belief within the intelligence community and military leadership that the enemy was neither inclined toward nor capable of a major nation-wide offensive. Just two and a half months later, these predictions would prove disastrously wrong. Despite numerous indicators—including captured documents and prisoners—the fact that Hanoi had, almost six months earlier, decided to stage just such a nation-wide offensive during the Tet holidays of 1968, was not believed by most senior US and South Vietnamese leaders until after the attacks had already commenced.

Although General Westmoreland in Saigon and Admiral Sharpe (US Commander-in-Chief Pacific) in Hawaii were convinced that the enemy "was no longer capable of

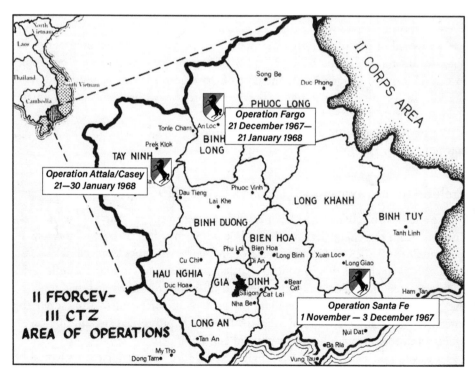

Map showing 11th Armored Cavalry Regiment operations in late 1967 and early 1968. (basic map, US Army)

a military victory," that did not mean that the troopers of the Blackhorse Regiment could sit back in the saddle and bask in the tropical sun. Quite the contrary, in fact.

Although the battles through mid-1967 had been ferocious, they were generally set-piece ambushes on main roads, firefights during recon-in-force operations, or contacts in base camps deep in the jungle. There were long periods of quiet in between. This pattern was to continue through the end of the year and for the first month of 1968. However, from that point forward, the squadrons of the 11th Cavalry—individually and collectively—were involved in sustained periods of combat until the end of August 1968. Contact with enemy squads, companies, battalions, and regiments was made virtually daily for weeks at a time. The troopers had passed their preliminary tests with flying colors; now came the mid-terms, which would establish the Regiment as the premier armored fighting force in Vietnam.

Most Blackhorse troopers spent Thanksgiving 1967 in the jungle on Operations *Santa Fe* and *Kittyhawk*. Their share of the 57,000 turkeys, 28 tons of cranberry sauce, 15 tons of mixed nuts, 8 tons of hard candy, and 33 tons of fruitcake (*tons of fruitcake?*) that Uncle Sam sent to Vietnam was prepared by the cooks in the Long Giao base camp and helicoptered out to the fire bases and night defensive positions along the length of Highway 1 and in the jungle near the May Tao Secret Zone.

Ninety-degree temperatures and 93 percent humidity made it feel less like Thanksgiving, but everyone made do as best they could. Troopers piled the familiar "turkey and fixins" onto their paper plates, and gave thanks for still being alive. The South Vietnamese could only marvel at food that was so foreign to them, but they too could understand the sentiment of being alive—and free.

About the same time, intelligence analysts at MACV believed that the build-up of forces they were detecting was an indicator of a renewed offensive in the border region only (not country-wide and not in the cities). Reports from local agents and villagers alike indicated the presence of regiment- to division-sized enemy units in the An Loc-Loc Ninh area. Squads and platoons of mostly NVA soldiers were visiting local villages and hamlets, confiscating government-issued ID cards, food, and money. The enemy soldiers spoke openly of an upcoming assault against Loc Ninh during the third week of January. While in hindsight, these reports are easily identifiable as part of the enemy's cover and deception plan, at the time they appeared to be real; they fit the pattern of the other indicators, including numerous small-unit contacts and newly constructed base camps.

So II Field Force Vietnam put together three brigade-sized operations along the border north of Saigon in late December to track down and isolate up to three enemy regiments thought to be there. The 11th Cavalry was dedicated to Operation *Fargo* around the already-famous Highway 13—Thunder Road. The mission was to engage and destroy enemy main force units, identified as the 271st, 272nd, and

273rd (VC) Regiments, clear and secure Highway 13 from An Loc to Loc Ninh, and to interdict further infiltration out of Cambodia.

In essence, the 11th Cavalry was tasked to open Thunder Road so that additional forces could reinforce Loc Ninh if needed (in case there was a repeat of the November 1967 assault there, as was expected), secure land clearing operations along the road to reduce the possibility of ambush, and find and destroy the enemy regiments responsible for those ambushes.

Unfortunately, the radio intercepts, prisoner interrogations, and agent reports were all part of the Communists' highly-successful deception plan for the Tet offensive. By the time the Blackhorse troopers arrived in the area near the Cambodian border, the enemy forces were either already on the outskirts of Saigon or back across the border in their Cambodian sanctuaries. As Regimental Command Sergeant Major Bill Squires described it, Operation *Fargo* was "a dry hole, no fortifications, no move[ment], no dinks, no nothing."

Contact with the enemy proved elusive. Although the area was honeycombed with trails, there were few signs of fresh activity. The 9th (VC) Division employed economy of force tactics effectively; plant a mine here, send out RPG teams there, but never get decisively engaged. John Longhauser recalls the few contacts they had involved chasing elements of the 274th (NVA) Regiment back across the border into Cambodia. Ominously, these were not ragged guerrillas but well-trained front-line soldiers. "The enemy was well equipped, tan uniforms, pith helmets and in large numbers. We learned later they were on their way to the Saigon area in support of Tet attacks." Dee Cuttell adds: "It was obvious to us after we'd been there a couple of days that the enemy had withdrawn back across the Cambodian border into his safe havens." As the official after-action report called it: "Viet Cong reaction to Operation *Fargo* was unexpectedly light."

Contact was even lighter during Operation *Attala/Casey*, initiated on 21 January 1968. As the 2/11 after-action report noted: "No enemy units were identified during the operation and the only significant intelligence matter was the knowledge of the enemy's extensive use of mines." Not only was the operation unproductive, it was also frustrating and costly. For example, in the course of ten days, 1/11 lost 8 troopers killed and 17 wounded due exclusively to mines—with only one VC base camp destroyed and no VC bodies to show for it.

Thus, the eve of Tet found the Regiment chasing phantoms across the central and northern tier of War Zone C—and far from the enemy's objectives of Saigon, Bien Hoa, and Long Binh. The 1st, 2nd, and 3rd Squadrons, along with four infantry brigades (2nd Brigade, 101st Airborne Division, 1st Brigade, 1st Infantry Division, and 1st and 3rd Brigades, 25th Infantry Division), were scouring the jungle for the elusive enemy. As the Big Red One division's after-action report for the period laconically states: "Operation *Attala*, a II Field Forces operation … aimed at locating and destroying the 165th NVA Regiment, met with no results."

The enemy's cover and deception plan had worked exactly as planned.

Tet '68: January to March 1968

The start of the biggest battle of the Vietnam War found the Blackhorse Regiment far from the action because US military leaders had been hoodwinked and were chasing ghosts.

Lieutenant General (LTG) Fred Weyand, commander of II Field Force, was a notable exception.

He worked hard throughout December 1967 and January 1968 to convince his boss that the enemy was not only capable, but also had the intention of conducting a large-scale attack on the South Vietnamese capital in the early part of 1968. While Westy's intelligence experts were telling him that Khe Sanh, not Saigon, would be where the heaviest blow would fall, and his political advisors were saying that the enemy would "never" conduct military operations during the sacred Tet holiday truce, Weyand—who served as an intelligence officer in the China-Burma-India Theater in WWII—argued otherwise.[3]

Perhaps because he was so focused on Khe Sanh, Westy allowed Weyand to stack the deck by scaling-back the border operation and bringing more battalions closer to the population centers around Saigon. Weyand said in an interview in 1988: "[O]ur radio intercepts began picking up the movement of units toward Saigon, which caused us to cancel a major multidivision operation we had planned to launch in the northern part of III Corps, about 100 miles north of Saigon. That really proved to be a stroke of good fortune, for if those units had gone north, the VC would have had a field day in Saigon."

While Weyand was convinced that the enemy would attack in strength against the population centers and military installations near his headquarters, he knew he could not simply ignore the potential threat near the border. Thus, he gathered his infantry and artillery strength for what he expected to be a set-piece battle around Saigon. He gave his most mobile units the task of tracking down the enemy forces near Cambodia, but kept them within a day's march of where he expected the action to be. While light infantry mounted in helicopters might be more mobile in such a situation, there were not enough helicopters available in all of his command to move more than a brigade's worth of infantrymen at one time. And, once the light infantry was on the ground, well, they were "light." The lack of heavy weapons was what gave them their battlefield mobility; it also meant they lacked the staying power to go toe-to-toe with a determined, well-armed, superb infantry foe.

The 11th Armored Cavalry Regiment, on the other hand, had superior mobility, heavy firepower, and a spirit that would help them prevail where others might fail. Weyand's aide de camp recalls: "He differed somewhat from other US general officers in Vietnam in that, despite his infantry background, he was a strong proponent of armor."

Consequently, he carefully allocated the mechanized forces available to him. He gave explicit instructions to the commanders of the 1st, 9th, and 25th Infantry

Divisions that they were to keep their mechanized infantry and armored cavalry units "on a string." They were the key to a quick reaction to whatever his counterpart in the enemy headquarters was planning; the division commanders could not commit these assets without first checking with Weyand. To Blackhorse 6, he made it clear that he might need his unit's mobility and flexibility, so be prepared for a change in mission.[4]

Tet '68 changed the lives of all Blackhorse troopers—then and since. As General Donn Starry wrote in his seminal work on armored forces in Vietnam: "For South Vietnamese and free world armored forces the battles of 1968 marked the acceptance of armor as an asset to the fighting forces in Vietnam. That acceptance was won on the battlefield by a demonstration of mobility and firepower that silenced all critics."

For the Blackhorse Regiment, Tet was *the* turning point of the war—and the acceptance of armor as "an asset to the fighting forces in Vietnam." From this point forward, the 11th Cavalry would be in the thick of the fight—every fight. It would become the "fire brigade" that many within the Armor community had advocated since the summer of 1966. No major operation was conducted, or battlefield victory won, in the provinces around Saigon until US forces withdrew from South Vietnam that didn't feature the Blackhorse in a prominent role.

That role was more than simple subordination to an infantry division, running roads, protecting convoys, and supporting dismounted assaults. Within a month of Tet, the Blackhorse was finally allowed to use the awesome firepower and mobility inherent in the Regiment.

But first, the Regiment had to "ride to the rescue." The settlers were being threatened and needed help. Like the cavalry on the western frontier, Blackhorse troopers mounted their steeds and came charging into the flanks of the enemy. Reminiscent of Major Howze's last mounted charge at Ojos Azules in May 1916, the ACAV-, tank-, and helicopter-mounted cavalrymen rode into the fight against another group of bandits with weapons blazing. The advantage turned to the allied side and the VC began their retreat, unable to accomplish any of their military objectives wherever they ran into the troopers mounted astride steel ponies.

Taking nothing away from those who were the first line of defense at the Long Binh logistics depot and the Bien Hoa Air Base, the timely arrival of all that firepower is what made the ultimate difference. The fight dragged on until nearly the end of February, but the outcome had already been decided. It was LTG Weyand's decision to rely on armor instead of helicopters for mobility and firepower that shaped the victory. And it was the tactical and operational flexibility of the Blackhorse Regiment that made it happen.

The story of how 4,000-plus Blackhorse troopers pulled out of ongoing operations, reversed course, moved into an unknown situation with minimal information—and virtually no maps—and defeated a numerically-superior force with many advantages (psychological motivation, initiative, clear objectives, and detailed plans) is a remarkable one. This is how they did it.

Riding to the Rescue: 31 January–15 February 1968

The 409th Radio Research Detachment (Long Knives) was never supposed to be the pointy end of the Blackhorse spear. True, they might be the first to know something was happening while listening to the enemy's communications, but they were never meant to be the first in combat. In Tet '68, the 409th was the first Blackhorse unit engaged in the defense of Long Binh.

Conversion of the Regiment's gas-powered Armored Cavalry Assault Vehicles to the safer, more powerful diesel version began in early 1967. The recon platoons were the first to get the M113A1s. The 409th's turn didn't come until late January 1968—precisely because the detachment was not expected to be in direct combat with the enemy except under extraordinary circumstances. Each of the Long Knives' vehicles had been individually modified before leaving Fort Meade to accommodate the radio research equipment; each one was a unique, one-off creation.[5] That meant they would require technical assistance to modify the new vehicles as well. Lee Gentry, the first 409th commander in Vietnam, recalls that "the racks and communications equipment were moved from the 409th's older M113 tracks to a new fleet of M113A1 vehicles obtained for the 409th's use" thus making 18 tracked vehicles ready just before the Tet offensive began on 31 January.

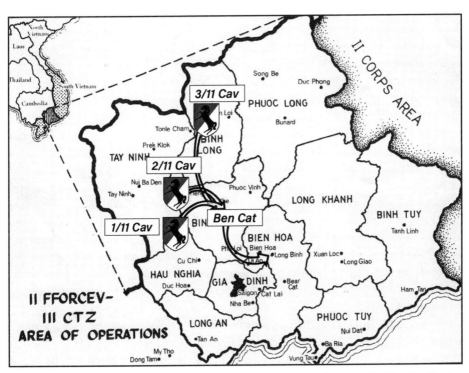

Map showing 11th Armored Cavalry Regiment's 'ride to the rescue' at the start of the Tet '68 offensive. (basic map, US Army)

Anticipating an attack on Long Binh that very day, the local commander ordered the 409th's ACAVs to the perimeter to supplement the existing bunker-based defenses. The satchel-carrying VC who attacked on the morning of 1 February were astonished to encounter withering fire from upgraded M113A1s. As Gentry observed: "The two [VC] companies were decimated and never penetrated the wire."

The bulk of the Regiment, however, was between 60 and 100 kilometers away when the shooting started—not far when you're out for a Sunday drive, but much further than it sounds when you're in the middle of impenetrable jungle and people are shooting at you. Blackhorse leaders at all levels were, for the most part, in the dark about the impending offensive. Higher headquarters did not pass the word down that things were heating up. Even when the Tet cease fire was cancelled on the 30th, the higher-ups did not inform all of their subordinate units about what they knew or suspected would follow.[6]

Early on the morning of 31 January, indications that something big was happening began to trickle in. India Troop's Lieutenant (LT) Charlie Locklin was located near the Cambodian border. He recalls that morning. First, he and his fellow troopers began to hear increased fire to their south. Initially, they ascribed it to the excessive celebrations that were common around Tet. But at 0200 hours, he and the other platoon leaders were called to the troop command post and told that Saigon was being attacked. They decided to be ready to charge into battle so, as Locklin recalls, the troopers better "clean their weapons and perform detail[ed] maintenance—they did and when we were call[ed] to secure ARVN III Corps HQ we were ready."

The regimental tactical operations center (TOC) was alerted of a change in mission mid-morning (1030 hours) on the 31st. They were told to "move to Long Binh area ASAP." At this point, no one in the 11th Cavalry had been told that the enemy had initiated his Tet offensive throughout South Vietnam; people in Washington knew before the Blackhorse troopers did. The troopers in the TOC only knew that something big was up and they needed to move—*NOW!*

The new orders from LTG Weyand's headquarters (nicknamed Hurricane and located in Long Binh) told Blackhorse 6 to turn his ACAVs, tanks, howitzers, and helicopters around and head south. Colonel Jack MacFarlane, who had taken command of the Regiment in December, recalled a few days later: "The details of the mission were lacking and the precise purpose for proceeding to Bien Hoa was not clear. However, the time urgency of the order indicated to me that it was essential to get all three squadrons on the road, moving as rapidly as possible, to Bien Hoa." He issued orders to his squadron commanders to "move south to secure Hurricane … more details to follow."

As previously noted, the three squadrons were operating in separate areas arrayed across two provinces on either side of Highway 13. The closest (1/11) to Long Binh was about 60 kilometers from its "ride to the rescue" objective (Hurricane Headquarters). Next was 2/11, nearly 65 kilometers away from the South Vietnamese prisoner of war (POW) compound. The furthest away was 3/11, with almost 100 kilometers to get to the headquarters of III (ARVN) Corps.

When the new mission came in about 1100 hours, Lima Troop and Mike Company were already in the rubber trees on a sweep with Big Red One grunts. They had to disengage from that mission, off-load the infantrymen, refuel, and then hit the road for Saigon. Third Squadron was on the road (Highway 13) by 1300 hours. Speed, Lieutenant Colonel (LTC) Neal Creighton told his troopers, not security, was of the essence, and nobody stopped for any longer than was necessary. Privately, Creighton thought to himself: "That's pretty good. I'm the lead element [for the Regiment] and I don't know where I'm going." Or what the enemy situation is. Or what the friendly situation is. But such trifles never stopped a determined cavalryman.

To get there, the Blackhorse had to fight its way through four regiments of first-line NVA regulars. Both the 7th (NVA) and 9th (VC) Divisions were tasked to make sure reinforcements were not allowed to reach the Saigon-Bien Hoa-Long Binh area.

These two vaunted enemy divisions failed to accomplish their mission. Miserably!

The post-war histories of the two enemy divisions are extraordinarily candid about this failure. For example, the 7th (NVA) Division's history says that its mission was "to cover the northern approaches to Saigon, a strategically-important sector in which were stationed the US 1st 'Big Red One' Division and the puppet [ARVN] 5th Division, both powerful enemy divisions, and the American 11th Armored Cavalry Regiment (ACR), the only American tank-armored regiment in all of South Vietnam which had tremendous mobility and powerful striking power." Only one of the division's three regiments (the 88th) even reached its forward assembly area in time. The division's history goes on: "Although some of the regiment's units fought hard … the regiment was unable to prevent a 200-vehicle enemy convoy [the Blackhorse] from driving down Route 13 toward Saigon on the night of 31 January." The 9th (VC) Division's regiments were caught up in fights on the way to their assigned blocking positions and also failed in their assigned missions.

The Blackhorse troopers encountered a number of unusual roadblocks along the way—such as logs, ditches, and stacked old car bodies—but pushed on.

Golf Troop's LT Al Bowen, recalls getting the call. "So the troop commander (Captain Rusty Russell) calls me, his message to me was: "Vietnamese sweep, get to the hard stripe [main road], turn right, I'll explain it when I catch up to you."[7] They followed orders and headed south. Somewhere along the way, the squadron commander landed his helicopter and said "we're going into Bien Hoa. Anybody got a map?" I had two of them, so I gave him one and kept one." Bowen had the maps "because I'm a pack rat."

First Squadron had the hardest trek—not the longest, but the hardest. They had to extract themselves from a heavily mined area that had cost them eight killed and nine seriously wounded just the night before and they also had a new commander (LTC Jack Nielsen), with less than 48 hours in the saddle.[8]

Nielsen remembers that 31 January started out as a "normal" day, with his troops scattered through the Ho Bo Woods conducting reconnaissance. Some were aware that the enemy had broken his own Tet truce, but the extent of their attacks was not yet known that far away from Saigon. As Jan Roberts recalls: "As a platoon leader I had no knowledge of where we were going or that the Tet Offensive had started. My first clue was when we entered Bien Hoa perimeter after an 8–9 hour march around 2 AM and saw soldiers armed and in the trenches. Been there many times and never seen any Bien Hoa/Long Binh soldiers with weapons."

LTC Nielsen was just two days on the job. He knew hardly any of his troopers. But he had been preparing for just such a situation all his professional life. He started out as a corporal driving a tank in the 2nd Armored Division in June 1944 in Normandy. By the time his outfit was the first US Army unit to enter Berlin about a year later, he was the company first sergeant. After being commissioned as a 2nd Lieutenant, he served in the Korean War—again in a tank company. So when Colonel MacFarlane told him that morning: "All hell has broken loose, they've attacked all the cities everywhere … I want you to do a 180 [degree turn] and get back to II Field Force as fast as you can make it," Nielsen didn't panic. He did realize this was no ordinary situation. He recalled: "When we were ordered to do a 180 and head south, I was amazed by the fine reaction to the squadron, and it broke out of the Ho Bo Woods and came all the way into the Saigon area in short order in spite of enemy opposition."

"Big Jim" Holt, a 1/11 Howitzer Battery forward observer (FO) working with Bravo Troop, remembers the radio call. "The day that Tet happened … the radio came on and it was essentially the colonel [Nielsen] and he was going, "Move out, all units move out. Saigon's being hit! 2nd Field's [Force] getting hit! Hue's getting hit! All the compounds across the country are being hit! … Move out! Move out! Move out!" … It probably didn't take 15 minutes and we were rolling."

SP5 Bill Barner, riding in 2/11 Howitzer Battery's fire direction center (FDC) track, wrote about the road march in his diary

> Word came for move out at 1215 [hours] … At 1500 we were at the checkpoint and at this time we were going S.W. [southwest]. At 1530 we went east to go on to Long Binh which was 55 miles away. It was a new plan and was such a shock. It took us 15 and a half hrs to make the trip and it was rough. We met 3 blockades and it slowed us down. It was 0530 when we pulled into a P.F. [Popular Force, South Vietnamese militia] POW camp that contained 2,000 VC. Outside it were 200+ dead VC which tried a ground attack.

Ben Cat (50 miles from the Long Binh-Bien Hoa goal) was a convenient place for Blackhorse 6 to provide the "details" of the new mission that he had promised his subordinate commanders on the radio. After a face-to-face meeting with LTG Weyand in which he received the new mission, Colonel MacFarlane borrowed four Bien Hoa-Long Binh map sheets from the headquarters staff. In longhand directly on the maps themselves, he depicted the friendly and enemy situation as it was understood at the time.[9] Getting back into his helicopter, he overflew the long reg-imental convoy to check its progress and status. En route, he wrote out the missions to his subordinate commanders on the four map sheets (one for each squadron and one for his own operations officer). Checking where the head of the column was, he told the squadron commanders to meet him at Ben Cat.

As vehicles continued to stream south, he held an impromptu pow-wow on the side of the road at about 1600 hours. MacFarlane gave his three squadron com-manders—Jack Nielsen, Garland McSpadden, and Neal Creighton—their orders. His parting words were: "In the event you encounter enemy resistance, you're to bulldoze on through, shoot as you continue, and get on to the area in which your assigned mission is located and accomplish your mission. Do not let minor enemy distractions en-route deter you from accomplishing the mission."

Each map had the specific squadron objectives. For the most part, these were the only maps that were available to them for the first 24 hours. They were sufficient to allow the squadron commanders to formulate plans and give orders—all on the radio to troop commanders who didn't have maps. Time was of the essence, so they moved out smartly, not waiting for the mostly-wheeled support vehicles that would have to catch up later.

Jim Holt reflects on what happened next.

> The thing I'll never forget is coming out of Lai Khe you hit a ridge and you kind of go down in the valley. We hit that ridge and it was like dusk … The sun had gone down but still sunset in the sky and everything. Everywhere you looked there were helicopters. I mean, it looked like every chopper in Vietnam was in the air and there was all this fire going on from these choppers down at various places and stuff, and my track was in the middle of this column and all I could see in front of me was tanks and tracks and all I could see behind me was tanks and tracks, the whole squadron.

If the view from inside the convoy was unforgettable, the view from above was nothing short of awe-inspiring. SP5 John Griffith was the crew chief of one of Thunderhorse's gunships flying cover along Highway 13. He remembers looking down and "seeing our guys below knowing if we got shot down we had them to kick ass and take names!"

Normally, night road marches in a combat zone are made with blackout drive lights.[10] But there was nothing normal about the road march made by the Regiment on 31 January 1968. The new moon arrived just two nights before, so there was no ambient light to speak of. As darkness fell, headlights came on and stayed on. SP5 Wes Slimmer remembers: "We traveled all the rest of the day, and then into the night. Every town or turn off we came to had Military Police waving us through and clearing the road—we were at full speed most of the time … We traveled into the night with our lights on, which was very odd; we never used our lights at night."

The VC were expected to continue their offensive after sunset, and the GIs and South Vietnamese soldiers and civilians inside the wire at Bien Hoa and Long Binh were depending on the armored might of the 11th Cavalry to see them through another long night. With Air Cav Troop scouts and gunships overhead, the paltry roadblocks and occasional sniper fire were not enough to warrant slowing down. As Colonel MacFarlane described it: "The regiment moved with speed, dash, and daring under difficult and hazardous conditions. It was a classic example of a boldly executed armored cavalry march."

As the first vehicles moved into the built-up areas of Bien Hoa and Long Binh, they came under fire. Captain Chuck Schmidt (India Troop commander) recalls entering Bien Hoa. "As soon as we got in the heart of the town, all hell broke loose. The Viet Cong were in all the buildings, on the roofs shooting down at us …" Following his boss' instructions, Schmidt told his troopers to "button up [close all the hatches] and keep going." With "rounds pinging off the tops from the rooftops," they continued toward III (ARVN) Corps headquarters.

Sergeant Jerry Mitchell was further back in the India Troop column. He, too, remembers that night.

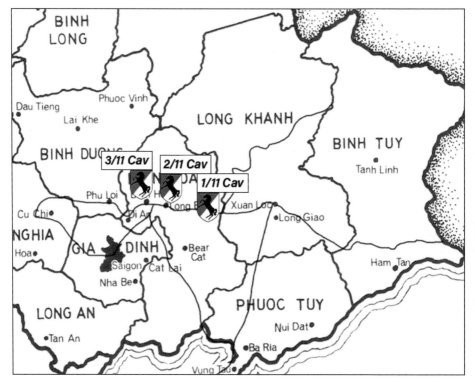

Map showing 11th Armored Cavalry Regiment objectives for 31 January–1 February 1968. (basic map, US Army)

The thing I probably remember the most is, when we got to the base, we had to fight our way into the base ... When we come in, there was one of those little [civilian] Vietnamese filling stations there ... outside the gate. We started receiving fire from it. There was a tank with us [from Mike Company] ... That tanker turned his gun towards it and obliterated that Vietnamese filling station. And I thought: "What kind of idiot stands behind a filling station, with all that gas, and starts shooting at you?" Obviously I don't have to worry about it, because he's not here anymore.

Rayford Smith was also there that night—inside the wire. He was assigned to the Alpha Company, 5th Special Forces Group tactical operations center, just down from the III (ARVN) Corps Headquarters.

Those of you who were there might remember the road junction just west of our compound at the CALTEX [filling] station. The VC/NVA held that entire pie shaped part of the village ... It was nip and tuck there all, or most of the morning ... I don't recall when you [11th Cavalry] arrived in our compound, but there was not one of our guys who wasn't happy to see you. So thank you all for what you men did that day.

As Lima Troop approached the gates of the III (ARVN) Corps compound about 2230 hours, soldiers from the 238th (VC) Battalion fired rifles, machine guns, and even some RPGs at the speeding armored vehicles. The harassing fire picked up as the rest of the convoy passed through the gates and assumed hasty positions along the perimeter. They were greeted by a bewildering sight. US (MACV advisors and GIs from C-2/47th Mechanized Infantry) and ARVN soldiers—who until just moments before expected VC swarming over the walls into the compound—were jumping around and slapping each other on the back. One observer said: "Then I heard this rumble ... Then comes M Company, and everybody was cheering and throwing beer bottles at them. It was like the liberation of Paris."

ACAV, tank, and howitzer crews, dust-covered and bleary-eyed after driving for 12-plus hours, were kept up most of the night. Between the desultory sniper fire, the nervous soldiers in the bunkers, and the on-again, off-again alerts for imminent VC attacks, the Blackhorse troopers were unable to sleep for very long.

Besides, there were plans to be made for the morning assault on the built-up area across the road. The intelligence was that a battalion of VC was holed up in the village and it would be up to 3/11, along with some paratroopers from the 101st Airborne Division, to dig them out. Apparently, the VC had seen the cavalry arrive too, because other than a few RPGs and sniper fire, there was no attack that night against the compound.

SP5 Armand Latour was with the 6th Psychological Operations (PSYOPS) Battalion on the same compound. He recalls what happened when 3rd Squadron arrived. "We could still hear rounds over head as snipers took up positions in the village across the road. At one point a tank was moved into the main gate and fired several rounds into the buildings." Several 90 mm rounds at point-blank range; return fire from the village ceased.

Over at the POW compound, things were getting desperate. When the 2/11 operations officer flew in, he found about 100 soldiers, half South Vietnamese and half from A-2/47th Infantry, manning the defenses. They were literally surrounded by the enemy. Inside the compound were about 1,100 Communist prisoners. A chain link fence and that small number of defenders were all that separated the prisoners from their comrades and liberation. Outside the compound, battalion-sized VC forces had been spotted in the villages east and west of the prison, with a large force also thought to be ready to attack from the south. Until, that is, the tanks and ACAVs arrived.

When Golf Troop crossed the Long Binh Bridge at 2100 hours, they got the order to move to the southeastern portion of the compound and prepare for a fight. By 2300 hours they were in position, on line and moving in the direction of the reported enemy concentration in the drainage ditch outside the fence and in the village. Apparently, the VC were not prepared to take on that much firepower, so the troopers cleared the area without incident. The squadron's ACAVs, tanks, mortars, howitzers, and command post vehicles moved into positions inside the compound fence.

Fox Troop's Staff Sergeant Jim Foreman recalls that "you could almost walk around that whole compound from one vehicle to another, it was so heavily fortified. Nobody could have taken that." Al Bowen remembers repeated VC assaults during that long night: "I'll tell you that trying to shoot RPGs through a 13-foot high chain link fence doesn't work. And charging guys with machine guns lined up, at ten meter basis between vehicles, is not right. They tried it anyway, but not [for] long."

SP4 Tom Thornburg probably spoke for many of the other troopers when he said: "One of my proudest moments in life was the night we protected and saved the 60 American guards at a POW Camp in Bien Hoa Tet 1968. They were on the line bracing for a 300–500-man human wave attack … coming right at them."

As noted above, 1/11 had the most difficult trek to get to its objective. Four hours of busting jungle was followed by another ten hours of eating dust (the squadron was the last unit in the column moving south). Joe Sedlachek has vivid memories of that move.

> Well, we packed everything up real fast and formed up in a real big convoy and proceeded south. I remember seeing tail-lights of vehicles for as far as you could see. A mile or two—then the dust got in the way and you could only see blurry red dots … All those ACAV's, jeeps, trucks and self-propelled howitzers moving along the road … We drove all though the night, changing drivers after about eight or ten hours … it was incredible.

Just at midnight, the first ACAVs from the First of the Blackhorse arrived at the II Field Force Vietnam compound (known as "The Plantation"). Bravo Troop, Delta Company, and Headquarters and Headquarters Troop, took up positions around the perimeter, while Alpha and Charlie moved across Plantation Road and out-posted Widow's Village, the next day's objective. Inside the perimeter, they found a motley—but incredibly effective—conglomeration of infantrymen, cavalrymen, engineers, intelligence specialists, ammo handlers, and an assortment of clerks, cooks, lifeguards, and other American GIs who had just been introduced to the real war.

Over the course of the next several days, Blackhorse mobility and firepower were telling. LTG Weyand and his staff reached out to the 11th Cavalry repeatedly, sending whole squadrons and individual platoons or troops hither and yon. As the regimental after-action report for the period notes: "Operations were characterized by a continuous parceling out of squadrons and troops at various times to the 1st, 9th, and 25th Infantry divisions, 101st Airborne Division (Screaming Eagles), 199th Light Infantry Brigade, and the 18th and 25th ARVN Infantry Divisions."

Wherever there was a serious firefight, Blackhorse troopers were in the thick of it. The Communist leaders—believing that the people would rise up *en masse*—told their subordinate commanders to hold in place rather than evade the inevitable counterattacks. Even though they had been reinforced with some heavy weapons, these VC infantry units were no match for the armored firepower of ACAVs, tanks, Zippos (flame throwing vehicles), howitzers, mortars, and gunships.

The regimental daily staff journals are filled with entries wherein various sized units were sent to check out reports of enemy activity. Most reports turned out to be either someone's vivid (or frightened) imagination, or the VC were long gone by the time the ACAVs and tanks arrived. However, some of the reports turned out to be accurate, resulting in major contacts.

The plan was for paratroopers from B-2/506th (Airborne) Infantry and Lima Troop to sweep west between the railroad and Highway 1 on the afternoon of 1 February. Coordination with the Screaming Eagles didn't start out well. Neil Creighton remembers going to the 101st division command post for orders. They were all airborne-spiffy, shined boots, freshly starched fatigues. Creighton walked in in jungle fatigues that were oil-soaked; they looked like he'd slept in them because he had. His fatigues were dirty, and so was he. Years later, someone told him that they remembered him walking in. "You were the dirtiest person we'd ever seen. Blood-soaked fatigues …" Another reinforcement of both stereotypes, cavalry and airborne infantry.

But things improved quickly. Creighton recalls:

> I was told to coordinate any action that I wanted to take with LTC Dave Grange, an infantry battalion commander [2/502nd Airborne Infantry Battalion] whose troops were moving through town towards III [ARVN] Corps Headquarters. It didn't take Dave Grange and I long to come to a meeting of minds of what to do. Before noon, L Troop and a platoon of M Company had joined up with Grange's Infantry and they were going through town … Contact was light until the Armor-Infantry team approached the area immediately in front of III Corps Headquarters and here they ran into heavy fire. The VC apparently had decided to make a stand. It was a poor decision, but it might have been their only choice as the only path of retreat for them was blocked by two ARVN battalions placed along roads to the south and west of III Corps. The fight didn't last long … It all came out very well for everyone except the VC.

This was the first time that the 3rd Squadron troopers had ever fought in an urban area. They discovered that just turning their vehicles in the narrow alleyways of Ap

Thanh village was difficult, but engaging VC snipers and RPG teams on the second and third stories of buildings was even harder. A PSYOPS bird had been flying over the village all morning telling the civilian inhabitants to *di di mau* ("get the hell out of Dodge") as the wrath of the Blackhorse-Airborne team was about to descend upon the heads of the VC. So when LTC Creighton was asked for permission to fire tank rounds into the VC positions inside the buildings, he said yes.

The results were impressive.

Five Mike Company tanks and about a dozen Lima Troop ACAVs lined up on a 1,000-meter-long stretch of the road between the III (ARVN) Corps compound and the edge of the village where the VC were hiding. Firing 90 mm canisters, .50-cal., and M60 machine guns, they rolled slowly down the hardtop. The flimsy wooden and poorly-constructed stucco buildings collapsed under the onslaught of "Made in America" ball bearings and armor-piercing bullets. Eyewitnesses described the scene:

> Viet Cong soldiers began to appear at windows, doors, and roofs of the first row of houses, just 15 to 20 feet from the armored vehicles. In what was described as the closest, most intense exchange of fire which L Troop had encountered, the Blackhorse soldiers literally decimated the enemy resistance before it. Houses began to break apart and crumble under the punishment of repeated cal. 50 bursts. Flames began to rage all along the line … For about five minutes these guys fired. And all of a sudden there was just dead silence. All you could see was Vietnamese [VC] running away and getting the hell out of the area—those that were still alive!

After ten platoon-volleys of canister, the battle was virtually over. The tanks and ACAVs stopped. Many of the VC who tried to escape were cut down by canister and machine gun fire. The remainder ran into the two battalions of ARVN infantrymen deployed behind them.[11] Just to be sure, helicopter gunships swept the smoldering ruins with 40 mm grenades and torrents of minigun fire. There was no further resistance from the village.

Don Patrick, Jr., was a member of the 537th Personnel Service Company (PSC), located inside the Bien Hoa Air Base wire near the village of Ap Thanh. Two VC battalions had tried and failed to breach the perimeter the night before. Retreating from the air base, the VC moved through the village, indiscriminately killing anything that moved. "The only forces in the way of Charlie were the MPs and the 537th PSC (also the 520th PSC)," Patrick remembers. That's when the cavalry arrived. Standing atop their bunkers, the personnel-specialists-turned-perimeter-guards-turned-spectators watched as the VC "exited the other side of the village, [where] they found themselves in a small valley between Long Binh and Bien Hoa. There they were quickly surrounded by the 3rd Sqdn, 11th ACR. I understand Charlie was being shot to pieces. They became frantic to get out of the valley … When the 11th ACR had beaten the two NVA battalions, they were wildly greeted as heroes."

The soldiers and airmen of Bien Hoa Air Base didn't take very long to show their appreciation. When asked what he remembered about the first few days of the Tet offensive, CPT John Longhauser wrote: "Fighting the NVA off the Bien

Hoa tarmac and out of the culverts—then a 2½-ton truck of cold beer and soda courtesy of the USAF."

And so it went in the weeks following the initial attacks. Alpha Troop reinforced the 1st Battalion, 18th Infantry (Big Red One) and threw two battalions of VC out of Thu Duc northeast of Saigon. Echo and Fox Troops fought a day-long battle alongside Screaming Eagle paratroopers in the village of Tan Phu against two companies of VC who allegedly wanted to surrender. As it turned out, they didn't, but they should have. India Troop, under the operational control (OPCON) of the 1st Infantry Division, helped to clear Phu Loi of residual resistance. Lima Troop (OPCON to the 2nd Brigade, 25th Infantry Division) had a major firefight with an enemy force moving west of Saigon; the VC never made it to their designated attack position. Thunderhorse gunships were engaged in virtually all of these actions. Golf Troop's SP4 Bruce Watson has his own recollection of that time. "In Bien Hoa, it reminded me of a World War II scene because there were bodies laying everywhere—and some of them were Americans."

The enemy concentrated a total of 35 battalions worth of mostly VC (with many NVA fillers) soldiers in and around the Saigon-Bien Hoa-Long Binh area. The Communist headquarters for South Vietnam (COSVN) was reinforced with several NVA units (two infantry regiments, six separate infantry battalions, and six artillery battalions, as well as sappers, engineers, signal, and other combat support units).

The Regiment's Long Khanh Province nemesis (the 5th (VC) Division) played but a minor role in the Tet offensive—at least in part because they had been rudely shoved out of the province and deep into northern War Zone D. They were a long way away from Saigon, thanks to the Blackhorse. They couldn't even mount an attack on the lightly defended Blackhorse Base Camp.

Despite its numerical strength, two elements of the "General Offensive, General Uprising" plan proved detrimental for the Communists in and around Saigon.

Instead of concentrating all their strength against a few targets, VC units were spread across the length and breadth of the area surrounding the capital. As a result, there were insufficient forces to reinforce success in the few places where it occurred. The second fatal flaw was the attempt to maintain absolute secrecy. This became an obsession with Communist planners and contributed directly to the failure of the 7th (NVA) Division to interdict the movement of the Blackhorse south toward Long Binh and Bien Hoa. They simply got their orders too late to execute them.

More than anything else, success for the VC depended on American reinforcements not being able to reach the allied military installations before they were overrun. Despite the fact that parts of two entire divisions (one VC, one NVA) were allocated to this task, American forces—the 9th Infantry Division from the south and west and the 3/4th Cavalry and 11th Cavalry from the north—succeeded in breaking the enemy cordon attempting to seal off the battlefield. Combined with the 15 battalions LTG Weyand had ordered back to the capital military region area in mid-January, these forces succeeded in ensuring that *none* of the enemy's military objectives were achieved. Weyand's assessment was that the "VC/NVA Tet offensive aimed at no less an objective than winning the war with one stroke aimed at the heart of political and administrative power in South Vietnam-Saigon. Militarily it was a complete failure for the VC."

The beleaguered defenders of Tan Son Nhut, Bien Hoa, and Long Binh were not the only ones to recognize the significance of the 11th Cavalry's ride to their rescue. Leaders and staff officers up and down the chain of command finally recognized that Vietnam *was* armor country, and that there *was* a role for armored forces to play in the ongoing fight. As LTG Bruce Palmer, then Deputy Commanding General of US Army Vietnam, wrote: "HQ II FFV [II Field Force Vietnam] in the north-central area of the same perimeter ... was so hard pressed that most of the 11th Armored Cavalry Regiment had to be called in to keep the II FFV command post from being overrun."

Everyone—from the highest-ranking generals to the private in the rice paddy—understood that the Tet offensive had changed the war. The *New York Times* characterized the change as "a new and much meaner war." People at home, following Walter Cronkite's lead, became increasingly disillusioned about why we were fighting a war that never seemed to end. The politicians began to question LBJ, whose legendary ability to coerce lesser men was failing him. The generals in Washington and Saigon understood that "1968 will be a pivotal year. The war may go on beyond 1968 but it is unlikely that the situation will return to the pre-TET condition."

While Hanoi lost the battle in South Vietnam, they won the post-battle war in Washington. Despite horrific casualties, the Communists claimed victory by just being able to pull off their surprise attacks. War-weary Americans—leaders and ordinary citizens alike—weren't able to counter that argument.

Mini-Tet and Beyond: May to June 1968

Tom White arrived in Vietnam in May 1968. He was assigned as a platoon leader in Mike Company, 3/11. Within just a few days, he recognized he was part of a special team. "The Regiment had been in constant combat since the start of Tet—I mean, hard combat. Lost a lot of people, but they were battle-hardened, tough people, the survivors. They knew what they were doing ... The Regiment was a real well-oiled machine at that point ... We had wall-to-wall talent ..."[12]

By the end of February, the enemy forces had withdrawn from their exposed positions surrounding Saigon. They did not go far. Hanoi had ordered a second round of attacks against the capital region, and the VC and NVA regiments designated to conduct those attacks needed to replace their personnel losses, retrain, and resupply. The units of the 5th (VC), 7th (NVA), and 9th (VC) Divisions fell back on prepared base camps and caches one- to two-days' march from Saigon.

Through prisoner interrogations and captured documents, Allied intelligence analysts divined these intentions fairly quickly. Military Assistance Command Vietnam and the South Vietnamese Joint General Staff launched two successive operations—*Quyet Thang* (Resolved to Win) in the provinces closest to Saigon in March, and *Toan Thang* (Complete Victory) throughout the region in April. The objective of the latter operation was to find and engage the forces that were thought to be preparing for a renewed attack on the cities and villages around Saigon. Almost 80 American and South Vietnamese maneuver battalions—split almost 50/50—scoured the 11 provinces that made up III Corps Tactical Zone. All three Blackhorse squadrons were part of *Quyet Thang* and *Toan Thang*. Initially, 3/11 was placed in direct support (DS) of the 25th (ARVN) Infantry Division, hunting down two of the 9th (VC) Division's three regiments. The remainder of the Regiment searched in War Zone D for residual elements of the 5th (VC) Division.

These operations were very successful. Caches of supplies stockpiled for the coming action were uncovered and destroyed. VC and NVA units were hounded from their base camps, interrupting training and disrupting timetables. Even the enemy acknowledged their success. The official post-war NVA history admits: "Beginning on 11 March, the United States and its puppets [Saigon government] massed 50 [sic] battalions to launch two successive sweep operations called "Quyet Thang" and "Toan Thang" in the region surrounding the city, causing a great many difficulties for our units trying to approach their targets." A captured NVA private put it in terms everyone could understand: "The greatest hardships since Tet were air attacks and sweep operations … Every three or four days we had to flee from sweep operations once we knew we hadn't enough strength to deal with the enemy's forces."

As if things weren't bad enough, another "difficulty" then arose. On 19 April, NVA Colonel Tran Van Dac surrendered to the South Vietnamese government. He had infiltrated from North Vietnam in 1962, joining the VC command structure in the provinces north of Saigon. By 1968, he was the senior political officer for the 9th (VC) Division. He told his interrogators that another country-wide offensive was scheduled to kick off within just days. However, he said that supplying the units in their attack positions was "very difficult," leading to units not having the requisite materiel to carry out their assignments by the 27 April. He speculated that his defection might cause the Communist leadership to reconsider some of their plans and timing.

Colonel Tran said that the offensive would start with attacks by fire (mortars and rockets) against major population centers and military installations across South Vietnam—reminiscent of the February offensive. However, unlike before, there would be only one major ground attack. The 9th (VC) Division would attack Saigon from the north and west, while the 5th (VC) Division, reinforced by the Dong Nai (VC) Regiment, would move against Long Binh from the north and east.

Colonel Tran stressed that the upcoming offensive had primarily *political* objectives.

The search for a site for the peace talks that started after the February offensive was stalled; Hanoi was dragging its feet. The Communists were hoping another Tet-like "victory" would give them the leverage to pick a site favorable to them. They clearly hoped to achieve a spectacular military and psychological triumph, demonstrating that Hanoi was in a position of strength and the Washington-Saigon position was weak. As Colonel Tran said, the political objective of the upcoming action—called the "Second General Offensive" by the Communists but dubbed "Mini-Tet" by most American GIs—was to "get a prevailing position, a more forceful position to support the negotiations … [T]he negotiations are resolved by the military victories."

But Hanoi couldn't wait any longer. Colonel Tran's defection and the capture of documents giving details of the upcoming offensive forced the Communist high command to give their troops the "go" order five days before the first negotiating session in Paris—and well before all of the assault units were in position.[13]

Based on the available intelligence, Lieutenant General Weyand directed the establishment of three defensive rings around the capital region. The inner-most ring, consisting primarily of South Vietnamese infantry, had the mission of defending the city of Saigon itself. The second ring, located about a day's march outside the Saigon-Bien Hoa-Long Binh area, included a mix of American and ARVN forces that were tasked with finding enemy base camps, staging areas, and caches, thus diminishing their offensive capabilities. The outer-most ring, nearest to the Cambodian border, was made up of mostly GI units, assigned the mission of interdicting the flow of supplies and personnel south from the Cambodian sanctuaries. The overall goal of this plan was, according to Weyand's operations officer, "aimed at destroying the VC and NVA units as far away from Saigon as possible while still maintaining a defensive ring of battalions close in to the city."

As the most mobile of Weyand's forces, the 11th Cavalry was given the mission to cut the supply and infiltration routes in War Zone D north of the Dong Nai River (Operation *Clifton Corral*). The Regiment was just a few days into this mission when an urgent message came in. The change in orders from LTG Weyand was succinct: "Intelligence indicates a probable VC attack in the Bien Hoa-Saigon area on 27 April. 11th ACR operations vicinity Bunard are terminated." For the second time in four months, Blackhorse troopers were called on to rescue the settlers. As had been the case in February, time was of the essence. Blackhorse 6 (Colonel Charles Gorder, who had taken command in March) was ordered to return "home" to Blackhorse Base Camp by the most direct route—a distance of over 150 kilometers.

The most direct route meant having to cross the formidable Dong Nai River. But there was no bridge on that route, and driving to the nearest existing bridge would cost time that was not available. So, Gorder asked the engineers to build a pontoon bridge across the 900-foot wide river. Doing so required virtually every float bridge in the entire corps area. Never before had such a massive mission been attempted in Vietnam. But the professionalism of the 168th Engineer Battalion (Combat) and attached bridge companies ensured that Operation *Allons* went off without a hitch; in a matter of hours (not days), 161 tanks, ACAVs, howitzers, command post vehicles, and recovery vehicles crossed on the most direct route to the objective.

As the enemy leaders were directing their forces into their final attack positions and American and ARVN units were rushing to defend the key installations around Saigon and Long Binh, people back in The World were preoccupied with other matters. Sports fans were thrilling to the classic NBA championship match-up between the Bill Russell-led Boston Celtics and Jerry West-led Los Angeles Lakers (Boston won, four games to two). The radical-chic musical *Hair* was premiering on Broadway, while Buffalo Springfield was appearing live for the last time in Long Beach. Most of all, people were still reeling from the assassination of Dr. Martin Luther King, Jr., an event that sent bad vibrations throughout society (even in Vietnam) and into the streets. All-in-all, what was happening—or about to happen—in South Vietnam was of only passing interest to an increasingly war-news-weary public.

Chief Warrant Officer (CWO) Charley Watkins joined the Blackhorse Regiment just as the mini-Tet offensive was kicking off. He'd already served a tour in Germany, where he graduated from the tough 7th Army Non-Commissioned Officer Academy. But he was fresh out of flight school; this would be his first assignment flying a Huey in a unit. Almost as soon as he'd arrived at Evans Army Airfield at Blackhorse Base Camp, he was thrown into the cockpit for a check ride. After post-flighting the aircraft, he was told that he was going on his first mission in 15 minutes. First Squadron needed a command and control (C&C) bird, and Charley was the only one available. "Three days later we get back to Blackhorse. I found my [duffle bag] right where I dropped it," Charley recalls.

To say that it was another busy time for the Blackhorse would be a gross understatement.

After crossing the Dong Nai River, the squadrons of the 11th Cavalry were deployed as part of the protective arc in and around the Bien Hoa-Long Binh complex. Intelligence estimates indicated that many of the targets that were struck in February were on the VC's hit list again. First Squadron was centered on Bien Hoa, with a recon troop protecting the Highway 1 bridge over the Dong Nai River, another guarding Widows Village and II Field Force headquarters, and one securing the III (ARVN) Corps POW compound. Second Squadron was located at the Blackhorse Base Camp, with the mission of screening the approaches to Long Binh from the east, as well as securing Highway 1 between Xuan Loc and Long Binh. Third Squadron was working for the 9th Infantry Division screening the northwestern approaches to Tan Son Nhut and Bien Hoa.

It was 2nd Squadron that would, this time, be in the VC's crosshairs.

Starting in late 1966 and continuing throughout its time in Long Khanh Province, the 11th Cavalry established and nurtured a special relationship with the village of Cam My—also known as Courtenay Hill for the rubber plantation on the edge of

Map showing 11th Armored Cavalry Regiment operations in April–May 1968. (basic map, US Army)

the village. The Regiment's 37th Medical Company hosted an annual Christmas party there for the children of Father John's Catholic orphanage starting in 1966, distributing clothing, food, medical and sanitation supplies, and presents to the children—some of which came from Americans back in The World, some of which came out of Army stocks, but many of which were purchased using donations by the troopers themselves.[14]

Medical personnel routinely visited Cam My for Medical Civic Action Program (MEDCAP) clinics, while others initiated English-language classes. At the request of the village chief, two platoons of Lima Troop provided security during the late-1967 national elections. The citizens of Cam My and four surrounding hamlets responded with a 100 percent turn-out of registered voters.

A mid-1967 regimental estimate assessed the population as divided into thirds: one-third pro-Saigon, one-third pro-VC, and one-third neutral. And even though the village itself was officially rated as "friendly" by mid-1967, it remained an island in a VC sea. Bill Neal was an advisor with the 18th (ARVN) Division in 1967–68. He recalls that the "area was considered a perpetually nasty area and a virtual no man's land from the perspective of Allied Forces."

The head of the local VC was 63-year-old Ba Quit, a native of North Vietnam who resettled in Cam My in 1954. He was sent there by Hanoi as an organizer of resistance. By 1964, his true sympathies became known, and he took to the jungle. His son was killed by ARVN soldiers, but his wife still lived in Cam My. The trail that ran through the rubber plantation near Cam My was known to the locals as "Ho Chi Minh Street"; the VC routinely used it as an east-west supply and com-mo-liaison route.

But things slowly began to change. Instead of sullenly looking on during MEDCAPs and civil affairs projects, villagers started coming to the troopers, telling of VC activities, where mines and caches were located, and who was part of, or supported, the local guerrilla units.

After a disastrous attack in early March 1968, the local militia (Regional Forces or RFs), facilities at Cam My were substantially upgraded. Not only were living and working conditions improved for those who served in the RFs, defenses were also strengthened. Red Devil engineers, individual troopers who had been carpenters, masons, and landscapers in civilian life, and others with big arms and bigger hearts pitched in to help erect quarters, build better bunkers, string more wire, and dig in crew-served weapons.[15]

As part of its Mini-Tet offensive, the provincial Communist party committee was directed to assault Cam My on the night of 4–5 May. The objective of this attack was to distract both the 11th Cavalry and the 18th (ARVN) Division from reinforcing the national capital region—allowing the 5th (VC) Division's attack on Long Binh and Bien Hoa to start unchallenged. The committee selected the 440th (VC) and 445th (VC) Battalions to make the attack. Under the motto of "Rush forward, this phase will be higher than the last," the 440th was to attack the militia compound and village, while the 445th arrayed itself in a ditch near the grass airstrip on the outskirts of the village. Their mission was "to strike the enemy disembarking from helicopters and to fire on their aircraft in the area to the southwest of the Cam My Special Sector."

The 440th (VC) Battalion kicked off the attack at 0400 hours with a blast from a recoilless rifle (RR) (about the same time the attacks on targets in Saigon began). The battalion history describes what happened next. "After the Battalion's recoilless rifles had fired, the troops simultaneously assaulted and took control of the battleground. After only 15 minutes of combat, our 5th Infantry Company and the Battalion reconnaissance element had brought down the Con Chim post [the militia compound], wiping out an enemy platoon dug in there. At the same time, the 9th Company and the 6th Company also took control of the strategic hamlet at the Cam My Special Sector."

The two battalions went about the business of occupying the village, treating their wounded, chasing militia stragglers, collecting weapons, haranguing the villagers with propaganda, and strengthening their positions. They thought they had at least six hours before any relief force showed up. In fact, they had less than two.

Second Squadron troopers were mostly "in the dark" that night—literally and figuratively. Rainclouds covered the half-moon as they left the base camp in response to radio calls for help from Cam My. As they headed for the sound of the guns, they didn't have a clue as to the size and location of the VC forces firing those guns. Hotel Company's Lieutenant (LT) Kent Hillhouse received a report that the Cam My position was on the verge of being overrun: "I recall thinking that this was going to be a BAD day." However, Hotel Company had run a recon to Cam My just two days before—just in case they were called upon to react to just such an attack. Knowing the lay of the land proved to be a huge advantage that morning.

Due to logistical shortfalls in country, Hotel Company had just turned in its diesel tanks for earlier models with gasoline engines. In addition to the increased risk of fire, they discovered that night that the wiring harnesses were faulty, causing severe issues with the radios. Just what they needed heading into what was sure to be a big fight—fire-hazard tanks with no communications.

The order of march that "chilly" (a wet 80°) Sunday morning for the seven kilometer run to Cam My was Hotel Company, Echo Troop, and Fox Troop. Second Squadron's Howitzer Battery, which had been firing in support of another attack

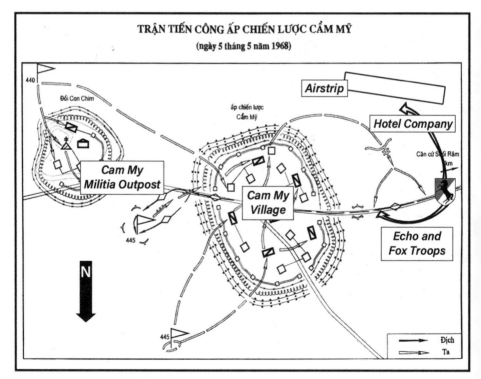

Viet Cong map of attack on Cam My on 5 May 1968 (with 2nd Squadron counterattack overlaid). (Ernest Chamberlain, used with permission)

on a village northwest of Blackhorse (a typical diversionary tactic by the VC), now switched its attention to the new target. To no one's surprise, the VC had mined the highway, and Staff Sergeant (SSG) Ron Charette's tank was disabled by one about halfway to the objective. His platoon leader remembers the "disgusted look on his face when we passed him … [H]e was another one who did not like to miss a fight." Ron's tank and his 11-months' experience in Vietnam would be sorely missed in the upcoming battle.

The rest of the column continued southward with barely a pause.

Specialist 4 (SP4) Dick Messier was driving tank H-36 that morning. "As I remember that rainy gloomy day, we were told to move out because a local village was taken over by N.V.A. Arvin [ARVN] soldiers were killed and the enemy soldiers were now wearing their uniforms, women had been raped and killed as well as the children. This time as we pulled out of our base camp we would head south knowing full well that we were in for a major ambush." Just outside of the village, the column halted, and Echo Troop took the lead. That's when the action started. SSG Dennis Creal remembers: "We were setting outside the gate of the village when all hell broke loose, RPG, automatic fire and then the mortar rounds started falling."

The track commander (TC) of tank H-36, Kent Hillhouse, continues.

> We turned on to the airfield at Cam My at about 0545 hours just at first light. E Troop was positioned in front of us at the main gate/entrance to Cam My. The lead platoon leader was walking forward to speak with one of the ARVN gate guards when suddenly the gate guard grabbed an AK [AK47 rifle] which was strapped on his back and pulled it into a firing position. The platoon leader was smart enough to hit the ground so the lead track commander could engage the NVA soldier who was wearing an ARVN uniform. At that point all hell broke loose. We found out that the NVA controlled the town and had our advisors pinned down in their bunker complex in the center of Cam My. Mortars started coming in from a SE [southeast] location and one of the Regimental scout choppers spotted the mortar battery's location. H Company was directed to move south and east through the rows of rubber [trees] to interdict the mortars. What we did not know at the time was that the NVA HQ's and their trains [logistics support] were co-located with the mortars.

Hotel Company's unexpected turn off the main road into Cam My—practiced when they did their earlier dry run—caught the enemy commander by surprise. He had deployed his engineer company along the main road, with the mission of delaying their arrival—using mines and RPGs. Platoon Sergeant (PSG) Glenn Nicholson in tank H-32 led the assault through the rubber trees toward the airstrip and away from the enemy engineers. When the tanks came close, the VC in a 600-meter long ditch that ran parallel to the airstrip, opened fire.[16] The two lead tanks were both hit by multiple anti-tank rounds. Dick Messier, driving the second tank, recalls:

> It was a bad situation as we raced into a potential ambush which we expected. I saw a flash of light from the right, I instinctively pulled the lever on my driver's seat, as it collapsed to its lowest position. My face burnt with shrapnel. We were hit by an R.P.G. It hit the turret right above my head as it penetrated through and wounded our gunner [SP5 Mike Reed] in the stomach … We fired canister rounds at our right flank but the enemy was dug in.

LT Hillhouse was thrown out of the cupola onto the back deck by that same RPG. He shook off the effects of the blast and climbed back into the turret. He recalls: "At first we tried putting a tank on top of the ditch but we found it more effective to rout the NVA by dismounting." Armed with his pistol and some hand grenades, Hillhouse did just that. "My biggest fear was that the NVA were going to over run our vehicles ... I grabbed a few grenades that had been stored on the bustle rack along with my Colt .45 [pistol] and headed towards the ditch with the intent of eliminating as many NVA as possible. After emptying all four of my .45 magazines and feeling pretty exposed, I started receiving covering fire from SSgt [Wayne] Scheu's tank."

At least 16 RPGs and 75 mm RR rounds hit the lead tank, severely wounding the entire crew—TC Nicholson and driver SP4 Freddie Cigar fatally. Sergeant (SGT) Peter Brum, who had ridden along that morning as an extra crewman, was also killed when he left the bustle rack to check on Cigar. The loss of Nicholson was an especially hard blow for the platoon. His was, as SP4 Mike Moynihan recalled, "the soft-spoken voice that kept our platoon going on course and was loved and respected by everyone."

As the Hotel Company tanks moved to envelop the village, the two recon troops (Echo and Fox) moved into Cam My proper. About the same time, two Air Cavalry Troop gunships arrived over the battlefield to add their special brand of firepower—miniguns and rockets. Over the course of the next several hours, 11 more helicopter gunship teams were engaged in the fight.

SP4 Ron Meadows was driving one of the Fox Troop ACAVs that morning. The VC occupied several of the newly-reconstructed bunkers in the militia compound. They waited until the vehicles were very close before opening fire. The ACAVs were so close to the bunkers that the machine gunners couldn't depress their weapons far enough to engage the enemy. Three ACAVs were hit in the initial barrage of RPGs and several individuals were killed or wounded including Meadows' TC.

The TC turned around in his cupola and motioned to him; he was trying to get Ron to come help him treat his wounds. But Ron thought he "meant go kill all the VC." Meadows dismounted his ACAV and charged into the blistering fire. When one of the VC popped up to fire, Ron was the quicker of the two and killed him. Another VC fired at him almost simultaneously, hitting him in the neck (and just missing his aorta). Ron fell into the enemy-occupied position from the force of the wound. However, he had the presence of mind to fire his .45-caliber pistol and killed the VC who was intent on stabbing him with his bayonet.

Two comrades of the man Meadows shot saw him fall and attacked him, using their RPG launchers as clubs. Ron fought back, and, despite his waning strength, knocked the two guerrillas to the bottom of the trench. He quickly crawled out of the trench and signaled to other Fox Troopers who were close by. The two RPG-armed VC were quickly dispatched while a medic dressed Ron's wounds.

Comrade Loi was one of the two VC that Ron Meadows fought in hand-to-hand combat. His exploits were considered so extraordinary that they became part of the D445 (VC) Battalion's legend.

> While engrossed in pursuing the enemy, Comrade Loi—a soldier in our reconnaissance element—became surrounded by enemy tanks. As he lifted his B40 [RPG2] to aim at an armoured vehicle, an American jumped down from another adjacent armoured vehicle. Loi turned, intending to strike the American on the head with his B40. However, the American was too tall and strong, and was able to snatch the B40. After a few minutes struggling, the American grabbed Loi's groin area and put his Colt pistol in Loi's back intending to capture him. With the special skill of a reconnaissance soldier, Loi flexed himself–then, suddenly raising his arm, stuck a swift and hard blow to the American's private parts. The American gave a loud roar, and then stumbled away. Loi still had time to grab his B40 and disappear into the jungle.

Among the dead was a VC captain who was carrying a map with the enemy operations order sketched in. The map had details of the Cam My defenses, including the location of all equipment and strong points in the village (undoubtedly provided by a VC sympathizer). In his shredded knapsack, troopers found a VC flag and several thousand South Vietnamese Piaster. Payday for the survivors of the Cam My battle would have to wait.

Higher headquarters termed the 10-hour long action at Cam My a "diversionary" attack; for the militiamen defending the village and the Blackhorse troopers who reacted in the middle of the night, it was the main event. It was, however, obvious that the enemy leadership had learned its lesson from their Tet offensive defeat in February. The attack on this village so close to Blackhorse Base Camp was intended to tie the 11th Cavalry down, preventing it from riding to the rescue of Bien Hoa and Long Binh.[17]

Unfortunately (for the enemy), their intelligence system failed them once again, as two-thirds of the Regiment's combat power was *already* near those key logistical and command and control installations. So the diversionary attack failed in its objective. They also didn't think that armored vehicles could reach Cam My so quickly. Here again, they were wrong.

Disastrously so.

Although the enemy claimed to have set "fire to 24 tanks and armoured vehicles" and killed 150 troopers, they admitted to serious casualties amongst their own troops, including two company commanders and one deputy company commander.[18] The post-war VC unit history concludes: "Our wounded and dead were carried back to the Suoi base for treatment or thoughtful burial. However, because the enemy [2/11] counter-attacked fiercely and—on the other hand, as our preparations for the fighting were not well-considered, we left a number of our dead comrades [104 killed and 5 captured] on the battlefield."

And so it went during the Mini-Tet offensive. Where the VC and NVA were able to make it through the three defensive rings thrown up between the Cambodian border and the Saigon-Bien Hoa-Long Binh complex, they were once again soundly defeated. Hanoi's claims of victory rang hollow. No advantage was gained on the battlefield or at the negotiating table.

India Troop, working for the 25th Infantry Division, was part of the successful interdiction of two of the enemy battalions that tried and failed to reach their objectives in Saigon. Over three days (3–6 May), a US task force consisting of three infantry battalions, a tank battalion, and India Troop, pinned large elements of the 271st (NVA) Regiment and the 267th (VC) Battalion against a swamp near the village of Bao Trai north of Saigon. Hundreds of VC were killed under 72 hours of nearly constant fire. LT Bill Suhre was there. "Our job was to try to find the enemy and then fight as best we could. We knew we had superior firepower ... We knew we'd win the battle once we found the enemy." After overrunning the enemy positions on 6 May, the India troopers found that some of the enemy soldiers had been chained to their weapons, explaining why they continued to fight despite such a massive bombardment.

In its own post-mortem, the North Vietnamese Army assessed the results of the Mini-Tet offensive in the following manner: "Carried out in a situation in which the enemy [US/ARVN] had brought in a large force, had organized a defense in depth, and was striking back at our forces in the outskirts of the city, this second wave of attacks by our armed forces against Saigon, and especially by our main force troops, demonstrated the tremendous resolve of our soldiers and civilians." Faint praise, indeed. Certainly Politburo planners had expected more than a "demonstration of resolve" in exchange for the huge expenditure in lives and resources during Mini-Tet. The enemy lost an estimated 40,000 soldiers during 1968—fully one-sixth of their pre-Tet strength.

The events of the first half of 1968, culminating in the start of peace talks and the May offensive, changed how many troopers perceived what it was they were being asked to do. Not during the fighting, of course, but at night, alone in the dark on guard or drinking beer with others. For the young men carrying the burden of the fighting, the start of the peace negotiations meant the beginning of the end, and Mini-Tet meant going back to the same places they had been in February to root out the same enemy all over again. Nobody wanted to be the last trooper killed in Vietnam.[19]

Recognition for the Blackhorse: March to June 1968

Ruth Neher, the chief of the Red Cross team at Blackhorse (affectionately known as "Donut Dolly 6") remembers the day the troopers came home as if it were yesterday. Although the enemy didn't launch an attack against the marginally defended base camp during Tet, there was some concern about how the "guest defenders" (from the 3/5th Cav, 9th Infantry Division) would perform if they did. "After serving lunch, and part way through our one hour program ... I said "Feel the ground" ... and a great whoop went up as all felt the tremor, and we all raced out to the main gate, where we saw the huge plume of dust in the distance, and heard and felt the *real* sound of Rolling Thunder!" First Squadron had returned home. The rear detachment cheered even louder than the "settlers" in Long Binh and Bien Hoa.

The unprecedented scale and ferocity of the Communist offensive over the Tet holidays changed the war forever. Before the attack, the motto was "no more Dien Bien Foos" (in President Johnson's signature Texas accent); afterwards, it was "no more Tets." Militarily, the VC and NVA were soundly defeated on every battlefield. The official history of the war written in Hanoi in 2002 speaks glowingly of the "great victory," but then struggles to identify any positive *military* outcomes save one: "our army had accumulated a great deal of experience in the organization of forces and the combat arts for urban warfare."

The authors then go on to acknowledge that "our preparations of supplies, spiritual preparations, and preparation of tactics were all insufficient ... We had somewhat underestimated the capabilities and reactions of the enemy [Allies] and had set our goals too high." In fact, Communist casualties were so severe—with the so-called "spearhead battalions" losing up to 50 percent of their strength—Hanoi ordered three new infantry regiments to move from the Central Highlands into the area north of Saigon.

In his memorandum to the president at the end of February, the Chairman of the Joint Chiefs of Staff stated that the margin of victory—survival even—over the VC at Tet had been "very very small." He went on to tell LBJ that all of the local commanders agreed that "the VC would have achieved a number of significant local successes at the outset, *except for timely reinforcement by U.S. forces* [emphasis added]." This statement places the Blackhorse Regiment's "ride to the rescue" in context. Without their timely arrival, the outcome could have been very different. The enemy had the forces in place, as well as the determination to inflict a serious defeat on American and South Vietnamese forces in Long Binh and Bien Hoa—one, the center of logistical support for all forces in the region and the other the busiest airfield in the world.

And then they tried it again in May.

In the space of about 90 days, the Blackhorse Regiment had moved a long way, both physically and figuratively. Individually, Blackhorse troopers had ridden a couple hundred kilometers; collectively, they had been transformed from bit players into headliners.

It was in the period between the Tet offensive in February and the end of the Mini-Tet offensive in May that the Regiment established the pattern of its future success. The recon troops and tank companies still got their share of convoy escorts and route recons, but the balance had shifted and these were no longer their *primary* missions.

Instead, the senior commanders finally realized that the mixture of ACAVs, tanks, and self-propelled howitzers, with organic scout and attack helicopters and armored engineers, all in one unit under a single commander was just what was needed—a self-contained combined-arms team that could move, shoot, and communicate, at a moment's notice, anywhere, and against anything the enemy could throw at it. For the rest of the war, the Regiment was away from its base camp more than it was there, operating from the fringes of Saigon to the far-flung corners of War Zones C and D, from the dusty rice paddies around Duc Hoa to the triple canopy jungle and rubber plantations around Loc Ninh—and all points in between.

From this point on, the Regiment never looked back. In General "Abe" Abrams (who took over from Westy in July '68), the 11th Cavalry finally had someone at the top who "got it"; someone who had started out as a horse cavalryman and who understood that giving Blackhorse 6 a mission and the support needed to accomplish that mission—and then getting the hell out of the way—was a sure recipe for success. Abrams had first tried that recipe with the 37th Tank Battalion in Normandy and on the Brittany Peninsula in 1944, adapted it during the carnage of the Falaise Pocket and assault river crossings of the Seine and Mosel, and then perfected it at Bastogne, across the Rhine, and into Czechoslovakia in 1945.

Now it was the Regiment's turn to add a trick or two. Several of his former subordinates, who had been trained by the master, were given the opportunity to show what they had learned. Colonels George Patton, Jimmie Leach, and Donn Starry (successive commanders of the Regiment in 1968–70) had all worked for Abrams before and understood how he operated and what he wanted. They did not disappoint.

The subordinates became masters themselves, each famous in his own right and in his own way. The troopers of the Blackhorse became most famous of all, adding to the legend and glory of the 11th United States Cavalry.

Recognition finally came to the Regiment. It came in the form of high praise from senior commanders who repeatedly asked to be reinforced by Blackhorse ACAVs, tanks, and helicopters. And it came in the form of official orders. US Army Vietnam (USARV) thought highly enough of the troopers' actions during Tet to issue General Orders Number 5069, awarding the Valorous Unit Award to the entire 11th Armored Cavalry Regiment.

The Army Valorous Unit Award was created to recognize particularly gallant actions by units. The Army regulation governing the award states that the gallantry must rise to the same level as that for awarding a Silver Star to an individual. That same regulation goes on to say that "only on a rare occasion will a unit larger than a BN [battalion] qualify for award of this decoration."

As an exception to its own policy, Headquarters, Department of the Army approved USARV's recommendation that the entire *Regiment* be cited for its actions between 31 January and 5 February 1968. The award highlights the Regiment's flexibility in responding to a dramatic change in mission. In an extreme example of Clausewitz' "fog of war," Blackhorse troopers charged into numerically superior enemy forces at multiple locations. Despite the lack of maps and having only mere hints as to the friendly and enemy situations, the 11th Cavalry "tore" into the enemy saving "countless American lives."

The Joint General Staff (JGS) of the Army of the Republic of Vietnam was genuinely thankful for what the troopers accomplished during Tet and Mini-Tet, awarding the Regiment the Vietnamese Cross of Gallantry with Palm. The JGS singled out the Blackhorse troopers for their contributions to both the safety and well-being of the South Vietnamese people. In the citation accompanying the award of the Vietnamese Cross of Gallantry with Palm, the 11th Cavalry was recognized as "one of the finest and bravest fighting units in Vietnam." The award cited the long string of operations from *Atlanta* in October 1966 until after Tet in 1968, during which the Blackhorse "demonstrated a degree of tactical finesse that was truly superb and resulted in a shattering of enemy forces in each of the battles."

But the ultimate recognition of the 11th ACR's prowess on the battlefield came with the award of Presidential Unit Citations (equivalent to a Distinguished Service Cross for an individual) to two of the Regiment's squadrons. In both cases, LTG Weyand sent what he considered the best unit available to accomplish a difficult mission under extraordinary conditions. Third Squadron was sent to Hau Nghia Province

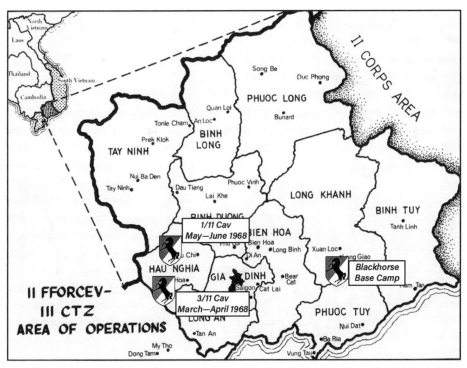

Map of 11th Armored Cavalry Regiment operations in Hau Nghia Province from March to June 1968. (basic map, US Army)

shortly after the Tet offensive sputtered to a conclusion in March. The troopers were tasked with hunting down the 9th (VC) Division and preventing it from renewing its attack on Saigon. What was extraordinary was that 3/11 was placed in "direct support" of the 25th (ARVN) Infantry Division—a command relationship that had never been tried before between American and South Vietnamese combat units.

Two months later, it was 1st Squadron's turn to clear Hau Nghia. The enemy was the same, and the command relationship was also the same. But what was not the same was the weather. The powder-dry rice paddies that characterized the province in March were now inundated with water. Knowing full well that this was not "armor country," the planners at Weyand's headquarters now had sufficient confidence in the Blackhorse to intentionally send its ACAVs and tanks off the roads and into the muck—expecting nothing short of mission accomplishment despite the difficult conditions. Blackhorse troopers did not disappoint.

3/11 in Hau Nghia Province

Colonel Kham, the commander of the 9th (VC) Division, had his orders. He was to disperse his three regiments and divisional troops into the far corners of Hau Nghia Province and prepare for the second general offensive of 1968. He was to take on replacements and supplies, train, and prepare for the offensive—and not do anything that would endanger the upcoming offensive. The senior Communist commanders guaranteed that the renewed assault would be so painful that the puppets in Saigon would collapse and Washington would sue for peace—just as the French had done back in 1954.

Kham's soldiers were holed up in the many small villages and hamlets of the province. The stands of bamboo and hedgerows that bordered these villages were perfect for digging; bunkers built into the hedgerows were virtually invisible and strongly protected. It would take a direct hit from the dreaded tank guns and air-delivered bombs to overcome his defenses. So Kham and his soldiers—more and more of whom came from the north rather than the local population—bided their time. Friendly villagers told them where the armored columns were headed, giving his units plenty of time to evade or, when trapped, to prepare their defenses.

Everything was new to 15-year-old Le Cong Lanh. Born and raised in North Vietnam, he had never been more than a few kilometers from his ancestral home. Now, here he was a soldier, a long way from home in a land that might as well have been the moon. Unlike the lush vegetation of his native north, this country was as dry as a bone. The rice paddies were familiar to Le, similar to those at home. But here, everything was so dry. The powdery white dust got into everything—his eyes, his weapon, even his meager ration of rice.

The training after being inducted into the army seemed like it was a lifetime ago. He was only allowed to spend a few days at home with his family before starting the long journey south. The political officer had told him and the others that they were beginning a great adventure, the first step in fulfilling their socialist duty. But for Le Cong Lanh, memories of home, not dreams of socialist destiny, made him put one foot in front of the other as they trudged up one more hill, across one more stream, through one more thicket of bamboo.

Finally, they arrived at a permanent camp. It was still in the jungle, but there were solid bunkers, clear water in the nearby stream, and even some free time to play volleyball, to write to his mother, or to dream of his village. But this interlude ended abruptly one day by the big news. They were all brought into the open-air classroom, when the political officers, beaming with joy, told them of the latest developments.

The freedom-loving people of the south had risen up against the hated Yankee invader. Liberation fighters, aided by soldiers like Le from the north, were very close to the final victory. Tens of thousands of Americans and puppet troops under the traitorous Saigon generals were dead as a result of the final offensive now underway. Saigon was aflame, Hue was in Communist hands, and Da Nang was next. Uncle Ho had declared that it was up to Le Cong Lanh and the other replacements now in Cambodia to provide the strength needed to overcome the last obstacle. So they cleaned their weapons, counted their bullets, rolled up their hammocks, and began to move again. They all smiled, dreaming of marching into Saigon as liberators.

As they moved south, even though it was at night, they heard the dreaded helicopters they had been warned about during training. The sounds of big guns went on almost all night, every night. Were those really the sounds of their socialist brothers relentlessly attacking the enemy? If so, they had never heard such loud explosions before.

But parading through Saigon was not to be their destiny. The revolution needed them here in Hau Nghia. This was where Le finally joined his unit. There was little time for formal welcomes and introductions. The sergeant told Le and his squad mates to dig defensive bunkers. There was a new sense of urgency to their digging.

They knew the enemy was close, so when the sergeant said dig, they dug deep, deep enough for Le and the other riflemen to stand while shooting out the narrow firing ports. Two to three men could fit in each position. They dug the defenses into the sides of the dikes along the edges of the rice paddies. These dikes had walls as much as three feet thick. The veterans said they were thick enough to absorb incoming rounds. The hedgerows on the village edge provided concealment; bamboo poles with two to three feet of dirt on top made the bunkers safe from the American artillery and bombs.[20]

They dug tunnels between the bunkers. These tunnels provided protection from the expected bombs, but also allowed them to move unseen from one bunker to another, to hit the enemy in the flank and from behind. Digging in the dry prickly heat was difficult, but what choice did they have?

It was the waiting, the anticipation of his first battle that occupied Le Cong Lanh the most. The battalion scouts reported back daily that the dragon-like armored vehicles were roaming through the area. Even an untested recruit like Le understood that it was only a matter of time before they would find his unit. How would he fight? Would he embarrass his mother and father, or would he do his duty? Would he die?[21]

The enemy used the terrain in Hau Nghia Province—acres and acres of rice paddies and pineapple plantations, surrounded by canals and swamps—to great advantage. When the VC went to ground after the Tet offensive, they dispersed their units. A battalion of 400 men could hide in a eight-square-kilometer area, with ten or fewer men in any one location. The flat terrain enabled the soldiers inside the villages to see any approaching allied forces a great distance away.

In early 1967, Hau Nghia was characterized as one of the most dangerous provinces in South Vietnam. A year later, the province was the scene of some of the worst setbacks suffered by the pacification program. In early January 1968, two VC battalions overran the provincial capital of Khiem Cuong, raising their flag for a major propaganda victory. Fearing the worst, village and hamlet chiefs began sleeping in Saigon rather than risking being the next victim of a nocturnal visit. Peasants hid their extra food as the VC levied new taxes on them.

The VC assaulted Khiem Cuong again on 29 February at the tail end of the Tet offensive, inflicting heavy casualties on the defenders and leaving a VC flag on the wall of the American advisors' compound. One post-Tet assessment stated flatly that for "all intents and purposes, it would appear that the pacification effort in Hau Nghia has ceased …" Major General (MG) F.K. Mearns, the commander of the US 25th Infantry Division—whose area of operations (AO) included the province—called Hau Nghia "the bed rock seat of National Liberation Front and Viet Cong resistance in III Corps."

At least part of the problem was that the 25th (ARVN) Infantry Division (3/11's partner for the upcoming operation) might "not only be the worst division in the Vietnamese army, but the worst division in any army." And that was the opinion of the chief of the South Vietnamese General Staff! The CIA agreed, calling those forces "the worst combat units in the Vietnamese Army."

Despite the willingness of some senior South Vietnamese leaders to cooperate, there were structural impediments that contrived to reduce the effectiveness of any combined operations. The ARVN infantrymen—rarely over five and a-half feet tall (66 inches) and weighing in at around 100 pounds—were still carrying M1 rifles (9.5 pounds, 43.5 inches long), Browning Automatic Rifles (16 pounds, 43 inches long), and tripod-mounted .30-cal. machine guns (31 pounds), all leftovers from WWII. Going up against AK47-armed VC and NVA regulars, the ARVN infantry units were simply outgunned.

The division's WWII-era weaponry and equipment only partially explained the operational deficiencies. Captain (CPT) Bill Camp was an assistant battalion advisor to the 2nd Battalion, 49th (ARVN) Regiment. His description of the standard operating procedure within the division provides insight into why they were so unsuccessful. "The division conducted extensive regimental size search and destroy missions during the daylight hours. At night, they would return to a defensive type posture around the villages and heavily populated areas." No multi-day operations. No overnights in the field. No nighttime patrols.

So, all the enemy had to do was to hide during the day and to conduct their operations unfettered during the night. They could pick their targets and the time to attack, then get away before the 25th (ARVN) could react.

The division commander, Brigadier General (BG) Nguyen Xuan Thinh, was politically reliable, an ally of President Thieu.[22] And, as the series of coups in the recent past had shown, it was not a "good" thing to have a unit this close to Saigon that was very combat effective. Officially, 3/11 was in direct support (DS) of the 25th (ARVN) Division.[23] The concept was for the squadron's troopers to work directly with ARVN battalions and regiments, thus by-passing the senior leadership. In the end, the new commander proved somewhat more capable than his predecessor ("mediocre" in the words of one report); most importantly, he gave LTC Creighton plenty of leeway in planning and executing the combined operations.

In mid-March, orders came from the enemy headquarters in Cambodia directing the 9th (VC) Division to prepare for the second phase of the offensive scheduled for early May. Commanders consolidated their units to infuse replacements, issue fresh supplies and equipment, and train for the new missions. The need to gather in one location made them vulnerable to attack. And that is exactly what 3rd Squadron and the theretofore lackluster 25th (ARVN) did. They attacked. They used their superior mobility and firepower to overcome the disadvantages of enemy familiarity with the area and the difficulty of the terrain.

Starting on 1 March, 3/11 was placed DS to the 25th (ARVN) Infantry Division on Operation *Adairsville/Andover*. Their assigned mission was likened to "the days when the cavalry chased one Indian tribe for weeks on end." Creighton was told to pursue the regiments of the 9th (VC) Division and the local VC, bring them to a fight, and destroy them—in other words, find the "bastards," then pile on. Above all else, the troopers were to disrupt the enemy's ability to attack Saigon in the anticipated second-wave offensive.

The concept of operation devised by LTC Creighton and Major (MAJ) John Getgood (the squadron operations officer), and "approved" by BG Nguyen Thinh, was aggressive. Two troop/company teams conducted recon-in-force sweeps with ARVN and militia infantry forces every day. The third troop/company team—paired with a South Vietnamese infantry company—established a separate night defensive position every night and sent out three platoon-sized ambushes.[24] On a rotational basis, one troop/company team secured Fire Support Base (FSB) Buffalo (where the squadron command post and howitzer battery were located) at night and performed maintenance during the day. This concept of operation ensured a 24-hour presence within the area of operations (AO), gave ample opportunity for "learning by example" for the ARVN and militia forces, and gave the enemy scant opportunity to conduct his own resupply and training missions.

The first few days in the new AO, the recon troops and tank company oriented themselves on the terrain, as the squadron commander and staff ironed out the wrinkles of the first-ever "direct support" command relationship with their ARVN allies. FSB Buffalo was mortared two days after it was occupied, with 40 rounds landing mostly outside the perimeter. The equipment had all been dug in, and there was minimal damage and only light casualties. Otherwise, the first 11 days in Hau Nghia Province were relatively quiet—perhaps too quiet. As the then-Headquarters Commandant says: "They [recon troops] found nothin' day after day. Then one time, it was the 12th of March ..."

After more than a week in the new AO, the presence of sizable enemy forces in the province was confirmed. Contact during the first part of the deployment had been limited to ambush patrols engaging small numbers of VC, a few sniper rounds, a couple of mines, and two attacks by fire. On 10 March, in response to heavy airborne sensor readings, Team A-352, 5th Special Forces (SF) Group, led a Civilian Irregular Defense Group (CIDG) patrol in the area 14 kilometers west of Duc Hoa. They ran into a VC battalion. The fight lasted four hours and included numerous air strikes and helicopter gunship runs. The "bastards" had been located and 3/11 was directed to pile on.

On the next day, the 2nd Platoon of Lima Troop (nine ACAVs) took the squadron surgeon (CPT James Nibler) and some of his medics to the village of Bao Canh Na, about five kilometers north of FSB Buffalo. There was nothing in particular to distinguish Bao Canh Na from the dozens of other tiny farming villages scattered through central Hau Nghia. Like all the others, it sat in the midst of bone-dry rice paddies; a few one-room hootches with thatch roofs, dirt floors, and no amenities.

But Bao Canh Na sat astride a well-known enemy infiltration and resupply route into Saigon. Troopers noted that there were no farmers or water buffalo in the fields getting ready for planting; everyone stayed in their houses, even after an interpreter announced the availability of medical assistance over a loud speaker.

Spider holes and freshly dug, covered bunkers were scattered around everywhere and one villager acknowledged that two NVA battalions had been in the area about two weeks earlier. About noon, the platoon leader declared the mission over, and the troopers gladly left Bao Canh Na.

Based on the information gathered on the 11th, LTC Creighton determined to run a recon-in-force operation around Bao Canh Na and two neighboring villages the next day. About the same time, an advisor with the Duc Hoa militia called and asked if 3/11 could provide an escort for two of his platoons. An informer had told them that there was a substantial cache of rice in the same village. The two missions were combined into one and scheduled for first thing on 12 March.

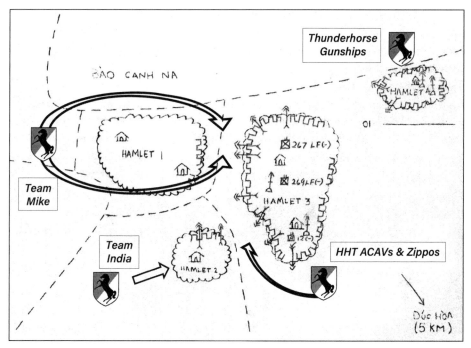

Map showing enemy dispositions and 3rd Squadron attack during battle of Bao Canh Na on 12 March 1968 (reproduced from the regimental after-action report). (basic map, US Army)

Squadron SOP was for a command and control bird to accompany the column, but all of the squadron's OH-23 helicopters were down for maintenance that day. Since it was expected to be a routine search, there was nobody flying overhead the next morning; everyone was expecting a "milk run."

Team Mike (two tank platoons and the 3rd Platoon of Lima Troop)[25] linked up with the 80 militia soldiers north of Buffalo and headed for the village of Bao Canh Na. The village was actually a cluster of four small hamlets. Each of the hamlets was ringed by hedgerows with bamboo planted atop them. The informer (who accompanied the militia) said the rice cache was located in the first hamlet. The armored cavalry-infantry team arrived at the first objective (Hamlet #1) and the militia soldiers dismounted. The tanks and ACAVs provided overwatching fires from positions to the west and north. There were 20 or 30 villagers inside Hamlet #1, putting most troopers at ease; normally, if the VC were in the area, the villagers wouldn't be present.[26]

During their search, the militiamen found the rice—a total of 1,300 pounds, much of it in bags marked "Hands Across the Ocean" and "Made in the USA." They also found several VC/NVA hiding in an underground bunker under a flower bed. The militia soldiers, who all lived in the neighborhood, did not recognize these men as locals and began to question them.

The prisoners didn't want to talk, but were convinced by the militia soldiers to do so (Mike Company platoon leader Tate Moorer called it "intensive interrogation").[27] They eventually revealed the presence of several other comrades in the same hamlet (a total of ten), as well as a weapons cache in the main village (Hamlet #3). The search and interrogation took about two hours. Up to this point, it was still a routine operation, a milk run. Specialist 5 (SP5) Tony Stanfa, the loader on tank M-66, recalled later that the prisoners "told us … there were a lot of weapons over there [Hamlet #3], but they didn't tell us that behind each weapon was a man."[28]

Not knowing for sure what lay ahead, CPT Don Robison (Mike Company commander) split his force along two axes for the approach to Hamlet #3. Four tanks moved in column to the north of Hamlet #1, while eight ACAVs swung to the south; once they reached the eastern side of the hamlet, they would be mutually supporting. The 18- to 36-inch tall dry rice paddy dikes made progress slow, especially for the lighter ACAVs. After crossing about half of the 800-meter wide open area on the other side of Hamlet #1 (just before 1300 hours), the northern column of Team Mike came under automatic weapons fire from their left front. Robison said over the radio "let's go get them," and the tanks came on line and rumbled toward Hamlet #3. The militia spread out on the right flank of the tanks. Robison called LT Jim Narrell, the leader of his attached recon platoon in the southern column, and directed him to head towards the sound of the guns.

The ACAVs had just entered the open area to the south of Hamlet #1 when they got Robison's call. At this point they were not receiving any fire themselves, so they continued in column between Hamlets #1 and #3. In so doing, they unknowingly flanked themselves to the enemy bunkers in the bamboo hedgerow that surrounded Hamlet #3. Soon thereafter there came a fusillade of anti-tank rounds from three sides. Most of the fire was coming from Hamlet #3, but there was even some from Hamlet #1 behind them. Both of Team Mike's elements were now under fire, some as close as from 30 meters away. The vehicles had to back off, because, as tank platoon leader Moorer recalled, "the anti-tank rounds became so intense that we could not even begin to equalize that volume of fire … We really received some raking over the coals, so to speak."

The mere fact that the enemy in Bao Canh Na was able—even temporarily—to gain fire superiority over nine M48 tanks and eight ACAVs is an indicator of just how heavily armed the 271st (VC) Regiment was. Neal Creighton reflected later: "What we had in front of us that day was probably the strongest force we ever did encounter. Main force guys, mostly NVA, well equipped, dug in, and ready to fight—and, at that point, they weren't very fearful of the tanks. They didn't know anything about the tanks and their power."

Don Robison radioed (in his usual calm and professional manner) that he estimated at least one, but maybe two enemy companies were located in and around Bao Canh Na and he was engaging. Please send help. In fact, there were at least two enemy *battalions* spread through the four hamlets.[29]

Fortunately, the volume of return fire from the tanks and ACAVs was such that the enemy gunners were not very accurate. As an example, of the dozen RPGs fired at the Lima Troop ACAVs, only one hit its intended target—even though the vehicles were initially flanked to the enemy (i.e., the RPG gunners were shooting at the flat sides of the ACAVs, not the much narrower canted fronts). The others were either too high or exploded in the ground short of the vehicles. The enemy was also using the RPGs like mortars. LT John Miller recalled: "Initially we thought that the VC were throwing sticks of dynamite at us; this later turned out to be that they were firing RPGs indirect."

Back at Buffalo, the staff swung into action. Calls were placed to Regiment (situation report), the Howitzer Battery and the mortars (fire mission!), the 11th Cav's Nile forward air controllers (FAC) (request for immediate air strikes), the on-call Air Cav Troop gunships at Duc Hoa (get flying to Bao Canh Na), the 25th (ARVN) Infantry headquarters (send more infantry), and to Team India (three recon platoons and the 3rd Platoon, Mike Company) protecting FSB Buffalo (start your engines, stand-by for orders).

Creighton—finally aloft in a borrowed helicopter—directed CPT Chuck Schmidt to deploy Team India from Buffalo to reinforce Team Mike. MAJ Getgood soon had artillery, tactical air (TacAir), and helicopter gunships on the way. Because there was insufficient infantry on the ground, not all of the enemy positions were cleared in Hamlets #1 and #2. As a result, the assaulting ACAVs and tanks were receiving fire from their front and from the flanks.

Within 15 minutes of leaving Buffalo, Team India joined the fight around Bao Canh Na. Attacking from the southwest through Hamlet #2 (and killing at least eight VC/NVA in the process), Schmidt brought his ACAVs and attached tanks on line on the right flank of Mike Company. Together, they raked the fortified positions in Hamlet #3. Howitzer Battery saturated the area with 155 mm high explosive and white phosphorous rounds, alternating concentrations with 2.75-inch rocket runs by Air Cav Troop (Thunderhorse) gunships.

India Troop's SSG Mack Bell had just taken over for his seriously wounded platoon leader (LT Frank Deusebio) when he—and most everyone else on that part of the battlefield—saw two water buffalo running between the lines. Undoubtedly frightened by the loud noises, they made a mad dash to get away. "We were standing up there on line and all of a sudden, a black cow, a brown cow started running out from the hootches. Right out in the middle of all the firing." Neither survived the fight.

The Nile FAC came up on the radio net and said he had fixed-wing aircraft inbound. The proximity to Bien Hoa Air Base meant that his requests for immediate air strikes could be answered in ten minutes or less. The Thunderhorse gunships expended their ordnance, the artillery checked fire, and the troopers on the ground popped smoke to fix their positions. The fast movers worked their magic. Several secondary explosions were seen in the target area as the jets pulled away. SSG Bob McNeil recalls the sight: "It looked like a million flashbulbs going off in the treeline."

By now it was 1500 hours, and it was time for another assault on the main hamlet. Teams Mike and India moved forward with all weapons firing, while Howitzer Battery provided a rolling barrage of artillery fire a few hundred meters in front. The militia, who had suffered three killed and a number of wounded, held back behind the vehicles. After the fight, Creighton said: "I don't much blame them. They were not a large enough force to … make an infantry assault and overrun what we had at that point."

Charlie still had plenty of fight left in him, though. As usual, the enemy had dug their holes deep and emerged after the airstrikes to engage the attacking vehicles. Platoon Sergeant (PSG) Tom Davidson, in his first firefight, recalled later: "I don't know how they do it, but it takes a lot of guts to stay in them holes and take all that pounding. The ones who do survive and when it stops to come out and fight again … They got plenty of guts."

Barrages of RPGs were coming out of the hamlets. Two Mike Company tanks were disabled, and enemy soldiers swarmed out of their holes trying to overrun them. M-66, the company commander's tank, was one of the damaged tanks; two or three RPGs knocked out all of the on-board weapons systems. Don Robison, still in the TC's cupola of M-66 and already badly wounded, took the assaulting enemy soldiers on with his M16 rifle. They were swarming out of bunkers and trenches just 40 meters away. He killed at least eight before being hit by a fatal burst of AK47 rifle fire to the chest.[30]

Loader Tony Stanfa was inside the turret trying to unjam the main gun. He recalled after the fight that Robison said over the intercom: "I need some help up here, get some help up here quickly." He then fell down into the turret. Tony noticed a chest wound and another near his left eye. "Shortly thereafter, his eyes closed and there was no heartbeat." PFC Richard Russell, the medic who treated Robison's initial wounds, was in his first action since arriving in Vietnam. He recalled later: "We all were just shocked you know. We couldn't believe that Captain Robison could get hit … We just couldn't believe it."[31]

LT Ed Howard's tank platoon, cross-attached with India Troop, was on the far right when the enemy attempted to outflank the attacking armored vehicles. His two tanks were firing a mix of high explosive, white phosphorous, and canister into the hedgerow where the bunkers were located; they were close enough to clearly see the bad guys in their NVA uniforms. Later, when Ed saw them trying to move around behind his platoon, he traversed the turret of M-34 and fired canister. "That was the last time we had any problems with the right flank."

The 3/11 Executive Officer (XO), MAJ Glenn Ryburn, wanted to recon the route that would be used to resupply the recon troops later that afternoon. Along with the Headquarters Commandant (CPT Terry Wallace), he organized a column of ACAVs and flame tracks (Zippos), and they started their recon before the first shots were fired at Bao Canh Na. Wallace recalls that the road to the objective was raised above an inundated marsh with reeds (not rice) "like cat o' nine tails." The side gunners on his ACAV kept seeing guys pop up amongst the reeds and took them under fire. They were well into their route recon when the fight in the village started.

Ryburn's column of ACAVs and Zippos from Buffalo arrived on the scene at a crucial time. They used the plumes of black smoke from the air strikes to guide on and, suddenly, were in the middle of the fight—literally. The combination of smoke, dust, and the need to get there quickly obscured the battlefield until it was too late. The six vehicles, approaching from the south, drove in between the enemy (in Hamlet #3) and the squadron tracks that had pulled back several hundred meters. Wallace says: "We had flanked ourselves to the enemy and were right in the middle of them. So we just kept firing, kept moving on through. It was too late to turn around. There was nothing we could do but move through." They ended up on the northwest side of Hamlet #3.

All of the vehicles moved about 200 meters away from the hamlet's edge as artillery, the rearmed Air Cav Troop gunships, and more US and Vietnamese Air Force aircraft came back on station to pound the target with bombs and napalm. The enemy brought at least five .51-caliber machine guns when they reinforced Hamlet #3; they engaged the aircraft, hitting several (all of which made it back to their bases). They made life for the rotary- and fixed-wing aviators very dicey that afternoon. Creighton called it "the heaviest flak that I'd ever seen, and when the US planes and the others coming in, they'd come in and they'd be shooting their machine guns and rockets, and these guys on the ground, they had anti-aircraft guns, and they were shooting right back at them … Years later when I asked the [VC] division commander, he said, "I had my anti-aircraft battalion with me.""

Two Zippo flame-thrower tracks moved in and swept the treeline around Hamlet #3 from just 50 meters away. For over two hours, Howitzer Battery (reinforced by the fires of a battery of South Vietnamese 105 mm guns), gunships, and fighter-bombers raked the target. While all this was happening, the tank crews were replenishing their turrets with ammo. SP4 Al Kruger recalled that his tank was down to two canister rounds and no 7.62 mm machine gun ammo before they were able to resupply from one of the damaged tanks. At the same time, crews were reshuffled to replace those who were wounded.

The ARVN 51st Ranger Battalion—with their distinctive purple scarves—arrived on the battlefield about 1700 hours, and Neal Creighton linked them up with the ACAVs and tanks for the final assault.

With dusk approaching, Creighton sent Teams Mike and India and the newly-arrived platoon of Kilo Troop and ARVN Rangers forward again to establish contact with the dug-in enemy. MAJ Getgood recalled the final assault as "real textbook tactics on the attack of a fortified position." The Rangers went from bunker to bunker, throwing in grenades and clearing the defensive line one position at a time.

About 1800 hours, the 51st Ranger commander called it quits; his soldiers had done enough fighting for the day. The lateness of the hour (sunset was at 1904 hours) and the day's 95° heat and 85 percent humidity undoubtedly played a role in his decision. Creighton was powerless to make him continue the assault. He recalled four decades later:

> I failed to convince the commander of the Vietnamese Ranger Battalion to press ahead just as the enemy line broke late in the afternoon. He was quite frank about his decision to stop the battle and go home so the troops could be with their families back in Duc Hoa. He pointed out to me that he had been in this war back when the French were fighting against the Viet Minh and expected to continue for many more years ... and that the enemy would always be out there to kill.

Sporadic fighting continued until about 2135 hours, when the enemy finally broke contact. There were not enough forces on the ground to establish an air-tight seal around Bao Canh Na.[32] So, despite a USAF "Moonbeam" flare ship overhead part of the night and frequent artillery salvos along likely avenues of escape, some got away.[33]

Teams Mike and India and the militia soldiers swept the battlefield the next day and found that the NVA had pre-dug graves behind the village. There were almost a hundred enemy bodies either in the graves or strewn about the hamlets. The eight soldiers (from the 267th and 269th (VC) Battalions) captured in Hamlet #1 indicated that their mission was to delay the armored vehicles for two days—probably to cover the operations of the regiments of the 9th (VC) Division and to give the rear service group personnel time to move caches and open new routes.

They fell 38 hours short of their goal.

The enemy commander had, perhaps, hoped that the marshy ground on three sides of Bao Canh Na would prevent armored vehicles from joining the battle. He was wrong. The large number of RPG rounds, launchers, and rice left behind were a sure indicator of the haste of the enemy's retreat.[34] A number of the dead enemy soldiers were found chained in position inside some of the almost 300 bunkers found in and around the four hamlets.

The searchers also found a line of bunkers dug into rice paddy dike walls about 50 meters forward of the bamboo hedgerow. These were so well camouflaged that the troopers had not seen them during the fight the day before. Most of the fire came from these bunkers.

There were two Blackhorse fatalities on 12 March—Don Robison, who died on the battlefield, and India Troop platoon leader Frank Deusebio, who died of his wounds several days later.[35] Another 25 Troopers were wounded, along with 30 of the dismounted militiamen and Rangers. The fighting was at such close quarters that most of the wounds were from AK47 rifles, not RPGs. Blackhorse 6, Colonel MacFarlane, was one of the wounded during this contact. LTC Creighton, who visited McFarlane at the battlefield aid station, recalls that "he looked in pretty bad shape, but would live." He was right.

The fight at Bao Canh Na successfully interdicted a major enemy supply and infiltration trail into Saigon. Two VC battalions tried valiantly to delay 3rd Squadron's aggressive recon-in-force operations and to keep the troopers away from their caches and supply routes. They failed in both missions. Intelligence reports through the remainder of 3/11's time in Hau Nghia indicated that the VC had to use alternate routes, forcing them into waiting ambush patrols. The 9th (VC) Division commander later told Creighton: "We had to make a stand somewhere. You were chasing us all over the place" … [adding that 3/11] really disrupted them as they were getting ready for the second Tet.

Over the next three weeks, 3/11 had contact with the enemy almost every day. Troopers fought five major battles in eight days against at least one NVA and three VC regiments. Over 400 enemy soldiers died in the month that the squadron was in direct support of the 25th (ARVN) Division.

Third Squadron's actions northwest of Saigon made a dramatic difference at both the tactical and operational level. Enemy units were hounded out of what they considered to be "secure" positions while suffering tremendous casualties. Allied and enemy assessments alike recognized the significance of the operations in Hau Nghia. The official NVA history of the war unequivocally states that Operations *Quyet Thang* and *Toan Thang* caused "a great deal of difficulties for our units trying to approach their targets. Because the enemy had discovered our intentions, the Front Command had to switch the primary direction of attack from the north-northwest of Saigon [Hau Nghia Province] down to the southwest of Saigon. During their advance toward the city our units were forced to fight as they marched and their forces suffered attrition." One regiment of the 9th (VC) Division, for example, suffered 30 percent casualties even before reaching its attack position, and thus was unable to accomplish its Mini-Tet mission.

The unique nature of the operation, the gallantry and superb leadership of the outnumbered 3rd Squadron, and the outstanding results led Department of the Army to award 3/11 (along with the 1st Platoon of Air Cavalry Troop, 2nd Platoon of the 919th Engineer Company, and the 11th Tactical Air Control Party, 19th Tactical Air Support Squadron) the Presidential Unit Citation for the 42 days in Hau Nghia Province in March-April 1968. In the words of the citation, "Although in each battle the 3d Squadron was numerically outnumbered by the enemy, superior tactics and the effective and relentless use of direct and supporting fires as well as the daring application of maneuver resulted in the successive defeat of each enemy force encountered."

1/11 in Hau Nghia Province

Two months later, 1st Squadron was assigned a mission similar to what 3/11 had accomplished in March. First Squadron troopers were directed to move as quickly as possible and assume a blocking position in Hau Nghia Province, southwest of Cu Chi and astride the infiltration route expected to be used by the 9th (VC) Division during one more anticipated follow-up attack on Saigon. Intelligence indicated that large enemy forces were moving out of Cambodia through Hau Nghia Province toward Saigon.

Captain (CPT) Dee Cuttell, the Bravo Troop commander at that time, recalls that the squadron moved into its designated blocking position in the vicinity of Bao Trai, astride the main infiltration route from Cu Chi to Tan Son Nhut Air Base. Some thought that the enemy had already withdrawn from the area and would not choose to fight anymore. "Little did we know that he stayed in the area ... The enemy was there—as a matter of fact, he was there in force and he was ready to fight. The First Squadron, 11th Cav made its name in that operation."

The main road along the enemy's infiltration route ran through a series of small farming villages spaced several kilometers apart. The infiltrating units were using the villages as way stations during the day, as well as for hiding supplies. Gerry Schurtz (1/11 operations officer) recalls that the first night they were in place, Air Cavalry Troop pilots, using the new-in-country night vision goggles, "picked up dismounted activity coming the other way just about half a mile from the road ... Ol' Jack Nielsen [squadron commander] told the guys to saddle up [on 13 May], and he and the rest of the combat guys went over there, and he led them on a sweep of that village and laid out a bunch of people. Decimated at least a battalion ..."[36]

Bravo and Charlie Troops—both reinforced with elements of the 3/49th (ARVN) Infantry Regiment—moved to where the aviators had seen movement the night before. Charlie Troop made first contact, charging into an inferno of RPGs and

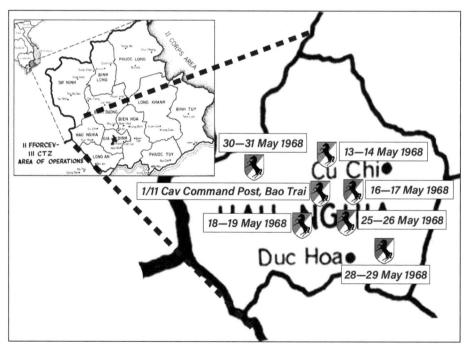

Map of 1st Squadron operations in Hau Nghia Province in May 1968. (basic map, US Army)

small arms at about 1000 hours in the hamlet of Ap Ben Long (about six kilometers northeast of the squadron command post). Two ACAVs were hit almost immediately, but artillery and close air support fire began to take effect on the estimated two VC platoons that were dug in. Shortly after Charlie Troop made contact, Bravo Troop came under heavy fire from an estimated enemy battalion from the 271st (VC) Regiment in heavily fortified positions.

LTC Nielsen describes the enemy fortifications: "The positions were so strong that an impromptu attack could seldom be successful ... I found through experience that the only thing capable of taking out the hedgerow position was a 750-pound bomb with delayed fuse."

Jack Nielsen witnessed it from on the ground. He didn't like to be up in the air; he wanted to be where the action was, just like when he was breaching the Siegfried Wall with the Hell on Wheels Division, in WWII and as a platoon sergeant in Korea. He'd been in command of 1/11 since the first of the year. He had a steady hand and a steady voice on the radio. About noon, he called for Delta Company to reinforce Bravo Troop.

By 1730 hours, after hours fighting in 95-plus temperatures and high humidity, Charlie Troop overran the enemy positions. But the Bravo Troop ACAVs and Delta Company tanks were still locked in heavy combat. Troop C moved in to reinforce. Dismounted ARVN infantrymen moved next to and behind the tracks. An after-action report describes the action.

> Immediately the volume of fire from the enemy increased, but the Squadron pressed on, penetrating the first line of defense. Continuing the attack, with not only track mounted weapons, but with hand grenades and small arms, the Squadron broke the enemy defenses crushing the enemy with the vehicles as they moved. The enemy fought to the last man constantly firing RPG's and small arms. By darkness, the objective was secured and Troop B and Team D laagered northwest of the objective prepared to sweep the area of the contact at first light. The enemy had been broken ...

Specialist 4 (SP4) Mike Sewell was driving a Charlie Troop ACAV that day. His recollections are from the perspective of the driver's hatch—and very vivid. The call to attack came just before dark. Sewell's platoon leader stressed that "we had to get through the hedgerow no matter what ... We no more than busted the bamboo open enough to even see what was inside when all hell broke loose. We got inside, of course. I mean, we hit it hard ... When we got in there, it was just overwhelming [enemy] firepower coming from, it seemed like everywhere. Each track was probably only ten feet apart, at some points even closer than that."

Sergeant (SGT) Doug Factora—nicknamed "Jerky" because his wife sent him lots of beef jerky in care packages—was on ACAV C-14 on Sewell's right. Doug didn't have to even be in Vietnam. He had already served his active duty commitment and was a member of an Army Reserve Special Forces unit in Hawaii. He volunteered for what he knew would be service in Vietnam. Laura, his widow, recalls: "He enjoyed the training and challenges. He also thrived on the respect and discipline of the U.S. Army ... Very adventurous ... He never feared danger."

The Army needed scouts more than snake eaters, so Doug was assigned to the 11th Cavalry.

SP4 Brian McDonnell went through the in-country training school with Factora and remembers him as "one of the 'happy pineapples,' always smiling, friendly, and good-looking." The two got together occasionally over the next ten months, comparing notes and catching up. In the spring, after they both had survived Tet, they met at the base camp for the last time. Factora "had gone home on R & R and his wife was pregnant ... Douglas told me that he was tired of being lead track. Mines usually killed the drivers and the TC's [track commanders] would lose their legs." These words still haunt Brian McDonnell so many years later.

On 13 May in Hau Nghia Province, Doug Factora proved his mettle. As the line of tracks approached the hedgerow, Doug fired his .50-cal. But once they broke through the bamboo barrier, the fighting was at close quarters. He began throwing hand grenades into the bunker entrances. When an RPG struck ACAV C-14, Factora was seriously wounded and thrown from his track. Despite his wounds, he climbed back into the cupola and resumed firing and tossing grenades. A second RPG took him and his vehicle out of the fight; the ACAV caught fire and melted down to the road wheels. Doug Factora was posthumously awarded the Distinguished Service Cross for his actions that day.

13 May set the pattern of operations for the next several days. Gerry Schurtz says: "Essentially the same cotton-picking things happened. Another regiment or battalion of NVA came down on the same infiltration route, and they were picked up by our helicopters." Each time, 1/11 moved out the following morning, found the "bastards," and piled on.

They did it again on 16 May.

Following up on a sighting of a large column of enemy troops moving northwest, Delta Company and Charlie Troop moved at first light toward the hamlet of Ap Tan Hoa, while Bravo Troop and the South Vietnamese 51st Ranger Battalion set up in a blocking position. The Delta Company tankers had to be especially careful where they drove; although the rain held off that day, the ground was becoming increasingly soggy as the rainy season was at hand.

The Air Cavalry Troop aviators were on the mark again—the tankers engaged a company-sized element just after noon, with first Charlie, then Bravo Troop piling on. Bravo, Charlie, and Delta again conducted a coordinated assault on the dug-in enemy, overrunning the position near sundown. Three Thunderhorse heavy fire teams of three gunships each helped to convince the enemy to finally break contact and scatter, leaving lots of weapons, ammo, and rice behind. And one prisoner.

Sergeant Ngo Xuan Do said he was a squad leader in the 9th Company, 3rd Battalion, 88th (NVA) Regiment. He said that his company was the rear guard for the regiment, tasked to slow down the pursuit by the dreaded "iron boxes bristling with firepower." He acknowledged that they were unable to accomplish that mission.

And so it went for the rest of May and into June. Unlike when 3/11 was in Hau Nghia in March, 1/11's sojourn there was marked by battles with both the enemy and the weather. Temperatures ranged from the mid-90s during the day to the mid-70s at night. The humidity matched the temperatures in the mid-90s, so even when it wasn't raining, jungle fatigues were as damp as if it was pouring.[37] The rice paddies that were so dry that they turned to fine white snow-like dust during the dry season, were now sloppy with knee-deep water and muck. As much as three inches of rain fell during the mornings, with thunderheads filling the afternoon skies. Howitzer Battery's LT Lee Pryor, who had less than two weeks in country when he came to Hau Nghia, recalls: "We were set up in a rice paddy. We had a helluva time getting the howitzers out of there. It just went from dust to mud in 24 hours."

But the 9th (VC) Division was definitely the more dangerous of the two enemies. The mud could make you mad; the enemy could make you dead. They were tenacious, fierce warriors with a seemingly endless supply of ammo. Delta Company tanker Private First Class (PFC) Ross Lyle recalls the time quite well. "There were so many RPGs coming at us we thought they had a 'belt-fed' tube." But they were not invincible; and they were not used to fighting mounted Blackhorse troopers. A prisoner captured on the 13th told his captors that "they had been taught that when they fired on the Americans, they would withdraw from the battlefield, thereby letting them escape after inflicting heavy damage. He said that this was the first time he had fought the personnel carriers with the tub in the middle [the TC's cupola]."[38]

Lieutenant General Weyand, the II Field Force Vietnam commander, wrote an assessment of the actions following Mini-Tet. While written for his entire command, his words are especially accurate for what 1st Squadron accomplished in Hau Nghia. "In the last few days of May the enemy attempted a weak attack on Saigon, presumably to establish a presence there, but by the end of May, the attack had been thwarted and the enemy routed."

In the period 11 May–3 June 1968, 1st Squadron suffered 21 troopers killed in action and another 174 wounded. The 9th (VC) Division, on the other hand, suffered at least 298 killed during the same period. Most importantly, the actions by 1/11 prevented the enemy from launching his planned late-May attack against Saigon from the northwest. The 9th (VC) Division was rated as "not-combat effective" for the next several months. The 25th (ARVN) Infantry Division displayed a new-found confidence subsequent to the combined operations conducted with the troopers of the Blackhorse. For these reasons, 1st Squadron was awarded a Presidential Unit Citation.

From this point forward, II Field Force operations planners placed the 11th Cavalry at the forefront of the most important—and yes, most dangerous operations throughout the corps area.

CHAPTER 5

The Bloodiest Year: 1969

In summary, the past eight months have proven the 11th Armored Cavalry Regiment to be the versatile, tenacious fighting machine that all cavalrymen knew it to be.

JIMMIE LEACH, BLACKHORSE 6, 1969

We didn't get attacked that often because we had a reputation, we thought, with the enemy in that we were something you didn't want part of. We were a hornet's nest.

BILL BARNER, HOWITZER BATTERY, 2/11TH CAVALRY

Their targets now are An Loc, Loc Ninh and Song Be.

MACV BRIEFING OFFICER, AUGUST 1969

You could tell almost right away that things were going to be different. The two men were almost polar opposites. One was urbane, suave, flamboyant, political; from the time he was a one-star, he called on members of Congress whenever he was in Washington. He always wore starched fatigues and never seemed to sweat. The other almost always had a chomped-on cigar in his mouth. He was gruff and always spoke his mind. He sought out sergeants and junior officers, wanted to hear their take on things. One Blackhorse officer said of him (with great affection): "His fatigues looked like ours, they weren't starched or anything else. It just looked like he got them out of an ammo container like we were used to doing ..."

Although classmates at West Point (Class of 1936) and sharing similarly distinguished service in Europe during WWII, William Westmoreland and Creighton Abrams could not have been more different—especially in their approach to the way GIs fought in Vietnam. One of the most visible changes was in how the war was conducted after General Abe Abrams assumed command of Military Assistance Command Vietnam (MACV) from Westy in mid-1968. His new strategy was an integral part of President Nixon's five-part plan for ending the war in Vietnam.[1] While Westy's "search and destroy" approach equated to a war of attrition, Abe's "clear and hold" strategy recognized that we could not beat an enemy who was willing to fight to the last man.[2] Instead, we would separate the enemy from the population and deny him his supplies.

As Abrams' new approach took hold in late 1968, that much-abused system of measuring success—the enemy body count—became less and less important.[3] The *Christian Science Monitor* quoted him as saying: "The body count [of Communist troops killed] does not have much to do with the outcome of this war. Some of the things I do think important are that we preempt or defeat the enemy's major military operations and eliminate or render ineffective the major portion of his guerrillas and his infrastructure—the political, administrative and para-military structure on which his whole movement depends."

This was the essence of General Abrams' "one war" strategy. The three theretofore parallel but separate efforts—combat operations to defeat the VC and NVA, stability operations to provide security for the population, and nation-building operations to establish a functioning South Vietnam—were brought together under one overall campaign plan and given equal weight and equal resources. An underlying tenet of that strategy was the preemption of enemy offensives by eliminating or interdicting the infrastructure—village-based Viet Cong infrastructure (VCI), supply caches, and infiltration trails. The whole hundred meters. Opening traditional enemy base camps, forward assembly areas, and routes of ingress and egress to observation through the use of land clearing by Rome Plows and B-52 "Arc Light" strikes was another high priority.[4]

The Rome Plow was a standard D7E engineer bulldozer with a special blade made by the Rome Plow Company in Rome, Georgia. In addition to the heavy-duty plow blade, the vehicle had a metal spike, called a "stinger," protruding from the front. A skillful operator could use the stinger to split larger diameter tree trunks into bite-size pieces, after which the blade could knock it down.

The number of tons of rice captured became a more meaningful measure of success than the number of bodies left on the battlefield. NVA regiments and divisions could not live off the land as their VC comrades had done. These conventionally-organized and equipped formations needed to be resupplied regularly. This made their lines of communication vulnerable to interdiction. And interdiction was something the 11th Cavalry did very well.

If an enemy commander didn't have enough to feed his troops and he couldn't get close enough to the villages and hamlets to get more, he wouldn't be able to threaten the South Vietnamese farmers and merchants. They could get on with their lives. The enemy commander, on the other hand, had to choose between starvation, surrender, or retreat to Cambodia.

The commander of the 275th Regiment, 5th (VC) Division is an example. In preparation for the second phase of the Winter-Spring Campaign in 1969, his unit was tasked to transport rice from distribution centers in Phuoc Long Province to forward caches in southern War Zone D. An entire regiment—one-third of the 5th Division's combat strength—allocated to transporting rice. But even that wasn't enough. Sweeps by the 11th Cavalry (and others) in the area northeast of Bien Hoa in December 1968 and January 1969 prevented the 275th from accomplishing its mission. Instead of the required 80 tons of rice, they delivered only 10.

For its part, the enemy headquarters opted to continue in search of the elusive major propaganda victory by mounting another offensive against Saigon around 1969's Tet holiday, albeit on a much smaller scale. Additional targets included the Vietnamization program ("de-Americanization" in Communist rhetoric) and the revitalized pacification program. But this was not simply a continuation of the 1968 campaigns. Things had changed, and not necessarily for the better from Hanoi's perspective. For one thing, the forces available were almost exclusively NVA; VC losses during 1968 could not be replaced through local recruiting.[5]

Another thing that had changed was a direct result of Abrams' clear-and-hold strategy. The NVA's rear service groups were incapable of stockpiling sufficient supplies far enough forward to support large-scale attacks. As a result, in the words of Hanoi's post-war history: "Most of our attacks would be small and medium sized attacks." Even these attacks (with a few exceptions) relied more on indirect fire and sappers than on massed infantry assaults. Numerous captured documents included instructions to subordinate commanders to conserve their units' strength. Further, unit commanders were directed to "deal the enemy painful, nasty blows, win great victories while suffering light casualties and consuming small amounts of ammunition."

Although the Communists continued to speak in terms of seasonal campaigns (e.g. Winter-Spring Campaign), in reality they were nothing more than a series of one- to two-day high points spread over several months.

The most significant development in the war in 1969—one that had a huge impact on the 11th Cavalry—was the steady movement of battlefield action away from the Saigon-Bien Hoa-Long Binh complex and toward the Cambodian border. After the lackluster performance of the 5th (VC) Division in February, there were no further coordinated attacks against the major population centers until 1975. The Communists could not sustain offensive campaigns that far away from their Cambodian sanctuaries. For the Blackhorse, this meant leaving their Long Giao base camp and conducting operations closer to Cambodia than to the capital of South Vietnam.

In the first six months of 1969, elements of the Regiment conducted operations in nine of the eleven provinces comprising III Corps Tactical Zone (III CTZ), serving virtually everywhere from the South China Sea to the Cambodian border and from the edges of the Mekong Delta to the slopes of the Central Highlands. During this time, the Regiment and individual squadrons/troops/companies worked for four different division commanders (two US, two ARVN), the Australian Task Force, the Capital Military Assistance Command, and the Bien Hoa Tactical Area Command.

The squadrons continued to conduct their fair share of route and convoy security missions, but these were no longer seen by higher headquarters as the primary mission or even as the optimal use of the 11th Cavalry. Colonel George Patton, who commanded the Regiment from July 1968 to April 1969, called the Blackhorse "the [II] Field Force Swing Force ... subject to employment in varying terrain and varying missions ... employed on short notice anywhere ..."

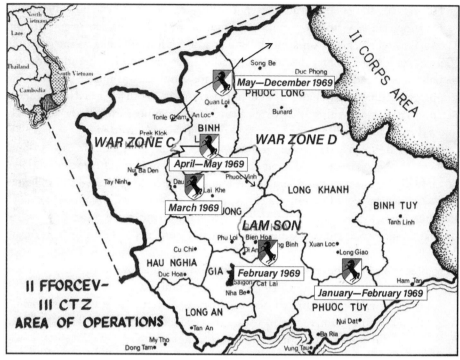

Map of 11th Armored Cavalry Regiment operations in 1969. (basic map, US Army)

Even the enemy recognized that General Abrams' ascension to command brought significant changes to the battlefield. In a captured document that reviewed the situation in 1969, the VC high command wrote glowing praise of the Blackhorse Regiment: "When Abrams assumed the position of Commander-in-chief of the U.S. forces in SVN [South Viet Nam], this regiment became a "cherished child" of Abrams. It was transformed into a mobile assault force of the II Field Force. The Commander of this Regiment is Colonel Patoon [sic] (a son of an American armor general)."

The year 1969 proved to be a tough one for Blackhorse troopers, with many hard-fought battles against a still-determined foe, but by the end of the year these troopers had written their accomplishments into the history books in bold strokes with indelible ink.

Tet '69: February 1969

The offensive began in the early morning hours of 23 February when the enemy launched over a hundred attacks by fire and on the ground throughout South Vietnam. According to a directive from the enemy headquarters (COSVN), the offensive was to be conducted in three phases over 34 days, with the first phase beginning on the

23rd and lasting for five days. Unlike the Tet '68 offensive, the initial attacks were intended as much to cover the advance of the forces designated to carry out the second phase during the week after Tet, as they were to achieve any battlefield goals. Another major objective was to influence public opinion in the United States, where anti-war demonstrations were growing in size and vitriol. Similar to the previous year's Tet offensive, Long Binh was one of the major targets for the Tet '69 attacks.

***

Back at home, race fans were gathered around their television sets watching LeeRoy Yarbrough, in his back-up car, pass Charlie Glotzbach on the final lap to win the Daytona 500. Yarbrough's average speed of almost 158 miles per hour was *slightly* faster than the M551 Sheridans (by about 110 mph) that had just been issued to 1st Squadron. But LeeRoy didn't have a 152 mm gun mounted on his Ford.

***

The enemy selected the location for his attack carefully. During the Tet '68 attacks, fuel resupply to GI combat units had become a major issue. As a result, a large number of tanker trucks, filled with various types of fuel (for wheeled vehicles, tracked vehicles, and aircraft), were parked overnight near the tank farm in a small valley located close to the southeastern perimeter. They were immediately available in case of emergency. The Long Binh heliport and US Army Vietnam (USARV) headquarters were within walking distance of the fuel depot.

The so-called "tanker valley" behind gate #10, tank farm behind gate #11, heliport, and USARV HQ were too attractive as targets for the enemy to pass up. Perimeter lighting had not yet been installed, so there were plenty of shadows in which to hide. The main attack struck the bunker line between gates #10 and #11. The enemy used Provincial Highway 317 that ran parallel to the southern perimeter of Long Binh Post to guide their approach.

Following a heavy rocket and mortar attack, elements of the 274th Regiment, 5th (VC) Division (an old acquaintance of the Blackhorse from 1966–67) commenced their ground attack against that part of the Long Binh perimeter about 0200 hours.[6] The 720th Military Police (MP) Battalion, responsible for post security, as well as an area of operations outside the wire, had placed three ambush patrols (AP) along likely avenues of approach south and east of the perimeter. These APs sighted the approaching enemy columns and engaged them with direct fire, while calling for artillery and gunships.

Corporal Tom Watson was a member of one of the ambush patrols that engaged the NVA on the night of 22 February 1969. He recalls that he and the other members of the MP ambush patrols "knew the attack had started and came to the sudden realization they were right in the middle of it." They found themselves caught in the crossfire between the attacking VC and the perimeter defenders—as Tom writes, "stuck between a rock and a hard place."

The enemy, late in arriving at their attack positions, was taken by surprise by these ambush patrols. As a result, their timetable and formations making the assault against the perimeter were disrupted. The attacking forces were thinned by artillery and gunships. Their assaults against the perimeter were pale imitations of those the previous year. The enemy soldiers were, nonetheless, determined. Perhaps they were motivated by promises of this being the "last battle" before the ultimate victory— after which they could go home (at least that's what the political commissars told them, anyway). Or maybe it was the promise of "all the C-Rations they could eat" that drove them forward.[7]

The mechanics, clerks, and chaplains' assistants inside the wire were overmatched. The perimeter bunkers did not have RPG screens[8] in front of them, so the enemy gunners had a clear shot at the defenders inside. M60 machine guns were few and far between along the perimeter, as were binoculars, compasses, body armor, starlight scopes, M79 grenade launchers, and radios (the bunkers were connected by landline to the base command post). The post commander, in charge of base defense, called for his Ready Reaction Force (RRF)—Task Force (TF) Privette.

TF Privette was originally formed in mid-August 1968 as a command and control headquarters for a two-recon troop RRF from the Blackhorse Regiment's 1st Squadron, with the mission of securing various sites in the Long Binh and Bien Hoa area.[9] After two months, TF Privette was disbanded. It was reestablished in early February 1969 in anticipation of the Tet offensive. The task force included 1/11's Alpha and Bravo Troops, as well as an infantry company from the 1st Infantry Division. It was under the operational control (OPCON) of the Bien Hoa Tactical Area Command.

The ensuing firefight south of Long Binh Post on 23 February was the M551 Sheridan's baptism-of-fire, matching Alpha and Bravo Troops (supported by Air Cav Troop gunships) against the sapper and heavy weapons companies of the K3 Battalion, 274th (VC) Regiment. These companies (filled mostly with NVA soldiers) had already been engaged by the MPs' ambush patrols. After daylight, contrary to normal SOP, the survivors did not melt back into the jungle but remained in close proximity to the huge logistics installation. They were waiting for the three infantry companies of the K3 Battalion to show up. They never did.

The reason they never did was due to Lieutenant (LT) Lee Pryor (the Bravo Troop Executive Officer) and the cooks, mechanics, and other headquarters section troopers. Troop routine was for the cooks to prepare a hot breakfast on post and then take it out to the troop night defensive position located off post. Just after daybreak that morning, they got to the gate and the MPs wouldn't let them leave because of reports of enemy activity. Pryor took the situation in hand and "opened it myself."

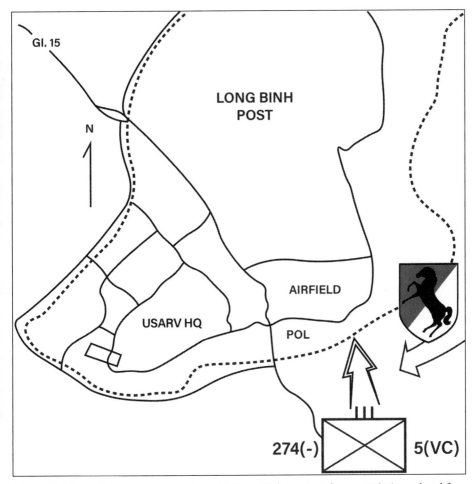

Map of Task Force Privette counterattack outside Long Binh Post in February 1969 (reproduced from the regimental after-action report). (basic map, US Army)

He allowed four PA&E[10] workers in, then took his makeshift column (an ACAV, a 2½-ton truck, another ACAV, and Pryor in his ¼-ton jeep) out. There was a slight rise in the road just outside the gate. Pryor stopped and had just picked up his radio mic to call the troop commander (Captain Jarrett Robertson) and say chow was on the way when RPGs and small arms fire "open[ed] up on my little convoy."

The rest of the convoy was slightly ahead of Pryor, down in a dip in the road crossing a creek. The intelligence specialists figured out later that the "lost" K3 Battalion was using the gully to infiltrate into their final attack positions. The rear elements of the battalion were cut off by the Bravo Troop vehicles; they probably saw the two ACAVs and felt they had been compromised.

Pryor recalls: "I was later told that what happened was, when my guys came down that road, the tail end people in that NVA battalion got trigger happy. They were not supposed to have opened fire. We were damn lucky, because at least two RPGs were fired; one missed the deuce-and-a-half in front and one in back." The K3 Battalion hunkered down in place in that gulley and was repeatedly engaged by fixed-wing and helicopter gunships. They played no role in the follow-on action.

About 0930 hours, LT Edwin Mendez, the MP Company XO, conducting a helicopter recon of the battlefield, sighted six enemy soldiers moving into dug-in positions outside the wire. He dropped a red smoke grenade to mark the spot and called in the cavalry.

While a company of infantrymen occupied a blocking position, the Alpha and Bravo Troop ACAVs and Sheridans (accompanied by MPs acting as dismounted infantry) assaulted the enemy positions. Bravo Troop Platoon Sergeant (PSG) Donald Kelly, one of the first on the scene, saw that the enemy force was in a trench line and bunkers along the ridge top. Other NVA riflemen were scattered across the area in spider holes. Kelly's Silver Star citation tells the rest of the story.

> The vehicles were brought on line and the troop assaulted the well-fortified positions. Sergeant Kelly surged slightly ahead of the other tanks, passed the first position and assaulted the second trench line, approximately forty meters long. Driving over the trench, he fired his fifty-caliber machine gun at point-blank range but still received intense automatic weapons fire and several grenades which bounced off the Sheridan tank. Realizing the immediate danger, he ordered a canister [flechette][11] round to be fired into the hostile soldiers, instantly killing fifteen.[12]

In the words of one Blackhorse Trooper, "it just stapled 'em."

Shortly thereafter, the enemy broke contact, leaving scores of their comrades dead on the battlefield, along with six wounded who were captured. The timely arrival of the Blackhorse troopers—and their newly-acquired 152 mm flechette rounds—prevented the enemy from renewing their attack against Long Binh Post and potentially setting ablaze the hundreds of thousands of gallons of fuel stored behind gates #10 and #11. As important as the heavy casualties inflicted on the enemy were the captured weapons—weapons that would never again be used against GIs. One after-action report concluded: "This action rendered the heavy weapons and mortar companies of the K3 Battalion ineffective."

CPT John Tillson had just taken command of Alpha Troop. He recalls that "A Troop was the reaction force for Long Binh post. My first engagement as a troop commander was outside the wire when I was supported by a company of MPs and [we] assaulted an NVA machine gun emplacement that was attempting to shoot down helicopters using the Long Binh post helipad. I was told that some of my .50-cal. bullets penetrated the USARV HQ building."

TF Privette was called upon three more times over the next week. On each occasion, the combined arms team of 1st Squadron ACAVs and Sheridans, Thunderhorse gunships, Big Red One grunts, and 720th MPs proved stronger than anything the enemy could muster. Once again, Hanoi's attempt to score a big psychological victory by occupying Long Binh had been stymied. The added firepower of the M551 Sheridans made the Blackhorse Regiment even more powerful than before.

Into the Michelin: March 1969

For as long as he can remember, Danny Connelly wanted to be a soldier. And not just any soldier. "I wanted to be a tanker. I didn't want to be in the infantry or artillery or anything else. I wanted to be a tanker." In 1960, he watched the movie *GI Blues*. When Sergeant "Tulsa" (Elvis Presley) was sitting in the tank gunner's seat and said "'On the way,' that pretty much cinched it for me."[13] Danny enlisted at 17, just so he could pick his specialty—tanker.

On 18 March 1969, Connelly had plenty of reason to be second-guessing his choice of careers. That's the day the 11th Cavalry entered the Michelin Rubber Plantation and ran into the 7th (NVA) Division. Ran *hard* into the 7th (NVA) Division.

And Connelly's tank was right up front. "Right before I got wounded, I felt the fear of God like I'd never felt it before. I thought I was gonna die ... I found myself on my hands and knees in the belly of a tank praying to God to let me live." Connelly was wounded that day; his tank burned up after he was medevaced, but all of the crew survived. It was the first in a series of hard-fought battles that ended with the 7th (NVA) Division scurrying back to Cambodia, unable to accomplish its mission of attacking Saigon.

Following the ineffectual late-February attacks, the enemy had four divisions spread across the northern and eastern sections of the III Corps area. MACV's assessment was that Saigon was still the Communists' "ultimate objective." The 1st (NVA) Division was thought to be in the northern half of War Zone C (east of Tay Ninh), probably with the mission of keeping the supply lines open and prepared to reinforce the offensive against Saigon if successful. The 5th (VC) was known to have filtered back into southern War Zone D astride the Dong Nai River after their "drubbing" (description used by the Associated Press) at the hands of Blackhorse troopers the previous month.

The 7th (NVA) was thought to be headed for staging areas around Dau Tieng, with the mission of renewing the offensive against the capital. The 9th (VC) was known to have bogged down, unable to accomplish its post-Tet offensive mission in Hau Nghia Province. They were thought to have retreated back across the Cambodian border in the Angel's Wing area shortly after Tet, but were expected to return to the battlefields west of Saigon by the middle of the month. The next "high point" was forecast for the third week of March.

The 7th (NVA) Division left its Cambodian base areas in early March. Their objective was the Michelin Rubber Plantation. The plantation was to be their forward staging area as they made final preparations for the next phase of the Winter-Spring Campaign. The Communist headquarters had given the 7th specific quotas for the campaign: "kill 10,000 enemy ... soldiers, put out of action one brigade or four or five ... battalions, destroy 200 assorted vehicles, and down 200 aircraft."

The Michelin was a favored assembly area for the enemy. Rumors circulated that the French planters had reached an agreement with the Viet Minh at the end of WWII. "Don't interfere with our business, and we will share a portion of the profits with you." It was said that the post-colonial government in Saigon had tacitly agreed to the same arrangement.

The plantation's rubber production provided a much-needed source of income for South Vietnam, so strict rules of engagement had been established that sought to minimize damage to the trees and workers' villages. The "unwritten" rules allowed units to return fire in kind, but not to employ artillery or air strikes. Ground operations were restricted to certain peripheral areas, and the enemy knew where they could send their units and remain unmolested.

The approach march took the 7th (NVA) Division's regiments about a full week, with movement limited to the hours of darkness. A near-full moon and cloudless nights provided ample illumination. With nighttime temperatures in the high 70s and low 80s, it was a relatively easy march, made easier by local VC guides who showed the northern troops the way. Intelligence reports indicated that the enemy was planning to stay in the Michelin until just before launching an attack on Saigon. One prisoner told the Blackhorse's 541st Military Intelligence Detachment interrogators that the 209th Regiment "was to stay in the Michelin at all costs."

The movement of the 7th (NVA) did not go undetected; radio intercepts, motion sensors, and helicopter recon flights tracked their southward trek. Eight sorties of B-52s dropped about three million pounds of bombs in an arc northwest of Saigon, above the Michelin. Once the 7th Division was safely inside the confines of the plantation, however, there were no more air strikes. But II Field Force did work up an operation to go after them starting on 19 March.

The original concept of Operation *Atlas Wedge* envisioned an armored cavalry squadron and an infantry battalion operating only on the edge of the Michelin. Because of the political and economic sensitivity of the plantation itself, no military operations inside the rubber were included in the original orders. Blackhorse troopers had never operated inside the Michelin previously, so Colonel Patton asked for, and received permission to conduct a visual reconnaissance on the periphery of the plantation on the 17th. The rules of engagement from higher headquarters allowed helicopters to return fire if fired upon (after being approved by the Big Red One commander, call sign "Danger 6"). They reiterated, however, that under no circumstances was heavy ordnance to be delivered into the areas planted with rubber trees.

In typical fashion, George Patton made a personal recon of the area starting just after midnight of the 16–17th. He was not disappointed. Within minutes, his

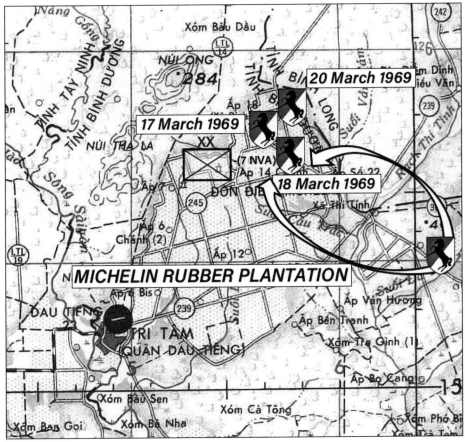

Map of 11th Armored Cavalry Regiment Operation *Atlas Wedge* in March 1969. (basic map, US Army)

command and control (C&C) bird was engaged by ground-to-air fire. The green tracers made identification unmistakable; there were definitely enemy forces inside the Michelin. Regimental Command Sergeant Major (RCSM) Bill Squires recalled that they were on the way to Dau Tieng to refuel when they just "happened"—*at midnight*—to overfly the AO for the upcoming operation.

> Green tracers buzzed around the chopper. Landing and refueling, the Regimental Commander [Patton] directed the pilot to fly back over the same area. Again, the chopper was greeted with intense fire, all aboard except the pilot returned with intense fire with the twin 7.62 machine guns on both sides of the aircraft, blasting away and tossing out CS [tear gas] grenades. The Regimental Commander sent the following message: "Receiving fire, taking hits, going in …" Then, with the mike off, added: "to kill the Bastards."

The response was predictable. Concerned that Blackhorse 6's helicopter had been shot down, Danger 6 authorized the use of aerial recon-by-fire in the Michelin. A

Thunderhorse pink team (one gunship and one scout) also just "happened" to be aloft and responded to Patton's call for help. The battle was on.

Four Air Cav Troop light observation helicopters (LOHs) and a C&C Huey, with a Nile forward air controller (FAC) overhead, conducted a follow-up recon on the morning of the 17th. It wasn't long before they found what they were looking for—just not where they had been told to look for it. The aero scouts spotted (in the words of Air Cav Troop's annual history for 1969) "groups of NVA troops literally lounging around in the rubber"—not in the area *outside* of the Michelin that had been apportioned to the 11th Cavalry for the upcoming Operation *Atlas Wedge*.

The intensity of enemy fire, as well as the size of the forces sighted by the aero scouts led the Regiment to request permission to return fire.[14] It took the 1st Infantry Division 90 minutes to finally get permission from higher headquarters to fire into the Michelin; Colonel Patton remembers them "as the longest one and a half hours of my life." But the ground-to-air fire grew, rather than diminished, in intensity. Even when the scouts were joined by gunships. It wasn't just AK47 rifles shooting at the helicopters, now it included .51-caliber machine guns with their softball-sized (in the eyes of the pilots being shot at, at least) green tracers. The estimated two companies of enemy soldiers "made little or no attempt to hide from the helicopters," so this was a target too good to pass up.

Blackhorse 6 requested authority to pile on by bringing in air strikes. After another long delay (two and a half hours), permission was finally granted. Under normal circumstances, the enemy would have been long gone four-plus hours after initial contact. But in this case, they were not. Whether it was a false sense of security due to the "sanctity" of the Michelin, ideological determination, or just bad leadership is unclear, but at the end of the day, the bodies of 30-plus NVA soldiers, 10 bicycles, and 6 tons of rice were strewn among the rubber trees, victims of nine air strikes and good shooting by pilots and door gunners. The Air Cav Troop commander, Major (MAJ) John 'Doc' Bahnsen, was quoted by a reporter as saying: "We are going to have good hunting here ... They are all over the place."

As a result of this target-rich environment, the 11th Cavalry's area of operations (AO) was extended into the rubber trees in the northeastern portion of the Michelin itself. The target was just too lucrative to pass up, political sensitivity or not. On the morning of 18 March (a day earlier than planned), 1/11 and 3/11 moved in from the east. The three US divisions (1st and 25th Infantry and 1st Cavalry) involved were otherwise engaged and did not have the same sense of urgency as Blackhorse 6. They did not deploy sufficient forces to *Atlas Wedge* in a timely manner. The western and northern sectors of the Michelin were left unguarded. Despite Air Cav Troop's best efforts to screen these areas, the bulk of the 7th (NVA) Division escaped. Those left behind, however, paid a high price for staying.

Much of the part of the Michelin in which the Regiment operated had been abandoned by the French owners for some time—*de facto* ceded to the Communists.

Unlike the typical rubber plantation, the area between the trees was not neatly groomed. Vegetation had grown up profusely, providing the enemy plenty of concealment for his always well-constructed bunkers. Four decades later, Bill Haponski still recalled: "During our attack the bunkers in the ragged undergrowth were as difficult to see in this neglected ... portion of the plantation as they were in the jungle surrounding it."

Air Cav Troop led the movement to contact on the 18th, sending in scouts and gunships, attempting to reconnect with the "bastards" from the day before. Dawn saw five scouts, two gunships, and a C&C bird in the air over the northeastern portion of the rubber trees. The aero scouts had recently added an M60 machine gun for use by the scout-observer, so they were ready for anything they found. United Press reporter Nat Gibson described what he and the aero scouts saw once contact was reestablished—just 15 minutes after reaching the plantation limits.

> A column of armor five miles long, moved toward the plantation ... The helicopters had no trouble finding the Communist soldiers. Heavy and light machine gun fire greeted them in several areas, and Communist troops could be seen dashing through the 25 square mile plantation. The pilots spotted piles of camouflaged equipment and bicycles and called in air strikes to pound the area with bombs ... Everywhere we flew we were either drawing machine gun fire or could see the NVA (North Vietnamese Army) running through the trees to bunkers ...

Colonel Patton predicted that the enemy body count would be high—not surprising in an area cluttered with clearly occupied bunkers. His boss for the operation, Major General (MG) Orwin Talbott, told a reporter: "I hope the enemy makes the mistake of trying to stand and fight."

Talbott got his wish.

The Regiment had a unique—and effective—task organization for Operation *Atlas Wedge*. First Squadron (minus Alpha Troop) was reinforced with two infantry companies. Third Squadron (minus India Troop) had Hotel Company (cross-attached from 2/11) and a company of air cavalrymen under its operational control, as well as an artillery battalion in direct support. The task organization changed on almost a daily basis, providing the on-the-fly flexibility needed to adjust to the fast-changing tactical situation. At one point, for example, the 1/11 commander (Lieutenant Colonel Merritte Ireland) had six troops/companies under his control (only three of which were organic to his squadron).

Lieutenant Colonel (LTC) John McEnery (3/11 commander) realigned his forces before starting out the morning of the 18th, cross-attaching ACAVs, tanks, grunts, and engineers in order to create four combined-arms teams based on Lima Troop, Mike and Hotel Companies, and the infantry company. Each was equally capable of executing any mission assigned. This was the ideal organization for recon-in-force sweeps, especially when the enemy situation was unknown but a fight was expected.

Teams L and M made contact with the enemy almost immediately upon entering the plantation. Team H made contact next in a base camp uncovered by the aero scouts. A furious, albeit brief (30 minutes), firefight ensued. Two M48 tanks were hit by RPGs, one of which—Danny Connelly's—burned. There were no friendly fatalities.

Team M had the most successful contact of the afternoon, however. Sustaining only one friendly casualty and no vehicular losses, they aggressively entered and cleared an NVA base camp. In addition to the bodies of 34 enemy soldiers and 5 prisoners, the tank-infantry team found numerous individual and crew-served weapons, ammunition, bicycles, and documents. The prisoners and documents identified the enemy as elements of the 209th Regiment, 7th (NVA) Division. The intelligence reports were right—the division was inside the Michelin in force. Third Squadron was "up to its armpits in enemy troops." It wasn't anything they couldn't handle.

Sweeping the contact areas, the troopers found signs of the carnage they had wrought, with additional bodies (some whole, some not), blood trails, drag marks, and equipment scattered haphazardly about—indications of both the sad state of leadership in the NVA division and the chaos of the firefights. One of the captured NVA soldiers was a first sergeant who provided unit identifications (209th Regiment), locations (northwestern Michelin), and missions (prepare to attack Saigon), all of which contributed to drawing up the operations plans for the 19th and succeeding days thereafter.

Over in 1/11's area, Bravo and Charlie Troops and Delta Company made contact with the enemy as soon as they entered the Michelin (about 1600 hours). The three units formed an armored wedge and pushed northwards into the undergrowth between the rubber trees as small arms and RPGs whizzed past. With Delta Company's tanks in the lead, Bravo Troop took the left side of the wedge and Charlie Troop the right. Cross-attached infantrymen rode on the outside of the vehicles. As they advanced on the dug-in enemy, the tanks, Sheridans, and ACAVs came on line to assault the NVA positions. The grunts dismounted and cleared the fortifications. Contact was broken at darkness.

Sergeant (SGT) George Red Elk was commanding one of the Delta Company tanks. He and a buddy had picked armor when they signed up, thinking "there's no tanks in Vietnam. Boy, were we wrong." In quick succession, Red Elk's M48 was hit by three RPGs—disabling the .50-cal. and wounding him in the right hand. Despite his painful wound, he traversed the turret and wiped out two RPG teams. Eventually, Red Elk blacked out. "I fought for about 45 minutes before I passed out from loss of blood and the pain ... I really don't remember it. My unit leader told me how I was shooting when it happened. I guess the Good Lord didn't want me to remember it."[15]

And so the action went for the next week—up close and personal. You could actually see the bad guys you were shooting at (and who were shooting at you). The situation was fluid and constantly changing. The nexus of attention moved to the northeastern part of the Michelin, as the 7th (NVA) finally recognized that their "safe" area was anything but. Unusually, instead of trying to flee, they hunkered down to fight it out—probably to cover the escape of the rest of the division. Documents found in base camps, prisoner interrogations, and radio intercepts identified new targets. B-52 Arc Light strikes—a total of 22 during *Atlas Wedge*—hit those targets overnight, and Thunderhorse pink teams (one LOH and one Cobra) followed up at first light. The Aero Rifle Platoon (ARPs) was inserted when there were more than just dead bodies lying around. Contact brought the inevitable pile-on forces of one or both squadrons, artillery, gunships, and tactical air (TacAir)—and another B-52 strike.

The fighting was intense, as the NVA regulars defended tenaciously. On the 20th, they were giving as well as they were getting—until John McEnery stepped in.

The ARPs had been inserted into a B-52 strike area and found a still-occupied base camp. Team Alpha (A-2/5th Cavalry, cross-attached with 3/11 ACAVs and tanks) piled on. The momentum of their attack began to falter, however, as vehicles were knocked out and communications broke down. LTC McEnery recognized that this was a critical juncture in the battle and landed his helicopter to take personal command. He mounted a still operational Mike Company tank, standing on the

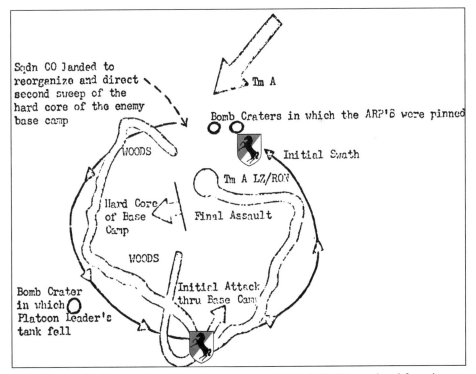

Map of Aero Rifle Platoon and 3rd Squadron contact on 20 March 1969 (reproduced from the regimental after-action report). (basic map, US Army)

back deck where everyone—including the enemy—could see him. Although exposed to intense fire, it was the only spot from which he could use hand and arm signals to form the ACAVs and infantry on line on either side of his "command" tank.

On his signal, Team A made one final charge through the heart of the enemy base camp. Although wounded by fragments from an enemy grenade, McEnery stayed in his exposed position directing the fight. When the last enemy resistance had been squashed, he insisted that all other casualties be treated and evacuated before he was flown out of the Michelin. Two Blackhorse troopers and one Alpha Company air cavalryman were killed in this fight and another 21 wounded, but 74 enemy soldiers paid with their lives during the all-day battle. No enemy soldiers were seen fleeing from the woods at the end of the fight.[16]

Most importantly, the 7th (NVA) Division was blocked from accomplishing its assigned mission of attacking Saigon.

The organization, equipment, flexibility, leadership, and gallantry of the 11th Cavalry made the operation in the Michelin an outstanding success. The harmonization of air-ground cooperation, pile-on tactics, and combined-arms teams provided an unparalleled flexible response to the constantly evolving situation. The operation was initiated a day early due to contact and changed from one squadron to two—and the Regiment was ready to go despite the last-minute change in plans and organization. There were substantial reorganizations "on-the-fly" as the situation required; command and control during pile-on operations was done mostly on the radio with fragmentary orders.

The reputation of the Regiment was a determining factor in gaining permission for artillery and air strikes—as well as extensive ground operations—inside the plantation for the first time. If Blackhorse scouts reported it, and Blackhorse 6 confirmed it, it was to be believed.

The 7th (NVA) stayed, fought, and died in large numbers, and when they left the Michelin for good, they left behind piles of weapons, bodies, ammo, food, supplies, and documents. When they finally did leave, it wasn't in the direction of Saigon, their campaign objective.

Three GI divisions—a total of ten battalions—were part of Operation *Atlas Wedge*. And yet, the pertinent reports hardly mention them at all. They couldn't seem to find the enemy, and when they did, he got away. They left the door open for the bulk of the 7th (NVA) Division to escape. The 11th Cavalry, on the other hand, found and soundly defeated the 1,350-man strong 209th Regiment. As the regimental intelligence officer (CPT John Kuntzman) noted in his after-action report:

> The significance of the operation was discovered through subsequent interrogation of PW's [prisoners]. The operation fixed the locations of the 141st and 209th NVA Regiments and the forward headquarters of the 7th NVA Division. The 209th was rendered combat ineffective, and the 141st Regiment was forced to relocate north of the Michelin. The threat to Allied installations along the Saigon River Corridor was diminished, and the southward movement of the 7th NVA Division toward the CMD [Capital Military District] was halted.

For the Blackhorse Regiment, this was proof enough of the effectiveness of how they found the "bastards" and piled on.

George Patton's assessment was, typically, succinct and to the point: "The first and third squadrons supported by our Air Cav Troop conducted themselves in a magnificent and soldierly manner; they found them and killed them."

Bustin' Jungle and Heads: April to June 1969

The 11th Cavalry had been working with the Big Red One almost continuously since June 1968, splitting its time between the southern half of War Zone D (the Catcher's Mitt and Lam Son) and the area between Bien Hoa and Blackhorse Base Camp. For the most part, these operations (when not engaged in direct combat with enemy units) were focused on pacification and destroying the Viet Cong Infrastructure. In mid-April, the Regiment was placed under the operational control (OPCON) of the 1st Cavalry Division, and its mission changed to interdiction of enemy infiltration and resupply operations near the border.

The missions assigned to the Blackhorse in the execution of the clear and hold strategy took advantage of the Regiment's strongest capabilities—mobility, firepower, and agility. Blackhorse troopers took the fight to the enemy, even (or especially) when the enemy was in his base areas resupplying, recouping losses, and retraining. The troopers executed their new mission aggressively; in the month of May 1969 alone they interdicted and captured 11 tons of rice and over 900 individual and crew-served weapons.

By mid-1969, the area around Saigon was considered sufficiently pacified to move the focus of operations closer to the periphery of the Corps zone. Even the enemy recognized that the battle for Saigon was lost, saying that a "number of units remained in the area on the outskirts of the capital, but they had to disperse into small elements that were constantly on the defensive and that suffered casualties and attrition from enemy air, artillery, and commando attacks."

The 1st Infantry Division—which had been protecting the close-in northern approaches to Saigon since 1965—was designated for redeployment to Fort Riley, KS, turning responsibilities over to the 5th (ARVN) Infantry Division. In his last assessment, the division commander wrote: "Within the 1st Infantry Division's area of operations, the last six months of 1969 were characterized by a sharp decrease in enemy-initiated activity." The division had, in effect "work[ed] itself out of a job."

This new situation didn't "just happen." It happened because 11th Cavalry troopers and Big Red One grunts went into the base areas and dug the enemy out. The fighting was fierce. The cost was high. Between March and July, 103 Blackhorse troopers were killed in action; in the first month alone, 45 died and another 240 were wounded. Eleven troopers were awarded the Distinguished Service Cross—three posthumously. Dozens of ACAVs, Sheridans, and tanks were sent to the scrap heap as combat losses.

Then came the new mission. With a new Blackhorse 6 in the saddle (Colonel Jimmie Leach, who had taken command of the Regiment in April), the Regiment, OPCON to the 1st Cavalry Division, pursued the decimated 7th (NVA) Division, as well as the newly-arrived 1st (NVA) Division, into their base areas in the thick jungles of War Zone C north of Dau Tieng all the way to An Loc. This was an area that had long served as a major staging area for enemy units moving to attack Saigon. Although dismounted infantrymen routinely conducted sweeps in the area, the sounds of tanks and ACAVs had been only infrequently heard.[17]

The Communist leadership liked it that way, and they told their subordinate commanders (seven regiments total) to defend the turf tenaciously. But after several intense fights, their determination—and ability to continue to defend against all those pile-on forces—waned. By the end of the summer, both of these enemy divisions scampered back across the border into the Kingdom of Cambodia.

The commander of the 1st Cav, Major General (MG) George Forsythe, got it. He knew what he had in the 11th Cavalry, and he used it accordingly. He wrote in his assessment for the period that the Regiment "granted the Division additional fire-power, mobility, and reaction capability." Troopers didn't just escort supply convoys or guard fire bases. They were the pointy-end of the spear thrust into the heart of the enemy's long-standing base areas. The Regiment was routinely reinforced with an airmobile infantry battalion—a virtual necessity in the dense vegetation common throughout the area.

Operation Montana Raider

Operation *Montana Raider* was the first of the sustained assaults against the NVA in War Zone C. It lasted for a full month (12 April–14 May) and involved two brigades of the 1st Cav in addition to two Blackhorse squadrons. *Montana Raider* was broken into three phases. The first phase was into an area west of the Michelin. Heavy contact was made on the very first day.

The area into which 1/11 and 2/11 deployed ranged from thick stands of bamboo to multi-canopied jungle. In most cases, tanks and aero scouts led the way. There were no roads and almost no trails, and there were no discernible landmarks visible from the floor of the jungle. Map reading was almost impossible. Pilots were called upon numerous times to help guide the ACAVs and tanks through the jungle because it was so dense. Red Devil engineers and armored vehicle launched bridges (AVLBs) were always close at hand, as the area was cut by numerous streams—many still dry, but wide enough to require a bridge. In the words of the Blackhorse operations officer (Major Jim Dozier), the AVLBs "proved to be absolutely essential … [They] facilitated cross-reinforcement and allowed freedom of movement in that pile-on tactics were employed."

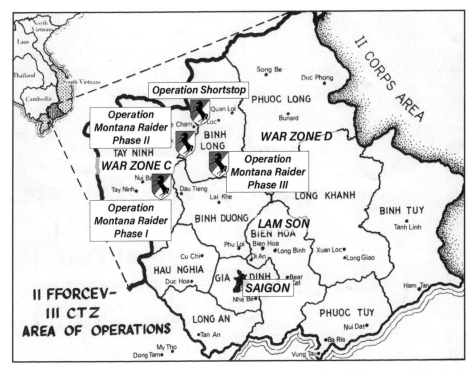

Map of 11th Armored Cavalry Regiment Operations *Montana Raider* and *Shortstop* in 1969. (basic map, US Army)

Phase I was, in the words of Blackhorse 6, "a helluva fight for us." Jimmie Leach had been in command just six days when the operation kicked off.[18] Even four decades later, the images remained imprinted on his mind:

> That Phase I though, that was a frightening experience because we ran right in the middle of a heavily, heavily defended area. We hit these guys with B-52s ... and then we went in between the craters ... Here's the B-52 attack, and we saw all these goddamn bombs dropping. And then the ARPs [Aero Rifle Platoon] went in ... These guys [NVA], a lot of them were groggy initially, but by God they were still alive and kicking. There were enough alive to give us trouble ... They were still fighting from the craters ... A lot of RPGs ... We were hurting.

Operation *Montana Raider*, named in honor of MG Forsythe who hailed from Big Sky country, was designed to conduct recon-in-force operations in three enemy sanctuaries that had not recently seen any action. The concept of the Phase I operation was to use massed B-52 strikes on suspected base camps, followed immediately by squadron-sized exploitation. The objective was twofold—kick the NVA forces out of the area and capture all of the supplies that were being stockpiled for the upcoming summer campaign.

Arc Light strikes played an enormous operational and tactical role in the operation. B-52s not only initiated contacts, they also broke them. As Captain (CPT) John Caldwell says: "The only way we could break contact was with a B-52 strike … There was bad stuff going on out there … [We] were in the middle of the North Vietnamese Army."

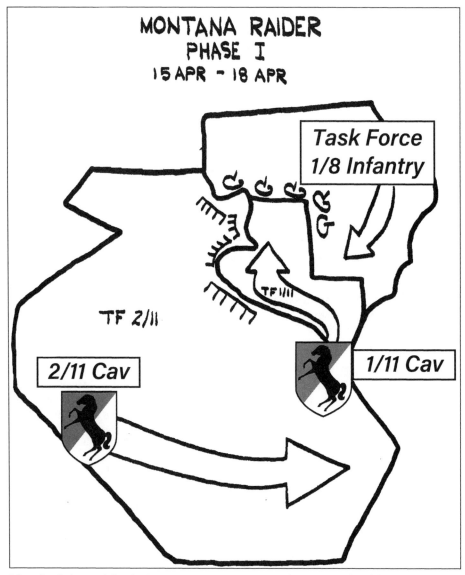

Map of 11th Armored Cavalry Regiment operations on 18 April 1969 (reproduced from the regimental after-action report). (basic map, US Army)

Fate determined that 1/11 troopers would be the ones to find the "bastards" most frequently during *Montana Raider* (2/11 troopers would have their "turn" in August, while 3/11 troopers were in the spotlight in November and December). First Squadron had contact each of the first six days of the operation. The last was on the 18th.

The squadron was never supposed to be in the area of the base camp that was discovered on 18 April. However, intelligence gathered on 16 April indicated that the enemy had relocated into the southwestern part of the area of operations (AO), known as AO Knife. An airmobile infantry company was airlifted into the area, and Blackhorse 6 told his new 1st Squadron commander (MAJ "Doc" Bahnsen) that he was expanding the 1/11 area to reinforce that company as they searched for elements of the 1st (NVA) Division. Another infantry battalion established five company-sized blocking positions, and the plan was for 1/11 to drive northward towards those positions. Charlie Troop was the first to make contact with the enemy. The entrenched NVA threw tear gas their way, so the troopers donned gas masks and pressed on.

Prisoners captured in this fight and another the next day were from the 18B Regiment, 1st (NVA) Division and the 82nd Rear Service Group. They included an Aspirant 2nd Lieutenant, who was the political officer for the C22 Transportation Company, and five NVA soldiers. Because of their work carrying rice and other supplies to combat units, they knew the locations of all three battalions and the headquarters of the 18B Regiment. They also revealed the location of several rice caches; more importantly, perhaps, they said that their unit had been out of rice for at least a month. This proved that the intelligence estimate was sound, and the troopers expected a tough go the following day if the rest of the 18B Regiment decided to stand and fight.

They did.

By 0930 hours on 18 April, both Teams Alpha and Bravo, each cross-attached with a tank platoon from Delta Company, were in heavy contact after a Squadron Aviation Section scout helicopter had been forced to land in enemy territory. Doc Bahnsen was in the air in an OH-6A light observation helicopter (LOH), urging his new command forward. Burning thickets of bamboo, ignited by artillery rounds and tracers, forced the troopers to alter direction several times throughout the day-long contact, but they finally succeeded in overcoming enemy resistance.

John Tillson, the Alpha Troop commander, recalls:

> This was a pretty typical day in RVN [Republic of Vietnam]. We went into a base camp and laid waste to the enemy. We did it the right way with the jungle box.[19] As darkness approached we pulled out of the base camp and established a NDP [night defensive position] some distance from the location ... I also had an infantry platoon from the 1st Cav attached to the troop. A staff sergeant led this platoon. I remember being impressed by the individual but unimpressed by a system that would place a junior NCO is such a position of responsibility so far from his parent unit.

There was another staff sergeant who distinguished himself on 18 April—Francisco Rodriguez. He was the acting platoon sergeant of the Delta Company tanks leading the attack. The jungle was so thick that the three tanks often had to back up and hit the jungle foliage twice or three times just to get through. The follow-on ACAVs and Sheridans had to back off so as to not get run over when an M48 suddenly went into reverse. Being up front, Rodriguez and his platoon were the first to receive fire from the well dug-in, almost invisible enemy. Post-contact analysis indicated that the NVA soldiers the troopers were facing were probably defending the headquarters of the 18B (NVA) Regiment.

NVA soldiers were everywhere, in front of and behind the tanks. There were even enemy soldiers popping up from spider holes between the tanks.

Despite "enemy bullets ricocheting off the side of the M48s, and several RPGs whizzing by close over his head," Rodriguez had the presence of mind to have his crew alternate the type of main gun ammo—high explosive to destroy bunkers and canister to kill soldiers. Using the radio, he directed the other two tanks to do the same. All the while, he kept up a steady beat of .50-cal. to keep the defenders' heads down. After briefly pulling back to regroup and link up with the ACAVs, Rodriguez again led the charge back into the base camp. An RPG team popped up on his flank and fired a rocket that missed his head by just inches (according to eyewitnesses); he traversed his cupola and dispatched two of the three rocketeers with his .50-cal. A main gun round then destroyed the bunker from which the team had emerged.

The action briefly calmed down somewhat (firing still continued), allowing Rodriguez to get a tow bar onto one of his platoon's tanks that was completely immobile. Just as he was starting to tow the tank out of the base camp, the NVA initiated a battalion-sized counterattack. At times fighting alone, Rodriguez and his crew beat off the assault with .50-cal., coax machine gun, and main gun fire.[20] He sustained a painful, bloody head wound about this time, but fought on.

Specialist 5 (SP5) Bob "Killer" Miner was near Rodriguez throughout the fight on the 18th. He says that "only SSG Rodriguez' extreme coolness under fire and continuous control of his elements insured an ultimate victory of the armored assault."

Francisco Rodriguez was not the only hero on the battlefield on 18 April. Alpha Troop's SP4 Ron Pongratz—who had already distinguished himself five days earlier—stood out amidst the carnage.[21] A wound from the fight on 13 April could have taken Ron out of the field; he chose to stay. He'd been in country with the Blackhorse for 20 months already. He understood that his experience and example were important. His platoon leader (LT Gary Calloway) said that his "ingenuity, diligence, and perseverance were almost unbelievable."

Pongratz' ACAV was on the right flank as Alpha Troop swept through the first line of enemy bunkers. His accurate .50-cal. machine gun fire took out an enemy machine gun that was causing no end of problems. His section leader, SSG Lane

Lauckhart, cautioned him that he might burn up his machine gun. Pongratz replied: "I know it, but there's dinks all over the place out here, and if I don't keep them pinned down, we're going to have more people hurt."

When they finally broke into the enemy base camp about three hours after the first exchange of fire, Pongratz dismounted and led a team clearing the bunkers. NVA soldiers in an unseen bunker further to the right opened up. Unhesitatingly—as he had done on the 13th—Pongratz assaulted the bunker. He fired his rifle until he was close enough to toss a grenade. There was no more return fire. Pongratz turned his attention to some wounded fellow troopers when fire came from yet another hidden bunker. This time, his luck ran out. Ron Pongratz was able to destroy the new threat with a grenade, but was shot in the head and later died from the wound.

Lane Lauckhart had been in Alpha Troop since it arrived in country in September 1966. He served continuously for three years, mostly as an ACAV track commander (TC). He'd survived numerous ambushes, Tet '68, and the 13 April mêlée. So, when he says that Ron Pongratz "dedication to the mission, to his people, to his job, and to his equipment, was more than impressive," you have to believe he knows of which he speaks. Lauckhart goes on: "I have seen scores of courageous acts performed by dozens of men ... I have never before witnessed an individual perform the equal of this."

Nine hours after initiating the fight, the NVA gave up and ran away. Jimmie Leach was quoted in the newspapers as saying: "The action was a good lesson for Charlie. He learned he can't mess around with the Sheridans and get away with it." John Tillson was a little more circumspect: "This was a very long day!"

***

There were many more long days ahead. In May, the Regiment completed Operation *Montana Raider*, then transitioned smoothly into Operations *Toan Thang*, *Shortstop*, and *Kentucky Cougar*. The three squadrons were almost constantly on the move, ranging from Tay Ninh to the Fishhook, back to the Catcher's Mitt, and up to An Loc. Blackhorse troopers had a series of running battles with NVA units attempting to infiltrate south from their Cambodian sanctuaries. These battles lasted a couple of days each, with the enemy disengaging and attempting to evade, only to be found again by Thunderhorse aero scouts. Skirmishes turned into major firefights with elements of the NVA's 1st and 7th Divisions. In addition to inflicting heavy personnel casualties, troopers uncovered three hospitals, a post office, and numerous over-stuffed caches. The enemy was deprived of tons of rice, hundreds of weapons, and thousands of rounds of ammo—all of which had been painstakingly pre-stocked for the summer campaign.

NVA units that were in desperate need of "down time" to recover from the Tet '69 offensive and to prepare for the summer campaign were hunted down in their base camps, attacked, and forced to melt even deeper into the jungle where food, medicine, and new recruits were difficult to obtain. The vast quantities of weapons and ammunition uncovered during these operations dramatically reduced the effectiveness of the enemy's combat operations.

Although Saigon was the enemy's stated goal of the summer campaign, the sweeps by the 11th Cavalry, 1st and 25th Infantry Divisions, 1st Cavalry Division, and ARVN 5th and 25th Divisions, combined with massive B-52 raids (based on targets uncovered during those sweeps), forced the enemy to retreat back across the border into Cambodia. Some small elements stayed inside South Vietnam (only three of nine enemy regiments), but they went to ground deep in the jungles of northern War Zones C and D, emerging only for hit-and-run attacks.

The sustained offensives that the Communists had originally planned for the period between June and November turned into a series of decreasingly effective "high points," each lasting just hours or a few days instead of the scheduled several weeks. According to captured documents, the so-called "Summer Offensive" was to last from mid-May to the end of July. In fact, there was a flurry of activity on the night of 11–12 May and again on 5–6 and 12–13 June. For the remaining 78 days of the "offensive," there was barely a stir.

After the war, the North Vietnamese explained the enforced slowdown in combat operations:

> Because of our difficulties in obtaining supplies and replacements and because the enemy [U.S./RVN] was conducting ferocious counterattacks against us, after the summer campaign of 1969 a major portion of our main force army was forced to withdraw to our base areas [in Cambodia] to regroup. In the rural areas the strength of our local armed forces was seriously eroded. The enemy exploited his advantage during the rainy [summer] season by moving into our areas, carrying out rapid pacification operations in the rural lowlands and attacking our base areas in the mountains and our supply corridors, creating further difficulties for our forces … The COSVN [enemy headquarters for operations in South Vietnam] base area was insecure and our supply routes from the lowlands were blocked.

In June, the Communists once again sought to regain the initiative by mounting an offensive against targets close to their Cambodian sanctuaries. But the combination of good intelligence and the mobility and firepower of the 11th Cavalry and the 1st Infantry Division thwarted that attempt before it even got off the ground. Elements of three enemy regiments were intercepted and thrashed as they approached An Loc. The attack fizzled and the NVA retreated across the Cambodian border.

The combined effects of the "clear and hold" strategy, unleashing the full potential of the 11th ACR, and the gallantry of the Blackhorse troopers had a telling effect on the enemy. Hanoi continued to boast of "glorious victories" on the battlefields of South Vietnam, but unit commanders were telling a different story. Such as the D440 (VC) Battalion.

> At that time, the … battlefield was especially tense and violent. Our base area regions became constrained and were constantly attacked by the enemy. Our communications were broken; and the passage of liaison information between villages, the Districts and Province was completely interrupted. Our reserves were nearly exhausted, and food was very scarce (rice was put aside,

and there were times when it was only counted out by small ... containers [about eight ounces], and reserved to cook gruel for the wounded).[22] The principal means of life for our cadre were those fruits and jungle vegetables that they were able to find—but these gradually became even scarcer as we entered the Dry Season [September] ... There were times when our wounded could not be moved, patients could not be treated or saved in time, and many comrades died due to a lack of medicines and even hunger.

For Hanoi, the future looked grim indeed. Ideology was being served instead of rice, Uncle Ho's exhortations in place of *nuoc mam*. Something had to be done. They decided to take a desperate risk, to throw the dice in a futile attempt to win at least a psychological victory. An Loc, defended by the 11th Cavalry, was the chosen target and mid-August the chosen timeframe.

But first, there was one more "high point" to play out.

Most Baby Boomers remember precisely where they were and what they were doing when they heard that President Kennedy was assassinated. For the members of 3rd Platoon, Charlie Troop, listening to the landing on the moon over 360,000 kilometers away while sweating buckets in that jungle clearing, is indelibly etched into their memories. Paul Baerman remembers well.

> Everyone stopped what he was doing and strained to hear the [Armed Forces Vietnam radio] station. One of our soldiers had a thermometer on his vehicle. The temperature was 116 degrees Fahrenheit and the sun was beating down. It was shortly after noon on July 20th, 1969 (just after midnight on the US East Coast) as we heard the announcer from Mission Control in Houston, Texas describe the actions of astronaut Neil Armstrong. When we heard Neil's words, "One small step for man, one giant step for mankind," we all cheered.

Memorable indeed, but not for the same reasons for everyone. Trooper David Connolly (Fox Troop), who joined the Vietnam veterans against the war movement after returning to Boston and used poetry while in Vietnam as a way "to stay sane, to try to make some sense out of what was going on around me," captured his memory of 20 July in a poem.

> Piercing the night, from the right
> the RTO whispered, "Brothers,
> an American is walking on the moon!"
>
> We all looked up, then forward,
> into some poor papasan's
> thousand year old rice paddy,
> pulverized by the planes
> into round puddles of puppy shit.
>
> Some dead serious, totally sane,
> nineteen year old boonie-rat said,
> "I don't see him out there."

If some pictures are worth a thousand words, then Bryant Nelson's picture of a 1st Squadron trooper standing in monsoon mud on the afternoon of 20 July 1969 says a dictionary's worth. While Neil Armstrong was leaving an extraordinary footprint on human history, Blackhorse troopers continued to put one foot in front of the other as they slogged through their year in hell.

Over twenty thousand kilometers away in Ferdinand, Indiana, Louann Nord (widow of India Troop's Staff Sergeant David Nord)—50 days a bride, 28 days a widow, and six months pregnant with her now fatherless son—watched and thought: "How can a country so great send men to the moon, yet my husband's dead, killed in a war?"

The Battle of Northern Binh Long Province: August to September 1969

In mid-1966, the newly established II Field Force Vietnam (IIFFV) headquarters conducted a war game of the defense of Loc Ninh. Even at that early date, military planners recognized both the significance (political) and vulnerability (military) of this district capital. Several of the vulnerabilities—especially the defensibility of the Special Forces/Civilian Irregular Defense Group camp and ARVN compound—were identified, and, in the wake of the major enemy campaign against Loc Ninh in late 1967, had been addressed. However, the wargamers identified one geographical and one topographical fact that could not be ameliorated: "The proximity of the Cambodian Border to Loc Ninh and the intervening good terrain for rapid, concealed movement presents special problems in the defense of Loc Ninh ... Forces moving by ground to reinforce or relieve Loc Ninh must traverse areas that provide excellent ambush sites." These prophetic words still applied three years later.

In late July, the 11th Cavalry was still in the midst of Operation *Kentucky Cougar*, which had been going on since the 23rd of June. Frustrating day followed frustrating day—conduct a recon, hit a mine, receive the random sniper round, shoot back, results unknown. But things changed perceptibly at the beginning of August. Prisoner interrogations, document analysis, and sniffer missions all pointed to something big on the horizon.

Kentucky Cougar was part of the outer "defensive belt" that protected both pacification and Vietnamization programs closer to Saigon. Calling it a defensive belt, however, was a bit of a misnomer. Offensive reconnaissance was the order of the day; "find the bastards, then pile on" still applied. The 1st Air Cav, with the Blackhorse (partnered with the 9th (ARVN) Infantry Regiment) under its operational control, was tasked with protecting an area along the Cambodian border that stretched in an arc from 100 kilometers northwest to 130 kilometers northeast of Saigon.

The first "defensive belt" along the border encompassed a tremendous amount of territory—about 150 kilometers of primary infiltration routes. A lot of ground for two airmobile infantry brigades and one armored cavalry regiment to cover.

As the intelligence picture emerged and revealed the enemy's intentions, however, Blackhorse troopers were able to focus specifically on An Loc and Loc Ninh.

Build-up

The battle of Northern Binh Long Province, as the actions around Loc Ninh and An Loc in the late summer of 1969 came to be known, began with a windfall of information. Over the course of six days, three NVA soldiers surrendered to the South Vietnamese cause. The story they told was of an elaborate plan by elements of four enemy divisions to strike Loc Ninh, An Loc, Highway 13, and the US and South Vietnamese military base camps near the Cambodian border in the first half of August. The plan was to seize and hold An Loc for one day, seriously embarrassing the Saigon government at the negotiating table, and inflicting as many battlefield casualties as possible.

The battle can be divided into three distinct phases. From late July until 6 August, there was a slow but steady build-up of enemy activity in the area. Starting on the 6th and lasting until the 11th, there was a flurry of enemy activity involving the movement of units from their secure base areas in or near Cambodia to forward positions throughout Binh Long Province (a build-up that was matched by US and ARVN forces). Finally, from the night of 11–12 August until the 16th, Blackhorse troopers, along with 1st Cav and 1st Infantry grunts, corps artillery redlegs, ARVN infantrymen and cavalrymen, and aviators wearing green and blue flight suits, waged pitched battles against elements of all four of the enemy's available divisions.

The terrain in the area north and west of An Loc is quite favorable for an attacking force. It offers both cover and concealment; thick jungles abut expansive rubber plantations. NVA units found the jungles ideal for their forward base camps, while the rubber plantations offered concealed high-speed avenues of approach to the towns and military installations on both sides of Highway 13. Most importantly, high-value targets were, in many places, just a couple hours' march from the Cambodian border. Long-established and well-stocked base areas inside Cambodia served as both jumping-off points and politically "inviolable" sanctuaries to run to after an attack.

The 11th Cavalry and 1st Cav were, despite the terrain disadvantages, able to watch the enemy forces as they made their way from their base camps. A series of contacts with air and ground scouts tracked the progress of the enemy battalions as they approached their objectives around Loc Ninh, An Loc, and Quan Loi. Technical assets—including side-looking airborne radar (SLAR), Red Haze (sensors that detected human urine), and radio intercepts—identified potential targets for attacks by flights of B-52s or individual helicopter gunships.

Warned in advance, the Blackhorse was ready for the Summer-Autumn Campaign. In addition to two of its organic squadrons, Air Cav Troop, and the 919th Engineers, the Regiment had operational control over two US infantry battalions and was responsible for coordinating the operations of five South Vietnamese infantry and cavalry battalions.[23] Three battalions' worth of various-caliber artillery supported the defense. Nine maneuver battalion-sized units under Colonel Leach's command and control, as many as a two-star general anywhere else in Vietnam—and more than the 1st (NVA), 5th (VC), 7th (NVA), and 9th (VC) Divisions had bargained for!

A major intelligence coup came with the defection of Lieutenant Nguyen Van An, a platoon leader in the H21 Sapper Reconnaissance Company, 272nd (VC) Regiment on 29 July. He was ultimately interrogated by Lieutenant (LT) Tom Kelly from the Blackhorse's 541st Military Intelligence Detachment.

He told Kelly that the 7th (NVA) and 9th (VC) Division had moved into the Fishhook area of the Cambodian border starting in late June. They took on supplies of ammo, food, and medicine, while training replacements from the north. In mid-July, these divisions began to search out potential targets around An Loc and Loc Ninh; in fact, the VC lieutenant said, he had been with his battalion commander on a recon of assembly areas, staging areas, and avenues of approach west of An Loc when he surrendered. He related that two regiments of the 9th Division, along with the local D368 (VC) Battalion, were planning to attack An Loc between 5 and 15 August.

An Loc was the Communists' main military and political objective. Elements of the 7th (NVA) Division would strike Quan Loi, Loc Ninh, and Bo Duc with secondary attacks at the same time. The NVA lieutenant had even heard that the 5th (VC) and 1st (NVA) Divisions were scheduled to "take care of" Tay Ninh Province and ambush convoys on Highway 13, thus isolating the An Loc area from reinforcement.

In light of these revelations, previously sketchy and confusing intelligence reports began to make sense. Nguyen Van An's story meshed with information from a series of small contacts west of An Loc and Loc Ninh in late July. Documents found after these firefights indicated the presence of soldiers from the 1st (NVA) and 9th (VC) Divisions, both of which were then thought to still be in their Cambodian sanctuaries further to the north and west.

Hard on the heels of this sensational story came yet another. Nguyen Van Sen, a member of the propaganda section of a local VC cell, surrendered on 2 August. He had been an ARVN soldier until he was abducted by an enemy squad in July 1968. When he saw his chance, he escaped and turned himself in to the 399th Regional Force (RF) Company. He said that his unit had been visited by advance teams from the 9th (VC) Division in mid-July and the D368 (VC) Battalion on 1 August. Each of these units asked for directions to Soc Tranh (about 12 kilometers southeast of An Loc). This, too, clicked with what LT Kelly had been told.

The intelligence picture became even clearer the next day, when Nguyen Van Thien defected to another militia platoon southwest of Loc Ninh. He was an assistant platoon leader of the C21 Sapper Recon Company, 209th (NVA) Regiment. He said that he had been wounded on 27 July in a contact with Fox Troop, 2/11; although he had managed to avoid capture at the time, his wound had gotten worse and he decided to give up. He stated that two battalions of the 209th were planning an attack against a small village on or about 7 August and then to ambush the reaction forces as they moved along Highway 13 from An Loc or Quan Loi. Other units from the 7th (NVA) Division were arrayed from north of Loc Ninh to Bu Dop preparing for the upcoming offensive.

Pieces of the intelligence jigsaw fell into place. Prisoners whose claims of belonging to advanced elements of the 7th (NVA) and 9th (VC) Divisions, initially dismissed, now made sense. Electronic sensor readings showing major movement south and east out of Cambodia fit the pattern of troop movements, now that the operators understood what they were seeing. Agent reports of well-armed bands of NVA west of An Loc, originally rated as unlikely, were upgraded to likely. Armed with this "inside" information, the regimental intelligence officer, Major (MAJ) Bob Foley, redirected his collection effort, while the operations officer, Lieutenant Colonel (LTC) Jim Reed, focused aerial and ground operations to the approaches from the north and west. Aero scouts now understood that they wouldn't be looking at empty jungle; the bad guys were down there, waiting to be found.

When Blackhorse 6 reported this new situation up the chain, he found that none of the higher echelons' formidable intelligence-collection resources had picked up signs of another "high point." MACV's periodic intelligence report for July noted some movement of enemy forces along the northern tier of the Corps area, but dismissed it as inconsequential. The report concluded: "The autumn campaign probably will be similar to his summer effort; that is, a generally low level of activity, occasionally punctuated by a surge or "high point" which will be primarily indirect fire attacks and limited-objective ground assaults."

Could it be that elements of four enemy divisions had moved out of their base areas to converge on the Loc Ninh-An Loc area without it being recognized for what it was? Could their mission be something other than a limited-objective attack?

The short answer to both questions was yes.

Fortunately, General Abrams had been Jimmie Leach's battalion commander in WWII, and Abe Abrams had implicit trust in his old company commander. They talked on the sidelines of the big awards ceremony at Quan Loi the morning of 7 August. They then went together to the 3rd Brigade, 1st Cav for a tactical briefing. The scene of the briefing is described in J.D. Coleman's book, *Incursion*.

> His briefing by the Cav's G-2 [intelligence] and G-3 [operations], usually a pro forma affair, was anything but routine this time. The briefers told Abrams about An the *Hoi Chanh* [defector] and the evidence they had gathered to substantiate his story. Abrams chomped down on his cigar as the briefing unfolded. "It was obvious," [Brigadier General] Shoemaker recalled, "that General Abrams hadn't had a clue about this from his MACV intelligence staff" ... Although the evidence was not overwhelming, Abrams, years removed from the turret of a tank, retained the tanker's basic philosophy of "let's get the show on the road." He had not gotten where he was waiting for technicians to present him with a picture-perfect analysis. It was the strong

endorsement by Colonel Leach that probably sold Abrams ... When the briefing concluded and the staff and commanders waited for Abrams's verdict, he unwrapped another cigar, fired it up, and told them that the Cav needed to get serious about the threat ...

Thirty years later, Jimmie Leach remembered what happened when Abrams returned to Saigon.

IIFF [and III (ARVN) Corps] responded immediately by sending reinforcements into the Blackhorse AO. The 36th ARVN Rangers joined Major "Doc" Bahnsen's 1/11 Cav under "Task Force Wright" (Lt. Col. Larry Wright—the Regimental Executive Officer). The ARVN 9th Infantry Regiment and 5th ARVN Division Cav. Squadron were placed south of An Loc, and the 1/16 Mech Infantry of the 1st US Division was placed north of An Loc. The 1st Division also added a troop of the 1/4 Cavalry and a battery of artillery to this force. All totaled, there were about 8,000 U.S. and South Vietnamese troops deployed in and around the Loc Ninh-An Loc-Quan Loi triangle.

The 1st Cav's Assistant Division Commander, BG Robert Shoemaker, called the exploitation of the information from defector Nguyen An "the best intelligence analysis that I ever knew over there ... [Be]cause of great intelligence work by the 11th ACR we were ready for them."

If there were any doubts left about the veracity of the rather detailed picture the "Three Nguyens" had painted, numerous contacts with enemy forces between 6 and 11 August dispelled them. Enemy forces were on the move throughout the area, and the reinforced Blackhorse found them.

The increasing number of contacts with enemy forces, coupled with the detailed revelations by the three defectors, led to an increase in B-52 Arc Light missions west of An Loc—two each on the 4th, 5th, and 6th, four on the 7th, seven each on the 8th and 9th, and another four on the 10th. Other strikes hit in the Fishhook area inside Cambodia. In just the last three days of this aerial onslaught, the B-52s dropped over 1,000 tons of bombs on suspected assembly areas and base camps. One of the strikes struck especially lucrative pay dirt.

The target area was around the Ton Le Trou stream (a source of water for an NVA base camp), 15 kilometers west of An Loc and close to the Cambodian border—right where Nguyen Van An said they would be. The B-52s struck around 1600 hours on the 8th, but heavy rains delayed Air Cav Troop's visual recon for another hour. CPT Ted Duck, the acting troop commander, was flying the command and control Huey at 1,500 feet, while LTs Fred Van Orden and Stephen Moushegian each flew a scout bird (LOH) at tree-top level. Above the C&C and LOHs was an AH-1G Cobra, just in case.

An hour into their aerial bomb damage assessment (BDA), they began to follow a trail in the cratered landscape. The trail led them to six NVA, armed with AK47 and Chinese SKS rifles, sitting by a tree—either dazed by the bomb strike or hoping that they wouldn't be spotted. In the words of the official after-action report: "The NVA's had every reason to hope that they could hide successfully. If one has the misfortune to be in a B-52 strike and then has the fortune to live through it, could not the Fates as easily will your escape from helicopters?"

The Fates decided to smile on the six NVA, but only for the remainder of this day. Low fuel levels and waning daylight caused the aviators to return to Quan Loi. They planned to come back the next day, sensing that there was more to be found in the area. That's when Colonel Leach "used some blue chips with Abrams to get another B-52 strike put in [the same area] …" SOP said that you didn't put bombs on the same target two days in a row, but this appeared to be a time for an exception. It was.

The Arc Light strike went into the same area in the early morning hours of 9 August (about the same time Charles Manson was telling members of his "family" to murder Sharon Tate and four others back in The World).

Due to low ceilings, Thunderhorse's BDA team wasn't able to depart Quan Loi until 0930 hours. The helicopters flew directly to where they had seen the six NVA the day before, but they were no longer there. However, dirt blown up by the bombs made it easy to see where people had gone after the strike. Numerous footprints were visible to the northwest and crossing the Ton Le Trou stream. At 1100 hours, Steve Moushegian spied six NVA (the same six?) sitting in the open by a fresh mound of dirt; his scout-observer engaged, killing one and seriously wounding another. Three minutes later, Fred Van Orden spotted five more NVA trying to hide in the bamboo. CPT Duck, hoping for prisoners radioed: "Don't shoot unless they try to run." Van Orden then reported locating eight additional NVA, with their weapons five meters away laying in the dirt. The aero scouts kept the now 14 NVA—apparently dazed and not making any attempts to escape—in sight, flying low, tight circles around them. Duck requested a pink team (one scout, one gunship) to maintain aerial coverage when he and the scouts refueled. CPT Jake Marshall, a Cobra pilot, recalls that "suddenly the entire troop was orbiting the area."

Duck envisioned sending in the Aero Rifle Platoon (ARPs) to capture the NVA and sweep the area for any additional live or dead enemy soldiers—standard Blackhorse operating procedure. If they found too many live ones, he wanted to make sure that someone could quickly come help the lightly armed ARPs. He called on the command radio net to the regimental tactical operations center (TOC) asking for a ground reaction force. He was informed that no ground forces were in the immediate vicinity, but artillery and air support were available. That was good enough for Ted Duck.

Steve Moushegian says: "It was a gutsy move on the part of the Executive Officer [Duck], because that thing could have gone south in a heartbeat."

The first problem was a 75-foot tree—that had miraculously managed to survive the two B-52 strikes—standing in the middle of the only possible landing zone (LZ) for Hueys for 3,000 meters in any direction. The Lift Platoon Huey tried every possible approach for over an hour, while the "NVAs sat and watched." Chief

Warrant Officer (CWO) Steve "Punjab" Gardipee, hanging out in the Thunderhorse operations bunker, suggested taking the minigun off a scout ship (thus reducing weight) and loading four ARPs aboard (this was well before Delta Force and the movie *Blackhawk Down*). The smaller OH-6A aircraft might be able to land where a Huey couldn't. At least, that was the theory.

Staff Sergeant (SSG) Rollie Port, Air Cav Troop's operations sergeant and former ARP platoon sergeant, dismissed the idea out of hand. When Duck heard it, Punjab recalls him saying that "he would consider this if we could find anyone stupid enough to do it." Enter 1LT Doug Rich. The ARP platoon leader asked for seven volunteers—he got all 18. Picking his best seven, they loaded on two stripped down LOHs and headed for the Ton Le Trou stream.

In the meantime, Blackhorse 6 sent a helicopter with a loudspeaker and the regimental civil affairs interpreter, Sergeant Thinh, aboard to broadcast a *Chieu Hoi* (surrender) message. "Don't be afraid, you will be treated fairly, given food and medical attention," Sergeant Thinh told the dazed NVA. They were instructed to rally to a yellow smoke grenade that was dropped near the intended LZ. At least one of the NVA was seen to move in that direction.

The two ARP-laden LOHs—with an empty third one to extract the anticipated prisoners—landed at 1150 hours. Gardipee, piloting the second OH-6A LOH, recalls: "The LZ was very small, tight. There really wasn't enough room to land safely but at this point we were committed to landing. We were a bit over gross [weight] and coming in hot!" Scout platoon leader CPT George Adams landed first, hitting a couple of tree limbs on the way in. Gardipee was close behind. "I also chopped through some trees and got my tail rotor stuck in some bushes … My aircraft was vibrating badly as I pulled out."

Team Leader SP4 John Montgomery was the pointman on the ground as they began to move through the area. He was followed by Private First Class (PFC) Bruce Stephens, LT Rich, and the five other ARPs. Almost immediately they captured an enemy soldier who didn't put up any resistance. In fact, he pointed out where two of his comrades were hiding. Montgomery remembers: "We looked into a bamboo thicket and found their company commander [a warrant officer] and one other guy playing dead." PFCs Rothie Brackins and Bruce Stephens were told to watch the prisoners.

The ARPs split into two teams and went in search of additional prisoners. Montgomery headed for a small stream where three enemy soldiers had been spotted. As the ARPs approached, the trio took off across the stream. "*Chieu Hoi, Chieu Hoi, Chieu Hoi* [give up]," the Troopers shouted. Two of the NVA faded into the jungle, while the third pointed his AK47 at the ARPs. Surprisingly, he then slung his rifle and started to swim across the monsoon-swollen stream toward them. Doug Rich waded in to pull the struggling NVA from the current.

SP4 Edward Cook spotted 15 NVA on a ridge on the other side of the stream, aiming their weapons at his LT. When Rich grabbed the drowning NVA, the 15

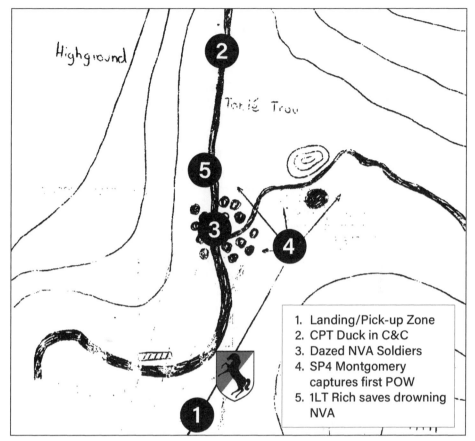

Map of Aero Rifle Platoon operation to capture six prisoners on 9 August 1969 (reproduced from the regimental after-action report). (basic map, US Army)

left the ridge and melted back into the jungle—Rich didn't realize until later that he had been in their sights!

SP4s Danny Bock and William Fergerstrom now joined the others with two prisoners of their own. Recognizing that they were greatly outnumbered and there was no immediately available reaction force, Rich led his seven fellow ARPs and six prisoners back to the three waiting LOHs. Somehow, even in their over-max weight condition, in close jungle and hot, humid air, the pilots were able to take off and fly to another LZ—three captives and one ARP aboard each OH-6A. There the ARPs and NVA prisoners were loaded aboard Lift Platoon Hueys for the trip to Quan Loi.

LT Rich told a *Stars & Stripes* reporter: "We would have been in bad shape if the enemy had known what was going on … They were so dazed by a heavy bombing attack by Air Force jets that they just milled around in a daze and couldn't organize a counterattack against us."

The assistant division commander of the 1st Cav was there to greet the returning ARPs and scouts when they landed at Quan Loi. BG George Casey told them that what they had just done was "probably the most gallant action that I have heard of during the entire war." High praise from a soldier with three Silver Stars, a Bronze Star for valor, and a Distinguished Flying Cross himself.

A day after the daring prisoner snatch, Thunderhorse aero scouts spotted a column of porters carrying 120 mm mortar rounds northwest of An Loc, not far from Fire Support Base (FSB) Eagle I. Eight more NVA soldiers were captured. Stephen Moushegian captured one of the enemy soldiers by hovering his LOH over him and using hand-and-arm signals to coax him to surrender. Two more prisoners were talked into throwing down their weapons and surrendering by the ARP platoon sergeant, SSG Homer Hungerford.

The prisoners confirmed that the objective was to take An Loc and establish the Provisional Revolutionary Government there—at any cost. For Hanoi, the appearance of a battlefield victory was a precursor for making progress at the Paris peace talks. As the official NVA history of the war states: "We could only win at the conference table what we had already won on the battlefield." A Military Assistance Command Vietnam briefing officer told members of the media: "Their targets now are An Loc, Loc Ninh and Song Be. If they could take them over for 24 or 48 hours and establish de facto control and a provisional government, it would be a psychological victory for them."

By the end of the day on 10 August, the picture was as good as it was ever going to get. Nguyen Van An's improbable story was proving to be, for the most part, on target. The 271st and 272nd Regiments (9th (VC) Division), supported by the D368 (VC) Battalion, were positively identified in forward assembly areas to the west of Highway 13, poised to assault bases in and around Quan Loi and An Loc. Battalions of the 101D and 209th Regiments (1st (NVA) and 7th (NVA) Divisions respectively) were located along Thunder Road with the apparent mission of ambushing convoys and cutting off reinforcements headed north to relieve An Loc. NVA soldiers from the 141st and 165th Regiments (7th (NVA) Division) were captured between Loc Ninh and Bo Duc (their anticipated targets), but their base camps had not yet been positively identified. Independent artillery, recon, and sapper units were known to be reinforcing these regiments across the board. These units could reach their attack positions quickly, using the jungle and rubber plantations to move unseen.

Blackhorse 6 took full advantage of the firepower and mobility of the 22 troop/company-sized maneuver units, two air cavalry troops, and multiple batteries of artillery under his control for the defense of An Loc. Friendly forces were deployed in positions to deter and disrupt the planned enemy attacks. Regimental headquarters, two recon platoons, and elements of the 919th Engineer Company (about 25 ACAVs and 3 tanks), along with two airmobile companies from the 1st Cav, were located at Quan Loi. Task Force Wright (elements of 1/11 and the 34th (ARVN)

Rangers) were deployed in and around FSB Jon, responsible (along with the local CIDG force) for the defense of Loc Ninh. The 2nd Squadron, 1/9th (ARVN) Infantry Regiment, and 15th (ARVN) Cavalry were screening the southwest approaches to An Loc from FSBs Aspen and Sidewinder. TF 1/16th Infantry (Mechanized) (with an airmobile infantry company (OPCON) and the 4/9th (ARVN) Infantry) were patrolling out of FSBs Eagle II and Allons II northwest of An Loc. The 2nd Battalion and Headquarters, 9th (ARVN) Regiment, provided close-in security at An Loc itself; Fox Troop, 2/11 and the 2/1st (ARVN) Cavalry (reinforced with a company from 1/9th (ARVN) Infantry) were outposted along Highway 13 south of An Loc. Alpha Troop of the Quarterhorse, on loan from the 1st Infantry Division, was the sole unit defending the eastern approaches to Quan Loi.

Eleven artillery batteries (including those of 1/11 and 2/11 and three ARVN 105 mm batteries) provided direct and general fire support (coordinated by 6/27th Artillery at Quan Loi) for the 11th Cavalry. These forces gave the Allies about a four-to-one advantage in personnel and an overwhelming advantage in firepower.

Colonel Leach directed his staff to develop a multi-optioned counterattack plan. The commanders of the maneuver units were assigned a range of counterattack options, with fire support plans for each. An overlay of named and numbered checkpoints was distributed down to troop/company/battery level, ensuring everyone had a common operational picture for when one or more of the options was exercised.[24]

Perhaps the enemy was counting on the effects of the rainy weather to diminish the 11th Cavalry's ability to defend Quan Loi, An Loc, and Loc Ninh. In fact, the Regiment's own cross-country movement charts showed "movement restricted during wet season" just ten kilometers either side of Highway 13 from the Cambodian border all the way south to the provincial boundary with Binh Duong. But, in August 1969, those charts were proven to have not taken the spirit of the Blackhorse trooper into account.

An Loc and Quan Loi

SP4 Marvin Gootee was with the 3rd Platoon, 919th Engineers (Red Devils), at Quan Loi. He wrote to his parents that the captured NVA soldiers "were an advance scout party (according to the information they gave us) for a massive enemy force just over the border that were preparing for an all-out attack on Quan Loi. The orders they had received from higher-ups was to take over our camp at all costs." Marvin's platoon was part of the rapid reaction force (RRF) the night of 11–12 August, and they were ready: "We've even had to sleep with all our clothes on. All day we have been working on our ACAV's, cleaning machine guns ..."

The troopers of Bravo Troop's 3rd Platoon—the "fighten'-est platoon" in Vietnam according to their platoon sergeant—considered themselves fortunate. Because their vehicle count numbered but four operational vehicles (three ACAVs and one

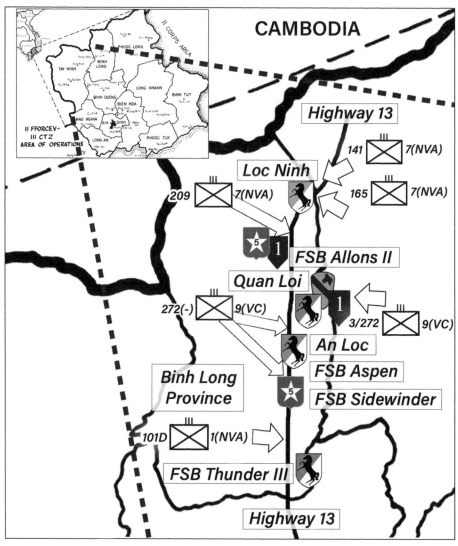

Map of friendly dispositions and enemy attacks during the battle of Northern Binh Long Province in August 1969. (basic map, US Army)

Sheridan), the troop commander (CPT Doug Starr) directed them to return to Quan Loi for a much-needed maintenance standdown. Although the enemy was known to mortar and rocket the huge base camp nightly, it still wasn't "the field." LT Ray DeWitt thought he was especially lucky. He'd been the platoon leader for exactly one week. As they pulled into the maintenance area near the airstrip and completely unloaded the tracks on the afternoon of 11 August, he thought this break in the action would provide him a chance to gather his thoughts and pick the brain of his platoon sergeant (who was on his second tour with Bravo Troop), SSG Ashbee Tyree.[25]

Boy, was he ever wrong.

The ominous silence and lack of enemy contact throughout the day of Monday, 11 August, seemed to confirm the suspicion that the attack would come that night.

Elements of the 1st (NVA), 7th (NVA), and 9th (VC) Divisions—"seething with the revolutionary fire of the August Revolution" (according to an NVA history of the fight)—made their way through the rubber plantations into their final attack positions after darkness on 11 August 1969. Despite some serious losses during their approach marches, about 2,000 NVA and VC soldiers initiated an attack in the early morning hours of 12 August. The same pattern repeated itself across the battlefield—a light mortar and RPG barrage, immediately followed by moderate to heavy ground attacks.

The attacks were initially focused on the An Loc area. The first assault came just 45 minutes after midnight. Following a barrage of mortars, a battalion of the 101D (VC) Regiment attacked the Chon Thanh airstrip astride Highway 13 south of An Loc. The defenders from the 2/1st (ARVN) Cavalry, according to the after-action report, "dug their heels in and fought the enemy back." Two Air Force AC47 "Spooky" gunships and troopers from Fox Troop, 2/11, roared into the fight, quickly chasing the attackers back into the jungle.

The Quan Loi base camp, about 20 kilometers away, received the next early-morning wake-up call by mortars and sappers. This action was designed to tie down any possible reaction force for the follow-on assault against An Loc itself, as well as to disrupt command and control.

The Quan Loi base camp sat atop a broad hill, 50 meters higher in elevation than the valleys around it. The defenders had burned off all of the vegetation down into the valleys, giving the impression of a bald, red-clay bump in an otherwise verdant green world. The perimeter bunkers, 25 meters apart, were partially dug into the side of the hill, half way between the hill's flat top and the valley floor. Four strands of concertina wire encircled Quan Loi base camp, the last strand actually at the base of the hill. Daylight visibility from the bunker line was good but, on a cloudy, moonless night, like the night of 11–12 August, visibility was ten meters or less. Night vision devices were almost useless; troopers occupying the bunkers could barely make out the first strand of wire, let alone the fourth. Illumination rounds and hand-held flares only reflected the gloom and served mainly to spoil night vision. Everyone had been briefed about the expected attacks and the perimeter line was on alert and nervous.

The first NVA rocket impacted 100 meters south of the Air Cav Troop operations bunker about 0105 hours on the morning of 12 August, followed in quick succession by three more scattered around the compound. Mortar fire (60 mm) followed 15 minutes later, striking two bunkers. The incoming rounds covered the approach of sappers already in the wire in the Green Sector (on the east side of the base camp manned by 1st Cav infantrymen). The sappers, "some of the best in the business" (according to a 1st Cav Division report), had been there since well before midnight. The defenders of bunker #61 were all killed (their weapons were found to still have safeties on after the battle), but the reaction force quickly deployed behind the bunker and prevented the sappers from moving any further up the hill. Fifty meters away, a direct hit by an RPG took out bunker #63, but the follow-on sappers tripped a flare and were halted by intense fire at the perimeter.

RPGs struck and knocked out bunkers #67 and #68 at 0237 hours. Simultaneously, probes began against the Blue and White Sectors on the west side of the perimeter. About this time, land-line wire communications were breaking down inside the base camp due to the incoming mortars.

The 919th Engineer Company was the base rapid reaction force that night, the final reserve force as it were. They deployed a mixed bag of combat engineers, mechanics, clerks, cooks, and cavalrymen on four ACAVs and two new Combat Engineer Vehicles (CEVs).[26] When the shooting started, they took their alert position behind the Red Sector. Radios were tuned to the base defense net and they could hear the mounting anxiety and confusion. Then the personnel manning the tower responsible for the Green Sector "started screaming on the radio that the enemy was in the wire." But the land-line was dead, and the RRF had strict instructions not to deploy until they were explicitly told to do so by the officer in charge of the base defense force. At that moment, however, that net was overloaded with excited voices proclaiming the end of the world from multiple sectors of the perimeter.

Chief Warrant Officer 2 (CW2) Clemens Duprey, an "old soldier," was in charge of the RRF—nicknamed "All Glory"—in this sector. Born in 1938, he had joined the Army while many of his troopers were still in grade school. They universally respected and looked up to him. He knew a bad situation when he saw/heard one and, on his own initiative, told RRF All Glory to march to the sounds of the guns.[27] Another "old soldier," Sergeant First Class (SFC) Ben Fields, was the senior NCO present; he was a Korean War vet. Marvin Gootee remembers him saying just before heading out to plug the hole in the perimeter: "I guess this is it. This is what it's all about."

SP4 Kerry Jones tells what happened next.

> The night wasn't dark and peaceful anymore. As we approached, flares turned the night to mid-afternoon and we began to get every kind of fire the enemy could toss at us ... Bunker 68 had been knocked out and the enemy was everywhere. They'd put a gap in the wire big enough for two tanks to drive through, and Charlie was in! They'd even dug into our berm and were firing rockets at us from there.

In quick succession, the All Glory command track was hit by three RPGs and a fourth hit one of the CEVs in the commander's cupola. At least three troopers were wounded; SP4 Fred Sheetz, a right-side ACAV machine gunner, was seriously wounded, as was

Ben Fields. Despite the intense rocket and rifle fire, the engineers kept to their guns and slowly gained fire superiority in the 200-meter-wide gap in the wire between bunkers #55 and #71. With two of the newly-acquired CEVs up front, Duprey directed their fire into the midst of the 30 or so NVA sappers and supporting RPG teams inside the wire. The effect of the 165 mm "demolition" guns firing medicine-ball sized plastic explosive rounds, 7.62 mm coaxial machine guns, and .50-cal. machine guns—at ranges of 30 meters or less—was both immediate and devastating.

Despite a broken left arm and numerous shrapnel wounds, Ben Fields (on his second tour with the Blackhorse in Vietnam), stayed behind his .50-cal., hosing down the enemy sappers.[28] SP5 Joe Rooney recalls that Fields was proud of his Native American heritage and his warrior spirit shone through that night. As one NVA sapper would mount the captured bunker, Fields' accurate machine gun fire would knock him off. He was seen to single-handedly eliminate several RPG teams. Both Duprey and Fields then aided in the evacuation of numerous wounded troopers until first light brought a break in the action.

Shortly after 0130 hours, the action shifted to the 11th Cavalry-defended Red Sector on the northeast side of the perimeter, manned by one platoon of nine ACAVs and a Sheridan from Bravo and Charlie Troops, 1/11, four ACAVs and the Golf Troop mortars from 2/11, three M48 tanks, and the Regimental Headquarters and Headquarters Troop (HHT). However, the element of surprise had been wasted and the sappers were caught still in the first strand of wire (almost two dozen bodies were found in the wire after daylight). The combination of tanks, ACAVs, and mortars (that fired about 700 rounds that night) was too much for the NVA. A group of mechanics, cooks, clerks, and other support personnel, made immeasurable contributions to the defense as well.

SP4 Dan Reid, a mechanic, was amongst those in the Red Sector. When the first enemy mortar and rocket rounds impacted, he was caught near the motor pool. Grabbing his .45-caliber pistol and several magazines, he crawled under one of the tracks to ride out the incoming barrage. That's when he spotted an NVA sapper moving from vehicle to vehicle, throwing satchel charges inside. As the sapper approached, Dan slid through the mud to the end of the vehicle. He shot the NVA soldier dead. A second sapper appeared, attempting to finish the job his comrade had started. He was just as unlucky. Reid killed him as well.

The Red Sector was closest to the air strip and the so-called "White House," now serving as the regimental HQ.[29] Several prisoners revealed later that the White House and air strip were the 271st (VC) Regiment main objectives. The 2/11 Howitzer Battery's mess sergeant, SFC Walter Hand, was in that area and rushed to the villa to help evacuate the wounded. As enemy RPG teams continued to fire their rockets into the building, Hand crawled outside. He spotted the flash from one of the RPGs, engaged the team with his individual weapon, and killed all three of them.

Just after 0230 hours, ground surveillance radar picked up heavy movement *away* from the Red Sector; there was just too much Blackhorse firepower for them to handle. The K3 Battalion moved from the Red into position to attack the White and Blue (northwest and west respectively) Sectors. The presence there of a rump platoon of ACAVs and a Sheridan from 1/11's Alpha Troop may have been enough to convince the NVA that any attack was doomed. It never came.

Three and a half hours after it started, the ground attack on Quan Loi ceased. When the smoke had cleared, the base camp was still in friendly hands. Only three snipers had reached the top of the hill. What could have been a giant fiasco ended with barely a squeak.

The firebases

Throughout the night of 11–12 August, four enemy regiments struck US and South Vietnamese bases across northern Binh Long Province. Task Force Wright at Fire Support Base (FSB) Jon outside Loc Ninh came under a heavy mortar and rocket attack, while Delta Company, 1/11, two kilometers to the southwest, was assaulted by the 7th Battalion, 209th (NVA) Regiment. TF 1/16 Infantry (Mechanized) at FSB Allons II simultaneously defended against mortar and ground attacks while preparing to react to several nearby bases under heavy attack. The 2nd Platoon, Alpha Troop, 1/4th Cav, in a screening position astride a vital crossroad southeast of Quan Loi, was under siege for two full hours, but prevented an unidentified enemy battalion from reaching its attack positions against Quan Loi. Infantrymen from the 9th Infantry Regiment, 5th (ARVN) Division, and militia soldiers from various provincial units, successfully defended the towns of An Loc and Loc Ninh, as well as several fire bases to the west and south.

But at FSB Sidewinder (4.5 kilometers south-southwest of An Loc), poor leadership ensured that the defending South Vietnamese cavalrymen and infantrymen (about 250–300 personnel total) were, despite ample warning, unprepared. There were no bunkers dug on the perimeter, no listening posts or ambush patrols deployed, and the ARVN soldiers were sleeping in above-ground tents; the wires to the few claymores set out were not connected. The six-man, one-ACAV, one-M577 liaison team from 2/11 (there to coordinate fire support and reinforcements) watched in amazement at 0100 hours as the South Vietnamese, awakened by the noise and light show to their south, strolled to the top of the perimeter berm, in their underwear, and watched the fireworks at FSB Aspen I.

About that same time, a radio call from Aspen gave specific information of an impending attack on Sidewinder.[30] Despite this 30-minute warning, the ARVN defenders took no additional precautions. Within moments, FSB Sidewinder was struck by the K3 Battalion, 271st (NVA) Regiment. There was virtually no return fire from the perimeter as South Vietnamese soldiers scrambled out of their tents looking for their uniforms and weapons. The 2/11 liaison team barely escaped total annihilation as the NVA quickly breached the perimeter and overran the base. PFC Bill Maks recalled: "I could see between 75 and 100 VC to shoot at all times."

Led by Regimental Commander Colonel William Cobb, the 11th Armored Cavalry Regiment comes ashore at Vung Tau, South Vietnam, on 7 September 1966. (US Army)

Organized chaos as more than 4,000 Blackhorse troopers settle in to the Long Binh Staging Area just after arriving in Vietnam in September 1966. (US Army)

Blackhorse Troopers prepare their 400-plus armored vehicles for combat in the Long Binh Staging Area in September 1966. (US Army)

The Regiment's 300 Armored Cavalry Assault Vehicles (ACAVs), with their three machine guns and 5-man crews, made the Blackhorse Regiment the most lethal brigade-sized unit in Vietnam. (US Army)

With 3,000 rounds of .50-cal. and 10,000 rounds of 7.62mm M60 machine gun ammunition, the ACAV crew (like these C Troopers in 1968) could sustain itself in virtually any firefight. (Phillip Michitsch)

The ACAV served as the crew's "mobile" home for months at a time, during the rainy (hot and muddy) and dry (hot and dusty) seasons alike. (Bryant Nelson)

The Regiment's 54 M48A3 "Patton" tanks (like this one from M Company in 1968) were armed with a 90mm main gun, a coaxially-mounted 7.62mm machine gun, and a .50-cal. machine gun atop the tank commander's cupola, providing heavy firepower and armored protection during the close-in fights that characterized the war in Vietnam. (Robert McNeil)

Each squadron had a battery of six 155mm M109A1 howitzers (like this one from 2nd Squadron's Howitzer Battery in 1969), each capable of firing four high-explosive rounds a minute at targets up to 18 kilometers away. (David Watters)

Each recon platoon had one M106 mortar carrier with a 4.2-inch mortar for immediate fire support during the close-in battle. (US Army)

The Regiment's nine M132 Flame Tracks (universally known as Zippo after the popular cigarette lighter brand) were used extensively to clear fields of fire around base camps, fire support bases, and night defensive positions, as well as enemy soldiers from their underground bunkers. (US Army)

Air Cavalry Troop's (Thunderhorse) mix of gunships (like this AH1G Cobra), scouts, lift, command and control helicopters, and an aero-rifle platoon provided third-dimensional capabilities to find the enemy and fix him in place until ground forces arrived. (William Powis)

The enemy—Viet Cong and North Vietnamese alike—hid in South Vietnam's and Cambodia's thick foliage, requiring the Regiment to "bust jungle" (like these M Company tanks in 1968) in order to "find the bastards." (Robert McNeil)

By 1968, the jungle had become slightly less challenging, as the combination of Rome Plows and aerial defoliation made movement by armored vehicle (like these F Troop Sheridans in 1970) a bit easier. (US Army)

Rome Plows (D7 engineer tractors with a special plow blade made in Rome, Georgia, attached), protected by armored vehicles (like this A Troop Sheridan providing security for the 60th Land Clearing Company in 1970), cleared the jungle to enhance both trafficability and visibility. (US Army)

In the dry season, South Vietnam's ubiquitous rice paddies slowed down, but did not stop, the Regiment's armored vehicles (like these 3rd Squadron ACAVs and tanks in 1968). (US Army)

Many proclaimed Vietnam as non-tank country due to the weather and terrain, but the Blackhorse Regiment helped to prove that wrong—most of the time (an M48A3 from D Company bogged down in the mud in 1970). (Tim Brooks)

In October 1966, the 11th Cav began the construction of their new home—Blackhorse Base Camp—with a perimeter over four miles in circumference, including 66 defensive bunkers and 13 towers, more than 500 buildings, an airfield, and almost 20 kilometers of roads. (Public domain)

This picture was taken on 20 July 1969 (middle of the rainy season in South Vietnam). After hearing the news that Neil Armstrong had stepped on the moon, Bryant Nelson felt compelled to record the moment for history. (Bryant Nelson)

While on operations, squadrons established fire support bases (like this 2nd Squadron FSB in 1969) that usually included the squadron's command post, headquarters troop, and howitzer battery, with a recon troop or the tank company providing perimeter defenses. (David Watters)

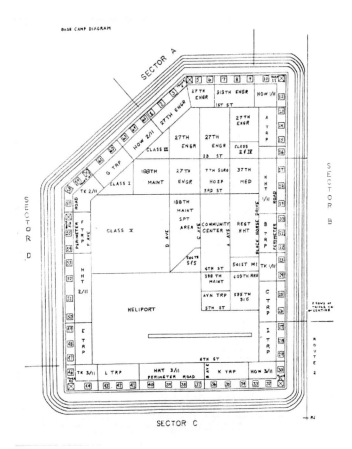

This diagram of Blackhorse Base Camp shows the location of each member of the Blackhorse family, including organic and attached units, support and tenant units. Most troopers spent very little time at the base camp—maybe a total of 30 days in a 12-month tour. (US Army)

Lieutenant (future 18th Secretary of the Army) Tom White performs maintenance on his M Company tank in the 1968 mud, proving that even the most routine tasks were more difficult in the rainy season. (Jim Tankovich)

Squadrons typically named their fire support bases after a recently wounded or killed trooper, a historical military leader or battle, or a traditional name associated with the squadron. Third Squadron—the "Bandit" Squadron—occupied FSB Bandit in 1970. (Public domain)

When individual troops and companies established night defensive positions (NDPs), all of the unit's armored vehicles "circled the wagons" (like these from I Troop in 1968), with weapons pointed outwards. A unit seldom spent more than 24 or 48 hours in an NDP. (US Army)

By mid-September 1966, the 11th Armored Cavalry Regiment (including these from A Troop preparing to move out on a mission in the fall of 1966) was deemed to be combat ready. The troopers' test-by-fire came quickly, as the 5th (VC) Division tried their best to return to the status quo. (US Army)

The convoy ambush along Highway 1 on 21 November 1966 proved that the firepower, armored protection, and counter-ambush tactics of the Blackhorse Regiment were effective, even when outnumbered, as well as that the ACAVs (like this one from B Troop destroyed in the ambush) were not impervious to anti-tank weapons. (US Army)

The 2 December 1966 ambush demonstrated the value of having M48 tanks as part of the convoy escort—especially when severely outnumbered. Even though one of the tanks had its tank commander's cupola and .50-cal. machine gun knocked off by an anti-tank round, the crew survived and kept the tank in the fight. (US Army)

The early combat experience also proved a long-standing cavalry tradition. Just like their predecessors on the western frontier, in the Civil War, and World War II, Blackhorse troopers in Vietnam (like these from 2nd Squadron in 1968) were just as likely to fight dismounted as they were mounted. (US Army)

During the multi-division combat operations *Cedar Falls* and *Junction City*, Blackhorse armor was paired with dismounted infantry (like these M Company tanks and 173rd Airborne Brigade Skytroopers) for major sweep operations—up to that time, an untested concept in Vietnam. A lesson learned from this operation was that the armored vehicles, not the infantry, should lead the sweep in jungle areas. (US Army)

The first Tet offensive in February 1968 caught virtually everyone by surprise. In true cavalry fashion, Blackhorse troopers (like this ACAV crew in Bien Hoa on 2 February 1968) "rode to the rescue" of the major headquarters and logistics bases that were under siege. (US Army)

The Regiment was called upon again in May 1968 to counter the enemy's second or Mini-Tet offensive. Here, Blackhorse M48 tanks cross the longest pontoon bridge built during the Vietnam War to reach Long Binh in time to crush that attack before it got off the ground. (US Army)

Following each of the two major enemy offensives in 1968, the Blackhorse kicked back—hard. In March, 3rd Squadron (including these ACAVs attacking a VC-held village) was awarded a Presidential Unit Citation for thwarting the 9th (VC) Division's attempts to storm Saigon from Hau Nghia Province. (US Army)

In February 1969, the enemy again tried to overrun the Saigon-Bien Hoa-Long Binh complex. They failed, in no small part due to the overwhelming firepower and maneuverability of the 11th Armored Cavalry Regiment (including these ACAVs from 1st Squadron near Long Binh). (US Army)

Over the course of 1969—the bloodiest year of the war—Blackhorse troopers (like the ones crewing this C Troop Sheridan) pushed the enemy further and further away from the population, food and tax sources, and battlefield victory. (US Army)

The arrival of the OH6A "Cayuse" light observation helicopter (like this one from 3rd Squadron in 1969)—a fast, quiet, and agile scout helicopter—completed the modernization of the Blackhorse aviation assets. Pilots literally spread the branches of the trees to see the enemy hiding below. (Greg Mason)

The air cavalry-armored cavalry team proved itself again and again, finding the bastards and piling on. This became more than just a motto for the 11th Armored Cavalry Regiment—it was a highly successful battlefield tactic that was copied by many other units throughout South Vietnam. (Richard Gilpin)

The year 1970 was highlighted by the cross-border attack into Cambodia in May and June. Blackhorse troopers (like these from C Troop) led the attack into the Fishhook north of Saigon. (US Army)

Four days into the Cambodia operation, the Regimental Commander received an order that every Cavalryman dreams of: break off your current operations, make a sharp turn to the northeast, and move at full speed—behind enemy lines—to seize the important cross-roads town of Snuol. Here, E Troop enters Snuol two days later. (David Watters)

Throughout the rest of May and June, Blackhorse troopers (like these from F Troop conducting recon-by-fire) protected the flanks of the infantry and engineer battalions emptying out the Communist warehouses inside Cambodia. Two enemy divisions tried as hard as they could to salvage some of the weapons, ammunition, and medicine, but to no avail. (US Army)

The Cambodia operation proved hugely successful from a military perspective. Not only were the stockpiles of supplies taken away or destroyed, the enemy units inside South Vietnam and Cambodia were so thoroughly disorganized and demoralized that they were unable to mount any substantial operations for over a year. Here, A Troop moves—unmolested—through its generally quiet area of operations. (US Army)

When the bulk of the Regiment went home in early 1971, 2nd Squadron and Air Cavalry Troop continued the fight for another year. In early 1972, the Blackhorse stood down. Here, E Troop Sheridans during the final "pass in review." (Bill Squires)

Over the course of five and a half years of combat service in Vietnam and Cambodia, almost 25,000 men served in the 11th Armored Cavalry Regiment. These three troopers are representative of those who proudly wore the Blackhorse patch. (US Army)

Vietnam was primarily a small-unit war. It was usually a recon platoon, commanded by a lieutenant with less than two years in the Army, who led a platoon of 45 to 50 mostly young men, that made the initial contact with the enemy. Here, Lieutenant Lou Reymann shows the effects of heat, rain, mud, lack of sleep, and the pressure of making life-and-death decisions. (Lou Reymann)

In the spring of 1967, the Regiment erected a monument, upon which were placed the names of every Blackhorse trooper killed in Vietnam and Cambodia. Today, that monument stands near the US Army Home of Cavalry and Armor at Fort Benning, GA. A total of 730 names are etched onto that piece of stone from Vietnam. (Pete Walter)

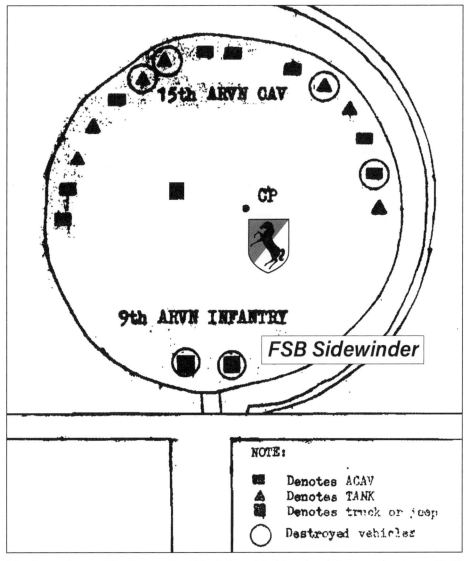

Map showing layout of Fire Support Base Sidewinder and 2nd Squadron liaison team location on 11–12 August 1969 (reproduced from the regimental after-action report). (basic map, US Army)

Most of the ARVN soldiers broke and ran, leaving their ACAVs and M41 tanks to be satchel-charged by the NVA. Enemy soldiers manned the .50-cal. machine guns atop the abandoned vehicles, harassing an AC47 Spooky and shooting down a 1st Cav Cobra that had come to help the defenders.[31]

The two 2nd Squadron vehicles were able to escape and head for FSB Aspen. They were chased by an enemy-commandeered South Vietnamese ACAV, which was destroyed by "friendly" (VC) RPG fire from inside Sidewinder (enemy gunners inside Sidewinder assumed the ACAV was manned by South Vietnamese and attempting to escape—it wasn't). The two Echo Troop vehicles took a total of 13 RPG hits before getting away. By the time the rest of Echo Troop was able to react (40 minutes after the initial assault), 44 ARVN soldiers had been killed and another 37 wounded. Some of those who ran away that night didn't make it back to their units for days.

Captain (CPT) Bob Hurt (Hotel Company commander) was inside Aspen and recalls that night vividly. Shortly after the mortar rounds started falling, there were numerous reports of ground probes at various points around the perimeter. But the Hotel Company tanks and Echo Troop ACAVs lined up around the berm were forewarned and easily handled them all. Hurt recalls the M577 from Sidewinder rushing into Aspen "with the damn [canvas] extension on the back, poles and shit flying everywhere."

The 1st Cavalry Division after-action report summarized the opening moves of the battle of northern Binh Long Province.

> It had been quite a night. In the space of less than two hours, from the time of the first attack on Chon Thanh at 0045 hours until the attack began in earnest on Sidewinder at 0241, the enemy launched major ground attacks, involving units of three main-force divisions, at six different points over the entire length of Binh Long Province. It was a challenge of unusual scope and ferocity, the first time the enemy has been able to mount such a coordinated effort on such a scale … He did not succeed in any of his ventures … Cumulative results of the day's operations show 467 enemy KIA, 12 PW and 15 *Hoi Chanh* [defectors]. The action resulted in 36 U.S. KIA, 231 WIA, and 8 MIA.

Counterattack

After daylight on the 12 August, the Blackhorse kicked back—hard. Counterattack Plan Alpha was executed, sending all units against suspected enemy strongholds.

Echo Troop's mission on the 12th was a continuation of its relief of the 15th (ARVN) Cavalry at Sidewinder and Aspen. The troop was on the trail of the NVA forces that hit the bases. But the 271st (VC) Regiment reoccupied a strong defensive position among the young rubber trees near the hamlet of Minh Duc, less than five kilometers from Sidewinder. When the 15th (ARVN) Cav ran into them, they called on the Blackhorse to, once again, rescue them.

CPT Jake Marshall was the Cobra driver for the Air Cav Troop team first to arrive on the scene. From the air, it was obvious there was a hell of a fight going on below. He recalls:

> And, no sooner had I turned in that direction than I saw battle smoke rising above one of the Michelin rubber tree plantations about three minutes away. I knew that was where to go and I knew there was bad trouble … I then radioed the US advisor to the ARVN regiment. Again I could tell that there was pretty intense fighting by the volume and the loudness of the rifle and machine gun fire coming across the radio … The US advisor told me the enemy was only 10 yards from his position and coming hard.

Marshall fired pairs of rockets into the dense foliage, hoping that he was hitting bad guys, not friendlies. "After about seven pairs had been fired and begun impacting, all of a sudden the American advisor keyed his mike screaming." Fearing the worst, Marshall tensed for the bad news. Instead, he heard: "'It's perfect! It's perfect! It's right on top of them!' Wow. From the lowest depths of emotion to elation!"

It was now Echo Troop's turn in the barrel. Heavily outnumbered by about 400 dug-in NVA armed with plenty of RPG7s, the troop fought for its life for the next six hours.

The initial fusillade struck Echo Troop's right flank. The troop's ACAVs and tanks made a "Right Flank, March" and charged with all guns blazing. The 1st Platoon entered the rubber trees first, followed behind and to the left by 2nd Platoon. The enemy commander had chosen his ground carefully, right where the old-growth rubber met the new-growth. The 200-meter long bunker line was dug in among terraced, young-growth, 14-foot tall rubber trees, with two-foot high irrigation dikes running throughout the area. The Echo Troop ACAVs were forced to enter the rubber trees at an angle across the grain, rather than straight down the rows. Each ACAV had to work its way between the trees and over the dikes, making relatively easy, slow moving targets for the numerous RPG teams.

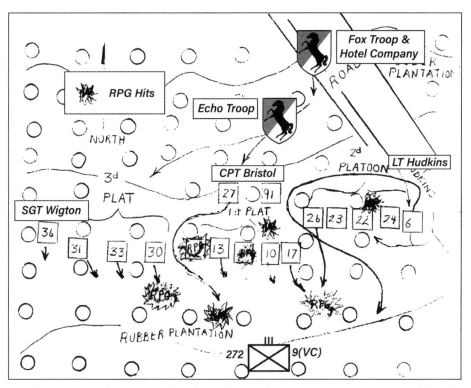

Map showing enemy dispositions and 2nd Squadron attack on 12 August 1969 (reproduced from the regimental after-action report). (basic map, US Army)

Two ACAVs were set ablaze shortly after entering the tree line. The enemy gunners were targeting the vehicles with two antennas first. CPT William Bristol (Echo Troop commander) reported to the squadron operations officer (Major John Gilbreath) circling overhead in a helicopter that both platoon leaders had been wounded and that the troop could not proceed further. Shortly thereafter, Bristol was severely wounded himself, leaving the troop without its normal leadership.

For LT Richard Hudkins, the 2nd Platoon leader, 12 August was a harrowing day. He was on the left flank as Bristol brought the troop on line to assault the entrenched enemy. They were met initially with just a few desultory shots. After a break of several minutes, Hudkins' ACAVs became the target for an intense barrage of RPGs and automatic weapons. Specialist 5 (SP5) James Foote, an ACAV driver, recalled shortly after the fight: "I've never seen anything like it! We were getting fire from all directions! PC's [personnel carriers] were getting hit all over the place. It was quiet and then all at once all hell broke loose!"

Radio communications between Bristol and his platoon leaders and between the platoon leaders and their track commanders (TCs) was lost early on in the fight (mostly due to antennas being shot off by the enemy fire concentrated against the leaders' vehicles). Command and coordination became exceptionally difficult. When Hudkins moved his ACAV in front of the formation in an attempt to regain control of his platoon, his track became a magnet for all of the lead flying about the left flank of the battlefield. A series of RPG hits disabled the vehicle, killed the driver, and seriously wounded both side gunners. A final RPG struck the front of the TC's cupola just as Hudkins was climbing out, knocking him off the vehicle and into the dense underbrush.

As the medics pulled the dead and wounded from the damaged and destroyed ACAVs, Hudkins lay nearby, unconscious and bleeding profusely—unseen and somehow unaccounted for. When the platoon medic finally found him, there was so much blood coming from his chest and groin, he thought his LT was dead. There were no signs of life, so the medic turned to treat those he thought could still survive.

At this point in the battle, the troop commander and three platoon leaders were all either dead or severely wounded, as were all of the platoon sergeants. The troop had suffered over 40 casualties (dead and wounded), and seven ACAVs had sustained one or more RPG hits. Sergeant (SGT) Charles Wigton, the TC of ACAV E-36, rose to the occasion. He and his crew had already taken out an RPG team that was maneuvering for a better angle to fire against the vehicles on line in the rubber trees. Recognizing that he might be the most experienced man left in action (he'd been in country eight months), he immediately assumed command of the remaining operational ACAVs. Lieutenant Colonel (LTC) James Aarestad (who had taken command of 2/11 in April) was over the contact and ordered Wigton to pull everyone back in order to call in artillery and tactical air strikes (TacAir). SGT Wigton and the crew of E-36 covered their withdrawal, then moved out of the bunker complex to safety.

Over the next 90 minutes, 105 mm and 8-inch artillery, Cobra gunships, and TacAir pummeled the rubber trees. Team Hotel, with two tank platoons and a platoon of ACAVs from Fox Troop, moved to the area of the contact to reinforce and help recover the friendly casualties. Team Hotel was under the command of CPT Bob Hurt—a self-described "'shake 'n' bake' captain with 26 months experience" in the Army. But Hurt had been in command of "Hell's Henchmen" for over five months (plus he had already commanded a recon troop in Germany for a year). He quickly took control of the situation.

First, he got everybody organized; "Who's in charge?," he asked. Silence. "Officers?" [silence] "Any NCOs?" SGT Wigton responded. Bob said: "You're the E Troop commander now." Hurt described his plan of attack and they mounted up for the renewed assault. The M48 tanks and ACAVs maneuvered amongst the new-growth rubber trees in the direction of the enemy bunkers. Visibility was significantly reduced because the trees were close together and there was lots of other vegetation. Hurt thought: "This is a great place to set up your defensive positions if you're the bad guy."

One of the tanks was struck almost immediately by multiple RPGs, and the entire crew had to be evacuated. The company communications chief, SGT Bill Percival, grabbed two other troopers, mounted up, and brought the tank back into action. They eliminated numerous NVA soldiers. Percival then directed his driver to crush first one, then another enemy bunker. Fifty-two tons of American steel caused return fire from these bunkers to cease—permanently.

When the Echo Troop-Hotel Company team disengaged from the fight late in the day, they left behind five ACAVs burning and five troopers unaccounted for. The loss of the troop's entire chain of command explains—but does not excuse—this unforgivable oversight. Three of the left-behind troopers were later found dead. One, John Sexton, was captured and held prisoner for two years. The fifth lived to tell quite a tale.[32]

When the severely wounded Richard Hudkins finally regained consciousness, he realized his precarious position—apparently the only one alive and in the middle of the enemy positions. Half-blinded by the blood from his head wound, he stumbled toward another ACAV (E-22), hoping that it (unlike his own) might still be operational. The good news was that it started; the seemingly bad news was that, disoriented, he drove the vehicle away from the friendly troops and further into the dense vegetation. The loss of blood and resulting state of shock eventually got to him, and he collapsed again into unconsciousness.

The vehicle ran all night until the fuel tank was empty. Drifting in and out of reality, Hudkins repeatedly called on the radio on both the platoon and troop frequencies, but never received an answer. When Echo Troop left those ACAVs on the battlefield—one of which was a platoon leader's vehicle—the squadron had to assume that the enemy was now in possession of all of their operating frequencies and call signs. In accordance with SOP, all units switched and began operating on new frequencies. No radios were tuned in to the old Echo Troop radio nets.

Three days later during a late-afternoon aerial recon of the contact area, MAJ Jim Bradin (Air Cav Troop commander) spotted an ACAV alone in a field, not where it should be. He reported the stray vehicle, and a team was inserted just before darkness. They found Hudkins inside and still alive.

Reconstructing the incident later, it became evident that the LT was a very lucky man. Because he drove the ACAV out of the immediate contact area on the morning of the 13th, he missed being caught in the middle of several artillery barrages and four air strikes—eight 750-pound and twenty-two 500-pound high explosive bombs, 14 napalm canisters, 386 rounds of 105 mm howitzer, and 46 rounds of 8-inch howitzer. Eight Cobras expended all their ammunition into the area during the same time period as well.

One eye-witness account noted that, when found, Richard Hudkins "was in pretty bad shape, as one can imagine, having been left for dead three days before, but he had enough energy left to ask his rescuers if he could please have a coke!"

Despite serious personnel (4 killed, 38 wounded, 1 missing) and equipment (4 ACAVs combat loss and 3 ACAVs moderate damage) losses, the Echo and Hotel troopers prevented the 271st (VC) Regiment from carrying out its follow-up mission—the complete destruction of the 15th (ARVN) Cavalry Regiment and the collapse of the western portion of the defensive ring protecting An Loc.

Wrap-up

Even while the major engagements were still raging in and around An Loc and Quan Loi, the regimental staff began to plan for cutting off the enemy forces as they made their inevitable "run for the border." Task Force 1/16th Infantry and TF Wright were deployed between the suspected post-battle NVA assembly areas and their Cambodian sanctuaries. These moves paid off handsomely. The already depleted ranks of the enemy infantry regiments were further thinned on 13 August in a major fight between TF Wright and the 209th (NVA) Regiment northwest of Loc Ninh. Alpha Troop and Delta Company, 1/11, and the 34th (ARVN) Rangers, supported by the 1/11 Howitzer Battery and Thunderhorse gunships, scattered the remnants of the 209th; another 140 NVA soldiers did not make it across the border.

Task Force 1/16th Infantry took on the rump 272nd (NVA) Regiment west of An Loc and further cut down its morning report strength. Individual VC and NVA soldiers were seen running from rubber tree to rubber tree. The infantrymen made contact on three separate occasions over the next 48 hours, scattering the survivors into the dense jungles where some made good their escape—others were not so lucky.

As to Hanoi's main political objective for the start of the Summer-Autumn offensive, the attack and "occupation" of An Loc itself was a complete bust. Starting about the same time as the assault on Quan Loi, a light barrage of mortars and rockets struck the periphery of An Loc and the surrounding villages. Although radar picked up the movement of a battalion-sized force southwest of the town about 0530 hours, the 214th Regional Forces Company defending that sector reported no contact. In fact, other than this radar contact and one other sighting by excited villagers of a "large" enemy force, there was no sign of either the 272nd (NVA) Regiment or the D363rd (VC) Battalion assigned the mission of attacking and seizing the provincial capital. Maybe they got lost in the dark.

About 0430 hours, a four-man VC propaganda team did enter An Loc's east gate and passed out leaflets. The message read: "Now that the U.S. soldiers are leaving, who will protect the ARVNs?" The VC team took one prisoner, then disappeared about a half hour after arriving. So much for establishing the Provisional Revolutionary Government in An Loc.

A total of 11 Silver Stars (1 posthumous), 2 Distinguished Flying Crosses, 48 Bronze Stars for Valor ("V"), 10 Bronze Stars for Service (posthumous), 20 Army Commendations Medals "V," and 2 Air Medals "V" were awarded to members of the Regiment for actions on 12 August 1969.

It was not mere coincidence that the Blackhorse was in the eye of the storm on 12 August. That decision was a direct result of the first battle of northern Binh Long Province two years earlier when, in late 1967, elements of four enemy regiments assaulted Loc Ninh and Bo Duc. Although enemy losses were horrendous, the battle was a close-won victory for the 1st Infantry Division defenders. Among the most salient lessons learned from that experience was that protecting this remote area required tactical mobility, organic firepower, and mental agility.

The 11th Cavalry was the only force available in the corps area with all three of these attributes.

The enemy, decimated by 18 months of severe losses—numbers that could be replaced, but not the experienced leadership—attempted to infiltrate the better parts of three divisions to make a statement, to capture a district or provincial capital, install a revolutionary government, and proclaim to the world—but most especially to the negotiators in Paris—that South Vietnamese Government claims of control over its own territory were a sham.

But superb field craft by the aerial and ground scouts of the Blackhorse Regiment, coupled with intuitive intelligence analysis at multiple levels (from prisoner interrogations by the 541st Military Intelligence Detachment to all-source information integration by the regimental intelligence officer and his staff), gave away the enemy's intentions. Tens of thousands of pounds of bombs dropped from unseen B-52s and "snake and nape" from all-too-well-seen F-100s rained down on the regiments of the approaching enemy divisions, while 2.75-inch rockets, 155 mm shells, and .50-cal. machine guns thinned their ranks.

The enemy did not accomplish even one of his objectives during the August high point, and the divisions involved were not seen in strength on the battlefield in Vietnam again during the remainder of the Regiment's service in Southeast Asia.

The battle of Northern Binh Long Province stressed command and control at all levels in ways that were not seen at any other time during the 11th Cavalry's combat tour in Vietnam and Cambodia. Over the course of the first 18 days of August 1969, Blackhorse 6 commanded no less than five US battalions (two organic squadrons and three infantry battalions) and controlled five South Vietnamese infantry and armored cavalry battalion-sized units in life-or-death combat. He was also responsible for coordinating fire support from three battalions' worth of artillery and two air cavalry troops. At the squadron-level, the squadron and battalion commanders and their staffs were tasked with establishing combined command posts with ARVN infantry battalions, while simultaneously conducting combat operations. Complicating matters even more was the location of 3rd Squadron at Blackhorse Base Camp, the turn-over of the base to the South Vietnamese, and the relocation of all of the Regiment's rear detachments to Di An—all while staving off fanatical attacks by 8,000-plus NVA soldiers.

For the remainder of 1969 and into 1970, the 11th Cavalry remained in the vicinity of the Cambodian border. The Long Giao base camp was no longer "home." The camp was turned over to the 18th (ARVN) Infantry Division in the fall, and the troopers found new homes in Quan Loi, Bien Hoa, and eventually Di An.

General Abrams' clear and hold strategy was so successful that there were no major battles for the rest of the year. The bulk of the enemy's infantry regiments were withdrawn across the border into Cambodia for resting, refitting, and retraining. The few VC and NVA forces remaining between the border and Saigon subsisted on grubs, roots, and propaganda.

The year 1969 was a dramatic turn-around from 1968. The enemy was able to launch only a few offensive operations, none of which reached the scale of the Tet and mini-Tet campaigns of 1968. In fact, because of their significant losses in men and material, Hanoi ordered a return to guerrilla war throughout South Vietnam.[33] Regiments and battalions broke down into company- and platoon-sized elements, learned sapper and attack-by-fire skills, and avoided major engagements.

The guerrilla had been separated from the people. Newly equipped and better trained South Vietnamese militia units kept the VC and NVA out of the villages, denying them food, recruits, and propaganda victories. The program of accelerated pacification was making real headway in bringing stability to the countryside.

The year 1969 was a year of extremes for Blackhorse troopers. In March in the Michelin and in August and September around Quan Loi, they fought two of the hardest, most sustained battles of the Regiment's entire service in Southeast Asia. One measure of the heavy combat faced by the troopers during the year is seen in the tally of citations for battlefield courage. Two of three Medals of Honor and almost half (12 of 29) of the Distinguished Service Crosses awarded to Blackhorse troopers between 1966 and 1972 were for action during 1969. Casualties reflected the intensity of the fight—187 Blackhorse Troopers lost their lives in 1969 (one-quarter of all troopers killed in five and a half years). The fighting was hard and bloody, but the enemy suffered even more. Most importantly, the 11th Cavalry had seized the initiative, taken the fight to the enemy and put him to flight at every turn. By the end of the year, we clearly held the initiative, especially in the area north of Saigon.

But 1969 was also a year of disappointment. Blackhorse troopers, from junior private to senior colonel, wondered what their sacrifices were bringing. Early in the year, the chief US negotiator at the Paris Peace Talks had said at a press conference that the United States "is not seeking a military victory in Vietnam." Not seeking military victory? Why, troopers began to wonder, am I risking my life for a "political settlement"? Did my buddies die just so some politicians could give victory away? Strong leadership and good citizenship ensured that these questions did not seriously undermine morale, but the questions didn't go away.

Blackhorse troopers continued to beat the bush, to find the "bastards" and to pile on.

CHAPTER 6

Expanding the War: 1970 to Early 1971

The most critical current issue is to reduce our involvement in Southeast Asia while minimizing the impact of our withdrawal on regional stability, encouraging conditions for the self-determination of the people of South Vietnam, and protecting our credibility for the future.

NATIONAL SECURITY STUDY MEMORANDUM 95, 1970

Man, this is for real, only scarier than you see in the movies.

RAY TARR, ALPHA TROOP, 1/11 CAVALRY

It was heavy-weight, big boy stuff.

JAKE MARSHALL, AIR CAVALRY TROOP

Summing up the year 1969, the North Vietnamese Army's official newspaper editorialized on 1 January 1970: "Many crack US units, such as … the 11th Armored Regiment, were heavily defeated." The paper further prophesized that: "1970 will be a year full of brilliant prospects for our people. It is obvious that we are in a winning posture while the enemy is in a losing one." A companion assessment for 1969, conducted by the political arm of the VC claimed that 19,000 American tanks and armored vehicles had been destroyed or damaged in 1969.[1]

The reality, however, was much different.

In July 1969, the Communist headquarters for South Vietnam issued Resolution 9, which directed subordinate units inside South Vietnam to break up into smaller detachments and conduct guerrilla-like operations against the increasingly successful pacification program. Although the directive still called for the ideologically obligatory "total victory," unit commanders were told to focus on "the withdrawal of all American troops, to liberate rural areas, to destroy the RVN pacification teams, and to upgrade and develop the Viet Cong revolutionary government"—far short of total victory.

Resolution 9 was tacit recognition that the Communists were losing the military part of the war. Their earlier "campaigns" had been reduced to widely-separated high points lasting one or two days at most. Virtually all of the battlefield action was taking place on the fringes of South Vietnam, far from the population centers. If controlling the population was the definition of success—and it is according to Mao's theory of people's war—then Hanoi was losing the war, politically as well as militarily.

A pattern of activity emerged in the last half of 1968 that repeated itself through mid-1970. The "neutral" government in Cambodia—under Prince Norodom Sihanouk—allowed Hanoi virtual free rein along the Ho Chi Minh Trail and in base areas close to the border with South Vietnam. Enemy divisions based in Cambodia would launch an attack into South Vietnam. They suffered heavy personnel losses, expended considerable resources, and gained nothing more than a few transitory headlines. They then crossed the border back to their sanctuaries, where they replenished, replaced, trained, and reindoctrinated—then repeated the whole cycle all over again.

However, each cross-border attack was conducted by smaller and smaller forces and was aimed at targets further and further away from the Saigon-Bien Hoa-Long Binh area. What started with the Tet offensive against the capital region in early 1968 had, by late 1969, regressed to objectives within 20 kilometers of the Cambodian border. In the course of two years, division-sized, nation-wide offensive campaigns had diminished to company- and platoon-sized, localized high points—most of which were attacks by fire with only an occasional, half-hearted ground assault.

The enemy had suffered significant battlefield losses during the previous 18 months (February 1968–August 1969). In one province in Military Region (MR) III,[2] agents reported the local VC as having "low strengths, low morale, lack of supplies and illness." The largest company in the province had but 24 members, while the other six averaged only nine guerrillas each. NVA battalions and regiments avoided engagements.

The economy-of-force strategy (minimum expenditure of resources to achieve maximum psychological and political results) Hanoi had implemented in 1969 was to continue in 1970, although there were signs of increased resupply activities from the north as the rainy season drew to a close. One report spoke of "as many as 15,000 trucks winding down the Ho Chi Minh trail in December [1969]."[3] The problem, however, was not getting the supplies into the Cambodian depots; it was in getting them from there to the hungry soldiers.

Abrams' one-war strategy aimed at cutting off the enemy's lifelines was working—at least on the battlefields of Vietnam. On the "battlefields" on America's city streets and in the Congress, however, Hanoi was winning. They just needed to hang on long enough for Americans to go home.

Prisoners and captured documents from early 1970 indicated that the Communists were planning two rainy season high points in 1970. The objective of these two high points (one in May, the other in July) was primarily political, not military. Hanoi hoped to influence the negotiations in Paris in a manner to force war-weary America to seek a way out of Vietnam—quickly. However, developments in Cambodia after the overthrow of Prince Sihanouk caused the Communists to change their plans. A flurry of enemy activity in April, which was initially intended to support the two high points inside South Vietnam, was refocused toward supporting military action inside Cambodia. Allied attacks into the enemy's sanctuaries in late April and early May changed Hanoi's plans once again.

Interdicting the Enemy: January to April 1970

In early 1970, there were three enemy divisions and five independent regiments arrayed north of Saigon. The 5th (VC) Division was located in southern War Zone D (north of the Dong Nai River). Its three infantry regiments were spread from north and east of Bo Duc to well east of Xuan Loc, well over 100 kilometers apart. In this disposition, the division was incapable of conducting unified action. Both the 7th (NVA) and 9th (VC) Divisions were based inside Cambodia, with only one regiment each located on the Vietnamese side of the border (in northwestern War Zone C). The five independent infantry regiments—all rated as marginally combat ready due to low numbers and lack of supplies—were dispersed north and west of Saigon. The Military Assistance Command Vietnam (MACV) estimated the average NVA battalion had only half of its authorized wartime strength.

Since mid-1968, three US and three South Vietnamese divisions, as well as six brigade-sized units (including the 11th Cavalry) occupied three defensive bands stacked outward from the Saigon-Bien Hoa-Long Binh complex. With the emphasis on interdiction of the flow of supplies and personnel from Cambodia, the enemy forces inside the inner two defensive bands were effectively cut-off. They were on their own. Everything they ate, fired, or medicated had to come from somewhere else—and the list of available "somewhere elses" was getting shorter by the day.

Lieutenant [LT] Ray DeWitt was the 1/11 intelligence officer in early 1970. He knew first-hand about the problems the enemy was having. After interviewing enemy prisoners, he shared some of his observations with the folks back in the States. "[M]y letters home indicate that my impression was that they were "young, scared, and not ready to fight." I recollect being told that they used sticks to practice attacks as the NVA was short of weapons; they were issued weapons only when they were about to enter a fight."

A meaningful measure of the success of General Abrams' strategy of interdicting infiltration and resupply can be found in the enemy's use of the major trail networks flowing south out of his base areas astride the Cambodian border. The trails (from west to east, Mustang Trail, Saigon River Corridor, Serges Jungle Highway, Adams Road, and Jolley Road) were the lifelines for all VC and NVA units located in the area.

By early 1970, all but one of these trails had been virtually closed, permitting only a trickle of supplies and replacements to come south. The interdiction portion of General Abrams' one-war strategy was having a telling effect on the enemy.

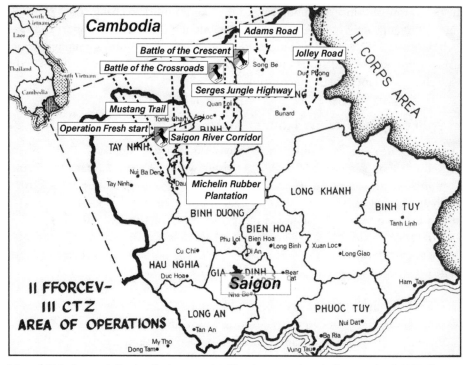

Map of 11th Armored Cavalry Regiment anti-infiltration operations in January–April 1970 (known infiltration routes shown in dotted arrows). (basic map, US Army)

The rest of Abrams' strategy was proving to be just as effective. Under the code name of *Dong Tien* (Forward Together), Blackhorse troopers were working closely with South Vietnamese Army battalions and local militia platoons and companies. Using both hands-on instruction and combined operations, troopers focused on improving their allies' military skills. This training led to more effective pacification efforts and to great strides in Vietnamization of the war. The Communists considered this to be the most effective program of all, describing it as:

> ... a ferocious, savage, destructive enemy [US/South Vietnamese] counter-offensive using combined force, but primarily political force, on the battlefields of the rural countryside. It was a "war to secure control of the civilian population," a "war of destruction" on a massive scale and employing extremely brutal methods that caused us [Communists] great difficulties and tremendous losses ... In this way, they [Saigon] recaptured virtually the entire rural countryside that we had taken during the 1968 Tet Offensive ...

Back in The World, the Pittsburgh Steelers were drafting LSU quarterback Terry Bradshaw as the number one overall pick in the draft. Non-football fans were flocking to theaters to see movies that covered a lot of emotional ground, including *Patton*, *MASH*, *Airport*, and *Love Story*. In Florida, Disney World opened its first facility in

January, while the Boeing 747 made its maiden commercial flight from New York to London. Most consumers were counting pennies as higher costs ate into their pocketbooks. Washington reported inflation at 6.1 percent, the worst in two decades.

The Paris peace talks, not the South Vietnamese battlefields, were capturing headlines at the start of the year. The lack of progress was highlighted by media reports that over 17,191 Americans—including 301 Blackhorse troopers—27,013 South Vietnamese, and 244,778 NVA and VC had been killed during the period between when the talks began on 13 May 1968 and 3 January 1970.

Colonel Donn Starry assumed command of the 11th Cavalry in early December 1969. In his first commander's column in the *Blackhorse* newspaper, he told his troopers what was in store for them in the Vietnamese Year of the Dog (1970). He had just come from the office responsible for planning the drawdown of American forces (working directly for GEN Abrams), so he knew what he was talking about. "First, we can expect US redeployments to continue and to be speeded up. There will be more work for US units remaining—including the Blackhorse ... This means killing more enemy, helping train more RF/PFs [militia], [and] working more with the ARVN ..."

And that's exactly what happened—only not just inside South Vietnam.

Battle of the Crescent

The first opportunity to find the "bastards" and pile on came just 20 days into the new year.

Blackhorse intelligence specialists had been tracking the 7th (NVA) Division for some time. They had first seen elements of the division move into northern Phuoc Long Province in November. Captured documents and prisoner interrogations revealed the division's mission to be reopening Serges Jungle Highway (a major infiltration trail network running south out of Cambodia). In late November and early December, the division launched a number of attacks by fire and limited ground assaults against bases in the Bo Duc area northeast of Quan Loi. They suffered high casualties and were forced to return to Cambodia to regroup. After taking on supplies and replacements and a short period of retraining, the division made final preparations to launch another campaign to reopen the desperately-needed infiltration route.

Air Cavalry Troop, reinforced by 1/11, tangled with elements of the division's 141st Regiment northwest of Loc Ninh in a day-long contact on 27 December. This fight fit the pattern, and commanders were told in early January to expect that Binh Long Province would be a primary target during the upcoming Winter-Spring offensive. That prediction was proven accurate by heavy contacts on 20 and 21 January.

Fire Support Base (FSB) Ruth, just outside of Bo Duc, was built and occupied by 2nd Squadron in early January. Sitting atop a small hill, Ruth was a strong defensive position. The tank turrets and ACAV cupolas were barely visible above the six-foot high berm. Troopers built bunkers with logs and sandbags for themselves and their ammo.

In mid-January, the enemy reappeared in the area in force. Two weeks into the year, agent reports and visual recon detected the presence of a rather sizable enemy force between Loc Ninh and Bu Dop. Ground and aerial scouts detected squad- and company-sized forces moving into the area, with agents reporting groups as large as 500 camped near the border. Airborne sensors confirmed the agent reports. Blackhorse intelligence specialists determined that a regiment of the 5th (VC) Division was relocating into the jungle immediately across the border (still inside Cambodia) north of Bu Dop, while two regiments of the 7th (NVA) Division were moving in north of Loc Ninh.

January 20th opened quietly for 2/11. The command post (CP) and howitzer battery were at FSB Ruth, Golf Troop was set up to provide convoy security along Highway 14A, Hotel Company was preparing to meet up with an airmobile infantry company to recon an area northwest of Bu Dop, and Fox troopers were looking forward to a maintenance standdown at Quan Loi. The first sign of enemy activity came just before 0600 hours, when a Golf Troop ambush patrol reported the sounds of digging and chopping wood about 200 meters from their location. They fired M79 grenades in the direction of the sounds and the noise stopped.

Forty minutes later, the quiet was shattered by a barrage of mortars and rockets aimed at Ruth. As it turned out, the action at Ruth was one of more than 50 attacks-by-fire and six ground assaults against allied bases and installations that same morning—most of them in the Cambodian border region.

At Ruth, about 50 rounds were fired in 15 minutes, most of which landed outside the perimeter. Blackhorse 6 was meeting with Lieutenant Colonel (LTC) Grail Brookshire (the 2/11 commander) at that moment, discussing the upcoming day's activities. They hopped in their respective helicopters and took off.

Brookshire flew to where the aero scout-gunship teams were searching for the source of the indirect fire. He tried an old trick. "I told my right gunner to fire along the treeline and for the pilot to turn sharply as if we had seen something. It worked. A whole bunch of NVA opened up on us." With a hard target now identified, the howitzers at FSB Ruth began firing. The enemy mortar fire stopped (for a while).

Indirect fire hit again about four hours later—this time over 40 rounds, including a number of 120 mm rockets. There was minimal damage and only a few troopers were wounded. Brookshire was in his helicopter and began to receive ground fire about the same time, but was not hit. He asked Thunderhorse aviators to check out the area. A pink team (one scout, one Cobra) responded to the call and flew into the open area south of the treeline known as the Crescent—and directly into the sights of the entrenched enemy. Heavy vegetation hid the well-designed enemy defense on three sides of the Crescent.

This area about six kilometers southwest of Bo Duc and about four from the Cambodian border had earned its name because of the crescent-shaped marshy open space several hundred meters wide and deep bordering the dense jungle. The area was inundated in the rainy season, but was mostly dry in January. A map recon shows that this is the only naturally occurring space for a multi-ship airmobile landing for many miles. The after-action report for the contact on 20 January describes the area. "This is a wild, physically harsh area. Its rolling hills are covered with jungle—single, double, and triple canopy jungle. The huge jungle trees are surrounded with tangled, impassable thickets, and bamboo forests with trees three and four inches thick, yet growing like blades of grass."

In retrospect, it is clear that the enemy was goading the GIs into responding to these contacts. The commander of the 209th (NVA) Regiment knew that the 1st Air Cav was operating in the area, and he expected that they would react in their usual manner. In response to being mortared and a helicopter taking fire, they would undoubtedly send in the helicopters. When the two Air Cav Troop choppers appeared in front of his carefully laid ambush, the NVA commander must have been salivating. Here was a chance to shoot down an American helicopter, almost guaranteeing that a flight of Hueys, each carrying a load of vulnerable infantry, would descend into the open area of the Crescent.

He planned to turn those same mortars and heavy machine guns—along with two reinforced battalions' worth of small arms and RPGs—on the defenseless helicopters and grunts, ensuring a victory for the revolution and glory for himself and his soldiers. The terrain between his carefully-laid ambush and the sanctuary of the border was covered with dense foliage, thus providing ample concealment for his soldiers' escape after the attack.

As Colonel Starry said: "Apparently what they had set up out there, looking at the thing later, was about six or eight .51-caliber anti-aircraft guns trying to entice us to come in and fight them in the crescent with an airmobile operation. They would have wiped us out."

So, the enemy commander gave permission to fire, and the Thunderhorse scout bird was shot down.

There was only one problem. The 7th (NVA) Division failed to inform the 209th commander that in addition to the helicopter-mounted 1st Cav, the area was also occupied by the ACAV- and tank-mounted 11th Armored Cav. Instead of thin-skinned helicopters and dismounted infantrymen, his challenge was answered by a combined arms team of armored vehicles, artillery, and armed helicopters. The tables were turned and the would-be ambushers became the targets. The 209th Regiment did not stand a chance.

Captain (CPT) Bill Paris (radio call sign White 6), the scout platoon leader, was slowly flying his OH-6A light observation helicopter (LOH) in the area where Brookshire had taken fire. Chief Warrant Officer (CWO) Roger Scott, a Huey pilot who wanted to fly scouts, was acting as scout-observer on this mission. Paris describes the action.

> We go down near the [target] box and I start sniffing around. Sure enough, I start cutting trails … It's single- to double-canopy jungle … I'm going along and I'm kind of crabbing. By

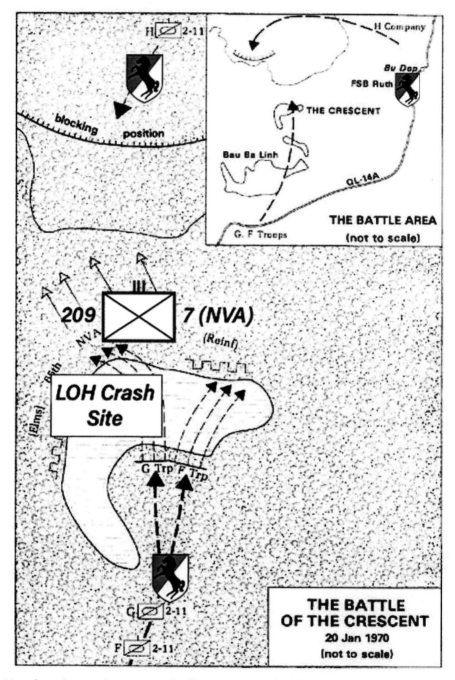

Map of initial enemy dispositions and exfiltration routes and 2nd Squadron attack during the battle of the Crescent on 20 January 1970 (reproduced from the regimental after-action report). (basic map, US Army)

that I mean I'm flying sideways trying to keep this trail in sight that I'm following … All of a sudden, I have never heard this before. I hear more shit. It sounds like there's a roar. It's a roar! I hear the cracking sound, but it's a roar. I mean I'm taking fire like you wouldn't believe … I could hear bullets hitting the blades, the skids, everything … Now, we're on fire … Of course, I'm highly stressed … I said, "We're going to crash. We're not going to make it."

When the LOH crashed, Bill Paris escaped the wreckage by crawling through the broken Plexiglas bubble. He scrambled into a bomb crater. Roger Scott was not so lucky.[4]

CW2 Vito Bubell, the Cobra pilot accompanying Paris, was relatively new in country, but his training took over. He first notified the 2/11 command post of the downed bird, then fired his rockets into the enemy positions. Despite the heavy ground fire, he continued to fly low-level over the Crescent looking for the downed LOH and its crew. Back at Quan Loi, the pilots of the gunship platoon had been listening to the radio as the situation developed. As soon as they heard that one of their own was down, they scrambled.

At this point, it was clear to Brookshire that there was more in the treeline north of the Crescent than just some mortars and a couple of heavy machine guns. He got on the radio and directed the Fox, Golf, and Hotel commanders to ride to the sound of the guns. The tank company, with engineers attached, turned westward along a small trail. Major (MAJ) Fred Franks, the squadron operations officer, was in an OH-6A adjusting artillery and heard his boss' plan

The Golf Troop ACAVs and Sheridans had already begun to outpost Highway 14A (that day's mission), so they assembled on the fly. They moved a short way down the road and then turned north into the jungle at a point that would take them directly into the Crescent. Fox Troop was on Highway 13 just north of Loc Ninh when they got the word. They turned around and retraced their steps to follow Golf Troop in the direction of the growing battle.

First on the scene after Paris and Scott were shot down were Thunderhorse Cobras from Quan Loi. CPT Carl 'Jake' Marshall (the platoon leader, call sign Red 6) was the aircraft commander and Lieutenant (LT) Art Smith, the gunner in the Cobra named "We the People."[5] They flew into the Crescent looking for Paris and Scott. They had been told that the two aviators were probably dead, but Marshall wasn't willing to accept "probably dead" without seeing it with his own eyes. "Part of our psyche [was] that we don't leave anyone behind. We take care of one another … In combat, the guy next to you is your brother. I didn't know how badly he was wounded, but I was going to do all I could to keep him alive."

Red 6 and an accompanying LOH (flown by LT Dave Porter) came in at treetop level doing about 115 knots—low and *fast*. They overflew the crash site twice; Porter reported seeing "just white ash remains of the crash." Marshall says:

> When I got to the point where I thought the crash site was, I snapped the Cobra on its side, peered down and saw the same white ash. No survivors. But as I was righting the Cobra, movement caught my eye. I looked towards the movement and saw Paris waving from the

bomb crater. Imagine the emotional surge of that. Someone who was dead was back alive!!! Without thinking, I keyed my mike and yelled, "He's alive! He's alive!" We were getting very heavy ground fire. With my emotions riding high, in an instantaneous decision, I knew I had to get him out. He was alive, but I didn't think he would be alive long. He had to come out!

Marshall pulled out of the Crescent and briefed his platoon quickly. He was going to mark the target and then go in to land. He could have directed Porter to land his LOH to pick up Paris; it would have made a lot more sense. But Marshall wasn't about to tell someone else to do something he wasn't willing to do himself. "I was the Cobra Platoon Leader ... [M]y intent was to lead by example." Marshall directed the other gunships to focus their fire on the treeline to the north where he had just fired, then radioed: "This is Red 6. I'm going in." He and his gunner had been flying together for some time. He still recalls today that "Smith and I became extraordinarily synergistic in battle. I would think something and he would do it!"

Marshall found a spot where he could hover close to the bomb crater in which Paris had sought refuge. He oriented his aircraft on the enemy-occupied treeline. Smith kept his finger on the minigun trigger as Marshall did left and right pedal turns. As Paris dashed across the bullet-swept ground, Smith popped his canopy. Bill Paris stood on the skid, half-in and half out of the Cobra. Smith recalled: "He jumped up a step on the side of the ship and fell backwards into my lap with one leg hanging over the side. I grabbed him around the neck with my left hand and kept my right on the gun triggers ... We pulled pitch [took off] with my hatch open and the rescued pilot only half in ..." With Paris on board, Jake Marshall lifted off.

Under other circumstances, Jake Marshall and Art Smith might have been court martialed. They attempted to take off with a grossly-overweight aircraft. The Cobra was designed for a two-man crew, no passengers. They undertook aerial flight with the canopy not secured. Regulations said that the gunship shouldn't be flown over 40 knots with the hatch open. Marshall, Smith, and Paris were doing between 80 and 100 knots on the way back to Quan Loi. But the Thunderhorse Safety Officer was willing to overlook these violations, under the circumstances. It was, as Brookshire said, "one of the greatest things I've ever seen." Franks still thinks it was worthy of a Medal of Honor. Marshall received a Distinguished Service Cross and Smith a Silver Star for their gallantry flying into the cauldron of the Crescent, rescuing one of their own.

The NVA commander almost got his wish at this point. According to SOP, the Aero Rifle Platoon loaded onto their Hueys and prepared to air assault into the Crescent to secure the downed helicopter. However, the troop commander (MAJ Charles Abbey) told them to hold tight on the Bu Dop airstrip (a short flight away) until the anti-aircraft machine guns could be suppressed. Bill Paris told his rescuers that he had seen with his own eyes that the treeline above the crash site was full of enemy soldiers and bunkers.

Fred Franks took control of the gathering force while Brookshire's helicopter went to refuel. After an initial firing run against the western edge of the treeline, Franks directed the Cobras to focus on the likely escape routes. He brought the artillery (the 2/11 Howitzer Battery and an ARVN 105 mm battery at Bu Dop) onto the entrenched enemy inside the jungle. Shortly thereafter, the first of 14 Air Force tactical air (TacAir) sorties arrived.

Franks shifted the forces and fires to encircle the 209th Regiment. He recalls the plan: "46 [Hotel Company] to the north, 26 [Fox Troop] and 36 [Golf Troop] from the south, air to the northwest, Cobras to the northeast, HOW Battery and ARVN 105 mm to the east … That's how we set up the attack."

The ground forces continued to move to the increasingly louder sound of the guns. Hotel Company was moving westward from near FSB Ruth, helped along by MAJ Abbey in his helicopter who guided them through the last several hundred meters of jungle into their blocking position. Golf Troop was making its way cross-country through the jungle when they encountered one of the many streams that crisscross the area. Undeterred, the troop commander (CPT Paul Dickenson) jumped from his vehicle and waded across the four-foot deep stream. The ACAVs and Sheridans followed. In the words of the after-action report: "Their speed was remarkable. In one and a half hours G Troop crossed the stream and busted about two kilometers of jungle to reach their objective."

Not to be outdone, Fox Troop was raising clouds of dust as they raced back up the road, following Golf Troop into the heavy vegetation. MAJ Franks guided Golf and Fox Troops through the last bit of jungle. They burst out of the treeline and came on line in the open area of the Crescent—Golf on the right, Fox on the left. The ACAVs and Sheridans opened fire and moved out!

Imagine what was going through the mind of the commander of the 209th (NVA) Regiment as he looked out from his bunker. Instead of the hulks of burning Hueys and the bodies of dying Americans, there were 50 or so armored vehicles blazing away to his front and 17 thundering tanks to his rear. More than 600 earth-shaking artillery shells, 14 TacAir sorties worth of 500-pound bombs, and 20 Cobra sorties worth of 2.75-inch rockets and minigun rained down on his soldiers' heads.[6] Helicopter gunships blocked his intended route of escape.

"What has happened to my carefully-laid ambush?" the enemy commander must have thought. "What else could possibly go wrong?"

The Blackhorse had one more surprise in store for the hapless NVA commander and his soldiers. MAJ Franks called for a short break in the artillery and Cobra fire. The battlefield grew still. The quiet was broken by the sound of a single Huey as it approached from the west. Under the direction of Chuck Abbey (on his second tour with the Blackhorse in Vietnam), the helicopter flew along the northern treeline, while members of the 33rd Chemical Detachment dropped 50-pound tear gas clusters every few seconds. The clusters opened at 100 feet, spraying their eye-watering contents on the dug-in enemy below. The after-action report picks up the story: "They dropped 13 clusters so that they opened and the men inside were preparing for the next run when they heard MAJ Abbey's voice over the radio say, "On the second run, come in just a little lower … no, wait … it's beautiful, they're running all over the place." The NVA, who had stayed in their positions despite the approaching doom, were driven from their bunkers by the tear gas and were running away, panic stricken.

This was the moment that Brookshire had been waiting for, so he unleashed the Furies. Fox and Golf Troops, with ACAVs and Sheridans on line and weapons blazing, executed a cavalry charge across the grassy meadow called the Crescent. MAJ Abbey was overhead in his Huey. "Much excitement is heard on the radio net as armored cavalry men near the crescent's wood line, break out, and CHARGE the far side. One of the most thrilling moments of my career is to observe this action! An honest-to-God mounted cavalry charge in combat! Judging from radio traffic on the command net, everyone feels this 'Charge' spirit."

In the middle of the field, CPT Dickenson radioed "Echelon Right," and his vehicles turned half-right and headed for the right half of the treeline. The Fox Troop commander (CPT Max Bailey) ordered "Echelon Left," and his vehicles mirrored Golf Troop's, heading for the left-most section of the jungle. Hotel Company got ready sitting in its blocking position to the northeast.

Platoon leader Bill Gregory remembers the moment when the first khaki-clad NVA soldiers appeared in an "organized retreat" heading toward the Hotel Company tanks.

> When we got to the blocking position … we were facing a large open area bordered on the other side of the clearing by thick jungle. At first there was nothing—nothing but the purr of Tank and ACAV engines, then we began to take fire from the wood line. I remember seeing tracers coming at my tank from what I believe was a .51-caliber machine gun position … I brought my .50 to bear on the source of the tracers and let go with a couple of 5 to 10 round bursts and the tracers from that spot stopped permanently. Next, the firing continued for a few minutes from both sides, then it intensified and a lot of NVA soldiers tried to advance across the clearing. Some made it further than others but none more than 10 or 20 yards before they were cut down. It is never wise to launch an infantry assault into that many machine guns and 90 mm main guns firing hardball canister rounds at what amounted to point blank range. We could not have missed them if we had tried. Whoever ordered them to advance sent them to a certain death. It did not last long, probably minutes …

MAJ Franks called "End of mission. Well Done." to the artillery. It was now dusk, and the ground units went into their night defensive positions. Second Squadron's annual historical report summed up the action: "The enemy, while expecting and fully primed for an Air Cavalry assault, received instead an Armored Cavalry assault which thoroughly disrupted his intentions and routed him. He limped across his refuge, the Cambodian border …"

One indication of just how soundly the enemy was defeated on 20 January was what he left on the battlefield in his haste to get away. The Communists prided themselves on clearing the area after a fight, not only to ensure that nothing of value was left behind, but also because of the psychological impact on the GIs. After a hard fight, it was disheartening to comb through the just-vacated bunkers and find no evidence of how badly the enemy had been hurt in exchange for however many troopers had been killed or wounded.

It was, therefore, especially gratifying to find that the soldiers of the 209th (NVA) Regiment had left behind the remnants of six .51-caliber machine guns, four 120 mm mortars, and four 82 mm mortars—a good portion of the weapons from the K22 Heavy Weapons and 24th Anti-Aircraft Battalions of the 7th (NVA) Division. Stockpiles of ammunition, strands of commo wire, and lots of individual equipment—including over 600 individual packs filled with food, medicine, and personal items—were recovered from the jungle over the next several days.

Colonel Starry summed it up succinctly when he called it "a perfect cavalry operation …"

On 21 January, Bravo and Charlie Troops tangled with the K1 and K2 Battalions, 141st (NVA) Regiment, less than 20 kilometers away from the Crescent. In a fire-fight called the battle of the Crossroads, the two enemy battalions attempted to ambush the recon troops, but the tables were turned in short order by overwhelming firepower—especially after 2/11 ACAVs and Sheridans and Thunderhorse gunships piled on. As was the case the day before, the NVA were seen scurrying through the jungle to reach the safety of their Cambodian sanctuaries.

The contacts on 20 and 21 January were part of the enemy's attempt to relieve the pressure on their resupply and infiltration operations. Both were abject failures. What was significant about these two battles—other than the fact that the enemy had returned to the battlefield for the first time since suffering severe casualties in August and September—was that the NVA commanders had carefully laid two traps, seeking to engage American forces on ground of their choosing. They had meticulously reconned and selected the terrain, established primary and back-up ambush positions, attempted to lure the helicopters, ACAVs, Sheridans, and tanks into their trap. They were soundly defeated in both instances. First and 2nd Squadrons had each engaged the better parts of an NVA regiment and came away with clear victories. In so doing, the Blackhorse had kept the enemy from reopening his routes of infiltration along Serges Jungle Highway and the Saigon-Michelin Corridor, enabling other US and ARVN forces to strengthen their pacification efforts. Combined, these actions made a significant contribution to accomplishing General Abrams' overall goals for 1970.

This is not to say that the enemy gave up. Far from it. The individual NVA soldiers continued to fight with enormous courage and tenacity. Senior NVA unit leaders continued to achieve tactical surprise through imaginative deployment of their forces and superior camouflage techniques. But, over the course of the first six months of 1970, it became apparent to Blackhorse troopers that the enemy was suffering the effects of the long-lasting war. Mortar rounds aimed at night defensive positions landed outside the perimeter. Gunners launching the new and improved RPG7s missed their intended targets. Long-serving guerrillas surrendered, saying they were tired of suffering the deprivations of life on the run in the jungle. In the face of overwhelming firepower, individuals and units left behind weapons, ammunition, equipment, and the bodies of their comrades as they evaded capture.

Operation Fresh Start

After these battles, there was no let-up in the pressure being applied by the 11th Cavalry and the three brigades of the 1st Air Cav Division as they scoured the border region for the enemy. The Regiment initiated Operation *Fresh Start* at the end of January. It lasted three full months. The objective was to open roads and enemy base areas to ground and aerial observation.

The value of armored cavalry-Rome Plow teams to clear out even the most difficult of the enemy's traditional base areas had been demonstrated throughout 1969. The Regiment was next pointed in the direction of the grandfather of all of the enemy's safe havens—War Zone C—and told to once again work its magic. Three companies of airmobile infantry reinforced the Regiment during the new operation, providing the much-needed infantry boots-on-the-ground to operate with the ACAVs, Sheridans, tanks, and Rome Plows in clearing the jungle, finding supply caches, and rooting the enemy from his base camps.

Donn Starry relates the genesis of Operation *Fresh Start*.

> So successful was the 2d Squadron Bo Duc operation [in December] that it was decided to carve up War Zone "C" with an extensive series of Rome Plow cuts using two squadrons of cavalry and two Rome Plow companies. In February the 1st Squadron (Lieutenant Colonel Jim Reed) moved to Tay Ninh, picked up an engineer-land clearing company and commenced operations north toward the Cambodian border. Once along the border, Colonel Reed turned his forces east and moved to link up with the 2d Squadron which had begun to cut west out of Binh Long Province along the trace of Highway 246. By mid-March both squadrons had made extensive cuts into enemy trail networks in northern War Zone "C": the 1st Squadron across the Mustang Trail, the 2d Squadron across the trail systems leading from Cambodia onto the Saigon River Corridor.

Recognizing the debilitating effect the Rome Plow cuts were having on their infiltration and supply activities, the NVA fought back with mines, hit-and-run ambushes, and indirect fire attacks against night defensive positions and fire support bases. There were a total of 21 contacts during the month of February alone, ranging from automatic ambush detonations (see below) to full-blown contacts with company- and battalion-sized NVA forces. Most of these contacts were enemy-initiated; they resulted from the Communist's fears that their access to the population was being slowly but surely severed. American and South Vietnamese forces had seized the initiative and Hanoi was forced to fight back at a time and place not of its choosing.

Over the course of 90 days, Blackhorse Troopers made the lives of the few VC and NVA remaining between Tay Ninh and the Cambodian border a living hell.

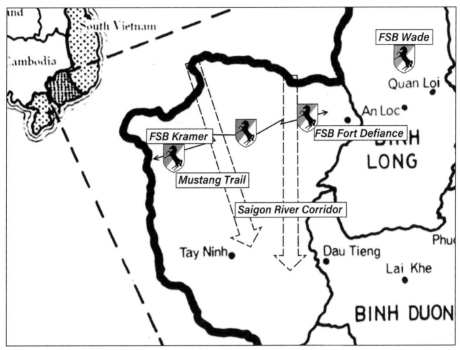

Map of 11th Armored Cavalry Regiment Operation *Fresh Start* in March–April 1970 (known infiltration routes shown in dotted arrows). (basic map, US Army)

Blackhorse 6 placed two squadrons abreast, straddling known enemy infiltration routes. First Squadron occupied an area from the Dog's Head eastward to just short of Ka Tum; 2nd Squadron picked up from there to the Ton Le Chon River.[7] Seventy kilometers from west to east; 70,000 meters is a lot of ground for two armored cavalry squadrons to try and screen—especially in the dense vegetation of northern War Zone C.

But the Blackhorse troopers didn't have to cover every square meter. Months and months of ground and aerial recons in the area by the 11th Cavalry and 1st Cav Division gave them a fairly detailed map of the major infiltration routes used by the enemy. The Mustang Trail and Saigon-Michelin Corridor ran generally north to south through the area. The squadrons established themselves astride these "highways." Recon troops fanned out on a daily basis, looking for evidence of recent usage, as well as caches and any new trails.

On 19 February, 2/11 moved to a new location and assumed the security mission for the Rome Plows along Route 246. As they were moving in, they intercepted a group of NVA soldiers intent on bringing in some much-needed supplies to their comrades further to the south. The operations officer happened to be flying overhead when he saw the enemy porters. Fearful of the helicopter, the NVA soldiers dropped their packs and scattered. The pilot landed and the scout-observer dismounted and killed at least two enemy soldiers (who resisted rather than surrender). He then secured two of the rucksacks. Inside, they found gold—a map of the area, detailing all of the trails being used for infiltration and resupply. This map served as the basis for operations over the next month.

Between early February and the end of April, Blackhorse troopers ranged across the length and breadth of War Zone C, hunting infiltrators, supply caches, and base camps. They employed every weapon available to them, including Rome Plows[8] to open up the enemy's infiltration routes to ground and aerial observation; automatic ambushes to strike fear into the hapless soldiers and porters moving through the dark night; and B-52 Arc Light strikes to destroy enemy hideaways.

For Rome Plow operations, the squadron commander or operations officer would designate the area to be cleared, based on intelligence reports, prisoner debriefings, or the results of aerial reconnaissance. Typically, a recon troop (ACAVs and Sheridans, reinforced with a platoon of infantrymen) provided security for the Rome Plows as they scoured the designated piece of jungle. Most days were long, hot, and boringly repetitive. Some days a plow would hit a mine. Other days, the enemy laid an ambush, hoping to scare the intruders away.

Bill Nash was the Alpha Troop 1st Platoon leader accompanying the Rome Plows on 7 February 1970 during just such an ambush. He recalls: "The cav-infantry-Rome Plow team was great! … The combined arms lesson that I took with me for my entire career started on the 7 February."[9]

French author Bernard Fall called the Rome Plow the "most incredibly impressive" of all the weapons used in the war, more impressive even than massed B-52 strikes. Quite a statement, coming from a man who had been on the Indochina battlefields for well over a decade and had seen it all before. The enemy apparently thought so too.

Saigon-born Tran Minh Dao was a Senior Captain and held a prestigious position in the staff of Sub-Region 1 in Tay Ninh Province. He was captured in mid-1969.

During his interrogation, Tran revealed that of all the tactics being employed against the VC, land clearing operations were the most perplexing. The Communist leadership had directed the main force regiments and battalions to break down into smaller sized units, to train in sapper and guerrilla tactics, and to move only at night in small groups along different trails to avoid detection in the newly cleared areas. These changes were a direct result of the Rome Plow operations. "They hurt the Main Force troops because they eliminate their ability to concentrate," Tran told his captors.

After the Rome Plows had opened up the trail network, Blackhorse troopers went to work interdicting them. But the enemy supply lines were so extensive that manned ambushes alone could not begin to cover them all. Enter CPT Sewell Menzel.

Sewell Menzel, the Golf Troop Commander, was said to be the originator of the automatic ambush—based on ideas from several Golf Troop NCOs. He described it as an economy of force measure: "A small number of troops can dominate a large number of enemy trail networks. They can inflict enormously disproportionate numbers of casualties on the enemy with minimal risk involved."

The automatic (or mechanical) ambush (AA) was one or more claymore mines (or other explosive devices) placed along the side of a trail. A trip wire, connected to a battery, was strung across the trail. In the dark, the trip wire was virtually invisible. When someone tripped the AA, an electrical circuit was completed and the mine(s) detonated

Golf Troop's Sergeant (SGT) Patrick "Destruction Inc." Murphy became his platoon's expert on the automatic ambush. Either the platoon leader or platoon sergeant would give him the general location for his AA, but he would always choose the exact location based on the terrain. He and at least two other troopers would go out near dusk to emplace the device. Sometimes, Murphy would link three to five claymores in tandem, while other times he would rig 30-pound shaped charges (wrapped in barbed wire) and a claymore together. If the AAs did not detonate after a day or two, he insisted on being the one to recover them.

Donn Starry (Blackhorse 6) recalls that the 409th Radio Research Detachment intercepted messages indicating a hard-pressed enemy regiment was going to be resupplied by a large carrying party from the 50th Rear Support Group. The 35-man carrying party ran into an automatic ambush, and they all dropped their 60-pound rucksacks on the spot and headed back to Cambodia. Along the way, they ran into two manned 2/11 ambushes and lost ten killed. According to Starry: "So we felt we had the [enemy] regiment … pretty well cut off and the route pretty well interdicted."

Starry—like his former boss, Abe Abrams—was a big believer in the B-52 as a tactical weapon. Between the scouts, prisoner interrogations, and sensors, the intelligence specialists determined that the NVA were using bicycles to medevac their wounded.[10] The same bicycles were used to bring supplies in and carry wounded out. Starry says: "You'd get these long bicycle convoys going up the trail headed north. They would strap the wounded on the bicycle and there'd be a guy pushing the bicycle."

He recalls one mission during Operation *Fresh Start* in particular. The strike was targeted against a known trail terminus along the Cambodian border. The strike was 45 minutes late. Blackhorse 6 had the authority to move the B-52 box up to one kilometer within 15 minutes of the time on target. He was already in the air in his helicopter when they sighted a convoy of bicycles headed north. He was able to adjust the Arc Light target in time. After the bombers dropped their loads, they flew in to assess the damage.

"My God, you've never seen anything like it," Starry recalled almost four decades later. "Here come the B-52s. Here come the bombs … What a mess! … We dropped the helicopter down to see what was going on. Bicycles hanging in the trees, bodies hanging in the trees."

The Regiment's three-pronged operations had severe consequences for the enemy, and he reacted in a predictable manner. His first attempt used the indirect approach, seeking to force the redeployment of one or both squadrons out of northern War Zone C and away from their vital supply lines and caches. The attempt came in the form of a series of attacks on 3/11 near Loc Ninh, but proved unsuccessful in either disrupting the squadron's operations or in relieving the pressure in War Zone C.

The enemy then shifted his tactics to a more direct approach, attacking throughout northern Tay Ninh Province. These attacks in late March, directed against elements of the Regiment, as well as the 1st Cav Division, culminated in major assaults against 2/11 at Fort Defiance on 9 April and against 1/11 at Fire Support Base Kramer six days later. In both cases, the assaulting forces were unable to penetrate the base perimeter, let alone scare the squadrons off.

The actions at Fort Defiance and Kramer marked the end of Phase One of the NVA/VC Campaign X (Spring-Summer 1970), which had begun on 28 March. The combined efforts of no less than two full NVA divisions, one rear support group, and numerous local VC units failed to deter the Regiment from clearing the cover and concealment so vital to the enemy's infiltration efforts. The enemy fled back across the border into his Cambodian sanctuaries, setting the stage for the cross-border operation that followed less than a month later. The Regiment's after-action report for the period concluded: "The enemy attempt to gain a victory near Loc Ninh failed. In addition, the losses he was suffering in War Zone C would continue to cause his units along the Saigon-Michelin Corridor to starve logistically."

The ultimate success of Abrams' strategy in 1969–70 was in wresting the initiative away from the enemy. At the tactical level, the Communists still chose the time and place for many of the contacts with Blackhorse troopers. But at the operational level, it was the 11th Cavalry and the 1st Cav Division that were dictating both the location and pace of operations. The enemy was no longer able to freely choose a target for his next offensive. Whereas, up through the end of 1968, Hanoi had our forces reacting to attacks across the length and breadth of the corps zone, by early 1970, it was the enemy who was reacting.

Into Cambodia: 1 May to 29 June 1970

The United States and South Vietnamese governments had long contended that Cambodia was serving as a sanctuary for NVA and VC units, headquarters, and supplies—a charge repeatedly and vehemently denied by the Cambodian head of state, Prince Norodom Sihanouk, and Hanoi. The fiction of these denials was proven when western journalists uncovered an enemy base camp four miles inside "neutral" Cambodia in late 1967. The camp, designed to house several hundred personnel, apparently served as a way station for the receipt and forwarding of war supplies into South Vietnam. A carefully engineered corduroy road had numerous signs of recent use by double-axle trucks and ox carts. Well-concealed parking areas for as many as 20 heavy trucks were located next to the road. A well-traveled road through the otherwise undisturbed jungle led from the camp straight to and across the border into northern Binh Long Province near Loc Ninh.

The Communists attempted to deny the report, labeling it as a "slanderous accusation, a vile and shameless threat of aggression," but from this point forward, they knew that we knew. They were confident that no politician in Washington would expand an increasingly unpopular war by systematically violating Cambodia's neutrality in order to do something about the bases. And Prince Sihanouk seemed to understand that publicly taking on Hanoi over this issue was tantamount to political suicide. Besides, by this point in the war, American and South Vietnamese operations had driven the major headquarters, units, and supply bases out of the Iron Triangle and War Zones C and D, forcing them to relocate onto Cambodian territory. The enemy's entire war strategy depended on the inviolability of these sanctuaries.

But in the early part of 1970, the whole house of bamboo began to crumble, opening a door of opportunity for allied forces. A report from II Field Force headquarters describes the situation:

> The abrupt change in the political posture of the Cambodian government, stemming from the removal of Prince Sihanouk as Head of State, and the announced plans of the new government to eliminate the Communist/NVA presence in Cambodia established the framework that permitted the GVN to conduct operations against enemy base areas which had long provided the enemy with a safe haven from which to launch offensive operations and to resupply his forces in the III Military Region.

In late March 1970, the Pentagon authorized the Military Assistance Command Vietnam (MACV) to begin planning for limited cross-border operations in Cambodia. The plan envisioned combined US-South Vietnamese operations in two general areas—the Angel's Wing/Parrot's Beak and the Fishhook areas of the Cambodian border. The initial concept of the operation had a brigade from the 1st Cav Division (reinforced with a mechanized infantry and tank battalion from the 25th Infantry Division), the ARVN Airborne Division, and the 11th Armored Cavalry Regiment attacking into the Fishhook and elements of III (ARVN) Corps into the Angel's Wing/Parrot's Beak area. The objective of these operations would be "the capture or destruction of enemy materiel and facilities." The operations overlay for the attack into the Fishhook prominently identified the Communist headquarters as the primary objective.[11] About 12,000 enemy troops were thought to be in the area—7,000 of whom were directly opposite the Blackhorse.

This plan is significant for two fundamental reasons. First and foremost, the plan divided offensive operations between South Vietnamese and US forces, with ten discrete operations led by the South Vietnamese and only two by GIs (*Toan Thang*

43 and 44). The main attack against the Angel's Wing/Parrot's Beak region of the border (Operation *Toan Thang* 42) was to be carried out almost exclusively by ARVN forces (American advisors accompanied the operation). The inclusion of a brigade of the ARVN Airborne Division in the attack against the Fishhook (*Toan Thang* 43) not only raised the South Vietnamese profile and ownership of the combat operation, it also meant that American and ARVN units would be working together as virtual equals. Dependence on South Vietnamese forces was an integral element of the plan, not only for the cross-border attacks, but also for the areas inside Vietnam vacated by the attacking units—all part of Vietnamization.

The second significant development in this plan was the prominent role assigned to the Blackhorse. In virtually all of the previous multi-divisional operations, the 11th Cavalry's role had been to support one or more of the US infantry divisions. The evolution of the Regiment's reputation from September 1966 to April 1970 was both dramatic and telling. After over four and a half years at war, senior leaders finally took advantage of the full potential of the 600-plus vehicles, 40-plus helicopters, and 4,000-plus troopers with an incredible mix of skills, experience, and courage.

Not everyone was flexible enough to deal with the dramatic change in mission and operational tempo of *Toan Thang* 43. Infantry divisions in fixed installation base camps with long-standing areas of operation (AO), for example. That was not the case for the Blackhorse leadership; as Armor Officers, they had trained for—and dreamed of—this opportunity all of their professional lives. As Donn Starry said: "We're playing Rommel."

This was a mission only the Blackhorse could have accomplished. Only the 11th Cavalry had the mobility, firepower, command and control, and inherent flexibility to move quickly, strike hard, change directions without so much as a pause to regroup, and still have the wherewithal to deal with any and all threats. Airmobile infantry did not have the staying power, air cavalry and tactical air force squadrons could not clear the enemy's jungle strongholds, and divisions were too "comfy" in their assigned AOs to quickly reorganize and refocus their efforts in the middle of an operation. Its size, organization, and leadership (from individual track commander to Blackhorse 6) made the Regiment the ideal tool in the higher commander's toolbox—and the swiftness of the 11th Cavalry's advance took even the forewarned soldiers of the 7th (NVA) Division by surprise.[12]

The enemy knew about the attack earlier than even some of the attacking units. With four days of warning before the first cross-border attack commenced on 29 April, the Communists were able to move some of their more critical elements (such as their main headquarters) and to make some troop adjustments. However, they were able to move only a miniscule portion of the supplies in their massive storage depots (one report estimated the enemy was able to remove only 400–600 tons of ammo before the attack).

How much the enemy knew, and when, was essentially a moot point for the 11th Cavalry. Colonel Donn Starry put it this way: "There is nothing stealthy about an armored cavalry unit ... The management [of the Communist headquarters] probably knew we were coming, but it takes a while for the word to filter down to Private Nguyen over in a bunker in the jungle." PVT Nguyen Xuan Ho, a medic with the 165th Regiment, 7th (NVA) Division, was a case in point. He told his Blackhorse interrogators that "his unit had been issued a warning order on 28 April to be prepared for an attack by ARVN forces in Cambodia although he indicated he was not aware of the impending American participation as well."

The initial concept for the attack into the Fishhook was limited in both scale and duration. II Field Force estimated the operation would last 14 to 30 days. Brigadier General (BG) Robert Shoemaker, the 1st Cav assistant division commander, designated to command the task force (TF Shoemaker) for *Toan Thang* 43, recalls:

> On a Sunday [26 April] ... General [Elvy] Roberts [1st Cav commander] and I were called down to II Field Forces which had a new commander, General Mike Davison ... In his office we talked again about going into the Fishhook area of Cambodia with a force consisting of the 11th Armored Cav, all three squadrons, and a couple of our air mobile brigades. I thought we were talking about a raid into the Fishhook or sometimes called the COSVN base area. I got the very clear impression from General Davison that there was a real possibility that this thing might go. I really didn't believe it ... When we left General Davison's office, he said, "Get prepared. If this operation goes, you'll get 48 hours' notice" ... On Wednesday [29 April] morning, I got a call from Shy Meyer the Cav Chief of Staff. He said, "It's on for Friday [1 May] morning."

The TF Shoemaker ad hoc planning staff did not include any armor or cavalry members. To their credit, however, they got it right. The plan for employment of the two squadrons of the 11th Cavalry was tactically sound, with missions that could be accomplished on the assigned terrain and in the time allocated.[13]

The forces chosen for the initial assault were mobility personified. US airmobile infantrymen and South Vietnamese paratroopers rode helicopters into blocking positions about 20 kilometers inside the Fishhook, then US and ARVN armored cavalry troopers charged across the border aboard their steel (well, OK, most were aluminum) ponies, pushing the enemy into the guns of the waiting infantry and helicopter gunships. Tankers and mechanized infantrymen protected the flanks, ensuring the main thrust was unmolested. Intrepid aerial scouts and gunships screened to the north, inviting the enemy to react. The NVA, with neither helicopters nor ponies of any kind, chose to run rather than fight. They scattered, leaving everything behind—their half-cooked breakfast, their laundry, and their stockpiles of military supplies.

Colonel Starry was notified just four days before the operation kicked off. He was able to tell the squadron commanders, his sergeant major, and a couple of staff officers, but no one else could be let in on the secret until the 29th. He directed 1/11 and 2/11 to cease their current operations and move to the area due south of the Fishhook. Third Squadron was released from working with the 5th (ARVN) Division near Lai Khe and headed north. Everything was done via fragmentary orders, given face-to-face whenever possible. Security was considered a big deal.

The concept of operation called for a limited-objective thrust into the Fishhook area by about 10,000 GIs and ARVN soldiers. BG Shoemaker told Starry "to neutralize the COSVN base area complexes and headquarters." The Regiment was to move north and link up with South Vietnamese forces that had been airlifted in, then "drill out the area." The target area had long been considered to be the heart of the enemy's logistic network for operations in War Zones C and D.

On 1 May, President Nixon announced that the operation would end in 60—not 30—days. BG Shoemaker recalls: "Up until that moment, I thought I was on a raid that would be over in about a week. No one had ever told me that we were going to muck around Cambodia until the end of June, and I was the Commander of the Task Force ..." Starry learned about the 30-mile limit of advance on Armed Forces radio.

> This may sound crazy, but I was sort of headed for Hanoi. I had some Naval War College classmates who were in Hanoi—naval aviators—who were in jail in Hanoi ... It was a long way, that was the only problem. I figured we had about 500 klicks [kilometers] to go. But I think we could have made it ... I thought: "Maybe I can go up the Ho Chi Minh Trail." I think that would have been great fun. So help me, we had an outfit that could have done that ...

On day two of the operation, the 1st (ARVN) Armored Cavalry, which had attacked west from An Loc, linked up with the airborne force. An additional 1st Cav infantry battalion was helicoptered into Cambodia to exploit a cache uncovered as the initial forces swept toward Highway 7. By 5 May, the bulk of the 1st Cav was committed to Operation *Toan Thang* 43. TF Shoemaker was dissolved, the 1st Brigade was thrown into the exploitation, and the 11th Cavalry was given the mission of striking northwards along Highway 7 to the key crossroads of Snuol in order to protect the flank and open Highway 13 for the transportation of captured enemy supplies. At this point, 13 battalions/squadrons were committed to the Fishhook fight.

Behind this brief summary lie the details of one of the Blackhorse Regiment's most significant battlefield accomplishments of the war.

Operation Toan Thang 43

On 28 April, after just 20 hours in a new AO near Bu Dop, the 1st Cav commander flew in to see the 3/11 commander (LTC Bobby Griffin) and told him to pack up and head into War Zone C. He was to rejoin the rest of the Regiment, mission to follow. Griffin thought this unusual and started thinking about what the new mission could be. He "put two-and-two together" and decided there was only one possibility. So, when the convoy reached Lai Khe, Griffin sent his intelligence officer to Saigon to get "400 maps of Cambodia, which, as it turned out, was a goddamn lucky guess."

The squadron arrived in War Zone C in the early morning hours of April 30th. Starry told Griffin about the Cambodia mission late that afternoon. He said that whichever squadron was in the best shape after arriving in the new area of operations would follow 2/11, which was already in position to lead the attack. So, after travelling almost 300 kilometers in less than 48 hours, 3/11 pulled into Fire Support Base (FSB) South II, repaired its vehicles, refueled, resupplied, and reported itself ready to go.

FSB South I (2/11) and South II (1/11) were built just for the Cambodia operation. Well, built is a misnomer; nothing was really built—no berm, no wire, no bunkers. Just two clearings in northern War Zone C selected because they were close to Cambodia. Located just three kilometers south of the border, South I and II contained 24 tubes of 155 mm artillery combined.

Mike Company's top NCO, 1st Sergeant Vernon Nevil, recalled that move almost three decades later.

> It was now the 29th of April, 1970, and we had an all-night road march from Bu Dop to Lai Khe, then on to west of Quan Loi ... Our Executive Officer in "M" Company knew we were coming, and we had a party in the Motor Pool where we resupplied with ammo, fuel, coke and beer. There were ice and clothes plus a lot of questions as to what was going on and why we were going west of Quan Loi again. We moved all day April 30th, and pulled into our parking place for the night. It was here that our Company Commander, Stewart Wallace, informed the unit that we were going to Cambodia the next morning ... and the troops were elated.

For the first time in anyone's memory, the tank and Sheridan crews drew HEAT rounds. High explosive and canister/flechette were the norm, appropriate for personnel and bunkers; High Explosive Anti-Tank rounds were designed to kill other tanks. The intelligence picture was murky; the Blackhorse leadership really didn't know for sure what they would find north of the border. But there had been rumors. Alpha Troop scout Tom Hudspeth believes they were "well inside the border" in Cambodia in March when he saw track marks that "weren't ours. Weren't 48s, weren't Sheridans, weren't ACAVs, weren't M88s." And Special Forces cross-border patrols had also reported hearing tanks and seeing tracks north of Loc Ninh and Bu Dop. So the tankers loaded the anti-tank rounds aboard and dreamed about engaging Communist tanks.

Over in 2/11, it took a while for the word to get down to the platoon level. But, as Hotel Company's 1st platoon leader recalls: "I mean, this wouldn't be some big secret. I mean, nobody told us. But I got suspicious when they assigned a sergeant from the Cambodian Army to my platoon as a scout. I'm going, you know, I mean ... I'm a Tennessee country boy, but I'm not that stupid. So I figured something's up, and so we moved, we kept moving. We moved up closer to the border."

On the 30th, they pulled into FSB South I, but didn't set up for a long stay. Finally, after dark, the Hotel Company commander called his platoon leaders and platoon sergeants together and says: "'Guys, at six o'clock in the morning, we're going into Cambodia in force.' And everybody was kind of like, you know, part of you was glad because we had been wanting to get in there and try to weed these guys out for months."

There was a huge thunderstorm the first night they occupied FSB South I. For those who knew about the plan and were watching the weather, the storm was ominous. For those who hadn't yet been let in on the secret, the thunder, lightning, and burning trees struck by lightning were even more ominous.

Crews checked their weapons one last time, then shifted into overdrive. The waiting was over. As Bobby Griffin remembered: "As you can well imagine, fever was running pretty high. We had no earthly idea what truly existed right across that imaginary border wherever it was … We were very interested in what we were liable to run into … [that] morning."

At 0718 hours on the morning of 1 May, the command net came alive; the preplanned air strikes were finished and it was time to move out. Steady rains had fallen the previous day, but 1 May dawned bright and sunny.

There was no doubt in Blackhorse 6's mind who would lead the attack into Cambodia. Second Squadron, under the leadership team of Grail Brookshire and Fred Franks, was a lean, mean, fighting machine. Donn Starry knew it—and so did the 2/11 troopers.

The line of departure (LD)[14] was the border itself, just a ten-minute drive north of FSB South I—but it really wasn't very distinguishable on the ground. As Specialist 4 (SP4) Charlie Carlson noted: "There was no sign that said: 'Welcome to Cambodia.'" Donn Starry recalled four decades later: "Brookshire said: 'I expect to be hit before the border.' I said: 'Well, since we don't know where the goddamn border is, it doesn't make much difference, does it?'"

In fact, the lead vehicles—Hotel Company tanks reinforced by ACAVs from Golf Troop—were taken under fire before they reached the border. Colonel Starry's ACAV was right behind the Hotel Company commander (LT Miles Sisson) tank.[15] When the RPGs started flying, Regimental Command Sergeant Major Don Horn said: "Maybe we should move." Starry said: "Nah, they'll hit the tanks first." The RPGs all landed short, they were just barely out of range. LTC Brookshire called in air strikes and multiple battalion volleys of artillery.

The fight was on!

The tankers buttoned up, concerned that some of the napalm—barely 150 meters from the lead vehicles—was going to splash up on the tanks. It did. And shrapnel from the 500- and 750-pound bombs pinged off the armor. Right after the last one dropped, Miles Sisson popped out of his turret and dropped to the ground. Starry and others joined him. "We traipsed through several hundred meters of crispy-crunchy dinks hanging on the wire, hanging on the bushes, what not. Napalm on the ground is awesome … Awesome. Spectacle, I guess would be the right word for it."

The rest of Golf and Echo Troops followed the spearhead, available to reinforce either the scouts or continue the attack led by the tanks. Fox Troop, Howitzer Battery, and Headquarters Troop would catch up later. LT David Watters was a forward observer (FO) with Echo Troop that day. He recalls: "[W]hen we first

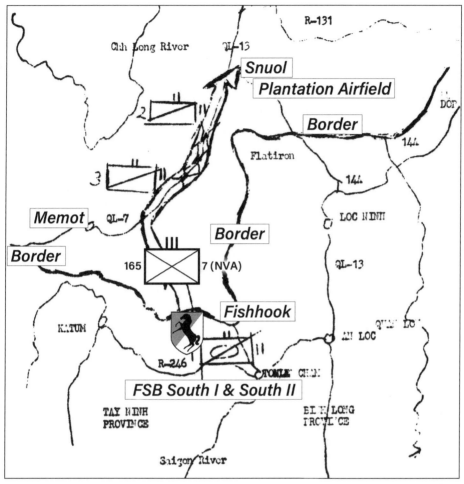

Map of initial enemy dispositions and 11th Armored Cavalry Regiment operations in Cambodia from 1 to 6 May 1970 (reproduced from the regimental after-action report). (basic map, US Army)

entered Cambodia … the only person in E Troop HQ with a map of the area was the CO [commanding officer] who, of course, rode on his own track. I kept thinking 'How can I call in artillery or air support, when I don't have a clue where we are on the ground?'"

Any NVA border watchers still alive were long gone by the time the first Blackhorse vehicles actually crossed the creek marking the boundary between the Republic of Vietnam and the Kingdom of Cambodia. The temperature was already well into the 90s, and the previous night's rain made the humidity almost unbearable.

The terrain was single-canopy jungle and bamboo, interspersed with marshy open areas. Standing water from the previous day's rain, along with huge bomb craters and still-smoking holes from the artillery prep, told the troopers that maneuvering off the trail in case of contact with the enemy would be iffy. So, the tanks, ACAVs, and Sheridans left the hard-packed surface—made so by the feet of thousands of North Vietnamese porters—only when they needed to check out possible ambush and cache sites.

As the lead squadron operations officer, MAJ Fred Franks was responsible for planning the attack. He recalls that the lack of information on where the enemy was and in what strength made things dicey on 1 May. "It was a reconnaissance in force, a movement to contact. We really didn't know what we were going to be up against."

The only enemy soldiers the Blackhorse troopers saw after the initial exchange of fire at the border were either already dead or, as SP5 Dan Atchison recalls, "walking on the roadway and they were dazed, they had no idea what was going on." These NVA soldiers were shell-shock victims of the B-52 strikes and artillery barrages. Hasty interrogation revealed little of tactical value, so they were shuttled to the rear for more intense questioning. As Dan remembers, these soldiers were "certainly not at their best."

Three hours later, the lead elements—following what the troopers called the "pig path"—reached the small Cambodian town of Phum Satum. The place was deserted—no NVA and no civilians in sight. Bunkers, trenches, and spider holes on both sides of the pig path outside of the village made it clear that the enemy had been here. The tanks, Sheridans, and ACAVs proceeded cautiously to the northwest, following a well-used trail with deep ruts made recently by heavy truck traffic.

With dusk approaching (sunset was at 1805 hours that day), LTC Brookshire told his troopers about 1600 hours to look for a place to establish a night defensive position for the night. Three kilometers north of the crossroads, Hotel Company came upon an elliptical open area; a burned-out meadow about 200 meters across. It would be a tight squeeze to get everyone in, but they only expected to be there overnight.

Just as LT Sisson was informing Brookshire of his recommendation, an aero scout flying over the clearing saw an enemy soldier in a trench on the eastern side. Golf Troop's 3rd Platoon maneuvered through the six-foot tall savannah grass and scattered scrub trees in that direction. The platoon leader (LT Frank Cambria) saw several NVA soldiers (from the 141st Regiment, 7th (NVA) Division) in the open, running for cover.

Cambria reported the enemy sighting and began to pursue them. Cambria's request to engage the fleeting targets was denied, however. LT Sisson was maneuvering his tanks to attack the flank of the enemy position, so the Golf Troop ACAVs were told to hold their fire so as to not accidentally hit the flanking M48 tanks. Cambria recalls: "Through the scattered trees ahead, I could see we were closing on a solid dark green wall of jungle. That was when I realized that the communists were "baiting" us into following them towards an ambush site. In approximately the same instant, I ordered my platoon to open fire and the enemy commander did the same."

Riding with the lead element, Blackhorse 6 said the ensuing firefight "looked like the fourth of July."

The NVA focused on what they perceived as the greatest threats—the Sheridans and the command vehicles with multiple antennas. When RPGs knocked out one of Golf Troop's Sheridans, several NVA soldiers broke cover headed for the smoking vehicle. They either intended to turn its guns on the other vehicles, or to steal the weapons and food.

Platoon Leader Cambria and his crew became the focus of enemy fire—RPGs and AK47 rifles alike. All aboard ACAV G-36 were soon wounded, and the platoon medic was killed. Using a combination of one M60 machine gun (fired by gunner SP4 Elwin Dillon with only one usable arm), a .45-cal. pistol (fired left handed by right-handed Cambria), a couple of M16 rifles (fired by driver SP4 Bill Brawn and one-handed by Cambria), hand grenades, tear gas grenades, a thermite grenade, and even hand-held flares launched directly into the enemy-held trench line, the crew of ACAV G-36 held off the NVA until the rest of the troop was able to maneuver into a position to finally gain fire superiority.

The quasi-ambush was over as quickly as it started. As soon as the rest of Golf Troop and the Hotel Company tanks closed on the enemy trench line, the NVA soldiers melted into the jungle. Two Blackhorse troopers were killed in the action.

The first day in Cambodia closed out with 2/11 north and west of Phum Satum, while 3/11 occupied positions on the eastern flank. The combination of adrenalin from the fight, excitement about being in Cambodia, and not knowing what the enemy was up to kept the guards alert that night. LTC Griffin was comforted by the B-52 strikes that were hitting around the squadron night defensive positions. Firepower is a glorious thing, when it's on your side.

The initial contact had not been as difficult as had been expected. SSG Myllin "Henny" Henrich, writing to his parents, reflected what many troopers felt—a mix of bravado and relief.[16]

> By now you have probably tired of hearing of Cambodia with all the riots etc., going on back there because of it. Don't know what all of you think of the move, but for us, although we didn't really want to go, because of the resistance we expected to meet, we sort of accepted it as being an inevitable fact of necessity. The NVA must have figured that we were coming because they just disappeared ahead of us. But then, with the entire 11th ACR driving towards you, I don't reckon that I'd want to stick around myself and fight if I was with them; not to mention all of the air power we had in the form of fighters with everything from napalm to 500 pound bombs.

BG Shoemaker, called the first day "an unbelievable first-class performance of a very complex operation ... [T]he most magnificent job of a real complicated thing I've ever seen."

Movement throughout the first day and over the next two days—after linking up with the ARVN airborne—was slow and deliberate.[17] First, the NVA was expected to defend the base areas tenaciously—at least that's what all of the intelligence analysts had predicted. And second, the orders from TF Shoemaker were to clear the area. These orders had two goals. Everyone was looking for the Communist headquarters, so the idea was to search every village, every bunker, and every hootch thoroughly. Prisoners were closely interrogated, documents carefully screened. Where were the NVA regiments and headquarters staffs and what were they up to?

Everywhere you turned, there were signs of the enemy. Enter a clearing and you were met with thatched huts covering hastily evacuated troop billets, mess halls, and pig pens. Encounter a trail and you found signs in Vietnamese pointing towards depots. Pull up a pineapple plant and lo and behold there was the entrance to a tunnel.

After it became obvious that the enemy had not established an air defense network (as had been initially feared), Air Cav Troop and 1st Cav Division scouts and gunships roamed the skies ahead of the advancing tanks and ACAVs, looking for bad guys and shooting at anything that moved. The lack of the forecasted heavy ground fire was one indicator that the Regiment had achieved tactical surprise. Trucks, bicyclists, and even individuals on the roads and trails, apparently unaware of the ongoing assault, were all fair game for the miniguns and grenade launchers mounted on the helicopters. Some were reminded of the black-and-white films from WWII where Thunderbolt pilots strafed German convoys behind the Normandy beachhead. It was a heady feeling.

The enemy was in disarray, but nobody on the allied side knew the full extent of their confusion. After the fact, captured documents made it clear just how much the armored and airmobile assault had affected them.

The enemy border surveillance force was established in depth, with small detachments—squad-size or smaller—spread along the border trace, mostly belonging to the 165th (NVA) Regiment. Their mission was to determine the location, size, and intention of any force crossing the border, report the information up to the 7th (NVA) Division, delay the attackers with a few quick volleys, and then to disengage and fall back on prepared defensive positions about a kilometer inside Cambodia. The next level of defenses consisted of company positions. The mission of these forces was also primarily to delay any assaulting forces, giving the battalions of the 165th time to gather their strength and occupy prepared defensive positions along the main avenue of attack. That is what happened to 2/11 on 1 May. But after the initial short delay at the border, and a somewhat longer (and intense) delay at Phum Satum, the NVA's defensive cohesion crumbled.

The artillery command (using the cover name of Doan 75) for the entire South Vietnam Liberation Army was located near where the Blackhorse crossed the border into Cambodia. In their official after-action report, the Doan 75 staff wrote:

> In early May, when our activity phase started and the U.S. and Puppets [South Vietnamese] recklessly conducted aggression against K [Cambodian] territory, our Doan did experience

difficulties in leadership and control of its units. This had bad effects on the situation of our depot areas and the ammunition supply efforts of friendly [NVA] forces. On 6 May 70, the Doan Command Post moved to the area north of Route 7 and reestablished contact with BO [probably their higher HQ] which had been interrupted for several days. After officially receiving the order from BO, Doan Headquarters and its subordinate agencies also moved to the same area. Not until 28 May 70 could Doan stabilize the activities of its agencies and units and its command system.

Sifting through the convoluted Communist-style rhetoric and propaganda, it is apparent that the cross-border attack resulted in chaos for the enemy. The highest level headquarters were forced to flee across Highway 7 and establish new bases in unfamiliar and unprepared locations. Command and control was lost between the higher headquarters and their subordinate commanders for about a week, and between the operational headquarters and their subordinate units for almost a month. Resupply operations broke down completely during all of May.[18]

Blackhorse troopers still had a mission to accomplish. For the next two days, troopers used recon-by-fire techniques and lots of dismounted scouting to look for the enemy headquarters and the stockpiles of supplies thought to be in the area. Along the way, they linked up with some Cambodian soldiers who were familiar with the region and acted as local guides.

But new orders arrived on the evening of 3 May, orders that would make any cavalryman smile. Higher headquarters was beginning to realize that the enemy was trying to get away and speed was now of the essence. Forget the base camps and caches (that mission was turned over to the infantry); airborne sensors and other intelligence assets indicated that the enemy was using Highway 7 to escape the ongoing onslaught. TF Shoemaker had two mechanized infantry battalions and two armored cavalry squadrons available to choose from—the choice was obvious.

Blackhorse 6 was told to attack northwest to cut Highway 7 (the main east-west line of communication) at the Memot Rubber Plantation. Once linked up with the 2nd Brigade, 1st Air Cavalry (which had made an airmobile assault into the area on both sides of Memot), Starry was directed to execute a hard, right turn and *Charge!* up the road to capture the important crossroads town of Snuol. The leading elements (2/11, followed by 3/11) were expected to initiate the attack on the morning of the 4th and secure the objective within 48 hours. First Squadron would follow. Air Force and helicopter gunships would secure the flanks.

Now get cracking!

In retrospect, it seems inevitable that someone would have to go to Snuol. Even though the initial plans envisioned a limited advance into Cambodia, the small town—and its airstrip—was just too important to be ignored. As the II Field Force commander, LTG Davison, said in an interview: "Snuol was the center of a road net and it was important to him [the enemy] as well as to us. We had to go there and he had to defend it." Prisoners said that the 141st Regiment was tasked by the 7th (VC) Division to protect both Snuol (1st Battalion) and Memot (2nd and

3rd Battalions). These units were at about 60 percent strength and reinforced with mortars, recoilless rifles, and heavy machine guns from higher headquarters units.

Finally, after almost four years in combat, the 11th Cavalry had a textbook armor mission. Using its inherent mobility and firepower, as well as the demonstrated flexibility and agility of its leaders and troopers, the Blackhorse Regiment was to exploit the confusion and loss of cohesion by charging into the heart of the NVA's rear area, sowing death and destruction as it went.

Over the course of the next 48 hours, TF Shoemaker was dissolved. Major General (MG) Elvy Roberts assumed command of the Fishhook operation as additional infantry battalions were fed into Cambodia to search and clean out the expanding number of supply depots being uncovered.

Although they were aware of the massive anti-war demonstrations, student strikes, and confrontations with National Guard troops starting to sweep across the United States, most Blackhorse troopers were too busy to pay them much attention. They had a job to do, and their lives depended on doing that job well. Success in Cambodia, most thought, would be more likely to end the war and get them home than would students protesting on campus and in the streets. As Colonel Starry said: "We weren't worried about what went on at Kent State; we were worried about Snuol."

Golf Troop led the charge, with Hotel Company close behind. Traveling on an NVA supply trail that (in the words of one participant) "resembled a well-used stateside road," the ACAVs, Sheridans, and tanks moved north. Minesweep teams were not used, applying the logic that the NVA would not mine their own trails (no mines were encountered). Besides, there was no time to lose. Many troopers found the terrain similar to that in the An Loc-Quan Loi area, much more open than the dense jungles of War Zone C. Red dirt topped with thin tracts of jungle, broken up by larger open areas with barkless white-trunked trees spaced up to 30 meters apart. Tall mahogany trees bordered fields covered with elephant grass. Craters from B-52 strikes pockmarked the countryside—some a day or two old, others months old.

As they approached Memot, they found orderly rows of rubber trees with small, neat villages of 30 to 40 huts where the plantation workers lived. Unlike in South Vietnam, bamboo thickets had been cleared here, making cross-country travel and line of sight/fire much easier. Things got especially complicated, however, when a combination of curious onlookers, refugees escaping the fighting, and exfiltrating Cambodian and NVA soldiers crowded the highway and the trails leading to it.

Memot itself was an anachronism for the jungle-hardened troopers. Thomas Hudspeth describes the scene: "The buildings were white, and the people were neat and clean. There were little businesses … There were these Frenchmen in Citroens with the most beautiful Cambodian wives you've ever seen, running Michelin rubber plantations. Huge, *huge* pineapple plantations. You've got to be kidding me, man. This doesn't look like a war zone. But it was."

An NVA battalion put up a brief fight outside of Memot, but air strikes quickly reduced the rubber factory in which they were holed up to rubble. Upon reaching the main road, the 2/11 tracks did a right pivot and headed toward Snuol. The terrain along Highway 7 became increasingly hilly. The fact that there were no mines was one more indicator of just how disorganized the enemy forces were. The troopers were happy about that.

This was about the only possible avenue of advance towards the key crossroads, but the 7th (NVA) Division was unable to establish any ambushes or roadblocks. And, since it would be obvious to the enemy commander where the column was headed, speed was of the essence. The Blackhorse vehicles reached speeds of up to 35 mph along the way to Snuol.

Franks and Brookshire realized there was some risk associated with the open flanks, but because of the theretofore light casualties and apparent disorganization of the enemy, they both concluded "it was worth the risk." Besides, 3/11 was right behind them, in position to react to whatever might be lurking on the side of the road. Speed was the order of the day.

Platoon leader Bill Gregory remembers that attack well. "H Company moved over to the main highway [Highway 7], an honest to God blacktop road and moved toward Snuol—fast! This was probably the most fun I had in Vietnam; a tank company flat out on the road moving to the objective! It was like something out of a World War II movie with Third Army's tanks moving toward Berlin!"

In one of the war's many ironies, Blackhorse troopers were listening to the Beatles sing "Let It Be" over Armed Forces Radio as they zipped up their flak vests and moved toward Snuol.

> And when the night is cloudy, there is still a light that shines on me, shine until tomorrow, let it be. Let it be, let it be …

Air Cav Troop scouts had checked out Highway 7 the previous day and identified three bridges destroyed by NVA sappers in an attempt to slow down the cavalry charge. The scouts thought that the first two chasms could be spanned by armored vehicle launched bridges (AVLBs) (they were right), but the third site would require something more substantial. The plan was simple, but daring. Members of the Aero Rifle Platoon (ARPs) were inserted into the site shortly after daybreak on the 5th, followed quickly by engineers from the 8th and 31st Engineer Battalions. A small bulldozer and a Class 60 M4T6 bridge (38-feet long) were airlifted by Flying Cranes into the position, and the engineers went to work.

Despite the engineers' best efforts, it soon became obvious that the bridge would not be completed until late in the afternoon. So Golf 6 was ordered to try and find a ford or an AVLB site.[19] The Golf Troopers found something 150 meters west of the destroyed bridge, and by shortly before 1300 hours, both Golf and Echo Troops had crossed the AVLB and were prepared to push on. Hotel Company was close behind. There were but inches to spare on both banks, but the AVLB remained in place long enough for first the ACAVs, then the M48 tanks to cross. The 48-hour deadline imposed by higher headquarters was fast approaching.

By this time, 2/11's column stretched 20 kilometers back down Highway 7. Echo Troop was followed by Fox, with the headquarters and Howitzer Battery in trail. In fact, the howitzers were so far down the road that they could not support the assault on Snuol. MAJ Franks landed his LOH at a 1st Cav position south of Snuol, occupied by the 1st Battalion, 5th Cavalry and a 105 mm towed howitzer battery. As luck would have it, the battalion commander—LTC Jim Anderson—had been Franks' upperclassman platoon leader during Beast Barracks at West Point. Anderson quickly agreed to "turn over his artillery" in direct support of 2/11.

The enemy planned to halt or at least slow down the armored column that was fast approaching. The 7th (NVA) Division's antiaircraft company was assigned the mission of establishing an ambush along Highway 7. However, according to a captured member of that company, his comrades "fled into the surrounding jungles when they heard the tanks moving up the highway."

Because of the information garnered from that captive soldier and some civilian refugees, LTC Brookshire knew that the NVA expected him to come straight up Highway 7 into the heart of Snuol. So, that's where the 141st (NVA) regimental commander set up his strong points and cut an anti-tank trench across the hard-surfaced road, waiting to ambush the arrogant Americans in their armored vehicles. But Brookshire fooled his counterpart from North Vietnam.

About four kilometers southwest of the edge of the town, aero scouts located a trail that bordered the rubber plantation. The trail ran east and then north, terminating at the grass airstrip built and used by the French plantation owner.[20] Thunderhorse scouts, dodging heavy .51-caliber anti-aircraft fire, confirmed that the town was occupied and well defended—as was the airstrip. As in the battle of the Crescent (20 January), the NVA was again expecting an airmobile assault.

The plan of attack had Echo, Fox, and Golf Troops, reinforced with Hotel Company tanks, move in column (but with flank security amongst the rubber trees) along the trail. As they approached the landing strip and plantation mansion, the ACAVs, Sheridans, and tanks would peel off to attack the NVA dug-in inside the town from the east flank, not the south as they had expected. Brookshire told his subordinate commanders: "Now, if we can get around these fuckers, we might have them bottled up down in this end of the rubber. They figure us to come right up Highway 7 ... We can always come up through the rubber through this draw. If you have to start knockin' down rubber trees, they go down easy."

Hotel Company's 1st platoon led the flanking maneuver. As they broke out of the trees, they saw the airfield and white-washed buildings of the plantation. Bill Gregory recalls:

> [W]e came across a plantation ... And you've got these five tanks surrounding the place ... I mean, it was beautiful. And this guy came out, a Frenchman and he was speaking in, in broken English ... He had his arms full of fresh pineapples and he says, "Great American Liberators. It's so wonderful that you're here" ... And he comes up to our vehicles and he's cutting these pineapples and giving us pineapple to eat. You know, fresh pineapple and it was good pineapple.

When Grail Brookshire talked with the plantation manager, he confirmed that the enemy indeed intended to fight. According to Jacques Louat de Bort,[21] who had managed the 12,500-acre *Société de Plantation de Kratie* for several years, the NVA attacked and defeated the Cambodian garrison on 22 April. After US troops crossed the border and headed toward Snuol, they told the Cambodian civilians "to leave Snuol because there would be a fight. They had intended to defend their position …" The 141st Regiment was thought to have up to 3,000 soldiers—three-to-one odds over 2/11.

De Bort told Brookshire that the NVA armed most of his 1,600 plantation workers as well. "They gave guns to the people and now they are fighting with the Viet Cong," he said. He went on. "The North Vietnamese were very impressive … They were well equipped and gave an impression of extraordinary mobility." Second Squadron was in for a fight.

Brookshire deployed his forces, telling them to work outwards from the plantation and search the surrounding villages for enemy forces and supply caches. Echo Troop was the first to make contact, running into dug-in NVA inside Snuol. This is how SP4 John Cody, a *Stars and Stripes* reporter riding with Echo Troop, reported the battle:

> This is a large, scattered town of neat, thatched houses and attractive stone buildings. Cambodians on the road as we came up told us there were 1,000 to 3,000 Communist soldiers in town and three ambush positions. When our 25 assault vehicles (ACAVs) and Sheridans rolled into the southern edge of town Tuesday [5 May] afternoon past the post office there were bullets from automatic weapons whizzing all over … A rocket-propelled grenade hit one of the Sheridans. All our vehicles had stopped and opened fire on the town. It was total noise, total din.

The center of resistance was in the schoolyard, where NVA soldiers had used earth moving equipment "liberated" from the plantation to dig bunkers and trenches in the backyards of the houses and along the streets. They engaged the approaching armor with mortars, RPGs, recoilless rifles, .51-caliber anti-aircraft and 7.62 mm machine guns, and AK47s. Troopers closed the Sheridans and ACAV hatches (buttoned-up) as shrapnel from the bombs and expended minigun casings from F4s and Cobras pinged against the armor. At times, 2.75-inch rockets from the gunships impacted within 20 meters of the lead vehicles.

An RPG struck the lead Sheridan just on the edge of the marketplace. Troopers exchanged fire with the dug-in NVA until another RPG struck the same Sheridan. Echo Troop pulled back. Brookshire recalls: "In Snuol, one of the Sheridans was hit and on fire, and the crew bailed out. I saw that it was still running, and the fire was out, so went back in with H Company to get it. That's when I called in the air strikes."

Memories of street fights against a determined enemy during Tet '68 were fresh enough to allow the guys with the really big bullets (USAF) to have first crack at the bad guys. *New York Times* reporter James Sterba listened in to the operations order briefing between the squadron and troop commanders. He made a recording, so we know his exact words. Brookshire told his subordinate commanders before the battle:

This is a reconnaissance in force to find out what's in there and also, if possible, to take the town—without destroying it … Now, if you take fire, return it. If you take heavy fire and you look like you've got prepared positions, back 'em out—shoot and back out. Shoot like a sonofabitch and back 'em out. Get 'em back out, and then we're just gonna have to start preppin' it [with airstrikes] or else we're gonna have to bypass it … If you're taking light fire and there are civilians in the area, try to return the fire without losing all the fuckin' civilians.

After strikes by Air Force F-4 Phantoms and F-100 Super Sabres, Hotel Company passed through Echo Troop and the combined M48-Sheridan-ACAV force moved past the burning gas station and the destroyed houses, overrunning the NVA strongpoint and clearing Snuol. Several other short-lived contacts were made while moving through the built-up area, but friendly casualties were light. The NVA, on the other hand, lost over a hundred soldiers—and the vital crossroads—during the encounter.

The biggest loss of the day, however, was back near the airstrip, where a determined NVA soldier tossed a hand grenade out of a bunker, severely wounding eight Blackhorse troopers.

Things were very fluid at the plantation airfield. In typical Blackhorse fashion, troops, platoons, and individual tracks were reacting to the evolving tactical situation. As it turned out, Blackhorse 6 in his ACAV "quite inadvertently" as he remembers, led the assault against several gun pits of the anti-aircraft unit ringing the airstrip. After Hotel Company and Echo Troop had overwhelmed the machine gun crews, they dismounted to take prisoners and clear one last bunker. Colonel Donn Starry and his sergeant major, Don Horn, led their crew in the dismounted attack.

As this was unfolding, MAJ Franks landed his helicopter and joined Starry on the ground. Franks recalls: "We were quite anxious to talk to the NVA we had captured and some more that were in the bunker, so I landed the helicopter …" It really would be good if they knew how many NVA were defending the town.

The South Vietnamese interpreter questioned the prisoner about where the rest of the units were, but he, according to Franks, "either didn't know anything or wasn't saying. Time was of the essence, so I started to get back in the helicopter … Somebody called: "Hey, Major, there are two more over here."" Franks was helping one of the troopers on the ground to move a log when the enemy soldier inside the bunker tossed out a grenade. Fred Franks didn't even see it.

Fortunately, Donn Starry did. Before the grenade exploded, Starry pushed Franks to the ground. He described what happened. "We almost ran into a gun pit with our track (armored personnel carrier) during the attack on the airfield … The sergeant major, myself and the crew dismounted, captured the gun and the people in the pit. But about that time someone threw a grenade at us from another nearby bunker."

At such close range, the grenade was very effective. Fred Franks was severely wounded (he would lose part of his leg eventually). Seven others, including Starry, were also wounded. When it happened, Starry did not have his flak jacket on—a big no-no in the Blackhorse since he had taken command. Four decades later, he said: "The Regimental Commander violated his own goddamn rule, and he paid the price for it." Starry, Franks, and the six other troopers were medevaced. Franks was the most seriously wounded of all.

The battle for Snuol went on without them.

Dusk was quickly approaching as the lead vehicles fought their way back into town. In the fading light, the tracks backed out to the outskirts and deployed into night defensive positions. Several vehicles were damaged during the fight. A dozen wounded troopers were treated; most were returned to duty that night.

Occasional contacts around Snuol with small groups of retreating NVA soldiers lasted until well after dark. There was no moon that night, so everyone was especially watchful. It was obvious that the NVA—from individuals to groups of three to four—were trying to get north of Highway 7 and escape beyond the 30-kilometer limit announced by President Nixon in his TV speech to the nation.[22] Some of them made it, but many did not.

After a PSYOPS broadcast by the civil affairs officer, MAJ Rudy Holbrook at 0800 hours on the 6th, 2/11 reentered Snuol from the south. Tanks, Sheridans, and ACAVs—this time reinforced with grunts on the ground—moved into the town center, ready for a fight. Too many times the troopers had seen the NVA emerge from their bunkers after being pounded by artillery and air strikes.

The troopers found trenches and spider holes and the remnants of a hurried retreat, but no live NVA soldiers. Only four of the town's 2,000 residents had remained in town during the fight, and their bodies were found where they were struck down in the street. The enemy had taken their casualties with them when they pulled out. The troopers found burning gas and oil cans behind the town's only Shell gas station. The station itself was a shambles, with gas pumps leaning left and right from a near miss.

While 2/1 was engaged inside Snuol, 3/11 was sweeping up the remnants of various NVA units that had been by-passed during the attack up Highway 7. With the help of gunships and artillery, 3rd Squadron troopers engaged numerous small bands of enemy from the tip of the "Flatiron" to areas northwest of the third blown bridge site. India Troop found the NVA ambush that had been intended for 2/11, but by that time the soldiers of the 141st (NVA) Regiment were only willing to fire a couple of volleys and fall back. Within about 15 minutes it was all over and the India Troop ACAVs and Sheridans, accompanied by Mike Company tanks, rolled up the highway and into the outskirts of Snuol.

The reporters who accompanied the Blackhorse troopers up Highway 7 wrote glowingly—almost admiringly—about the hastily-planned, violently-executed operation. It reminded some of the heady days of WWII, with phrases like "lightning armored thrust" and "50-mile dash" describing the move, and "determined North Vietnamese resistance" and "making their stand" recounting the enemy's actions.[23]

The 1st Cav Division's public information officer wrote: "Barney Seibert, veteran Saigon UPI correspondent, offered this comment on the use of armor in Cambodia: 'Almost every newsman in the world would like to know who planned the brilliant thrust into Cambodia. But one thing is certain—the planner knew when and how to successfully employ armor. This was the one new factor introduced in that phase of the war. Armor did magnificently well. It made the difference between success and failure on the ground.'"

It had been a "lightning advance" into the unknown. Accurate intelligence was hard to come by in the fast-moving attack. So, the Blackhorse troopers remained vigilant, prepared for anything. They accomplished the mission with minimal casualties. The enemy fled, his vital supply lines now in friendly hands.

Over the course of the next seven-plus weeks, Blackhorse troopers scoured the Cambodian countryside for the booty left behind when the NVA abandoned their depots. All three squadrons were, for the most part, under the command of Blackhorse 6—a rare occurrence.[24]

By the end of May, seven 11th Cavalry troopers had been killed inside Cambodia. But the Regiment had accomplished its mission—and then some. Two enemy divisions were in total disarray, unable to coordinate a successful defense or mount a counter-attack. The screen of Blackhorse armor protected the northern and eastern flanks, as grunts, engineers, explosive ordnance disposal (EOD) specialists, truck drivers, and platoons of VIPs and photographers scoured the jungle and cleaned out the shelves of the NVA's massive warehouses—including "The City," "Rock Island East," and "Shakey's Hill."[25]

June saw the Blackhorse troopers conducting operations similar to what they had done on a daily basis for the previous four years of combat. The squadrons occupied a series of temporary bases named Iowa, North Dakota, Sisson, Sabre, Hammerstone, Susan, and Carlson until the surrounding areas had been thoroughly checked. Troops conducted daily recons throughout the Fishhook and the Flatiron areas of the border region, looking for bad guys and their caches. Some swept the roads for mines and escorted the daily convoys on Highway 13, while others provided security to engineer work parties. Rome Plows cleared vegetation around NVA base camps and cache sites, as Sheridans and ACAVs provided overwatch. For his part, the enemy also reverted to his old habits with frequent mines, sniper fire, and hit-and-run RPG attacks.

From 1 June onward, everyone counted the days toward President Nixon's self-imposed deadline of 30 June. Then everybody went "home" to South Vietnam.

And what a homecoming it was. As the ACAVs, Sheridans, M48s, and all the other vehicles of the Regiment rolled by, the 25th Infantry Division band played. Gathered on the roadside were three Donut Dollies passing out cold sodas and winning smiles. ABC had a reporter and cameraman on the scene as a Kilo Troop ACAV passed, adorned with shaving cream writing on the gun shield ("K Trp, First In") and on the side "11 ACR." The troopers showed a mix of emotions as they rumbled by—smiles for having made it, grimaces for the lucky GIs clustered around the round-eyed women, and weariness for all they had endured.

One unnamed trooper was quoted in the Blackhorse newspaper as saying: "I feel a lot safer now that I'm in Vietnam."

Valorous Unit Citation: 1 May to 29 June 1970

The cross-border operation into Cambodia "to crush Communist sanctuaries" reminded many of WWII. The similarities to free-wheeling armored operations in Europe were no more evident than in the initial mission assigned to the Blackhorse: punch through the enemy's covering force along the border, link up with airborne forces dropped behind enemy lines, make a forward passage of lines, and then bypass any resistance in a headlong advance to a suspected strongpoint in a built up area deep inside enemy territory. Once the objective had been seized, provide flank security for the Corps. Classic armor missions executed to perfection by the Army's premier armored cavalry regiment.

Just as the ground elements of the Blackhorse Regiment accomplished several traditional armored cavalry missions during the Cambodia operation, so too did Air Cavalry Troop. In addition to their by-now standard role of conducting aerial recon of potential enemy locations and the terrain, the LOHs and Cobras conducted a vital screening mission out to the 30-mile limit imposed by President Nixon. Scout-gunship teams deployed on a daily basis searching for any signs that the enemy had recovered from his initial disorganization and was moving forces into position for an assault on the airmobile infantry and engineers engaged in evacuating the captured enemy equipment, food, and supplies. The ARPs were inserted on numerous occasions to uncover caches, secure downed birds, and check out potential hot spots.

Troopers of the 11th Cavalry reflected on what they had accomplished over the past two months. While the 1st Cav got the lion's share of the publicity cleaning out "The City" and "Rock Island East," Blackhorse troopers and their ARVN airborne allies slugged it out against NVA soldiers, thick jungle, and monsoon rains. The *LA Times'* Jack Foisie captured it well when he wrote on the day the last trooper left Cambodia: "Although their actions were little publicized, the ARVN airborne units and the American 11th Armored Regiment had the hardest fighting of any outfit after the allies invaded the enemy sanctuaries in Cambodia's eastern provinces."

Inevitably, those who were not there pose the question: Was it all worth it? Was the violation of a supposedly "neutral" country's border worth the social and political backlash from inside and outside America? Was the "expansion" of the war (though how the Allies were "expanding" the war by entering an area long occupied by the enemy remains an unanswered question) justifiable at a time when the Communists appeared to be getting serious about a negotiated settlement, and at a time when American citizens appeared to be focused more on "bringing the boys home" than they were on "peace with honor"?

SP5 Jim Leatherwood, a door gunner in Air Cavalry Troop, may have captured the feeling of most Blackhorse troopers in a letter to his hometown newspaper. "When my troop went into Cambodia, we were a little scared, but we were also glad to be able to go in and clean up the Communist strongholds in our assigned area. We've often chased Communist soldiers till they crossed the border and then we became helpless till they decided to strike again. President Nixon's campaign changed that."

Droves of military historians and political analysts have offered their opinions on these issues since shortly after the first troops crossed the border into Cambodia. But for most troopers who were there, the statistics resulting from their work—and what that meant in terms of effects on the bad guys they would meet on future battlefields—were the most important answer.

In the end, American and South Vietnamese troops who took part in the Cambodia operation racked up an impressive score in things that mattered:

- We killed, captured, or induced to surrender almost 9,000 enemy soldiers (380 by the 11th Cavalry).
- We captured enough individual weapons in two months to equip 74 full-strength NVA battalions and enough crew-served weapons to equip 25 battalions of Hanoi's finest. That meant there would be fewer NVA soldiers and VC guerrillas with rifles and machine guns shooting at us.
- We captured enough ammunition to supply all NVA and VC units in Military Regions II, III, and IV for 16 months. Of special interest to the Blackhorse were the 140,000-plus RPGs, mortar and recoilless rifle rounds, and almost 5,500 mines that were captured. That meant that even those enemy soldiers who did have weapons would not be quite so liberal with the number of bullets—including the big bullets—they fired. Not so many mines would be found "the hard way"
- We captured 14 million pounds of rice—enough to feed all enemy personnel in South Vietnam for four whole months, or the three enemy divisions facing the Blackhorse for a full year. A hungry NVA soldier was certainly less effective than one with a full stomach.

The commander of II Field Force, the man who gave the 11th Cavalry its missions during the Cambodia operation, believed that all these captured and destroyed supplies would affect the enemy in three ways. First, it would take the Communists months (if not years) and great amounts of resources (people and supplies) to replace the lost weapons, ammunition, and food.[26] Second, command and control was severely disrupted. The main enemy headquarters itself had to move, dispersed in the jungle and out of communications with its subordinate units. Moreover, Blackhorse troopers, along with the other US and South Vietnamese soldiers, had uncovered virtually all of the infiltration and resupply routes leading out of Cambodia; some were Rome plowed, others mined, the rest placed under routine surveillance. As a result, it would take a long time for the enemy to establish new trail networks, while the NVA and VC inside South Vietnam were on their own.

Finally, even the most fervent Communist ideologue had to be having second thoughts about their "inevitable" victory. The NVA had been thrashed, their stockpiles ransacked, and their communications disrupted. The effect on the morale of troops far from home fighting a seemingly endless war was predictable.

What did the enemy think? What was their opinion about the effectiveness of the cross-border operation? A 2005 history published in Hanoi gives us the answer.

> COSVN Military Headquarters issued a number of specific, detailed instructions regarding protecting our logistics facilities in the border area, but because of the massive enemy attacks we suffered heavy losses of our logistics resources: we lost one-third of our rice reserve stockpile, and we also lost 700 tons of weapons and ammunition, 60 tons of medicine and medical supplies, and 80 percent of our transportation equipment.

But the more lasting effect of the operation inside Cambodia was on the NVA itself, both officers and soldiers. No longer were they "safe" inside their Cambodian sanctuaries. Commanders at all levels now had to develop security plans, not just against aerial observation, but against the possibility of renewed ground and artillery attacks. Even though the United States was winding down its participation in the war, the South Vietnamese continued to operate inside Cambodia for the next two years. The "highways" that NVA engineers had opened between the Cambodia base areas and the units deployed forward inside South Vietnam were found, and many were closed permanently. Along the others, the tolls became so high as to be debilitating in terms of supplies lost and the morale of those tasked to travel southward.

In fact, the lowering of enemy morale may have been the biggest effect of all during the operations in May and June 1970. NVA Lieutenant Colonel Nguyen Van Nang was the deputy commander of Sub-Region 2 (SR-2), located in Tay Ninh Province. On 20 May, he decided that he had had enough of living in the jungle and defected to the South Vietnamese government. The story he told was of plans waylaid, orders disobeyed, and loyalties betrayed. He spoke of "an already harsh life … [becoming] cruel and hard."

The former SR-2 deputy commander then described the effects of the allied attacks on those who had not been killed or captured. According to him, even before the cross-border attacks began, the alert that an attack was expected caused about one-third of the personnel assigned to SR-2 to "openly agitate about returning home" to North Vietnam. He estimated that 800 "men refused to fight, including six battalion commanders and four company commanders."

In the long term, the efforts of Blackhorse troopers in Cambodia helped to shorten the Regiment's time in country. Reducing the combat effectiveness of the VC and NVA forces substantially reduced the threat to Saigon and the surrounding population and economic centers. The reduced enemy presence and influence in the countryside enhanced stability and strengthened the South Vietnamese government's hold on the people. The men in ARVN units that fought in Cambodia came back better, more confident soldiers.

Their morale soared. They had beaten the NVA in every battle, on his turf, and stolen his supplies. Senior South Vietnamese commanders learned to operate large formations in the field for extended periods of time. The essential premise of Vietnamization was that as South Vietnamese security forces improved and "normalcy" returned to the rice paddies and rubber plantations, ARVN units would replace American units on the frontlines. Success in Cambodia led to the replacement of the 11th Cavalry on the frontier by the end of 1970 and let the entire Regiment come home by early 1972.

Colonel Donn Starry summarized his feelings about Cambodia and the Regiment's part in it.

> We made ourselves a little history this past month … We got into his base areas and now we've set his operations back at least six months. Possibly even longer. But it wasn't easy, and the fact that we did so well is proof of the fact that everyone was up tight and ready to fight. We've done what the President set out for us to do, and done it well. No one can ask more than that. So, for those of us who were there, the Cambodian operation is our little piece of history that we made, and no one can ever take from us. I'm proud to say again—Well done Blackhorse!

During its 59 days inside Cambodia, the Regiment did what no other unit assigned to MACV could have done. Using their organic mobility, firepower, and communications, Blackhorse troopers took and held ground that was critical to the job of uncovering and clearing the massive storehouses of weapons, ammunition, food, medicine, and other war-making materials stockpiled by the NVA over a full decade. The First Team and Tropic Lightning found those jungle warehouses—and got all the headlines. But it was the 11th Cavalry that held Routes 4 and 7 and 13 open. It was the 11th Cavalry that held the 7th (NVA) Division at bay, preventing it from executing their assigned interdiction mission. It was the 11th Cavalry that secured the Rome Plows and engineer bridges and heavy road-making equipment until all of the war booty could be transported south. And, it was the 11th Cavalry that screened the withdrawing US and ARVN forces.

The cost for the Regiment was high—14 Blackhorse troopers were killed and 74 were wounded in the last week in Cambodia alone. Overall, 40 troopers died while operating on Cambodian soil—just over five percent of the 730 who died serving their Nation in the 11th Cavalry between September 1966 and April 1972. Another 322 were wounded in action. Their sacrifice contributed to allowing their brothers to come home, as the South Vietnamese assumed a greater combat role and the Regiment stood down.

These actions earned the troopers of the 11th Armored Cavalry Regiment another Valorous Unit Award.

Standing Down: January to March 1971

The Regiment was notified on 20 December 1970 that 1st, 3rd, and Provisional Squadrons would leave Vietnam less than three months later. Second Squadron (minus Hotel Company, which would redeploy with the rest of the Regiment), Air Cavalry Troop (reinforced with direct support aircraft and avionics maintenance support), a platoon of the 919th Engineers, and a platoon of the 37th Medical Company were to continue the fight against the 33rd (NVA) Regiment in Binh Tuy Province, under the operational control (OPCON) of the 3rd Brigade, 1st Cav Division.

There were good reasons to select 2/11 to carry on the Blackhorse legacy in Vietnam. The squadron had recently completed a thorough maintenance and personnel standdown and was, therefore, in good shape. Lieutenant Colonel (LTC) John Ballantyne, the 2/11 commander, had the longest of the three squadron commanders still to serve in command. Finally, the squadron already was working with the 1st Cav, so command relationships were well established and functioning.

First Squadron said farewell to the 274th (NVA) Regiment and began its final standdown at Di An base camp on 1 February 1971. Third Squadron gave the one-finger salute to the Regiment's long-time nemesis, the Dong Nai Regiment, closing Di An to begin its standdown one week later. In accordance with the regimental plan, both squadrons engaged in combat operations until the day they left the field.

Standdown was a busy time for all. Since only a representational colors detail would redeploy to the States, personnel were reassigned to 2/11 (which was brought up to 100-plus percent strength for the first time in anyone's memory), infused into other units still in country, or got the good news that they would be going back to The World early (up to 60 days early!)—maybe even accompanied by an early out from the Army. There were plenty of volunteers to stay on in country, so the 2/11 leadership had its pick of troopers. As John Sherman Crow recalls: "We had a lot of guys volunteer to stay with Second Squadron ... Too many volunteers. All ranks ... They loved the Regiment ... There's something unique about the Blackhorse."

End-of-tour awards were prepared and processed, efficiency reports were written, and pay records were reviewed and updated. Every trooper was briefed on the service of the Regiment—and their individual troops, companies, and batteries—in Vietnam and the meaning of wearing the Blackhorse patch on the right shoulder.[27] Each departing trooper received the thanks he so richly deserved. Di An base camp was unlike anything most troopers had seen. Special Services bands played three nights a week, movies were shown every night (three a night when a band wasn't playing), the pool was open, mini-golf, horseshoes, volleyball, basketball, baseball, and flag football were available to burn off energy, the post exchange was open for business, and the clubs were open late.

Tom Molino remembers Christmas 1970 as a memorable one.

I was given the mission of being the Officer in Charge (OIC) of a couple of Chinooks full of troopers flying into Long Binh to attend the Bob Hope USO Show. First Lieutenant Al Bumbry was my assistant—Al was a great lieutenant and I approved his early release that spring so he could attend training with the Baltimore Orioles … When we entered, I was aghast at the number of folks packed into the stadium—a mortar round would have killed hundreds. We wouldn't let troopers get in a crowded chow line and here were thousands packed shoulder-to-shoulder. I don't remember much about the show itself except it closed with everyone on their feet singing "Silent Night" in the 90+ degree heat of the mid-day sun. There wasn't a dry eye in the place.

All regimental equipment had to be accounted for, transferred to 2/11, or turned in. Everything—tanks, helicopters, rifles, ammo, radios, lawn mowers, stoves, generators, pillows, desks, etc. The top priority was to make 2nd Squadron as healthy as possible. The regimental operations officer recalls: "The major mission was to commission Second Squadron with the best, low-mileage equipment we had in the other two squadrons." The same was true for stockpiles of weapons, repair parts, tools, and maintenance equipment.

Prior to turn in, all equipment had to be prepared—pre-washed at the two Di An wash racks, tools cleaned and boxed, and log books reconciled before the road march to Long Binh. The wash-down of vehicles and equipment was done to prevent "exotic" (i.e., invasive) species of animal and plant life from being transported back to the US.

The turn-in and disinfection of vehicles required extensive—and exhaustive—efforts on the part of vehicle crews, unit maintenance sections, and the teams of experts who helped. The dirt, mud, dust and all manner of detritus from the areas that had accumulated on and in vehicles of 11th during five years of operations had to go.

India Troop Executive Officer, LT Jim Bartlett, recalls how some items were accounted for:

Every day, our Supply Sergeant prepared inventory cards for items to turn in … some were there, some were not. I needed about 100 or so metal army bunk beds to turn in. Probably had half that. We used to take 20 beds to Long Binh, off load into the pile, but load 10 beds back on the truck and explain to gate guard that we did not have paperwork for them. We continued this shell game until we had all beds accounted for. They were just going on a scrap heap anyway.

The bottom line—over 3,000 troopers were out-processed by the time standdown was complete. The squadron and regimental logistics sections turned in 523 wheeled and 420 tracked vehicles, over 4,600 weapons, and almost 40,000 other items of equipment collected by the Regiment since September 1966. And, oh by the way, it was Tet, so the 93 perimeter towers and bunkers had to be manned day and night until the South Vietnamese took over the Di An base camp late in the standdown period.

Those troopers departing and those remaining had shared so much together over the past months—mud and dust, red ants, bad chow (or no chow), RPGs, mines, jokes, and the loss of fellow troopers. They were more than just friends. They were brothers. They all made promises to keep in touch, but who knew. California and Michigan and Texas were so far away from Pennsylvania.

In the 5 March 1971 ceremony closing out the Regiment's first four-plus years' service in Vietnam, Colonel Wally Nutting, who had just taken command in December and was the last Blackhorse 6 in Vietnam, summarized the accomplishments of the Blackhorse troopers.

> As the Blackhorse Regiment takes leave after 1,639 days of combat in Vietnam and Cambodia, we salute the 24,421 officers and troopers who have served so faithfully and valorously. To those who have fallen, we owe an unpayable debt. To the many who have fought beside the Blackhorse and supported the Regiment, we thank you. We do not say farewell, for the spirit of the Blackhorse Regiment remains with the 2d Squadron, 11th Armored Cavalry Regiment. Allons!

The "spirit of the Blackhorse Regiment" wasn't the only thing that stayed with 2nd Squadron. The National Colors and Regimental Standard remained in Vietnam as long as Blackhorse troopers served there.

CHAPTER 7

Mission Accomplished:
November 1970 to March 1972

Vietnam remains in the 1970s, as it was in the 1960s, a focus of US interests, energies, and resources.

CONGRESSMAN LESTER WOLFF

We heard the 1st & 3rd [Squadrons] were going home and we believed we were screwed.

PATRICK MURPHY, GOLF TROOP, 2/11 CAVALRY

How would you like to fight a war without getting anyone killed?

UNNAMED PENTAGON SPOKESMAN

Congressman Lester Wolff, a member of the House of Representatives Committee on Foreign Affairs, visited Asia on behalf of the committee in early 1971 to obtain an on-the-ground view of what and how we were doing in that part of the world. Although his report of the visit to Vietnam started with a statement about the war-torn country still being a focus of American interests, the rhetoric quickly turned political.

> While US search and destroy missions in Vietnam are all but ended, and while the Congress has prohibited the use of US ground forces in Cambodia and Laos, it would be incorrect to assume that we have therefore effectively deescalated the war. We may make the US role more one of air support and less one of direct ground combat involvement, but there is precious little evidence that US disengagement—of the kind now receiving majority support in every public opinion poll here at home—is really close.

The report concluded: "Despite the great sacrifices the United States has made in South Vietnam, the South Vietnamese Government continues to ignore our interests and wishes in much that it does. And it often times appears that our own officials are as disinterested in true US interests as are the South Vietnamese."

The view from Military Assistance Command Vietnam headquarters was, not surprisingly, quite different. The official MACV history for 1971 starts out with two statements that are at the opposite end of the reality spectrum from Congressman Wolff. "The Republic of Vietnam today," the history states, "is markedly different from the Vietnam of earlier years." In every sector—military, political, diplomatic, economic, humanitarian, and administrative—US and Free World Forces had, according to the MACV history, achieved remarkable success. Foremost amongst the accomplishments stood the two premier US Government policy objectives. "The process of Vietnamization has largely been achieved, and the withdrawal of US forces is well underway." Rather than ignoring Washington's "interests and wishes," it was Saigon's forces—not GIs—who were now doing the bulk of the fighting.

Thanks to General Abram's overall strategy and the effective Allied operations in Cambodia, Hanoi's main focus had shifted from the battlefield to the negotiating table, where they hoped to win the war through political, diplomatic, and public opinion means. The VC were decimated; virtually all enemy units in Military Region (MR) III were composed of soldiers recruited and trained in North Vietnam. The battlegrounds chosen by the Communists starting in mid-1969 and continuing through the end of 1971 were the villages and hamlets of rural South Vietnam (as opposed to the major cities targeted in 1968). Counter-pacification was, according to captured documents, the main effort for 1971. The Communists also needed to recoup their personnel and equipment losses from the previous two and a half years, so attacks by fire and limited ground assaults against isolated territorial outposts replaced the multi-battalion attacks of the past.

Continued withdrawal of American servicemen resulted in a mere 2 and 2/3 division-equivalents remaining in all of South Vietnam by mid-1971—less than had been deployed around Saigon alone when the Blackhorse arrived five years earlier. Only 7,500 GIs in five maneuver battalions (plus support) were assigned to MR 3.[1] The brass called the operational strategy for the remaining GIs "dynamic defense." Blackhorse troopers called it combat. It still required finding the "bastards" and piling on—only with far fewer resources for both the finding and the piling.

The primary mission of 11th Cavalry troopers throughout the remainder of their service in Vietnam was to clear areas that could be used by the NVA as secure base areas, as well as to conduct combined operations with South Vietnamese security forces to enhance their professionalism. This mission evolved from the overall military mission contained in the 1971 Combined Campaign Plan. "Combined operations stressed mobility and interdiction of enemy LOC [lines of communication]. Specifically, military forces were to conduct sustained, coordinated, and combined mobile operations against VC/NVA forces, base areas [BAs], and logistical systems in RVN [Republic of Vietnam]." These operations were designed to isolate the enemy's main force units in areas away from the population, to destroy them piecemeal, and to enable indigenous security forces to eliminate the VC infrastructure in the villages and hamlets. Armored cavalry was the ideal force for this mission—they could move anywhere quickly and survive anything the Communists had left.

Within the context of the continued withdrawal of American forces and the political need to keep GI casualties to a minimum, 2/11's organization and equipment was well-suited for this economy of force role. Two of the enemy's most prominent base areas—BA 302 along the Long Khanh-Binh Tuy Province boundary and BA 355 along the Saigon River Corridor near the Ho Bo and Boi Loi Woods—were the primary areas of operation for 2nd Squadron troopers in 1971. Two NVA main force regiments, the 33rd in BA 302 and the 101st in BA 355, became targets for the Blackhorse ACAVs, Sheridans, howitzers, mortars, and gunships.

Staff Sergeant (SSG) Daniel Wilson was just starting his third tour in Vietnam when he joined Fox Troop in August 1971. All three tours were in the same area— with the 25th Infantry Division in '66–'67 and with 1st Squadron's Delta Company in '70. He was in a unique position to judge how much the war had changed.

Blackhorse troopers, Wilson realized, were still trying to "find the bastards" during their last year in Vietnam, but there were a lot more restrictions on what they could do to accomplish that mission. For example, there were fewer free fire zones on his second tour with the Regiment than on his first. This did not go down well with the troops. Wilson recalls: "That was the spooky part, because they'd [enemy] stand out there and shoot at you, and technically you weren't supposed to shoot back. A lot of us didn't like that. There might have been some instances where we shot first and *then* called [for permission to shoot]."

SSG Gene Johnson noticed some differences as well when he returned to Echo Troop in late 1970. He had already done one tour with the troop in 1967 and he started noticing changes as soon as he arrived at Long Binh. "They were threatening people at the 90th Replacement Battalion who didn't follow orders to be assigned to the 11th Cav ... Obviously, the 11th Cav had acquired quite a reputation as a combat unit. Being aggressive about finding the enemy and running his ass down ... Combat-wise, my second tour was much more active than my first tour."

But Gene "detected that the Vietnamese people had lost the will to continue the fight. They were at the point where they didn't care who won. They just wanted it to be over. And the morale among the [American] soldiers was at rock bottom ... Nobody wanted to be the last guy to die in Vietnam ... It was hard to keep people motivated." What did get people motivated was "the enemy. And we had a lot of them."

Carrying On: Late 1970 to Early 1971

In March 1971, 2/11 (minus Hotel Company), along with Air Cavalry Troop (reinforced with detachments from the 398th Transportation (Aviation Maintenance) and 124th Avionics), engineers (919th Engineer Company), and medical personnel (37th Medical Company), assumed responsibility for representing 70 years of Blackhorse tradition.

They proved themselves well qualified to assume this role.

Starting in the closing months of 1970, as the rest of the Regiment was focused on getting ready to redeploy to The World, the troopers under the command of LTC John Ballantyne were focused on clearing the two provinces east of Saigon. They were deployed there to provide the airmobile grunts with additional firepower as they battled the 33rd (NVA) Regiment for the harvest in the rice-rich area of eastern Long Khanh and western Binh Tuy Provinces (the so-called "rice bowl"). Simultaneously, the GIs were there to strengthen the South Vietnamese government's pacification efforts, a prime Communist target.

The squadron was working for the 3rd Brigade Task Force, 1st Cav Division.[2] The brigade had been shifted from the Cambodian border area as part of the program of Vietnamization, replacing the departing 199th Light Infantry Brigade east of Saigon. The task force was charged with eliminating enemy forces, keeping the enemy from using the Dong Nai River, destroying his base areas, and interdicting the flow of replacements and supplies into Long Khanh and Binh Tuy Provinces.

The Blackhorse returned to those two provinces that they had known all too well earlier in the war. By the fall of 1968, the provinces had been considered "pacified" and turned over to ARVN. In the intervening years, however, enemy units had filtered back into the area. Blackhorse ACAVs, Sheridans, howitzers, and helicopters were once again in demand, so 2/11 deployed to eastern Long Khanh on 9 September 1970. They immediately began constructing Fire Support Base (FSB) Bolen.[3] The enemy consisted of the regimental headquarters (including ten combat and combat

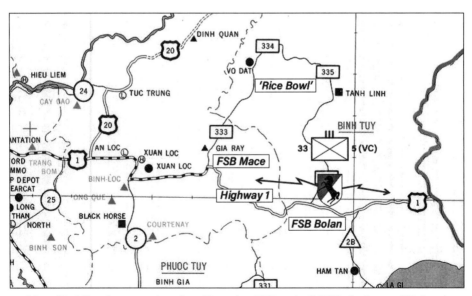

Map of 2nd Squadron operations from November 1970 to April 1971. (basic map, US Army)

support companies) and the 1st Battalion of the 33rd (NVA) Regiment, thought to be holed up in the vicinity of Nui Ong Mountain. These units mustered around 1,300 soldiers total in the fall of 1970. The Australians, who had been fighting the 33rd for over a year, considered it to be "the most effective NVA Regiment ... [A] seasoned and battle-hardened force to be reckoned with."

Six months later, after tangling with the Blackhorse and the 1st Air Cav grunts, the 33rd was down to about 400 soldiers.

Second Squadron established a recon screen north of Nui Ong, generally along Highway 1 southeast of Xuan Loc. Fox Troop made the first contact in the new area of operations three days after the screen was initiated, beginning a running battle with the NVA. The 33rd Regiment was gradually forced to relocate to the Nui Chua Chan area—a location known as Signal Mountain. The running fight lasted into early 1971.

As the enemy units moved to avoid contact, so too did 2/11. The squadron moved to FSB Mace, a large 1st Cav base on the east side of Nui Chua Chan Mountain, late in 1970. Staff Sergeant (SSG) Ken Smith was on his second tour with the Blackhorse when 2/11 made the trek back to the area around Xuan Loc. He recalls that he was "one of few" who knew his way around from his first tour.

The location of FSB Mace (near the old Gia Ray rock quarry) was a real problem; more problematic was a lack of understanding by the 1st Cav leadership as to how to employ 2/11. Ken Smith recalls that the airmobile infantrymen "didn't have a clue what to do with armored cav ... They expected us to do things that just didn't work. Like, "Can you climb this hill and rescue one of my platoons that's in contact?" Jungle, all the way up the hill. At night. *Sure*, and we would lose all the vehicles trying to get up the hill from thrown tracks and everything else."

But the 2/11 troopers found a way nonetheless. For example, they successfully employed automatic ambushes (AA) against the NVA, inflicting casualties and disrupting the enemy's nighttime resupply activities. During November 1970, Fox Troop was remarkably successful while emplacing AAs along suspected enemy resupply and infiltration trails. Over one 11-day period, a total of 16 VC/NVA were killed by these booby traps, all without any friendly casualties. Because the interdiction operations were so successful, especially the AAs, the NVA started using dogs. The intelligence specialists determined that the enemy was afraid to use the trails, so they used dogs to find the claymores and tripwires.

Simultaneously, Air Cav Troop was in high demand. The troop was one of only five air cavalry troops left in the area around Saigon. Although technically under the command and control of the 2nd Squadron commander, Air Cav Troop's primary mission was support to the South Vietnamese.

But Thunderhorse aviators never forgot which patch they were wearing, and when 2/11 said they needed support, they found a way to provide it. Thus, while gunships and scouts flew into Cambodia on a daily basis supporting the ARVN divisions as they fought hard to hold the NVA at bay, both command and control (C&C) birds and Cobra/LOH teams were virtually always overhead (or on call) as Echo, Fox, and Golf Troops roamed their piece of Long Khanh and Binh Tuy Provinces.

The operations of the 3rd Brigade Task Force and 2/11 east of Saigon in late 1970 and early 1971 successfully countered the enemy's plans in the area. Not only was the 33rd (NVA) Regiment's intended attack against Xuan Loc stymied before it could get started, the decimated regiment was forced to retreat into its most secure jungle base camps. The rice harvest went on unabated, with most of it going to feed the South Vietnamese people—not the enemy. The situation had stabilized sufficiently by the end of the first quarter of 1971 to allow the redeployment of 2/11 back into Hau Nghia and Tay Ninh Provinces, where the 101st (NVA) Regiment was threatening Saigon.

Once again, Blackhorse troopers were serving as the commander's fire brigade. The role the entire 11th Cavalry had played for II Field Force in 1969 and 1970, 2/11 was now playing in 1971 for Third Regional Assistance Command (TRAC).

Clearing Out the Nests: April to August 1971

Back in The World, the latest fashion rage was hot pants and boots—a welcome distraction from the seemingly constant negative news from the anti-war movement, publication of the *Pentagon Papers*, reports of increased drug use within the United States (including alarming numbers of GIs returning from Southeast Asia with heroin habits), the death of The Doors' lead singer and counter-culture icon Jim Morrison, and charges of American war crimes highlighted by the conviction of LT William Calley for the massacre at My Lai.

In Hau Nghia Province, South Vietnam, no one was wearing hot pants and boots. The US 25th Infantry Division stood down in early 1971. The 25th (ARVN) Infantry Division took sole responsibility for the area of operations (AO). The work of clearing the Ho Bo and Boi Loi Woods—long-time enemy redoubts—went on. The area had been previously cleared by Rome Plows, but the secondary growth was inexorably reclaiming the land. Infiltration trails were no longer visible from the air, so the land clearing engineers were sent back in. Two Rome Plow companies (one American, one South Vietnamese) razed the jungle astride the Saigon River Corridor in big bites, day-in and day-out. However, the ARVN company assigned to provide security had neither the mobility, nor the firepower to accomplish their assigned mission.

Both land clearing companies sustained heavy casualties in men and materiel. LTC John Ballantyne, the 2/11 commander, recalled that the US plow company was taking losses, while their ARVN counterparts refused to leave the motor pool and continue the mission.[4]

That's when they called in the Blackhorse.

Second Squadron moved in just north of Trang Bang and established (with the help of the 919th Engineers) Fire Support Base (FSB) Warrior at the intersection of Highway 1 and the road to Tay Ninh in mid-April 1971. Two 8-inch artillery pieces joined 2/11 from TRAC. They were soon put to good use.[5] In a harbinger of things to come, the column came under sniper fire almost as soon as it left the highway en route to set up the new FSB.

The Boi Loi Woods had been an enemy stronghold for as long as anyone could remember. The French tried to establish a rubber plantation there in the 1930s, but gave up due to staunch resistance by local Viet Minh. Early in the 1960s, elite South Vietnamese forces (rangers and airborne) tried several times to clear the area of guerrillas, only to have their noses bloodied on each occasion. They gave up. US forces, primarily the 25th Infantry Division, repeatedly attacked the woods with every weapon in the arsenal—dismounted infantry, ACAVs, tanks, mortars and artillery, helicopter gunships, tear gas, Rome Plows, napalm, incendiary bombs, Agent Orange, and B-52s. All to no avail. Charlie just waited a while and came back to reoccupy or rebuild his bunkers, tunnels, and caches. After a few months, he would then launch new attacks from the friendly confines of the Boi Loi Woods.

Map of 2nd Squadron operations in the Ho Bo and Boi Loi Woods in 1971. (basic map, US Army)

The plan was to use Rome Plows to cut wide swaths of the jungle vegetation away, thus denying the enemy refuge from aerial and ground observation. For the South Vietnamese government, the operation had an additional, quite significant goal. Ever since the enemy had occupied the Ho Bo and Boi Loi Woods, the surrounding land had lain fallow; the peasants would not work the rice paddies because they knew the enemy soldiers would come and tax them, kidnap their sons, and sow mines that killed as many civilians as they did soldiers. Saigon wanted the area cleared so that the peasants would return and strengthen the economy.

The NVA and residual VC in the area were not expected to just allow this to happen without a fight. These expectations were met—and exceeded—in the next 60 days.

Initially, 2/11 was OPCON to the 25th (ARVN) Infantry Division. Just as 1/11 and 3/11 had experienced in 1968 when they were in direct support of the same division in Hau Nghia, there were lots of growing pains associated with this command relationship. LTC Ballantyne recalls that the Vietnamese didn't understand how to employ armored cavalry. There were "misunderstandings on the part of the ARVN of what our strengths and capabilities were. They overestimated our ability to send troops out here, there, and everywhere."

Ballantyne finally went to Major General (MG) Jack Wagstaff (TRAC Senior Advisor) and said: "Us being OPCON to the 25th ARVN is not working. We need to work out an arrangement where we'll work with them; they've got an area, we've got an area, and we won't get in each other's hair." Wagstaff worked his magic, and 2/11 was assigned its own AO. In addition, the two Rome Plow companies and the ARVN recon company were placed OPCON to Ballantyne, who now reported directly to Wagstaff. "That worked just fine," according to Ballantyne.

The standard operating procedure (SOP) established by 2/11 was to have a recon troop with each of the Rome Plow companies and one securing FSB Warrior. Ballantyne describes how things worked on a daily basis. "I selected the areas day by day to be cleared and assigned the troops to run the mission. Troop commanders were then in charge. We never divulged each day's mission to the ARVN or RF [militia] commanders until early morning of each day's mission [security measure]. On those occasions where the 25th ARVN or the Province C.O. [commanding officer] gave the squadron OPCON of their infantry companies, those units were a big help."

As expected, the enemy didn't just fade away. The first toe-to-toe engagement came early—and was repeated often.

After spending a night together at Di An (2/11's rear area), Echo and Fox Troops moved out on 16 April to conduct an initial recon in the new area of operations. Three casualties resulted from mines and booby traps, so the troopers were especially alert the next day as they sought to gain first-hand knowledge of the terrain and the enemy. Entering the southern edge of the Boi Loi Woods, Captain (CPT) James Kelley set his two Fox Troop platoons in an echelon left formation, a diagonal arrangement that provides maximum firepower to both the front and to the left side where any enemy forces might be hiding. Kelley recalls that "there was nothing but low grass on our right flank with a very slight rise. On our left flank was a wall of low shrub 3 to 5 feet high … Any contact would have come from that flank as there was no real cover and concealment on the right side … We stopped the column because we had come across a tended garden right next to the shrub line."

Suddenly, two Vietnamese in light blue uniforms popped up and disappeared into the woods. Sergeant (SGT) Wayne Watts, commander of Sheridan F-25, saw them. "I was looking through my binoculars and saw an NVA regular soldier standing in the center of the hedge row motioning for us to come on in. I called Lt. [Phillip] Lee [2nd Platoon leader] and advised that we had NVA on the left. (To this day, I can still see that NVA pith helmet and the star with the round circle on it.) We immediately traversed to the left and got on line for an assault."

Soon after entering the wooded area, the platoon came under an intense barrage of automatic weapons fire and RPGs from the 3rd Battalion, 101st (NVA) Regiment. First a Sheridan and then LT Lee's ACAV were hit by RPGs, knocking both vehicles out of action. The RPG that hit his ACAV wounded Lee—but didn't kill him.

SGT Allen Burnworth was the thumper (M79 grenade launcher) gunner on the rear deck of the Sheridan (F-28) that was hit first. He was pumping rounds into the bamboo hedgerow when he saw it. "I happened to look over to the left and I saw something fly out of the shrapnel vest of Lieutenant Lee. At that point, it was slow motion … It took a moment for me to realize that he'd just been shot and that was the bullet that came out the back." The bullet had cut across Lee's shoulder blades and severed his spinal cord.[6]

CPT Kelley looked in LT Lee's direction and saw

> … he was slumped over his .50-cal. [machine gun]. I couldn't figure out what had happened. I leaped off my track and bounded up the side of his. In hindsight I probably shouldn't have done that as I left my commo … I couldn't leave him unprotected in the open. I dragged/carried him to a defilade spot where the medics were calling me. He was unconscious the whole time, but I didn't know why … I got back on my track and got the platoons on line to assault. Then everything cut loose. Within minutes I was hit by AK-47 fire. (A spent bullet stuck in my hand). My left elbow was shattered and I lost use of my left arm and hand. I tried to contact Lt [Thomas] Christian [3rd platoon leader] to take over command.

The crew of Sheridan F-28 fired over a dozen main gun rounds—152 mm flechette—in quick succession, but then had to wait for compressed air to build back up before they could fire again. The delay proved deadly. While waiting, they were hit by an RPG. Ken Smith recalls that the RPG hit "right over the top of the driver's hatch and underneath the gun [the ideal aiming point]. I mean, this guy must have been an expert, right?" The heat from the blast welded the driver's hatch shut.

Smoke started billowing out of the turret. At least one main gun round ignited and flames came out of both turret hatches. F-28 "rocked back like it had shot three rounds at one time," according to Burnworth. Platoon Sergeant (PSG) Rudolf Beck came out of the turret and said in his German accent: "'Get the hell out of here.' He didn't have to tell me twice, because it was on fire." The driver couldn't escape, however.

Specialist 5 (SP5) Tony "Doc" Balas was everywhere that day, attending to LT Lee and the others on his ACAV, then moving to help Beck and his crew. Despite the withering enemy fire, Doc Balas saved five lives on that Boi Loi Woods battlefield on 17 April 1971.

CPT Kelley's ACAV was hit by at least one RPG. Clearly, the NVA gunners had listened to their instructors and were aiming for the vehicles with two antennas, the sign of a command vehicle (Kelley and Lee's ACAVs and Beck's Sheridan). This left LT Christian in command; he ordered the troop to withdraw, leaving the three damaged vehicles behind. By this time, it was obvious that the troopers had found a numerically superior, well dug-in enemy force and it made sense to let the artillery and gunships pound such a position before assaulting it again. Besides, there were a number of casualties that need to be evacuated and there was the command arrangement to get sorted out. CPT Floyd McGough, flying the 2/11 C&C bird, made the first of his ten landings to evacuate the most severely wounded.

The question of overall command was settled when MAJ Don Borden (2/11 operations officer) landed and took command of the troops on the ground. After evacuating the wounded, Borden led five ACAVs in a direct assault on the enemy bunkers, as the rest of Fox Troop attacked from the flank. The objective of this assault was to retrieve the damaged vehicles and recover anyone who was still alive. However, in the words of an after-action report, the "enemy held its fire until the assaulting vehicles were within fifty meters of their position, then once again laid down a heavy volley of RPD [machine gun], RPG and AK47 fire. As he reached a position twenty meters short of the disabled Sheridan, Maj. Borden came under intense RPG fire and his vehicle was hit. Immediately, the vehicle began to burn."

Despite the heavy fire, Fox Troopers were able to hook tow cables to the two damaged ACAVs and haul them out of the contact area. Borden switched to another ACAV and pulled everyone back to allow the artillery (air strikes were not available at the time) and gunships to work over the enemy fortifications again.

Three times, the howitzers and helicopter gunships blasted the target area, and three times the ACAVS and Sheridans of Fox Troop, reinforced by two platoons from Echo Troop, assaulted the NVA bunkers. The 2/11 Howitzer Battery alone fired more than 200 rounds into that small piece of Vietnamese real estate. Finally, on the third assault, the two Echo Troop platoons broke through the line of bunkers and swept across the objective. CPT Tom Gray, the Echo Troop commander, told his two platoons to establish blocking positions on the far side of the bunkers, while Fox Troop covered a third side and helicopter gunships completed the fourth side of the box.

The enemy, now completely surrounded, fought on with RPGs and AKs, so Gray sent in dismounted teams to clear them out. Fox Troop's SGT Mike "Chief" Aguilar was one of those in the dismounted element.[7] His ACAV had been engaged by an NVA soldier in a bunker; he'd pop up, shoot, and drop back down when the ACAV returned fire. Aguilar grabbed some hand grenades and jumped off the track. His track commander (TC) asked: "'Chief, where you going?' He said: 'I'm going to get that SOB' ... Chief had no fear." Aguilar threw a grenade into the bunker; it exploded with lots of smoke. There was a female NVA soldier inside, still alive. Aguilar and the other dismounts thought she was dead.

SGT Allen Burnworth (with his M79) had joined the troopers on the ground sweep. He says: "Chief reaches down in for what he thought was a body and she was still alive enough that she bit him. He swore and said: 'She bit me. Give me that M16' ... After 20 rounds, she didn't bite anymore."

The contact lasted for three hours. All but one of Fox Troop's officers were casualties on 17 April; the first sergeant had to temporarily assume command of Echo Troop, as all of their officers were also wounded.

Even four decades later, John Ballantyne recalls the events of 17 April, a day he describes as "the most nerve-wracking day during my tenure with the squadron." For the previous five months, the troopers had been engaging mostly loosely organized units that did not stand and fight. The NVA soldiers encountered on their first day in the Boi Loi Woods were professionals. As Ballantyne recalls:

> We were clearly up against better organized and more determined NVA units with plenty of local VC support ... [It was] a learning experience for the squadron ... Prior to this contact, our mindset had been to instantly react to contact and charge in with weapons blazing ... We adjusted our tactics accordingly and made it SOP to precede any movement into contact with suitable artillery and air preparation.

Allan Burnworth summed up the day's action. "We really did have our things together that day—but more so after that ... After that, our crews worked like a well-oiled machine."

There was one other lesson learned—but it was one the squadron couldn't do anything about. The absence of Hotel Company and its 17 M48 tanks was felt during the first contact in the Boi Loi Woods, as well as in all subsequent fights. The armored staying power and bunker-busting firepower of these tanks were, according to Ballantyne, "sorely missed." The Sheridan was fine, but some jobs just called for 52 tons of American steel.

One week later, it was Golf Troop's turn to tango with the 3rd Battalion, 101st (NVA) Regiment. The 25th (ARVN) leadership wanted to start a Rome Plow operation in the neighboring Ho Bo Woods. CPT Jim Randles (Golf Troop commander) was given the mission to recon the area and find a good place to start the clearing operation. By mid-morning, the scouts had uncovered a well-camouflaged 6'×6'×4' bunker with 2-foot concrete walls and 1-foot overhead cover. This was clearly a good place to start clearing the woods.

Golf Troop, later reinforced by Fox, ran into a battalion-sized NVA base camp just inside the treeline about noon.[8] An ACAV and Sheridan were knocked out in the first volley of RPGs. For the next seven hours, troopers fought outnumbered against the determined NVA battalion. LT Robert George was awarded the Distinguished Service Cross for his actions during this fight. He went to the aid of the crew of the disabled ACAV, then pulled the damaged Sheridan out of the line of fire. When CPT Randles was wounded by an RPG, despite his own painful head wound that caused the loss of vision in one eye, George assumed command of the troop, pulled everyone back and helped orchestrate a 90-minute barrage by artillery, Thunderhorse Cobras, and F4 Phantoms. He then led the final assault from the right flank that cleared the enemy base camp.

Post-battle estimates were that the NVA battalion lost almost half of its soldiers on 24 April. The two contacts—one week apart—sent a signal that was received "loud and clear." LTC Ballantyne told his troopers to get ready for more. They were in for a fight.

Another serious contact came a mere five days later, when Echo and Fox Troop (working with two militia companies) tangled with the Gia Dinh 4 Sapper Battalion trying to interfere with the Rome Plow clearing operations northeast of Trang Bang. The combination of armored firepower and dismounted infantry had a telling effect during this contact in which there were no friendly fatalities.

The next firefights occurred on 19 May, when Fox and Golf Troops (both reinforced with militia infantry) got into separate actions north and east of Trang Bang. The enemy fired over 300 RPGs (so much for a shortage of supplies!) in four minutes against Golf Troop. The 2/11 Howitzer Battery countered with 250 rounds of 155 mm high explosive; the 8-inchers from 2/32nd Artillery added 50 rounds of their own.

When Golf Troopers finally overran the NVA defenders after nine hours of hard fighting, they found proof of long-term Communist residency in the Ho Bo Woods. It was a 200-bunker complex and a cache of almost 150 command-detonated mines. Near the center of the complex, troopers found the command bunker, described in the after-action report as consisting of "four levels of chambers below ground, protected by 18-feet of overhead cover—sandbags, logs and hard-packed earth. Radiating outward in all directions from the command bunker were tunnels leading to other bunkers ... Telephone wire connected the bunkers, indicating that the enemy had extensive communications capability within this complex."

The next fight came at 0300 hours on 25 May—under a new moon and intermittent monsoonal rain—when sappers from the K9 Battalion, 101st (NVA) Regiment assaulted the Echo and Fox Troop and 984th Engineers (Land Clearing) night defensive position near the Ho Bo Woods. The lack of moonlight allowed the sappers to get close to the perimeter of ACAVs and Sheridans—some within just 20 meters. Despite this advantage, they did not penetrate the laager; they did, however, damage six vehicles (three ACAVs, two Sheridans, and one M548 cargo carrier). The soldiers of the 25th (ARVN) Recon Company, dug-in between the armored vehicles, acquitted themselves well in this fight.

SGT Allen Burnworth was inside the ring of steel. He recalls that the NVA put a mortar observer in a tree that stood alone to the front of the F-26 track. Based on experience gained back on 17 April, the troopers knew the enemy liked to put spotters in trees, so the tree became a target. The next day, they found numerous bodies in and under the tree. Not only had a spotter climbed the tree, the sappers headed toward the perimeter were using it as a guidepost. "It was not their lucky day," Burnworth says. Ken Smith was there too. Forty-plus years later, an AK47 round from that night was still in his ankle. "A couple of the vehicles got hit, even though we had RPG screens ... As daylight came, the dinks broke contact and moved out, but they left a hell of a lot of bodies behind."

John Ballantyne could see the night fight from FSB Warrior a couple miles away. The next day, he overflew the battlefield. "Some of the attackers (dead bodies) had crawled up to within 20 to 30 yards before being detected and then hit by small arms fire from our troops. I attribute our troops' success in large measure to the continuous and effective illumination we provided from both our mortars and howitzers at the FSB Warrior."

As always, mines were a serious threat in the Ho Bo Woods. The 101st (NVA) Regiment, in fear of losing its long-time sanctuary, used them liberally trying to halt progress by inflicting casualties on the war-weary Americans. That effort failed. Despite the near-constant danger, the 2/11-Rome Plow-South Vietnamese militia teams cleared 10,000 acres of Boi Loi and Ho Bo Woods in under two months.

The assault on 25 May was the 101st (NVA) Regiment's last gasp. During subsequent operations through the end of October, enemy actions decreased dramatically; contacts were primarily against local VC only. Second Squadron's assessment was: "Reconnaissance operations and intelligence reports indicate that there has been a major shift of enemy unit dispositions in the TAOR [Tactical Area of Responsibility] to the eastern side of the Saigon River indicating the success of squadron operations aimed at interdicting enemy infiltration in the western portion of the Saigon River Corridor."

Even though the majority of the Regiment had gone home, the remaining Blackhorse firepower and mobility was sufficient to disrupt the enemy's conduct of operations and deter any major offensive actions by him. Even though the 101st (NVA) Regiment and 429th (NVA) Sapper Group tried their best to disrupt the South Vietnamese presidential election on 3 October 1971, combined operations between 2/11 and the 25th (ARVN) Infantry Division allowed the people to travel to the polling stations and vote. With 83 percent of the voters participating, the election amounted to a virtual referendum in support of the government and a rejection of the North Vietnamese-backed insurgency.

MG James Hollingsworth (who had replaced MG Wagstaff as TRAC Senior Advisor) recognized 2nd Squadron's performance in clearing Hau Nghia Province as something special. This three-war veteran knew something about gallantry—he was the recipient of three Distinguished Service Crosses, four Silver Stars, and six Purple Hearts. He was the real deal. He summed up 2/11's accomplishments.

> In the following weeks, the 2d Squadron inflicted heavy casualties on the 101st NVA Regiment. The 101st Regiment was driven from the area and land clearing operations were permitted to continue at an accelerated pace ... At the conclusion of these operations, the complexion of the Saigon River Corridor had been radically changed. Hundreds of enemy bunkers and the lush vegetation which provided ideal enemy sanctuaries had been eliminated. Were it not for the gallant efforts of the "Blackhorse" Troopers of the 2d Squadron, 11th Armored Cavalry Regiment, this task could not have been accomplished.

Thunderhorse Carries On: February to December 1971

As part of the standdown of the Regiment and reorganization of the forces that would remain in country, MAJ Roy Wulff (Air Cav Troop commander) did a detailed assessment of his troop. Because of personnel policies being applied across the 11th Cavalry (e.g. early return home for troopers with less than 60 days to go on their tour), the Aero Rifle Platoon lost 70 percent and the Aero Scout Platoon lost 50 percent of their experienced personnel between February and April 1971. This

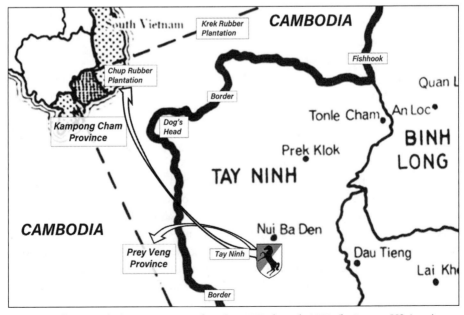

Map of Air Cavalry Troop operations from late 1970 through 1971. (basic map, US Army)

loss in combat experience meant that both platoons required extensive retraining. But neither unit could afford the luxury of a period of standdown; they both had ongoing combat missions.

Wulff's carefully organized plan to address these issues was based on the assumption that his aircraft and rifle squads would be used primarily in support of 2/11 east of Saigon—as envisioned in all of the guidance provided to the Regiment prior to and during standdown. However, starting in February and lasting until August 1971, Air Cavalry Troop was used mostly to provide support to South Vietnamese forces operating in northern Tay Ninh Province and southeastern Cambodia. For most of that time, the Thunderhorse crews were under the operational control (OPCON) of 3rd Squadron, 17th (Air) Cavalry, working in direct support of the ARVN 5th, 18th, and 25th Infantry Divisions.

Air Cav Troop's basic mission remained pretty much the same as before the rest of the Regiment stood down. Only now, they were finding the "bastards" and reporting to ARVN, not Blackhorse commanders, for the pile on.

The troop received an increasing number of missions that took the pilots and crews into Cambodia. While Cobra/LOH teams continued to provide almost daily support to 2/11 recon and land-clearing operations, there was a noticeable increase in enemy pressure on South Vietnamese units north of the border. Blackhorse aviators flew across the length and breadth of northern War Zone C and southeastern Cambodia, from the Dog's Head to the Fishhook. They spent almost as much time in Cambodian airspace as in South Vietnamese.

Chief Warrant Officer 2 (CW2) Bill Reinhart recalls: "We were given the area around the Chup [Rubber Plantation] and it was a hot bed of heavy anti-aircraft fire. We lost a few loaches and slicks. We also had some cobras shot up pretty bad."

The South Vietnamese showed their appreciation for the support. Air Cav Troop was cited with the Republic of Vietnam Cross of Gallantry with Palm for the very intense period of combat between 24 February and 19 May 1971.

Flying over northern Tay Ninh Province and southeastern Cambodia was dramatically different than around Xuan Loc and Hau Nghia. For one thing, there was a serious, conventional-style war going on between regular NVA divisions and ARVN regiments. The enemy's air defenses were unlike anything Thunderhorse crews had seen up to that point. Everywhere you flew, it seemed, there were .51-caliber machine guns. And where there was one, you could bet there was at least one or two more. Bill Reinhart describes what it was like to be in the sights of an AA gunner. "We would sit up there at 3,500 feet, watch stuff come at you that was like two streaks from somebody's eyeballs. I had them [.51-cal. rounds] through the rotor blades. But survived it ... They looked to me about the size of a softball. They were right outside the door."

Another challenge in the Thunderhorse AO was the terrain. Eastern Long Khanh Province was characterized by large tracts of heavy jungle. But there were recognizable landmarks to aid in navigation—like Nui Chua Chanh (the mountain near the Gia Ray rock quarry), May Tao Mountain, Xuan Loc, and Highway 1. But once you flew north of Tay Ninh, everything looked about the same. Lots of green jungle, rubber plantations, and dry stream beds. There weren't very many towns and even fewer roads. And the border? Forget it! In the days before satellite navigation, you had to be a damn good map reader to know if you were still in South Vietnam or Cambodia.

Except for all the .51-calibers. That meant you were definitely in Cambodian airspace.

Such was the case during the battle for Krek in late September–early November 1971. Thunderhorse aero scouts were among the first to notice the enemy build-up in the area, providing III (ARVN) Corps sufficient warning time to develop plans and marshal its forces. Fire Base Alpha, east of Krek, was besieged by two NVA divisions bent on kicking the South Vietnamese out of Cambodia. An ARVN armored task force moved up Highway 22 from Tay Ninh and defeated the enemy forces. American air power was decisive for the victory, including almost a hundred B-52 sorties, 2,500 tactical air strikes, and over 3,600 helicopter gunship sorties from the 11th Cavalry and others. A reporter described the action: "AH-1 Cobra helicopter gunships spread out over the rubber trees as four South Vietnamese Ranger battalions and two squadrons of tanks and armored personnel carriers pushed onto the plantation ..."[9]

Throughout the latter half of 1971 and into 1972, Air Cav Troop gunships and scouts flew daily missions in support of ARVN units on the offensive—and eventually defensive—in Cambodia. Some even returned to the skies over Snuol. It was in this area that T34 and PT76 tanks had been seen, harbingers of a Communist offensive intended to end the war in April 1972. Blackhorse and other 3rd Brigade Task Force crews flew over 300 sorties in the span of just 48 hours in late November. Some of these missions were flown at night against NVA sappers and mortars assaulting fire bases on both sides of Highway 7 about ten kilometers across the border.

Later analysis determined that the enemy's major operations in the region stretching from the Dog's Head to the Fishhook were in preparation for the Easter Offensive the following April. Three divisions (the 5th (VC), 7th (NVA), and 9th (VC)—all old "friends" of Blackhorse troopers)—and two independent regiments occupied positions just inside Cambodia. Between November and the end of March, they retrained and reequipped for the upcoming thrust down Highway 13 against Loc Ninh and An Loc.

One of those independent regiments—probably the 271st (VC)—occupied positions around Dambe, west of the Krek Rubber Plantation about 15 kilometers inside Cambodia. They were part of the enemy's deception plan for the upcoming offensive. Their mission was to try and convince the South Vietnamese that the major thrust into South Vietnam would be made against Tay Ninh, not An Loc. This mission dictated absolute secrecy.

On 19 December 1971, CWO Tom Skiles was piloting an OH-6A on a bomb damage assessment mission near Dambe. Lieutenant (LT) Peter Forame was in the left seat acting as his scout-observer. They were part of a Thunderhorse gunship/ scout team (call signs White 1 and Red 4). A C&C Huey was overhead. About 30 minutes into the mission, the Huey, piloted by CWO Robert Rowland and CPT Alton Bailey, started taking fire at an altitude of about 2,100 feet. They dove for the deck (the trees were 10–20 feet tall in this area). The enemy then concentrated multiple .51-caliber machine guns and AK47s on White 1 which was skimming the tree tops. Skiles managed to clear a stand of bamboo before crashing into an open area. The aircraft burst into flames upon impact. Red 4 made two gun runs on the area from which the fire was coming, but was hit and had to evade.

When the word came into the Air Cav Troop operations center that two of their own were down, Blackhorse birds flocked to the area. Several crews attempted to land to see if anyone had survived. They were driven off by heavy ground-to-air fire, including RPGs. The next day, another crew observed two charred bodies at the crash site where only a two-foot section of the tail boom remained recognizable. They, too, were shot down (and later rescued). Numerous air strikes and gunship runs pummeled the surrounding treelines over the next two days—all to no avail. There was no way the enemy regimental commander was going to allow GIs on the ground to uncover his unit's secret plans.[10]

Thomas Skiles and Peter Forame entered the rolls of the missing in action from this long war.

Completing the Mission: August 1971 to February 1972

Over the course of what came to be known as the "Ho Bo Cut," 2/11 paid a high price. A dozen Blackhorse Troopers were killed and another 116 wounded in action. Their sacrifice did, however, bring some impressive results. The traditional "secure" bases of the Ho Bo and Boi Loi Woods were opened to aerial observation and ground interdiction. The VC and NVA units that had occupied these long-standing base camps were driven out and their bunkers destroyed. South Vietnamese militia soldiers were trained in the art of reconnaissance, although there was much more needed before they could assume full responsibility for their own security. In effect, 2/11 troopers were slowly, but surely, working themselves out of a job.

The reduction in enemy activity inside South Vietnam itself was clear. Major NVA forces withdrew across the border to prepare for the upcoming offensive. VC forces, from battalions to guerrilla cells, went to ground for military and political reasons alike. On the one hand, the inability of the rear service groups to get supplies and replacements to these units severely restricted their offensive capabilities. On the other hand, the leaders in Hanoi did not want to give President Nixon any reason to slow the pace of GIs going home. LTC Bill Stokes recalls: "Major contacts by 2/11 were rare from the summer of July '71–March '72 … Contacts were down, I believe, because of 2/11's operations from March '71 on and deliberate efforts by

VC/NVA to pull back into Cambodia and prepare for Easter Offensive '72—just a few days after 2/11 stood down."

General Mud became as much of an enemy as General Giap. Fire Support Base Warrior became affectionately known as "Lake Warrior." MAJ Joe Cizmadia was on his second tour with 2/11, this time as the squadron Exec. He recalls:

> So as the rainy season weathered on, the inside of the firebase [Warrior] became a quagmire beyond belief. I mean, there was a gray slurry of muddy stuff about the consistency of syrup, chest deep, all around the inside of the berm … ACAVs swam in the main entrance to the berm, it was that deep … From the air, it's just amazing to see this lake [and] this little island that was kind of in it with canals of Venice running through it.

Allen Burnworth remembers the mud to be "somewhere between peanut butter and maple syrup" in consistency. Because of tactical requirements—and the mud—FSB Warrior was abandoned and a new base, FSB Andrews, was established on higher ground.[11] It was better, but not much.

CPT (Chaplain) Bill Karabinos recalls the first time he saw FSB Andrews in October 1971: "Never in all my days did I imagine that American troops would be living in such squalid surroundings. Mud and water was almost knee deep with only an occasional knob of high ground. Even the mess tent had water over your ankles." Those troopers who were lucky enough to read a copy of the 20 October 1971 edition of *Pacific Stars & Stripes* while living in such "squalid surroundings" stared in disbelief when they read the headlines: "Vietnam: It Can Be Fun." The article went on to describe the "71 swimming pools, 12 beaches with lifeguards, 160 craft shops, 99 service clubs, 159 surfaced basketball courts …" Well, you get the picture.

All that mud notwithstanding, the beat went on. At the end of September, an additional mission was assigned to 2/11. As part of its efforts to push ARVN forces out of southern Cambodia, the NVA initiated a series of attacks on the US firebases north of Tay Ninh. GI artillery units, protected by infantry units from the 3rd Brigade Task Force, were providing long-range fire support for the South Vietnamese infantry and armor units across the border around Krek.

As they did so often during the war, the Communists chose a significant date on the calendar to initiate a major offensive. In this case, it was the South Vietnamese presidential election scheduled for Sunday, 3 October. Although there was only one name on the ballot, Hanoi couldn't pass up the opportunity to try and embarrass the Saigon government. If they could evict the last remaining South Vietnamese troops from Cambodia prior to the election or capture a major town inside South Vietnam, the Thieu Government, so their logic and propaganda said, would be shown as weak and ineffective without the support of the "imperialist" Americans.

For his part, President Thieu understood that, in order for his reelection to have any legitimacy, the Army of the Republic of Vietnam would have to demonstrate the ability to stand on its own. To President Nixon, success on this battlefield would validate the Vietnamization plan and allow the continued withdrawal of all GIs from Southeast Asia. To the troopers of 2/11, it would be another opportunity to prove they had earned the right to wear the Blackhorse patch on their right shoulder.

The battle lines—military, political, and ideological—were drawn and the players were on the field when the opening shots were fired a week before the South Vietnamese election.

The Communist offensive was a big operation—one of the biggest, and perhaps one of the most important—since the drawdown of US forces had begun. Appropriately, the response to the offensive was an operation largely conceived and run by the South Vietnamese. US combat support forces (artillery, helicopter gunships, tactical air strikes, and B-52s) and combat service support forces (mainly logistical resupply elements) assisted them, but it was an ARVN-run show.

The mission to relieve the artillery at the former Special Forces camp at Ka Tum (less than ten kilometers from Cambodia in northern Tay Ninh Province) and escort Bravo Battery, 2nd Battalion, 32nd Artillery (Proud Americans) was a key part of the operation. Ka Tum sits astride Highway 4, and elements of two enemy divisions—the 5th (VC) and 7th (NVA)—reinforced with sappers, artillery, and anti-aircraft machine guns (about 20,000 troops total) were attacking southwards from Cambodia, guiding on both Highways 4 and 22 (located about 20 kilometers to the west) as their axes of advance.

There were numerous reports of NVA tanks being sighted in the Chlong River Valley around Snuol and along Highway 7 near Memot. A number of troopers were still around from the Cambodia operation just over a year earlier, and they well remembered how easily tanks could move north—or south—along the Highway 7-Highway 4 network.

The ARVN forces assembled to blunt the NVA attack included the 18th and 25th Infantry Divisions, two brigades of the Airborne Division, the 3rd Armored Task Force, and several Ranger Groups—about 50,000 troops total.

The South Vietnamese forces were receiving artillery support from the 175 mm and 8-inch guns of 2/32nd Artillery located at FSB Ka Tum on Highway 4 and FSB Pace on Highway 22, as well as at the old French Fort on the outskirts of Tay Ninh City. But the North Vietnamese attackers were coming too close to these forward bases; the artillery battalion reported that both fire bases were under virtual constant mortar and rocket fire starting on 26 September.

Ammunition expenditures for the battalion's 350 separate fire missions in September were in excess of 3,000 rounds and over 4,600 in October—an almost unheard-of amount at this point in the war. The NVA responded in kind, pounding Pace during the same period with over 2,300 rounds, while about 100 rounds per day were striking Ka Tum. SSG Paul Cibolski, a section chief at FSB Pace, remembers his battery commander telling them that they "were cut off and surrounded by 5,000 NVA." It was just as dire at Ka Tum.

For both military and political reasons, it was time to pull the long-range cannons out before they were overrun. Second Squadron was given the mission of getting Bravo Battery out of Ka Tum before the enemy could surround them. A company of 1st Cav grunts was helicoptered into FSB Pace to help defend it against an expected enemy assault.

The "Proud Americans" artillery had been supporting the Blackhorse Regiment virtually since they came ashore in 1966—*Cedar Falls, Junction City*, War Zone C, Fort Defiance, and Cambodia. Now, it was time for the cavalrymen to pay the 2/32nd Artillery redlegs back for all the times those huge shells had caused the enemy to keep their heads inside the bunkers as the ACAVs and Sheridans rolled forward.

On September 26th, the day the North Vietnamese began their offensive, over 1,000 mortar rounds and rockets rained down on FSB Pace, Ka Tum, and ten other positions inside Cambodia and northern Tay Ninh Province. There was a sapper and infantry attack on South Vietnamese armored cavalry and ranger forces defending the rubber plantation town of Krek, about ten kilometers north of the border. Battlefield reports from ARVN headquarters in Tay Ninh indicated that Highway 4 had been cut by the North Vietnamese pouring south out of Cambodia.

Intelligence reports indicated a large number of enemy troops had already slipped south of Ka Tum in the direction of Tay Ninh City, and the allied command directed B-52 strikes—guided by radar as they flew through heavy monsoon clouds—against them on 27 and 28 September. Almost 300 tons of bombs were dropped in this area, while other B-52s attempted to disrupt the southward movement of enemy reinforcements and supplies.

It was onto this hot and wet battlefield that 2/11 troopers moved, establishing a forward assembly area near the old French Fort on 29 September. Whether Highway 4 was cut by the enemy between there and Ka Tum was unclear. What was clear was that Ka Tum was receiving lots of incoming and that enemy ground forces had been seen in virtually every direction. The arrival of enemy tanks was a real possibility at any moment.

It was obvious that this was a serious situation and time was of the essence; 2/11's move from FSB Andrews to Ka Tum was a fast-paced affair on wet, muddy roads. The weather was acting as the enemy's ally. Heavy rain and thick clouds—caused by Typhoons Della and Elaine off the Vietnamese coast—hindered close air support and aerial reconnaissance.

The rescue mission was an unqualified success. Other than some damage caused by mines and a small number of wounded requiring evacuation, 2/11 accomplished the mission by delivering the redlegs to the more friendly environs of Tay Ninh. On a larger scale, the squadron contributed to the denial of every aspect of the enemy's plan.

President Thieu was reelected following a record turnout (over 87 percent) of the voters nationwide. The North Vietnamese did not overwhelm or even embarrass the South Vietnamese on the battlefield. Quite the contrary, in fact. Three regiments of the 5th (VC) and 7th (NVA) Divisions were turned away at each of the fire support bases they attacked with heavy casualties. The *Chicago Tribune* wrote on 6 October 1971 that the South Vietnamese had "trapped and routed [the enemy] in the worst defeat suffered by the North Vietnamese this year."

LTC Bill Stokes summed up the operation:

> I was very pleased with the professional way in which the squadron rescued the 2-32nd Artillery elements at Katum … [I]t did show quite clearly our capability to react rapidly and successfully to an important contingency task, while continuing to maintain a major fire base in the Boi Loi Woods … The entire squadron was responsible for the success of our operation, not just the field elements. A real pat on the back is due the individual trooper throughout the squadron; it was his performance that carried the day.

Following the mission around Ka Tum, 2/11 (along with the rest of the 3rd Brigade Task Force) was pulled back into a "dynamic defense" posture in the Saigon-Bien Hoa-Long Binh area. The squadron's primary mission was to conduct recon-in-force and dismounted ambush patrols to prevent enemy infiltration into the national capital region. Precluding attacks by fire from the rocket belt was a secondary mission. The low level of enemy activity throughout the area of operations meant that contact was sporadic—which suited the troopers just fine. Most of the work consisted of setting up night defensive positions which served as operating bases for dismounted patrols and ambushes. The troopers also blew up enemy tunnel and bunker complexes wherever they found them.

Second Squadron closed out the last full year of the Regiment's service in Vietnam receiving kudos from one of the most senior officers in the South Vietnamese military. Lieutenant General (LTG) Nguyen Van La, the Deputy Chief of the South Vietnamese Joint General Staff, wrote to General Abrams that 2/11 troopers "disregarded dangers and fought bravely, resulting in 223 enemy troops killed in action and 14 others captured and the seizure of 437 assorted weapons and a large quantity of ammunition, foodstuffs, military clothing and equipment."

By this point in the war, leading American soldiers into combat had become quite a challenge. Predictably, all of the ills of American society at large—loss of respect for authority, drug abuse, racial strife, and generational disparity—affected the US Army. On top of these trends was the fact that people were trying to kill you in a war many no longer agreed with or believed in. The fact that everyone was armed with a weapon made leadership even more of a challenge. Winding down the pace of the war resulted in fewer casualties, but simultaneously increased both the sense of futility (why be the last to die in a war our leaders had given up on) and the "off-duty" time available to get into trouble.

Platoon leader Hawk Ruth joined Fox Troop in August 1971. He recalls the relatively slow pace of operations. "Once in the field the soldiers and the NCOs were very professional and focused. The enemy knew we would be leaving soon and we felt that they were keeping a low profile, very little activity, until the Squadron would be standing down …"

By January, 2/11 was opening Fire Support Base Fiddlers Green. Brigadier General James Hamlet, the 3rd Brigade Task Force commander, described the tactical situation at the time: "In December and January enemy activity remained light, the enemy concentrating on resupply, training, and rice collection from the Binh Tuy "rice bowl" ... Local force units used mines, booby traps, attacks by fire and terrorism to harass friendly forces within the Brigade's area of operations." One of those attacks by fire was a 20-round mortar barrage that hit Fiddlers Green on the evening of 7 January. Eighteen Troopers and an ARVN interpreter were wounded.

The last day of February 1972 (it was a leap year) dawned pretty much like every other day in the dry season in Vietnam—clear, with promises of being HOT! But 29 February was a special day, nonetheless. This was to be Blackhorse troopers' last full day in the field. After 1,939 straight days in combat, the last of the Blackhorse was standing down. But there was one more ambush patrol to be run. Staff Sergeant (SSG) James Nelson—"SGT Rock" to his troopers—was picked to head up the patrol for 3rd Platoon. Specialist 4 (SP4) Arthur "Tennessee" Likens was one of the troopers who volunteered for the mission.

Earlier in the day, the troop had uncovered a small bunker complex, so CPT Tom Meriwether (the Fox Troop commander) specified that as the ambush location. The patrol was compromised almost from the start; things went downhill in a hurry. Private First Class (PFC) Louis "Skip" Brown, another volunteer on the patrol, says: "I was sitting right next to Tennessee when this tragic scenario unfolded, when he earned the title of "last Blackhorse trooper killed in Viet Nam." To his family and friends and especially his sons, let it be known that Tennessee died a hero, and I am here today because of his actions."

The following day, Fox Troop made the journey to Phu Loi for standdown. Tennessee's body was already in the hands of graves registration personnel.

The South Vietnamese created a task force of 13,000 men to fill the void when the 8,000 men of 2/11 and the 3rd Brigade, 1st Air Cav left Vietnam. The task force consisted of five Ranger groups and an armored cavalry brigade with 150 armored vehicles. The events surrounding the Easter Offensive that started less than a month after 2nd Squadron departed demonstrated more than any survey could have that the sacrifice of the Blackhorse troopers had not been in vain. Hanoi waited until virtually all American combat units had gone home, before launching a major land invasion along three separate axes from Cambodia, Laos, and North Vietnam. Each of these separate assaults was soundly defeated by *South Vietnamese* forces. Nowhere was that defeat more telling than in the area around An Loc.

During the three-month long battle of An Loc, soldiers from the 5th (ARVN) Infantry Division and militia from the Binh Long Province held off the combined forces of three NVA divisions, reinforced with tanks, heavy artillery, and sophisti-cated anti-aircraft weapons. These were the very same soldiers and militiamen that Blackhorse troopers had trained and operated with for the previous three years. Their battlefield prowess and courage was, at least in part, due to the professional skills and personal example demonstrated by members of the 11th Cavalry in 1969 and 1970. The virtual destruction of two NVA divisions by the brave defenders of An Loc ensured that South Vietnam would live to fight another day.

The South Vietnamese Government recognized what the 2nd Squadron troopers had achieved in their final year in Vietnam. The Joint General Staff cited 2/11 twice—once for overcoming "all terrain difficulties ... and intense enemy firepower by fighting gallantly, smashing many North Vietnamese Communist regular units, thus inflicting serious personnel casualties and weapons losses upon the adversary" between 1 November 1970 and 18 December 1971. A second Republic of Vietnam Cross of Gallantry with Palm was awarded to 2/11 for its operations around Ka Tum in late September and early October 1971.

In March 1972, just as *The Godfather* was premiering in New York City, "Godfather" Uncle Sam made Blackhorse troopers an offer they couldn't refuse— go home! As early as the third week in February, LTC Stokes had been given a "heads up" that the order to stand down was imminent. CPT Wayne Glass (the squadron logistics officer), was the pointman for turning in five and a half years' equipment—and then some. He recalls the process was very detailed and the rules were very stringent.

> We had guys with metal detectors combing the motor pools, staging areas, all around the airfield and in the troop billet areas, looking for anything buried or left behind ... I remember when we were standing down, somewhere at Phu Loi or nearby, they found an M88 [recovery vehicle] that had been buried ... Also, the 1/17 Aviation was located at Phu Loi and there was a lake next to their headquarters. We had a real dry spell about the time the stand down began, so the water in the lake receded a lot and suddenly one day you could see the rotor head of a helicopter sticking out of the water ... We had extra weapons and other assorted items from many years of being in Vietnam. We were instructed to just turn everything in.

Down at the troop and platoon level, things were a bit chaotic. A "monumental task," according to Hawk Ruth. "Property accountability, as expected, was extremely poor, and few people cared. Vehicles required a tremendous amount of attention for cleanliness so they could be returned back to the States even though we knew they were going to be scrapped anyway."

Turning in the vehicles followed the same procedures as 1/11 and 3/11 had faced a year earlier. Air Cavalry Troop crews were not exempt either, as by this point in the war, helicopters, like everything else from file cabinets to tanks, were being withdrawn from South Vietnam by the boat load. The journey of "Heart Breaker," a 2/11 Howitzer Battery M109A1 howitzer, was typical of the rest of the squadron's vehicles.

Not knowing what the future held, Heart Breaker made the short trip from Fire Support Base Fiddlers Green to Phu Loi. The troopers who had loaded and fired her life-taking (for the enemy) and life-saving (for the Blackhorse) 155 mm shells since

1967 would undoubtedly have shed a tear had they seen black paint being smeared over the bold red letters of her name stenciled on the long barrel. Crewmembers like Sergeant Rick Byrd unloaded their gear, turned in their M16 rifles and gas masks and poncho liners, leaving Heart Breaker's turret barren and empty. They then mounted up, cranked her 450-horsepower Detroit Diesel and headed for Long Binh—smiling and laughing all the way. They were going home. How proudly Heart Breaker paraded down Highway 1, not realizing that this was to be her last convoy.

But then the real indignities were inflicted on her. Heart Breaker was stripped to the bare metal skin, inside and out, blasted with high-pressure water hoses until her cosmetics started to chip. She was scrubbed, scraped, and scoured until the muck and grime of five faithful years of service to "her boys" were washed away. A gang of undignified strangers poked and prodded her, peering into her very soul for any vestiges of the combat missions she had endured. They filled out reams of paperwork, describing all her faults and missing pieces. Heart Breaker's final humiliation came when she was sprayed with insecticide; traps laced with rat poison were inserted into her engine compartment and under her floorboards. She was sealed up and trundled away to a Saigon dock, where she awaited a long ocean voyage in the dark hold of a sea-tossed ship.

Upon reaching Okinawa, she was unceremoniously taken to a depot where she faced an uncertain fate at the hands of US and Japanese technicians. They were tasked with integrating her back into the society of Army equipment. Alone in the dark, she wondered what became of all those young men who had treated her with such loving care over the years.

Not much of a thank-you and not much of a homecoming for a war hero.

The Blackhorse Goes Home: March 1972

Given that the first person to report in to the just-formed 11th United States Cavalry at Fort Myer, Virginia, in March 1901 was a chaplain (Charles Pierce), it was perhaps fitting that the last person assigned to the Blackhorse Regiment in Vietnam was Chaplain Blandon Karabinos.

Throughout the weeks of turning-in vehicles and equipment, 2nd Squadron and Thunderhorse Troopers were leaving in droves. Some caught a Freedom Bird, others were reassigned to new units. Bill Stokes held his last command and staff meeting on 20 March 1972. The colors (2/11's and the Regiment's) were flying out the next morning on their own Freedom Bird. Stokes had just one official act left. Someone had to stay behind and accomplish the last-minute actions to complete the standdown. Chaplain Karabinos recalls:

> One officer was to remain behind to conduct the road march [Phu Loi to Bien Hoa], account for that equipment exchange, see that the troops got the necessary transportation, sign orders and complete the paper trail that the Army thrives upon … Colonel Stokes looked around the

room one more time and the only officer not headed to Saigon with the Colors in the morning was indeed the Chaplain. He swallowed hard and then stood silently and stared in shock at the Padre for a long time and in complete silence. Major Paul Foley, Deputy Commander, broke the silence and with a smile said, *"why not"* ... Reluctantly the Colonel agreed—he had no one else. Thus the Chaplain became the last Commanding Officer of the Squadron's "rear guard" as it made its final march through Southeast Asia.

As the color guard with the colors was flying to Tan Son Nhut, Karabinos (with the help of several superb troopers) road marched the last vehicles and troopers to Long Binh. For the next seven days, "Sergeant [Ralph] Jordan efficiently and effectively took care of the logistics, and I signed everything he put in front of me, as ... *Captain (Chaplain), Commanding.*"

> The appointment of Chaplain, Commanding, Karabinos did not sit well with a furious Brigadier General, who deplaned from a helicopter that swooped in and landed just as the troops were boarding the last bus. "'Who the hell is in charge of this outfit.' He was steaming and when I stepped forward and he saw the Chaplain's cross on my uniform he was even more furious ... he got word that a chaplain was commanding an Armored Unit and if the media ever found out there would be hell to pay." After the one-star departed, "All that was left was our farewells and then Sgt. Jordan uttered something like: 'well our work is done here Kemo Sabe, time to ride on.'"

On the 27 March 1972, Karabinos returned to being "just" a chaplain. He commandeered the last 2/11 jeep and drove to the 229th Assault Helicopter Battalion to serve out the rest of his tour.

So, like their predecessors from the Regiment's first Asian war, a mere shadow of the combat-effective organization that boarded ships in Oakland in 1966 returned to the United States in 1972. In April 1904, less than 400 members of the 1,000-man 11th United States Cavalry Regiment sailed into San Francisco harbor, more than two years after departing for the Philippines. In April 1972, the 15 members of the color guard of the 4,400-man 11th Armored Cavalry Regiment flew home, more than five and a half years after departing for Vietnam. The color guard flew into McChord Air Force Base in Washington, then drove to nearby Fort Lewis.

When Major Joe Cizmadia arrived in Washington at the head of the 2/11 colors detachment, he got off the plane expecting to be met. No one was there. He was able to arrange transportation to Fort Lewis for the colors and troopers. He went to post headquarters and asked for the senior operations officer. A Department of the Army civilian came and said: "I'm it."

Cizmadia told him that these were the colors of the 11th Armored Cavalry Regiment which has been in combat in Vietnam since 1966. Surely there must be a ceremony planned. The civilian said there were no units then at Lewis, so no soldiers to conduct a ceremony. "What should I do with the colors?" Cizmadia asked. "Just bring them to my office" was the answer.

No brass bands, no tickertape parades, not even a thank-you or welcome home.

Blackhorse Forever: The Legacy

Henry Morris went to West Point in the fall of 1968. He was just back from his tour as the Fox Troop commander and was looking forward to some quiet time, some family time. In September, he received a call from a survival assistance officer asking if he was willing to go to a funeral for David Embrey in Rockfish, Virginia.

Before leaving Fox Troop, Henry had appointed five troopers as acting sergeants. He sent a letter to each trooper's family telling them what he had done and why. "I had to send the letters when people died. I hated doing that. So I got a chance to do something good, instead of it being bad news." Mary Embrey kept that letter, and when she learned of her son's death, she asked the survival assistance officer if he could find this Henry Morris and ask him to come to the funeral. Of course, Henry said yes.

At the church, Joe Embrey (David's father) invited Henry, in uniform, back to the house for the wake. "There were lots of people there. Everybody knew the Embreys." Later, Joe asked Henry—still in uniform—if he would go with him to feed the pigs. Henry dug some coveralls out of his car trunk, and together they went to feed the pigs. Very few words passed between them, but Henry apparently passed the test. As soon as they got back to the house, Joe invited him to spend the night. When Henry protested that there were a lot of close friends and relatives, Joe said: "'No, we've got room for *you*.' I stayed three days and three nights."

Since then, Henry's become a part of the Embrey family. He's attended David's younger sister's and brother's weddings, the Embrey's 50th wedding anniversary, and Joe's funeral. Mary Embrey attended the Louisville reunion of the 11th Armored Cavalry Veterans of Vietnam and Cambodia in 2007. She met the medic who worked on her son David in Vietnam. She, in turn, became part of the Blackhorse family.

In June 2009, General (Retired) Donn Starry told a gathering of Blackhorse troopers and their families: "While wars are fought for many causes, most often those of us who have fought come to believe that war's message is likely more divine than it is profane. That in battle's ever-present uncertainties of terror and destruction, the only things worth remembering are the leaders [and] the brave warriors who are our comrades in arms." Henry Morris and David Embrey are the embodiment of this principle. But they are not the only ones.

Those who served with the 11th Armored Cavalry Regiment in Vietnam and Cambodia came home to The World to find a place that was very different than the one they left. If you came back in 1967 and 1968, you found family and friends to be skeptical at best, but often openly questioning of "what was the United States doing in Southeast Asia anyway?" If you returned in 1969 and 1970, you were advised to not wear your uniform in public, as skepticism and questioning had turned to open hostility. By the early 1970s, when you came home you found your contemporaries who had not served either afraid or downright contemptuous.

For all Blackhorse veterans who returned from the war, the Fifties were gone forever, replaced by a new world that was, in their eyes, not necessarily better. In any case, it was a world that was not very interested in what they had done. They had gone off to war in their fathers' footsteps; most expected to be welcomed home like their fathers had been. They weren't. *Time* magazine described it as "an adjustment problem unique among US war vets."

Adjustment problem indeed.

Most Blackhorse veterans—like their contemporaries from other units—got on with their lives. Their sacrifices, memories, and medals were put away, in an attic trunk, in a comrade's burial plot, or etched into a black granite memorial. They got married (some more than once), went to work at Sears or driving a truck, and tried to forget. As Kilo Troop's Carl Strieter said: "I never had no problems. I just kinda got married and got on with my life."

It took a decade and a half before the first of those troopers realized that they had nothing to be ashamed of; to the contrary, in fact. They had answered their Nation's call, honorably, and made a difference. Not all of their contemporaries saw it that way, but they found in their fellow Blackhorse veterans a common bond of shared understanding of what they had been through (during and after the war) and a mutual sense of service.

Danny Connelly sums up what many have come to believe: "My whole year I spent in Vietnam was my most memorable experience, because it was the most meaningful thing I'd ever done—and it still is." Patrick Kelliher says quite simply: "For me it was the defining point in my life."

Welcome home, brother!

The 11th Armored Cavalry Regiment: Then and Now

Just two months after Joe Cizmadia delivered the regimental colors to Fort Lewis, they were unfurled again—back in Germany, along another hostile border. The 11th Cavalry took the place of the 14th Cavalry along the East-West German border in May 1972.

For the next 22 years, Blackhorse troopers conducted ground and aerial patrols along the border every day—24/7/365.[1] Garrisoned in Fulda, Bad Kissingen, and Bad Hersfeld, troopers stood watch along Freedom's Frontier in the closing years of the Cold War. The fall of the Berlin Wall in 1989 and the dissolution of the Warsaw Pact two years later signaled "Mission Accomplished" for the 11th Cavalry.

On 26 October 1994, the Blackhorse returned to Fort Irwin, CA. Long a training center for large units, elements of the Regiment had trained here each summer for three years in the early 1950s (while stationed at Camp Carson, CO). But this time, the troopers did not come to be trained; rather, they became the instruments for creating a professional, well-trained Army for a new era of global instability. The Cold War was over, but that did not mean the end of the Army's—or the Regiment's—mission. To the contrary. It meant that the 11th Cavalry now had to train other units how to cope with the uncertainty, ambiguity, and fog of a new type of war.

The Regiment—with 1st, 2nd, and Support Squadrons active, rounded out by the 1/221st Armored Cavalry Squadron (Nevada National Guard) and the 1/144th Field Artillery Battalion (California National Guard)—developed the reputation as the best trained unit in the Army. In addition to acting as the opposition force (OPFOR) for the Army's brigade combat teams and selected allied units, the 11th Cavalry must maintain readiness as one of the Army's three remaining armored cavalry regiments. In 2004, the Nation called upon the Blackhorse to, once again, move to the sound of the guns.

The Blackhorse Regiment began to deploy to war in June 2004 when the 58th Combat Engineer Company—a direct descendent of the "Red Devils" of the 919th Engineer Company—was attached to the 10th Infantry Division, spreading out through Baghdad in search of roadside bombs and their makers. The rest of the Regiment followed about a year later.

Prior to that deployment, a dozen troopers who served with the 11th Cavalry in Vietnam arrived at Fort Irwin to see their successors off to war. In a regimental formation, they exchanged guidons with Bravo and Echo Troops. These two units went on to serve their tours in the combat zone in Iraq under the same guidon as these veterans had in Vietnam. The idea was that the *mojo* from that guidon, stained with blood, washed in monsoon rains, and bleached in the blazing Vietnamese sun would help protect those younger versions of themselves while in Iraq.

A year later, the Blackhorse troopers returned to Fort Irwin. The *mojo* worked. Today, the 11th Cavalry continues to serve as the opposing force at the world's premier military training facility, the National Training Center.

The Blackhorse and the Future of the Army: The 11th Cavalry Leads the Way

Those who served in the Blackhorse in Vietnam as junior and mid-grade NCOs saw first-hand how "their Army" was affected by exaggerated body counts, lowered professional standards, and the lack of public support. Many vowed to stay in the Army and fix these problems. Danny Cline was a staff sergeant in Delta Company in 1967–68.

Twenty years later, as the command sergeant major of US Army Europe, he helped reestablish the high standards of professional conduct and unit performance that had prevailed when he first joined the Army. Paul Curran was the Hotel Company first sergeant in 1969–70. As a squadron command sergeant major, he helped to train the 2nd Cavalry Regiment that performed so magnificently during Desert Storm. Collectively, these Blackhorse veterans—and countless others—led by example. They applied their hard-earned battlefield lessons learned and made the Army better.

The experience of Blackhorse leaders—as well as those for whom the Regiment worked—in Vietnam affected first armored cavalry doctrine, equipment, and organizations, and then the Army as a whole well into the 1990s and even the 2000s. There is a direct tie between the post-Vietnam doctrinal and equipment evolution and the Vietnam experience. Two years after relinquishing command of the Blackhorse in Vietnam, then-Brigadier General Donn Starry wrote: "Vietnam experience also proved armored cavalry to be much more than the reconnaissance and security force doctrine prescribed as its primary role. The cavalry role in Vietnam was as a combat maneuver force; it was the most cost-effective such force on the battlefield in terms of killing power per man exposed to hostile fire."

By the time Starry was at the Armor School, Lieutenant General Bill DePuy had been put in charge of post-Vietnam development of doctrine and training. He, too, thought it important to maintain some of the tactics that had worked, even if they were in a counterinsurgency rather than a conventional war environment. The use of firepower, for example. In 1979, he said: "It is an appreciation of heavy direct fire suppression, which most of our light infantry has never seen done. It's not in their bones. Some have seen it, but very few … What bothers me is that the US Army has been led mostly by light infantry generals like myself, for a long time." He went on to add: "Thank goodness for the General Starrys."

These doctrinal precepts are directly (albeit not exclusively) tied to the experiences of DePuy as the Big Red One commander and Starry as the commander of the Blackhorse in Vietnam. Together, they brought about a revolution in military affairs within the Army. Other facets of that revolution included the close integration of air and ground assets, emphasizing the importance of engineers to enhance maneuverability, "heavying" the armored force by replacing M113s and M60s with M2/3 Bradleys and M1 Abrams, and integrating electronic sensors into front-line units. While the first post-Vietnam capstone field manual—*FM 100-5 Operations*—did indeed change much of the Army's direction (e.g., away from counterinsurgency and toward conventional war), the manual retained the combined arms team, balance of firepower, armored protection, and mobility, and need for flexibility that the 11th Cavalry had proven to be so effective in Southeast Asia. The manual called it "synchronization"; in reality, it was "piling on." Army leaders were taught that once the "bastards" were found, they were to synchronize all of the assets they had to "pile on" and defeat the enemy.

Fred Franks served in the 11th Cavalry three times in his 35-year career—as a platoon leader and troop commander in 1960–63, as the 2/11 operations officer in 1970, and as regimental commander from 1982 to 1984. Despite his severe combat wounds, he sought out the most challenging assignments. By late 1990, he had successfully completed command of the 1st Armored Division and was now in charge of VII Corps. When Saddam Hussein made his huge mistake by invading Kuwait, Franks led his corps into one of the most lopsided victories in modern warfare. In just 100 hours, the Jayhawk Corps destroyed 14 Iraqi divisions and helped to liberate Kuwait—with less than a hundred friendly killed. The similarities between the attack in the desert in 1991 and on Snuol in 1970 are striking.

By his own admission, Tom White "was not your model [West Point] cadet ... I fought the system. And I wasn't sure when I got out of West Point whether the Army was for me in the long term." A tour with the Blackhorse in Vietnam changed all that. "But my first tour in Vietnam in the 11th Cav really sold me that it was something I really wanted to do ... It was a turning point in my life." Tom White never forgot his roots. He became the commander of the Regiment in 1986. In 2001, President George Bush, with the advice and consent of the US Senate, appointed Tom White as the 18th Secretary of the United States Army.

Donn Starry, Fred Franks, and Tom White are the best-known of the Blackhorse leaders who went on to change the Army for the better. But they are, by no means, the only ones. Dozens of troopers who served in the 11th Cavalry in Vietnam went on to pin on general's stars and sergeants major stripes in the 1970s and 1980s. As Tom White told the author in 2013: "One of the great stories in the history of the Army is the 20 years between the last shot fired in Vietnam and Desert Storm—rebirth." This rebirth was a direct result of "Starry and that bunch of guys, then us junior guys falling in."

Together Then, Together Again:[2] BHA and 11th ACVVC

The Blackhorse Association (BHA) and the 11th Armored Cavalry Veterans of Vietnam and Cambodia (11th ACVVC) are the veterans associations of the 11th Armored Cavalry Regiment. Both organizations include thousands of members, and both hold annual reunions.

In the spring of 1968, a small group of 11th Cavalry veterans gathered at Fort Knox, KY. All recently returned from Vietnam, they organized the Blackhorse Association with the objective "to foster and strengthen regimental traditions and comradeship and to assist the survivors of regimental members." The BHA was given its purpose by a promise made by Regimental Command Sergeant Major Bill Squires to a dying Blackhorse trooper.

As Bill tells it, while he was flying in a helicopter near Chanh Luu in 1968, a 3/11 ACAV struck a mine "which wounded the two side-gunners and the track commander." Squires directed the pilot to land the helicopter to help medevac the wounded troopers. The two side-gunners' wounds were not as bad as the track commander's (TC), who was seriously wounded in the legs and stomach. Squires took his head in his lap as they took off. En route to the hospital, the TC "began to talk to the Regimental Sergeant Major, telling him that he was not going to make it … The track commander squeezed Sergeant Major Squires' hand and asked him to promise him two things … to 'not let people forget us' and 'please, take care of our kids.'" As Bill told the young trooper that he would keep his promise, the "track commander squeezed the Sergeant Major's hand again and died."

When Squires and George Patton both returned to Fort Knox in the spring of 1969, they helped establish a BHA scholarship program for the children of Blackhorse troopers killed in action or incapacitated by wounds. Patton provided the seed money for the fund. Over the years, the association has grown in numbers and in scholarship contributions. The first scholarship was presented in May 1971 to Michael Wickam, the son of Jerry Wickam, the 11th Cavalry's first Medal of Honor recipient. Since then, the BHA's 13,000 members have donated more than $800,000 in scholarships "to help educate the children of Blackhorse Troopers killed in action or incapacitated by wounds" (later expanded to any child of a member or former member of the Regiment).[3]

Ollie Pickral attended the ceremonies in Washington, DC, dedicating the three soldiers statue on Veterans Day, 1984. He visited the BHA-sponsored hospitality suite and "had a great time … I met about 50 troopers there and was so impressed with the camaraderie of the guys I decided that us Vietnam vets of the 11th Cav needed our own reunion. It was in October of 1985 that I founded the 11th Armored Cavalry Veterans of Vietnam and Cambodia (11th ACVVC)." Ollie and his wife sat on the floor and hand addressed about 150 envelopes. They rented a room in a one-story motel in Arlington, TX. A local beer company donated some left-over beer, Ollie bought some chips, and "we had the first reunion." About 175 Troopers and family members showed up.

Ten years later, over 2,000 Blackhorse troopers and their families attended the 'Mother of All Reunions' in Louisville, KY.[4] Ollie recalls thinking: "What are we going to do with all these people?"

Allen Hathaway received a call in 1986 from a fellow Blackhorse veteran. Did Allen know about the upcoming reunion? Allen thought getting together with other troopers was a grand idea. Just because he had hung up his spurs and put away his uniform, didn't mean that he had forgotten his fellow troopers and the history they had made as the only armored cavalry regiment to serve in the Vietnam War. Allen went on to become one of the driving forces in the 11th ACVVC. He's served as president and membership chairman for the organization. Through his efforts, the ACVVC has identified the names of 20,000 of the estimated 25,000 troopers who served in the Blackhorse between 1966 and 1972. Allen and his team of volunteers also combed the National Archives records to ensure every Blackhorse trooper killed in Vietnam or Cambodia is identified and honored. But Allen didn't stop there. He went back to the archives and did the same for Blackhorse Troopers who had died while serving in the Regiment during the Philippines Campaign in 1902, in World War II, and in Iraq.

***

Bobbie Fry, who served as a nurse in the 7th Surgical Hospital at Blackhorse Base Camp and departed just after Tet '68, recalls the feeling of

> ... homesickness for the people and places that had been my home for a year ... The Vietnam Veterans Memorial and the Vietnam Women's Memorial started the healing process. But nothing has touched me more than a letter that was delivered to me a few years ago ... It had the Blackhorse patch on the envelope and on the inside was an invitation from Allen Hathaway to become a member of the 11th ACVVC. I don't know how he found me but—Now I'm finally home!

From those humble beginnings, the 11th ACVVC has become one of the largest and most-admired veterans' associations in the United States. Divisional associations draw hundreds to their annual reunions; the 11th Cavalry reunions always have around a thousand or more attendees. They come because they once were, and will always be, Blackhorse troopers. Like the vast majority of their generation, they answered the Nation's call, did their duty, then got on with life. And like many others, when a buddy called, they answered "here I am" again, gathering together with fellow veterans to make sure what they did receives the recognition it deserves.

We have replaced our fathers as the old men sitting around drinking beer and swapping war stories/lies (the two are interchangeable, especially as the hour gets later) about what we did as younger men. We, too, bring our wives and kids (and, shudder, grandkids—how did we get this old?). Somewhere, in between the stories and chuckles and tears, a metamorphosis occurs. There's undoubtedly a scientific name for it, but for the troopers who attend these reunions the psycho-babble name is unimportant. For us, the understanding that what we did in our youth *matters* is all that matters.

Glossary

AA (1)	Automatic Ambush
AA (2)	Anti-Aircraft
AAF	Army Airfield
AAR	After-Action Report
AB	Air Base (USAF or multi-national base in a foreign country)
Abn	Airborne
ACAV	Armored Cavalry Assault Vehicle—a modified M113 armored personnel carrier designed by members of the Blackhorse Regiment and Food Machinery Corporation prior to deployment in the fall of 1966
ACR	Armored Cavalry Regiment
AGI	Annual General Inspection
AH	Attack Helicopter
AIT	Advanced Individual Training—where soldiers are taught the basics of their MOS
AO	Area of Operations—the area in which a unit operates during a specified period of time (hours, days, weeks); the operations order generally assigns the timeframe and the boundaries of an AO
AOR	Area of Responsibility—the area assigned to a unit on a semi-permanent basis. The unit is responsible for security in its assigned AOR (also TAOR—Tactical Area of Responsibility)
AP	Ambush Patrol—a mounted (usually between two and ten tracks) or dismounted (usually 10–15 personnel) group of soldiers with the mission of setting up an ambush not far (usually within a kilometer or two) from an NDP or FSB, usually at night; the mission of the AP was to ambush enemy soldiers moving along known or suspected infiltration routes, at cache sites, or approaching the NDP/FSB
APC	Armored Personnel Carrier (M113/A1)
ARA	Aerial Rocket Artillery (see Blue Max)

AR/AAV	Armored Reconnaissance Airborne Assault Vehicle—M551 Sheridan
Arc Light	USAF codename for B-52 strikes
ARCOM	Army Commendation Medal
ARP	Aero Rifle Platoon—the infantry platoon organic to the 11th ACR's Air Cavalry Troop; colloquially, any member of the aero rifle platoon was called an ARP; sometimes called the "Blues" (blue is the tradition US Army color for infantry)
ARVN	Army of the Republic of Vietnam—the ground force established by the Saigon government for the defense of South Vietnam; colloquially, "Marvin the ARVN" was any South Vietnamese soldier
ASAP	As Soon As Possible
AT	Anti-Tank (as in AT mine or weapon)
ATF	Australian Task Force
AVLB	Armored Vehicle Launched Bridge
BA	Base Area—areas in South Vietnam or Cambodia where enemy units or activities were known or suspected (as in BA 350); these areas were used for stocking supplies, receiving replacements, and conducting training
Base Camp	Base Camp—a semi-permanent position occupied by a unit (usually brigade/regiment or larger) for extended periods of time; the "owner" of the base camp was responsible for its security, administration, and management
Basic	Basic Training—where recruits are taught the fundamental skills needed to be a soldier
BDA	Bomb Damage Assessment
BG	Brigadier General O7
BHA	Blackhorse Association—the veterans association for men and women who served in the 11th Cavalry Regiment at any time during their military careers
BHTAC	Bien Hoa Tactical Area Command—the US headquarters formed after Tet '68 for command and control of units providing security for the Bien Hoa-Long Binh area
Big Red One	1st (US) Infantry Division
Bn	Battalion
Boat People	The troopers of the 11th ACR who deployed by ship to Vietnam in 1966
Builder	919th Engineer Company (Armored)
C&C	Command and Control
CEV	Combat Engineer Vehicle (M-728)

CG	Commanding General
Chinook	CH-47 Chinook helicopter (also "Hook" and "Shithook")
Chieu Hoi	Vietnamese for "open arms," the program to repatriate VC and NVA soldiers to the side of the South Vietnamese Government
CIB	Combat Infantryman Badge—awarded to troopers with MOS 11B (infantryman), 11C (mortarman), and 11D (scout) and officers (1542) who served at least 30 days in close contact with the enemy, but not to other troopers, even if they were accomplishing the same mission
CIDG	Civilian Irregular Defense Group—mercenaries recruited by special forces to conduct long range patrols and base camp defense
CMAC	Capital Military Assistance Command—headquarters established after Tet '68 to coordinate defense in the Saigon-Bien Hoa-Long Binh area
CMD	Capital Military District—the immediate area surrounding Saigon
CO	Commanding Officer
COL	Colonel (Col. in the Air Force) O-6
Combat Loss	Vehicle deemed not economically repairable due to enemy action and washed out of the inventory
Combined	Multinational operations (see Joint)
Commo	Communications
COMUSMACV	Commander, US Military Assistance Command Vietnam
COSVN	Central Office of/for South Vietnam—the headquarters established by the Politburo in Hanoi to guide military action in most of South Vietnam
CP	Command Post
CPL	Corporal E4
CPT	Captain (Capt. in Air Force) O3
CS	Riot control agent
CTZ	Corps Tactical Zone—the geographical area corresponding to the Armed Forces of South Vietnam I, II, III, and IV Corps; after 1971, redesignated as regional assistance commands; the 11th ACR served most of its time in Vietnam in III CTZ around Saigon; 2/11 was deployed to I CTZ between April and October 1967 as part of Task Force Oregon
CWO	Chief Warrant Officer
CW2/3/4	Chief Warrant Officer 2/3/4
DEROS	Date Eligible to Return from Overseas
DFC	Distinguished Flying Cross
DMZ	Demilitarized Zone
Doc	Affectionate name given by troopers to virtually all medics

Donut Dolly	Nickname for female American Red Cross Clubmobile workers
DS	Direct Support—a command and control arrangement, used primarily (but not exclusively) for artillery; a DS unit provides support to the supported unit whenever the supported unit's commander requests it
DSC	Distinguished Service Cross
11th ACVVC	11th Armored Cavalry Veterans of Vietnam and Cambodia—the veterans association for men who served in the 11th Armored Cavalry Regiment in Vietnam or Cambodia between 1966 and 1972
FAC	Forward Air Controller—an airborne USAF officer responsible for coordinating air strikes in support of the Regiment; 11th ACR FACs used the call sign "Nile"
FM	Field Manual—Department of the Army publications describing official doctrine
FMC	Food Machinery Corporation—producer of the M113-series of vehicles (later changed to just FMC); located in San Jose, CA
FM	Frequency Modulation—the primary type radios used by the 11th ACR in Vietnam (as opposed to AM)
FO	Forward Observer—an officer or NCO from a squadron's howitzer battery temporarily or semi-permanently assigned to a recon troop or tank company for the purposes of fire support planning and execution
FSB	Fire Support Base—a squadron-sized position that generally included the HHT, CP, artillery (organic and supporting), combat trains, and a troop or company for perimeter security (frequently the squadron's tank company); squadrons generally occupied the same FSB between three days and two weeks (although occasionally longer, depending on the mission and threat level)
Ft.	Fort (as in Ft. Defiance)
GEN	General O10
Grunts	Foot-mobile infantrymen
GS	General Support—units that provided support to all units in a geographical area (as opposed to DS to a specific unit)
GVN	Government of (South) Vietnam
HE	High Explosive
HEAT	High Explosive Anti-Tank—tank round used against vehicles and bunkers
HHT	Headquarters and Headquarters Troop
Hoi Chanh	Enemy soldiers and VCI who defected to the South Vietnamese government under the Chieu Hoi (Open Arms) program

Horn	Nickname for a tactical radio—e.g., "Get on the horn and call ..."
HOW	Howitzer Battery—used exclusively to refer to one of the organic howitzer batteries of the 11th ACR (as in First-HOW, the howitzer battery of First Squadron, 11th ACR)
Huey Hog	Nickname for a UH-1B/C helicopter gunship
intel	Intelligence
JGS	Joint General Staff (VN)
Joint	Multi-Service operations (see combined)
KHA	Killed by Hostile Action—US and allied soldiers killed in combat
KIA	Killed in Action—enemy soldiers killed in combat
LFT	Light Fire Team—two helicopter gunships (also Red Team)
Light Damage	Damage to a vehicle that did not render it inoperable
LOC	Line of Communication—roads and waterways used for civilian or military transportation needs
LOH	Light Observation Helicopter (also LOACH)
LRRP	Long Range Reconnaissance Platoon (or Patrol)
LT	Lieutenant—nickname for lieutenants that emerged amongst GIs during Vietnam; as in "Hey, LT" as opposed to "Hey, Lieutenant" or "Hey, Sir." O1/2; pronounced "El Tee"
LTC	Lieutenant Colonel (Lt. Col. in the Air Force) O5
LTG	Lieutenant General O9
LZ	Landing Zone
(M)	Mechanized—as in 2/2nd Infantry (M) (also Mech)
MACV	Military Assistance Command, Vietnam—the headquarters for all American military units in Vietnam
MAJ	Major (Maj. in the Air Force) O4
Mech	Mechanized
MEDCAP/ DENTCAP	Medical/Dental Civic Action Program
MG	Major General O8
MOS	Military Occupational Specialty
MP	Military Police
MR	Military Region—name for the US headquarters providing advice and assistance as of July 1970 (formerly Corps Tactical Zones—CTZ); MR was usually followed by a number; pronounced as "MR Three"
NCO	Non-Commissioned Officer
NDP	Night Defensive Position—a platoon/troop/company-size position usually occupied late in the day; Blackhorse units rarely spent more than 48 hours in the same NDP
NVA	North Vietnamese Army—regular soldiers in the People's Army of Vietnam

OH	Observation Helicopter
OIC	Officer in Charge (also NCO in Charge, NCOIC)
OPCON	Operational Control—a command and control arrangement developed during the Vietnam War; the gaining commander assumed responsibility for the tactical deployment of the OPCON unit, but the OPCON unit's parent unit retained responsibility for providing logistical and administrative support; in reality, the gaining unit frequently assumed logistical support responsibility as well
PF	Popular Forces—South Vietnamese militia recruited to defend their home village or hamlet
PFC	Private First Class E3
Pink Team	One helicopter gunship and one aero scout
POW	Prisoner of War
PSG	Platoon Sergeant E7
PSYOPS	Psychological Operations
PUC	Presidential Unit Citation
PVT	Private E1/2
R&R	Rest and Relaxation
RCSM	Regimental Command Sergeant Major—after 1967, the senior most enlisted trooper in the Regiment (previously named the Regimental Sergeant Major)
Recon by Fire	Firing weapons into suspected or likely enemy ambush locations
Red Devils	Members of the 919th Engineer Company (Armored)
Redlegs	Artillerymen—comes from the time when artillerymen wore a red stripe down the outer seam of their uniform trousers
REMF	Rear Echelon Mother Fucker—derisive term used for those who were stationed in major bases in Vietnam (such as the lifeguard assigned to the swimming pools at Bien Hoa AB)
RF	Regional Forces—South Vietnamese militia recruited to defend a specific area (e.g., district or province)
RIF	Reconnaissance in Force
RPG-2/7	Rocket-Propelled Grenade 2/7 (also B-40/B-42)
RR	Recoilless Rifle
RSM	Regimental Sergeant Major—prior to late 1967, the senior NCO in the Regiment
RS-1	Regimental S-1—the Regimental Adjutant and senior personnel officer in the Regiment (in other Army units, S-1/G-1; J-1 in a joint headquarters)
RS-2	Regimental S-2—the senior intelligence officer in the Regiment (in other Army units, S-2/G-2; J-2 in a joint headquarters)

RS-3	Regimental S-3—the senior plans, training, and operations officer in the Regiment (in other Army units, S-3/G-3; J-3 in a joint headquarters)
RS-4	Regimental S-4—the senior logistics officer in the Regiment (in other Army units, S-4/G-4; J-4 in a joint headquarters)
RS-5	Regimental S-5—the senior civil affairs officer in the Regiment (in other Army units, S-5/G-5; J-5 in a joint headquarters)
RVN	Republic of Vietnam (South Vietnam)
Secret Zone	An area used by the VC for training, rest and recuperation, organizing for combat operations, and other administrative activities
SF	Special Forces
SFC	Sergeant First Class E7
SGM	Sergeant Major E9
SGT	Sergeant E5
Shake "n" Bake	A graduate of the Army's Non Commissioned Officer Candidate Course; named after the then-popular seasoning mix that produced oven-baked "fried" chicken in a short amount of time
SP	Self-Propelled (as in the Howitzer Batteries howitzers were self-propelled, not towed)
SP4	Specialist 4th Class E4
SP5	Specialist 5th Class E5
Spooky	USAF AC47 gunship mounted with three 7.62 mm miniguns, ten .50-caliber machine guns, and a flare launcher (also called "Puff the Magic Dragon")
SSG	Staff Sergeant E6
TacAir	Tactical Air (usually as in TacAir strike)
TAOR	Tactical Area of Responsibility—a geographical area defined by a unit's higher headquarters within which the unit is responsible for conducting operations; commanders must request permission to enter another unit's TAOR
TC	Track Commander
TF	Task Force—a battalion-sized or larger force formed for a special mission or period of time that generally was formed around a tactical unit (e.g., a squadron), reinforced with other arms appropriate to the mission
Thumper	M79 grenade launcher (also Blooper)
Thunderhorse	Air Cavalry Troop, 11th ACR
Thunder Road	Nickname for QL 13 between Lai Khe and the Cambodian border

TOC	Tactical Operations Center—also called the Command Post; usually consisted of the S-2 and S-3 tracks (M577), the Fire Support Element, the Air Liaison Officer, and liaison officers/NCOs from attached or OPCON units
TO&E	Table of Organization and Equipment—the Department of the Army approved list of personnel and equipment and how they are organized; every tactical unit in the Army has a TO&E, while non-tactical units have TDAs (Table of Distribution and Allowances)
IIFFV	II Field Force Vietnam—the corps-sized headquarters controlling all American forces in III Corps Tactical Zone (pronounced Second Field Force) (also IIFFORCV)
UH	Utility Helicopter
USAF	United States Air Force
USARPAC	United States Army, Pacific
USARV	US Army, Vietnam—the nominal headquarters for all US Army units in Vietnam; USARV had very little operational responsibility and served primarily as a logistical and administrative headquarters
"V" Device	Device attached to a medal (ARCOM, BS, AM) showing the medal was awarded for valor; in other Services, the V device may designate only that the medal was awarded in a combat zone
VC	Viet Cong—guerrilla soldiers who were members of the People's Liberation Armed Forces
VCI	Viet Cong Infrastructure
WIA	Wounded in Action
WO	Warrant Officer—officers who rank between Commissioned Officers and Non-Commissioned Officers, who are technical experts in their field (such as aviation and maintenance); Warrant Officers are generally not expected to serve in leadership positions
The World	Euphemism for any place other than Vietnam (as in "back in The World …")
WWII	World War II
XO	Executive Officer
Zippo	M132 flame thrower

History and Patch of the 11th United States Cavalry Regiment

Blackhorse History

In 1900, the United States was still adjusting to its new role as a world power. Victory in the Spanish-American War of 1898 brought with it possession of overseas territories in Cuba and the Philippines. The Army, tasked with quelling incipient rebellions in both of these new possessions, found itself woefully undermanned to accomplish the mission. As a result, Congress authorized the raising of five new infantry and five new cavalry regiments in 1901.

The 11th Cavalry, the first of the new regiments, was established at Ft. Myer, Virginia, on 2 February 1901. Ft. Myer was unsuited for training a full regiment of cavalry, so as troopers for the new squadrons were recruited, they were shipped out for training elsewhere. First Squadron trained at Jefferson Barracks, MO, and Second Squadron at Fort Ethan Allen, VT. Third Squadron remained at Ft. Myer.

By the end of the year, the 11th was deemed combat ready. Under the leadership of Colonel Francis Moore, the 1st Colonel of the Regiment, 2nd and 3rd Squadrons shipped out from New York City and 1st Squadron from San Francisco Bay in late 1901–early 1902. Sixty days later, the regimental headquarters and all three squadrons had arrived in the Philippines. It was not, however, the 11th's destiny to serve together as a regiment. First Squadron was deployed on the island of Samar where the most truculent of the *insurectos* continued to resist Governor General William Howard Taft's administration. Second Squadron was dispatched to another rebellious hotspot in Batangas Province, while Third Squadron settled into northern Luzon.

Within a year, the rebellion had been quelled. The 11th Cavalry was awarded its first campaign streamer, "Samar 1902."

The Regiment returned to the United States in early 1904, assigned to Ft. Des Moines, IA. Garrison duty in the country's corn-belt included Saturday dress parades for the citizens of Des Moines, weeks-long cross-country rides in troop and squadron strength, demonstrations of riding skills at county and state fairs throughout the mid-west (great opportunities for recruiting new troopers), and annual cavalry maneuvers at Ft. Riley, KS.

It was during the 1906 Riley maneuvers that the 2nd Colonel of the Regiment, Colonel Earl Thomas, was notified that 2nd and 3rd Squadrons were being sent to Cuba to put down another revolt.[1] After a hurricane-tossed voyage to the island (in which over 100 mounts were lost at sea), 2nd Squadron deployed outside Havana, while the regimental headquarters and 3rd Squadron were sent to Pinar del Rio—the heart of the uprising. The troopers quickly settled into a routine of searches for arms caches and show-the-flag rides through the Cuban countryside. Some even found time for an occasional sip of rum and a cigar.

The 3rd (and longest-serving) Colonel of the Regiment, Colonel James 'Galloping Jim' Parker, brought the 11th back from Cuba. The new president, William Howard Taft, insisted that 'his boys' be part of his inauguration. Troopers made the climatic transition from tropical heat to a blinding snow storm, riding in the inaugural parade on 4 March 1909. The Regiment was then sent to Ft. Oglethorpe, GA (near Chattanooga), which it called home for the next decade.

That is not to say, however, that the troopers of the 11th Cavalry 'stayed' at Ft. Oglethorpe. Quite the contrary, in fact. In 1911 and again in 1913, the entire Regiment entrained for Ft. Sam Houston, TX, spending several months both times training, patrolling the southern border, and preparing for war with Mexico. In 1913, 1914, and 1917, 11th Cavalry troopers were dispatched to the scene of severe labor unrest, as close as Chattanooga and as far away as Colorado. In 1913, the entire Regiment rode from Oglethorpe to Virginia's Shenandoah Valley to participate in cavalry maneuvers.

But the troopers' longest absence from their Georgia 'home' was in the early spring of 1916. Mexican *banditos* under Pancho Villa crossed the border and raided Columbus, NM. President Wilson ordered the Army to hunt them down and punish them. Brigadier General John 'Black Jack' Pershing led an expedition of five regiments of cavalry, four regiments of infantry, and one of artillery 400 miles into the high Mexican desert. On 5 May 1916, 11th Cavalry troopers overwhelmed a large group of *banditos* at Ojos Azules. This turned out to be the last mounted US Cavalry charge in the history of the Army.

Upon return to the United States, troops and squadrons were scattered across the continent, from Virginia to Wyoming. In mid-1919, the 11th Cavalry Regiment was reunited and sent to its new garrison at the Presidio of Monterey, CA. Over the next two decades, troopers worked—and played—hard in the California sun. Frequent cross-country maneuvers, training ROTC cadets and National Guard units, and border patrols south of San Diego alternated with polo matches, casting as extras in Hollywood movies, and displays of horsemanship at county and state fairs.[2] It was during the 11th's time in California that it became known as the Blackhorse Regiment.

By the eve of World War II, the Regiment (now stationed at Camp Lockett in southern California) had started the process of transitioning from horses to armored vehicles. That transition from "horse to horsepower" was dramatically accelerated after the Japanese bombed Pearl Harbor. Between December 1941 and mid-1943, the 11th Cavalry Regiment (Horse) was deactivated, with individual troopers and whole units serving as the foundations for three major and numerous smaller organizations. Regimental Headquarters & Headquarters Troop formed the headquarters of the 11th Cavalry Group (Mechanized). The 36th and 44th Cavalry Reconnaissance Squadrons were attached to the group. In that configuration, the 11th Cavalry Group (Mecz) fought in Europe from December 1944 to May 1945, primarily as part of XIIIth Corps, Ninth Army. First and Second Squadrons were disbanded at Ft. Benning, GA in July 1942, serving as cadre for the 11th Armored Regiment (later renamed the 11th Tank Battalion). These troopers served in combat from September 1944 to May 1945 as part of the 10th "Tiger" Armored Division. Troopers from 3rd Squadron formed the 712th Tank Battalion, which served in combat from July 1944 until May 1945 as the lone armored battalion in the 90th "Tough Ombres" Infantry Division.

Notably, then First Lieutenant Leonard Holder commanded Baker Troop, 44th Cavalry Reconnaissance Squadron. Holder's troop was the first 11th Cavalry Group unit to land in Europe. Holder returned to the Blackhorse in 1968 as the 37th Colonel of the Regiment.

Following the war, the 11th Cavalry Group (Mecz) was redesignated the 11th Constabulary Regiment and assigned to occupation duty in the American Zone near Weiden in southern Germany. Off and on for the next 46 years, Blackhorse troopers patrolled the Frontier of Freedom between democracy and communism.

After a period of inactivation, the 11th Armored Cavalry Regiment stood up again at Camp Carson, CO, as part of the mobilization for the Korean War. In 1957, Blackhorse troopers returned to southern Germany, assuming the border patrol mission along the border between West Germany and East Germany/Czechoslovakia. The squadrons were based in Regensburg, Straubing, and Landshut. These were the days of the Cuban missile crisis, multiple Berlin crises, and repeated border provocations. It took stalwart troopers—the likes of George Patton and Fred Franks (later the 39th and 50th Colonels of the Regiment respectively)—to keep the Cold War from heating up to a boiling point.

In 1964, the Regiment returned to the United States and was assigned to Ft. Meade, MD. Two years later, Blackhorse troopers returned to Asia for the first time in over six decades. For the next five and a half years, they fought against the Viet Cong and North Vietnamese Army in South Vietnam and Cambodia.

When the Regiment stood down in March 1971, the regimental colors remained in Vietnam, but the 11th ACR (minus 2/11 and Air Cav Troop) was inactivated. Shortly after 2nd Squadron came home, the 11th ACR was reactivated, assuming the border surveillance mission from the 14th ACR in Fulda, Bad Kissingen, and Bad Hersfeld, Germany. That mission abruptly ended when the Berlin Wall fell

(1989), Germany was reunified (1990), and the Soviet Union and Warsaw Pact disintegrated (1991).

The 11th ACR officially remained in Germany until 1994, but there were a number of expeditionary missions to be accomplished before the Blackhorse troopers came home. When Iraq invaded Kuwait in August 1990, individual Blackhorse troopers and two scout platoons from Echo and Kilo Troops deployed as part of Operation *Desert Shield/Desert Storm*. The end of the war did not bring an end to the troop deployments. Task Force Thunderhorse (Combat Aviation Squadron) and major elements of Combat Support Squadron deployed to southeastern Turkey as part of Operation *Provide Comfort* in support of Kurdish refugees from Iraq.

In the spring of 1991, the 11th ACR deployed to Camp Doha, Kuwait, as part of Operation *Positive Force*. The mission was to deter any of the regional forces from taking advantage of the post-Gulf War chaos. That mission ended in September, when the Blackhorse returned to Germany.

The 11th ACR assumed the mission of being the US Army's premier training force at the National Training Center at Ft. Irwin, CA, in October 1994. Virtually every Army unit that deploys on an operational mission anywhere in the world is first put through its paces by Blackhorse troopers. Training rotations at the NTC have the reputation of being more challenging than the subsequent combat missions—due in large part to the professionalism of these Blackhorse troopers.

The Regiment had the opportunity to test this premise in 2005–2006 when the regimental headquarters and 1st and 2nd Squadrons went to war as part of Operation *Iraqi Freedom*. Although not deployed as a regiment, the 11th ACR acquitted itself admirably in separate task forces in Baghdad, Babil Province, and Mosul. Regimental Support Squadron was tasked with continuing to support the deployed troopers over 7,500 miles away, while also helping the Regiment's round-out unit (1/221st Cavalry, Nevada National Guard) provide the opposing force at the NTC. All missions were accomplished in true Blackhorse style, and the 11th ACR returned to Ft. Irwin in 2006.

Blackhorse Patch

The appellation "Blackhorse Regiment" started back in the 1920s and 30s, when the 11th Cavalry was stationed on the West Coast. It was peacetime, and troopers spent a lot of time riding in parades, participating in local horse shows, and demonstrating their riding skills at local, county, and state fairs. The 11th Cavalry polo team was a force to be reckoned with up and down Highway 101. Troopers were even featured in a number of movies, both silent and talkies. In 1923 they worked as extras in the chariot scene in Cecil B. DeMille's epic, *The Ten Commandments*. Four years later, Troopers mounted up for the film *Troopers Three*—written by one of their own, former 11th Cavalry trooper and WWI veteran, Arthur Guy Empey.

Many of these roles were filled by the troopers stationed at Fort Rosecrans (1st Squadron's Bravo Troop in the latter 1920s and early 1930s), near San Diego. Officially, they were there to patrol the Mexican border, but many hours were dedicated to their "unofficial" missions—support to Hollywood producers, Pasadena parades, and local county fairs. In a tradition that started as early as the days at Ft. Oglethorpe, some troops were mounted on horses of the same color. Troop A, for example, was mounted exclusively on sorrel-shaded horses, Troop B was mounted on black horses, and Troops F, K, and L were all mounted on brown horses. In a publicity-savvy town like Hollywood, it didn't take long for Bravo Troop to become known as the "Black Horse" Troop. By 1938, the troopers were no longer at Ft. Rosecrans, but they rode their black horses alongside megastar Ronald Reagan in *Sergeant Murphy*, filmed in the sagebrush-covered hillsides outside the Presidio of Monterrey. From that time forward, the 11th Cavalry Regiment was known throughout the Army as the Blackhorse Regiment.

Because of its nickname, unit signs frequently depicted a black horse on them.[3] Unit histories indicate that such a black horse was used "on the cover sheet of FTX's/ CPX's in Germany '62–'64 and also on a yellow shield presented as a Regimental Maintenance Award." Soldiers intuitively understand that such a black horse could not be simply standing or even cantering—it had to be rearing. And, most importantly of all, there could be no mistake that the black horse was a stallion, not some mare or—shudder—a gelding.

Most combat units in Vietnam had their own distinctive shoulder patches. All of the divisions did for sure (such as the 1st Infantry Division, which was first authorized to wear its easily recognizable "Big Red One" shortly before the end of WWI), as did some other brigade-size units (such as the 199th Light Infantry Brigade, which began wearing its distinctive shoulder patch in June, 1966). Cavalry regiments, while having their own unit crests, wore the patch of the unit to which they were attached—generally a numbered corps or army. While at Ft. Meade, for example, troopers of the 11th ACR wore the Second Army Patch. However, upon arrival in Vietnam, the Regiment was directed to wear the patch of its new higher headquarters, US Army, Vietnam.

Without detracting from USARV's record as an administrative and logistical headquarters, no self-respecting combat trooper wanted to wear the same patch as all those rear-echelon types who populated Long Binh, Bien Hoa, and Saigon. Since the Blackhorse crest was not worn on jungle fatigues, there was no way (other than perhaps the dirty uniforms and scruffy boots) to distinguish the members of the only armored cavalry regiment in Vietnam from, say, the staff of the US Army Highway Traffic Center, also part of USARV. Or the orderlies in the general officers' mess. Or the clerk-typist at the R&R processing center. Or the life guard at the Long Binh Post swimming pool.

One of the first units that the Regiment conducted combat operations with was the 173rd Airborne Brigade. No one could confuse them with clerks and life guards.

The Skysoldiers of the 173rd weren't wearing the rather non-descript tri-colored shield and sword of their higher headquarters. They had their own blue and red and white patch, with a stylized Pegasus wing grasping a red bayonet. Truly a patch worthy of a combat soldier. Why, the Blackhorse troopers asked, can't we have a patch of our own?

It wasn't long after the first members of the Regiment arrived in Vietnam on a liaison visit that the leadership came to realize that they would need a patch of their own to distinguish themselves from the REMFs. MAJ Norm Kelly, the regimental operations officer and leader of the Advanced Planning Group that went to Vietnam in July 1966, remembers: "The 11 ACR Patch design was proposed by the members of the Advanced Planning Group and consisted of the Black Horse sewn on [a] 1st Inf Div Patch by a tailor shop at Di An. It was forwarded to the S1 still in Fort Meade with a recommendation that the background be red and white to represent Cav colors."[4]

That said, troopers had been clamoring for a unit patch for at least as long as the 11th ACR had been at Ft. Meade. John Casterman, a platoon leader in Mike Company with a degree in graphic design, spent many off-duty hours in the post library researching the Regiment's history, as well as the art and science of heraldry. He came up with two draft patches in early 1966—a rearing black horse on a shield, one on a solid yellow background, the other on a red and white background.[5] Others were developing similar designs at about the same time, so the sample sent back by the Advanced Planning Group was based on ideas that had been floating through the Regiment for a while. But MAJ Kelly and his troopers had access to Vietnamese tailors who were wizards at embroidering all sorts of things at reasonable prices—so, it is likely that they came up with the first three-dimensional model of the patch.

Colonel Bill Cobb (Blackhorse 6 at that time) recalls how he felt about needing a patch worthy of the combat troopers of the Blackhorse Regiment. "When we arrived in Vietnam, we wore the USARV patch, the same one worn by all rear echelon troops. That was reason enough to intensify efforts to gain approval for our own patch." He sponsored a contest while still at Ft. Meade. As noted, John Casterman's design was remarkably similar to the one sent back by the Advanced Party.[6] The 34th Colonel signed an official request for an exception to policy, which was submitted on 18 September 1966—just eleven days after the first ramps dropped on the beach at Vung Tau.

The design that was submitted showed a black horse—clearly a stallion in the original version—rearing against the traditional cavalry guidon colors of red-over-white on a shield. This was a distinctive patch, unlike any other patch in the Army, and one each Blackhorse trooper could wear proudly. Even in the combat version, subdued with only black and olive drab (no red or white), the rearing black horse stood out, recognizable anywhere. The Regiment was convinced that the Army Chief of Staff would decide in their favor; so certain, in fact, that during the first days of

Operation *Atlanta*, as the squadrons made the move into what would become the Blackhorse Base Camp, leaflets scattered across Long Khanh Province were adorned with a depiction of the proposed patch. Crews painted the Blackhorse on a red and white shield on the noses of their Hueys. Signs at the new base camp at Long Giao included the draft patch design. Some troopers were so eager to show off their new patch that they had local tailors create one-of-a-kind versions.

The 37th Med's Larry Doyle remembers the first time he saw the patch.

> When I joined the Blackhorse in Vietnam in 1970 the patch … was quite distinct. It was a black horse reared up on its hind legs with his, quite prominent … how shall I say, John Thomas, pointing the way. "Wow," I thought, "This is so cool. We get to wear these?" I really didn't want to be there, but this was way cool. I thought it unlikely at first that the Army would allow an anatomically correct logo, but then these were real men. And, real horses are hung like … well, horses.

The entrenched Army bureaucracy was opposed to making an exception for the 11th ACR, even though the USARV commander had recommended approval. The official response from Department of the Army arrived on COL Cobb's field desk shortly before the Chief of Staff of the Army, GEN Harold Johnson, visited on Christmas Eve, 1966. Johnson was already aware of the issue, as MAJ Dave Doyle had sent him a letter complaining about the disapproval. COL Cobb mentioned the patch during his private conversation, but the Chief did not commit himself either way. He did, however, tell the assembled Blackhorse troopers (to a roar of approval): "Your Regimental Commander tells me that you have submitted a request for your own shoulder patch, and it has been disapproved by my staff. Well as soon as I get back to the Pentagon I'll check on it."

Perhaps it was the same logic train that had caused Johnson to override the request from Westmoreland for a mechanized brigade instead of the 11th ACR about a year earlier. Or perhaps he just understood how illogical the policy was that allowed separate brigades to have patches but not cavalry regiments. Or maybe it was more personal; his former enlisted aide (Allen Hathaway) now served with the Blackhorse. In any case, Johnson overruled the Army Staff and the patch was approved.

Three days after the 21 May 1967 ambush, the Regimental Adjutant sent a letter on behalf of Blackhorse 6 telling all subordinate units that the shoulder patch had been approved. The Regiment initiated action with the local tailor "to procure machine made patches" in the approved design, but the Adjutant's letter cautioned: "Care must be exercised to insure that all patches worn conform exactly to the specifications" of the approved version.

Shortly thereafter, "official" Blackhorse patches started arriving in country. Delta Company's Tom Currie recalls "that the US Army issue full color and subdued patches (made in USA not Viet Nam, carried at the Clothing Sales Store and PX) were still visibly a stallion (although not dramatically so) in August 1969." Over time, however, the already politically correct artisans of the Army's Institute of Heraldry magically transformed the stallion into a gelding. Currie continues: "[T]he totally gelded version of the full color patch was starting to show up around then. By the end of 1969 all the official issue full color patches were the gelded ones."

Stallion or gelding, the Regiment finally had its patch!

Bob Merriman tells the story of when he was at Ft. Benning attending a course two decades after he left Vietnam. He was approached by a CIB-wearing veteran of the 101st Airborne Division. Noticing the Blackhorse combat patch Bob was wearing, the airborne trooper said:

> "You know … the first time I saw that patch was in January of '68. My platoon had been fighting all day. Just before dark we heard this humongous noise behind us. I went out to the road and saw a tank, and behind that tank were these APCs."[7] The Screaming Eagle soldier continued his story: "I walked up to the tank … and looked up at the tank commander. 'What kind of patch is that?' I asked. The tank commander just looked at me. '11th Armored Cav,' he said. 'Well,' I said, 'We have been fighting all day and we're glad to see you.' The tank commander said, 'We just fought through 26 miles of gooks and we're glad to see you too.'"

If Bob Merriman, or that anonymous tank commander, had been wearing the USARV patch, the airborne soldier would probably not have made the connection that these were real fighting men, just like he was.[8]

One interesting sidelight arose about the patch. Just as no self-respecting cavalryman would want to wear the same patch as a rear area staff puke or life guard, no trooper wanted to wear a patch that had the horse showing its rear end to the enemy. But when the Blackhorse patch was sewn onto the right sleeve of the uniform (the proper place for the patch of the unit with which you served in combat) the horse was facing to the rear. Some enterprising troopers decided that this was definitely wrong, so they had a Vietnamese tailor make some patches that were mirror-images of the original. In this manner, the rearing black stallion faced forward, toward the enemy. Such patches were officially banned, but in the "so what are they going to do, send me to Vietnam" days of the late 1960s and early 1970s, many Blackhorse veterans wore them anyway.[9]

In fact, George Patton—in the interim promoted to major general—wore one as the 2nd Armored Division Commander. And Donn Starry was photographed at Ft. Leavenworth in 1972 wearing just such a patch on his right shoulder—even though he was, at that time, assigned to the Army staff in the Pentagon.

Firepower Comparison

WEAPON	REGIMENTAL CAVALRY TROOP*	US INFANTRY COMPANY	NVA INFANTRY BATTALION**
Rifle	83 M16 (5.56 mm)	161 M16 (5.56 mm)	~400 AK47 (7.62 mm)
Pistol	18 Cal .45	15 Cal .45	20 9 mm
Grenade Launcher	19 M79	24 M79	40 RPG-2/7
Machine Gun 7.62 mm	61 M60/M73	6 M60	3–5 RPD
Machine Gun Cal .50	27 M2	None	3–5 Cal .51
Recoilless Rifle	None	3 (90 mm)	1–3 (57 or 75 mm)
Mortar	3 (81 mm or 106 mm/4.2")	3 (81 mm)	10–15 (60 mm) 3–5 (82 mm)
Tank Main Gun	5 (90 mm)*** 9 (152 mm)****	None	None

* Routinely cross-attached with a platoon of M48 tanks
** Armored cavalry troops and infantry companies routinely engaged VC/NVA battalions reinforced with heavy weapons from regimental level
*** Before 1966
**** After 1969

Blackhorse Medal of Honor Recipients

Three Blackhorse Troopers were awarded the Medal of Honor during the Regiment's five and a half years' service in Southeast Asia. Corporal Jerry Wickam and Sergeant First Class Rodney Yano both died in the acts that earned them the medal. Captain Harold Fritz survived. (all US Army)

Jerry Wickam

For conspicuous gallantry and intrepidity in action at the risk of his life above and beyond the call of duty. Cpl. Wickam, distinguished himself while serving with Troop F, 2d Squadron, 11th Armored Cavalry Regiment in the Republic of Vietnam. Troop F was conducting a reconnaissance in force mission southwest of Loc Ninh when the lead element of the friendly force was subjected to a heavy barrage of rocket, automatic weapons, and small arms fire from a well concealed enemy bunker complex. Disregarding the intense fire, Cpl. Wickam leaped from his armored vehicle and assaulted one of the enemy bunkers and threw a grenade into it, killing 2 enemy soldiers. He moved into the bunker, and with the aid of another soldier, began to remove the body of one Viet Cong when he detected the sound of an enemy grenade being charged. Cpl. Wickam warned his comrade and physically pushed him away from the grenade thus protecting him from the force of the blast. When a second Viet Cong bunker was discovered, he ran through a hail of enemy fire to deliver deadly fire into the bunker, killing one enemy soldier. He also captured 1 Viet Cong who later provided valuable information on enemy activity in the Loc Ninh area. After the patrol withdrew and an air strike was conducted, Cpl. Wickam led his men back to evaluate the success of the strike. They were immediately attacked again by enemy fire. Without hesitation, he charged the bunker from which the fire was being directed, enabling the remainder of his men to seek cover. He threw a grenade inside of the enemy's position killing 2 Viet Cong and destroying the bunker. Moments later he was mortally wounded by enemy fire. Cpl. Wickam's extraordinary heroism at the cost of his life were in keeping with the highest traditions of the military service and reflect great credit upon himself and the US Army.

Since starting Operation *Fargo* in the middle of December 1967, 2nd Squadron troopers had been looking for the enemy around Loc Ninh. But the recon troops and tank company just couldn't seem to pin the enemy down. There had been plenty of mines, RPG teams, and sniper fire, but nothing substantial. The Hotel Company commander, CPT Don Saari, recalls that "we had contact on a daily basis," but these did not develop into major contacts. The intel specialists kept saying that there were at least three regiments of the 9th (VC) Division out there—*somewhere*. But day after day, in unrelenting heat and choking dust, the sweeps kept coming up empty.

On the 5 January 1968, Echo Troop was the latest to move through an area that looked promising; it turned out to be another dry hole. The area was near a small village near the Cambodian border. But the 2nd Squadron commander, LTC Garland McSpadden, was determined. He *knew* there was something in there; his gut feeling was confirmed by the results of an airborne radio direction finding flight that same day. So he told his operations officer to work up a plan for the whole squadron to search the same area the following day.

Team Hotel (one tank platoon and two recon platoons) was selected to lead the 2/11 advance on the 6th. The team's mission was to move down an old French colonial outpost trail in the direction of the Cambodian border. This was the area—based on the previous day's radio intercept—that held the suspected enemy base camp. CPT Saari decided to let his organic tank platoon (three operational M48s under the command of LT Kent Hillhouse) lead the column. He placed his own and the second headquarters tank behind the lead platoon, followed by the platoons of ACAVs from Fox and Golf Troops.

LT Ed Jones' 1st Platoon, Fox Troop was cross-attached with Hotel Company for the mission. Eight of the platoon's ACAVs were operational on 6 January. Two scout ACAVs led the platoon, followed by the LT in his ACAV (F-16). CPL Jerry Wickam was the track commander (TC) of ACAV F-10 immediately behind the platoon leader.

About three-quarters of an hour into the mission, the second M48 in the column was hit by an RPG-7 just as it entered a large clearing. The enemy gunner's aim was true; the rocket entered the turret on the left side—just below where the loader was standing. PFC John Martin, Jr., was killed instantly as the warhead penetrated the turret and sent shrapnel bouncing around inside. The TC was severely wounded (but survived). The undamaged tanks immediately returned fire, as LT Jones' ACAV crews visually searched the tall grass. The RPG team was, however, long gone.

The contact ensured that everyone was alert and looking for bad guys left and right as they moved out again. Past the clearing, the vegetation grew right up to the edge of the trail. Visibility was cut to no more than three to five meters, giving the enemy a decided advantage; they were experts at camouflage. Nonetheless, the lead tank crew spotted another enemy position about 200 meters further down the trail. SSG Dennis Creal, the TC of H-13, the lead tank, saw "a cloud of dust" on the side of the road up ahead. That "cloud" turned out to be an NVA soldier engaging his tank with an AK47; Creal says "he was very good." Rounds peppered the driver's vision blocks and struck smoke grenades strapped to both sides of Creal's cupola. By the time the tank stopped, they were already past the spider hole. CPT Saari's crew (the next tank back in the column) could not see it, so he had his driver (SP5 Mike Schaefer) back up. Creal carried an M14 rifle, which he used to shoot into the spider hole. The movement stopped momentarily.

Hotel 6 herringboned his M48s on the trail and told LT Jones to dismount some scouts to check out the area to the north. CPL Wickam dismounted, then said to SP4 Charles Henry: "Let's go Henry, let's go check out this bunker." Henry brought his M60 with him, and he used it (according to Schaefer) to "hose down" the hole. They found an enemy soldier who had been shot by Creal. They pulled his body from the hole. That's when they heard, in Charles Henry's words, "a popping sound and a sound like a fuze burning." Jerry Wickam recognized it as the sound of a Chinese grenade being charged. Someone was still alive inside the spider hole. Jerry yelled "Get back Henry, he just pulled a grenade" and pushed his buddy out of the way. He threw his own body across the entrance just as the grenade went off. Fortunately, neither trooper was wounded by shrapnel, but the same could not be said of the enemy soldier. He unwittingly committed "grenadacide."

About the same time, a side gunner on F-12 noticed a second bunker on the south side of the road. He fired a magazine's worth of M-16 ammo into the hole. Jerry Wickam came running and added another clip's worth from about two meters away. LT Jones and SSG Don Carter dismounted and joined them on the ground. Jerry pulled one body out, only to discover a second enemy soldier playing possum inside. As SSG Carter covered him with his pistol, Wickam pulled the enemy soldier—an assistant RPG gunner from the 2nd Battalion, 88th (NVA) Regiment—out of the hole by his collar and made sure he wasn't armed. They found an RPG launcher and four live rounds inside the position; these would never be used against a Blackhorse tank or ACAV.

Just at that moment, Ed Jones remembers, "all hell broke loose." The tanks and ACAVs came under intense automatic weapons, RPG, and 75 mm recoilless rifle fire from the left (south). The response was instantaneous; 90 mm canister, .50-cal., and M60 machine guns blasted the jungle in all directions. But one of the RPGs had found its mark, killing SSG Creal's loader, PFC Troy Battles.

About this same time, the air support Saari had requested arrived. Four F-4s dropped their bombs and napalm into the jungle, followed by a flight of Huey gunships, miniguns blazing. Artillery was next, although it hit so far in the jungle that it could not be seen, only heard. The jungle was so thick that even the accompanying

Zippo could not burn off enough foliage to see what was hidden amongst all that green.

The Blackhorse troopers had stirred up a hornet's nest, and Saari wanted to see what else was in there. LT Jones organized a 14-man dismounted patrol, with Jerry Wickam volunteering to take the lead. Jerry's father had taught him to hunt deer and pheasant while he was growing up in rural Illinois, so he knew what he was doing. He wasn't about to let someone without the right skills be on point. For Phillip Parrish, who served with Wickam for five months, this was typical for Jerry. "He always was looking out for other people, to see that everyone was alright. He always took the most dangerous missions to protect his men."

As they moved deeper into the jungle, they found numerous empty spider holes and fighting positions. Soon, however, the trees and vines and underbrush grew so thick that visibility was cut to less than a meter. Moving in a crouch with weapons at the ready, the dismounted troopers advanced cautiously. The patrol came under small arms fire and went to ground. LT Jones moved forward to be next to his pointman.

Jerry's eyesight was better than most in the jungle, despite the thick black-framed Army glasses he wore. He was the first to spot the two-man bunker about ten meters away. He pulled the pin on a grenade and let it fly into the entrance of the hole. LT Jones recalls counting the seconds, hoping that the enemy wouldn't throw the grenade back at them. They didn't. After the explosion, Jerry Wickam and Don Carter rose to charge the position. They immediately came under heavy and effective AK47 rifle fire. Jerry Wickam was hit in the side, grunted, and fell to the ground. Don Carter rushed to his aid. His Silver Star citation relates: "Although only a few meters from the enemy positions, Sergeant Carter gallantly gave first aid to the dying man and began to pull him back to safety through heavy automatic and semi-automatic weapons fire. While engaged in his mission of mercy, Sergeant Carter was hit four times by sniper fire and seriously wounded."

Other members of the platoon were able to rescue SSG Carter, but for Jerry Wickam it was too late. The medic tried mouth-to-mouth resuscitation, but he was already dead.

Shortly after his death, MAJ Don Martin, the 2nd Squadron Executive Officer, began the process for the award of the Medal of Honor to Jerry Wickam. He interviewed some of the troopers who had fought alongside him. Many years later, Martin reflected on what he learned.

> My only knowledge of Corporal Wickam had come through hearing his fellow soldiers speak of his behavior on that fateful day. I can still hear the inspiration in their voices as they described his courage and leadership ... I don't know what went through Corporal Wickam's mind as he faced a determined, well-armed enemy manning camouflaged bunkers only a few meters in front of him. I do know that he ran the race of a soldier with honor, leading the assault on bunker after bunker, even when severely wounded, until he collapsed on the field of battle ... I do know that he exhibited at that moment of crisis the utmost faithfulness to his comrades-in-arms, to his unit and to his country.

When she was in Washington to receive Jerry's posthumous Medal of Honor from Vice President Agnew on 18 November 1969, his widow, Suzanne Wickam, was quoted as saying that "even if the war came to an end today, I still would not feel that Jerry had died in vain. He believed in what he was fighting for, and that's all that matters." She explained further that after Basic and AIT, Jerry was sent to Germany. The couple was childless at that point, but they both wanted to raise a family. "He asked God to give us a son," Suzanne told a reporter, "and he made a promise that he'd volunteer for Vietnam if the prayer was answered ... I was for it. I knew how much it meant to him. He couldn't have lived with himself if he hadn't gone." Four months into his Germany tour, their prayers were answered, and Jerry was true to his pledge. He volunteered for duty in Vietnam.

John Maville said of his best friend and high school classmate: "Jerry had what few young people have today, discipline and responsibility."

Amen, brother!

Rodney Yano

> Sergeant First Class Rodney J. T. Yano, United States Army, who distinguished himself on 1 January 1969 while serving with the Air Cavalry Troop, 11th Armored Cavalry Regiment, in the vicinity of Bien Hoa, Republic of Vietnam. Sergeant Yano was performing the duties of crew chief aboard the troop's command-and-control helicopter during action against enemy forces entrenched in dense jungle. From an exposed position in the face of intense small arms and antiaircraft fire he delivered suppressive fire upon the enemy forces and marked their positions with smoke and white phosphorous grenades, thus enabling his troop commander to direct accurate and effective artillery fire against the hostile emplacements. A grenade, exploding prematurely, covered him with burning phosphorous, and left him severely wounded. Flaming fragments within the helicopter caused supplies and ammunition to detonate. Dense white smoke filled the aircraft, obscuring the pilot's vision and causing him to lose control. Although having the use of only one arm and being partially blinded by the initial explosion, Sergeant Yano completely disregarded his welfare and began hurling blazing ammunition from the helicopter. In so doing he inflicted additional wounds upon himself, yet he persisted until the danger was past. Sergeant Yano's indomitable courage and profound concern for his comrades averted loss of life and additional injury to the rest of the crew. By his conspicuous gallantry at the cost of his own life, in the highest traditions of the military service, Sergeant Yano has reflected great credit on himself, his unit, and the US Army.

Rod Yano shouldn't even have been there that New Year's Day. He was the senior technical inspector for Air Cavalry Troop, not a crew chief or a door gunner. But the troop commander's fill-in crew couldn't find their regular door gunner, so SSG Yano—typically—volunteered to take his place. Besides, it was a routine 15-minute flight from Saigon back to Alpha Pad and the holiday cease fire was still in effect. To make things even better, there were rumors that three American POWs might be released this Wednesday, an auspicious start for 1969. But en route to Bien Hoa, a Blackhorse pilot radioed that they had contact with a large enemy force in bunkers near the Dong Nai River, about 13 kilometers northeast of Alpha Pad. Doc Bahnsen (the troop commander and pilot of the Huey) never shied away from a fight—and neither did "Pineapple" Yano.

Born Rodney Jamus Takahashi Yano in Kaelakekua, Hawaii on 13 December 1943, he entered the Army after graduating from Kona High School in 1961. He served in Germany and pulled a tour in Vietnam as a Green Beret. When he returned home, he joined the Hawaii National Guard. His younger brother, Glenn, remembers: "I was originally on orders to leave [for Vietnam] when he came back off his tour. I was in jungle training when he said he was going instead … He said that he had two tours of experience and it was better for him to stay another tour than for a guy like me to go."

Rod Yano was assigned to Air Cav Troop at Ft. Meade. He was an SP5—a quasi-NCO, but a real soldier and leader by any measure. Gene Johnson, a newly-assigned LRRP, looked up to him. "Rod (Pineapple) was a friend of mine. Before we left Fort Meade, we had a spot near the Air Cav Troop Barracks that we called the Hobo Jungle, where we gathered to drink beer. One night I wrecked my car on Fort Meade. Pineapple got a jeep from the motor pool and drug it back to the parking lot. It may still be there today."

That's just the kind of guy Rod Yano was. But he was also one hell of a good helicopter mechanic. His word was the ultimate authority along the Thunderhorse flight line. As one of his former commanders said: "He knew his business and when he inspected a helicopter and gave his okay then it was safe to fly. When he grounded a helicopter, it was grounded for good reasons."

Over the contact site, Doc Bahnsen took charge. He adjusted artillery and called up some fast-movers from nearby Bien Hoa Air Base. Ground-to-air fire was intense, but the scout bird was down at tree-top level keeping eyes on the target. At a slightly higher altitude, Bahsen's C&C bird circled the bunker complex, receiving heavy machine gun fire. Rod Yano and the door gunner, SP4 Carmine Conti, hammered back with their M-60s. Rod Yano didn't like the standard door gunner set-up. The fixed pintle restricted his ability to engage the enemy as the pilot maneuvered to avoid being shot down. He could often be seen standing on the skids outside the aircraft, firing away with his machine gun mounted on the old-fashioned bungee cord; the Army said this was dangerous, but (in this case) Rod Yano knew better than his beloved Army. He was professionally loyal and personally absolutely fearless.

When the jets arrived on station, there was so much smoke that the pilots couldn't identify the target. So Doc flew his Huey over the target at about 150 meters altitude while Rod hung out of the open troop door to drop white phosphorous (WP) grenades to mark the bunkers. Heavy AA-fire stymied their first two attempts, so they went back a third time. That's when everything started to go wrong. Just as Rod was about to drop a WP grenade out the door, it exploded prematurely. SP4 Conti recalls the moment.

> Staff Sergeant Yano … instinctively drew a white phosphorous grenade, pulled the pin, readied himself for the throw, and tossed it from the aircraft as we again approached the enemy position on our marking run. As the grenade left the grasp of SSG Yano's hand it instantaneously detonated, spewing fragments and burning phosphorous throughout the cockpit and over all the occupants. SSG Yano, closest to the grenade at the time of detonation, absorbed the brunt of the explosion witnessed by the loss of his left hand and burning phosphorous consuming his entire body, to include partially blinding him.

The cabin immediately filled with heavy, toxic white-gray smoke.

Doc declared an emergency, radioing: "Mayday! Mayday! This is Thunderhorse Six. I'm on fire. We're going in." Although the exploding grenade had left Rod Yano bleeding profusely, partially blind, and in severe pain, he kept his composure. He understood that he needed to get the remaining smoke and hand grenades out of the helicopter before the white-hot residue caused them to detonate. Despite the still-smoldering bits of WP on his face and uniform, Yano quickly cleared the helicopter of all explosives and extinguished all of the fires. He used his still-good right hand. He used his barely-attached left hand. He had to use his hands because he couldn't see much. He pushed and kicked and shoved until everything explosive or burning was out the door. Carmine Conti recounts: "Although the phosphorous continued to burn through layer upon layer of his exposed flesh, SSG Yano never once uttered a cry of pain or showed a sign of fear for the wounds he had sustained."

Wind through the open doors cleared the smoke out of the aircraft and Doc headed straight for the 93rd Evacuation Hospital at Long Binh. Pilot 1LT Bill Maestretti recalls: "Landing at the hospital, SSG Yano was carried to an awaiting stretcher. At this time, disregarding his own pain, he asked if everyone else was all right."

The WP smoke he had inhaled and the burns proved to be too much. Rodney J.T. Yano died later that same night. Bahnsen visited him in the hospital while he was still alive. True to the great soldier and leader he was, Rod immediately asked how the rest of the crew was doing. When told that all had survived, he told Doc: "Don't worry about me, sir."

Mike Gorman remembers that day vividly. He and the rest of the Air Troop personnel sat around Bien Hoa waiting for word on their beloved Rod Yano. John Wayne and his pseudo-A Team were winning the Vietnam War single-handedly on the screen, but no one was really watching (or making the usual smart-ass remarks that typically accompanied showings of the film). Almost three decades later, he recalls:

> A long time into the movie the word reached us that he had died … The word passed through the troop by jungle telegraph. It seemed we all knew at once … And it occurred to me then, and I have never forgotten it since, that I had witnessed a tragedy as terrible as any, anywhere. That this was War, with all its terrible Irony and all the gutwrenching pathos. And Yano's death was something I could only hope to put behind me, and something I hoped I would never forget."

George Patton was the regimental commander when Rodney Yano accomplished these remarkable deeds. He noted that the "pressures of war breed the unusual, but the unusual became the commonplace in the units of the 11th Cavalry … This is the Yano story which will endure as long as history lasts."

Sixteen months later, on 7 April 1970, President Nixon presented the Medal of Honor to Rod's parents, Richard and Lillian Yano, in a ceremony at the White House. But, as SP5 Haig Tufankjian says: "His Medal of Honor Citation explains in detail his bravery and commitment to duty. But not his humanity, intelligence and ability to brighten any NCO club he entered."

The Huey that Yano was in on that fateful day survived the war. After sustaining damage on two other occasions, the aircraft was evacuated from Vietnam in May 1969. Following extensive refurbishment, the helicopter was shipped back to Vietnam 1971, then returned to the States about a year later. That helicopter is located today at the 11th Armored Cavalry Regiment at Fort Irwin, CA.

Harold Fritz

For conspicuous gallantry and intrepidity in action at the risk of his life above and beyond the call of duty. Capt. (then 1st Lt.) Fritz, Armor, US Army, distinguished himself while serving as a platoon leader with Troop A, 1st Squadron, 11th Armored Cavalry Regiment, in action against enemy aggressor forces at An Loc, Binh Long Province, Republic of Vietnam, on 11 January 1969. Capt. Fritz was leading his 7-vehicle armored column along Highway 13 to meet and escort a truck convoy when the column suddenly came under intense crossfire from a reinforced enemy company deployed in ambush positions. In the initial attack, Capt. Fritz' vehicle was hit and he was seriously wounded. Realizing that his platoon was completely surrounded, vastly outnumbered, and in danger of being overrun, Capt. Fritz leaped to the top of his burning vehicle and directed the positioning of his remaining vehicles and men. With complete disregard for his wounds and safety, he ran from vehicle to vehicle in complete view of the enemy gunners in order to reposition his men, to improve the defenses, to assist the wounded, to distribute ammunition, to direct fire, and to provide encouragement to his men. When a strong enemy force assaulted the position and attempted to overrun the platoon, Capt. Fritz manned a machine gun and through his exemplary action inspired his men to deliver intense and deadly fire which broke the assault and routed the attackers. Moments later a second enemy force advanced to within 2 meters of the position and threatened to overwhelm the defenders. Capt. Fritz, armed only with a pistol and bayonet, led a small group of his men in a fierce and daring charge which routed the attackers and inflicted heavy casualties. When a relief force arrived, Capt. Fritz saw that it was not deploying effectively against the enemy positions, and he moved through the heavy enemy fire to direct its deployment against the hostile positions. This deployment forced the enemy to abandon the ambush site and withdraw. Despite his wounds, Capt. Fritz returned to his position, assisted his men, and refused medical attention until all of his wounded comrades had been treated and evacuated. The extraordinary courage and selflessness displayed by Capt. Fritz, at the repeated risk of his own life above and beyond the call of duty, were in keeping with the highest traditions of the US Army and reflect the greatest credit upon himself, his unit, and the Armed Forces.

Colonel James Parker was the 3rd Colonel of the 11th Cavalry Regiment (1907–1913). He was well respected within the Cavalry community, as well as the Army at large. He had won his spurs fighting the Indians on the western frontier, and a Medal of Honor in the Philippines. His nickname—Galloping Jim—said a lot about the man and his character. So, when he published an article in the *Cavalry Journal* in 1909 proposing changes to Army regulations governing the Cavalry, people took notice. In that article, he wrote something that applied to his Regiment in its first decade of service to the Nation, as well as to the same Regiment five decades later. "Cavalry in its work of exploration [reconnaissance], is particularly exposed to ambush."

In early January 1969, 1st Squadron's Alpha Troop was operating along Highway 13—the infamous Thunder Road. The troop was located at Fire Base Thunder III, south of Quan Loi. Platoons, on a daily basis, swept the road for mines and then escorted the daily supply convoy as it made its way north. Everyone knew that this stretch of road was one of the enemy's favorite places for an ambush.

But the intel briefing on the evening of 10 January was that all seemed relatively clear. There were no indications of anything out of the ordinary for the morning of the 11th. About the only thing unusual was that 1LT Hal Fritz, normally the Troop Executive Officer, would be filling in as the 2nd Platoon Leader the next day. Hal was 'short'; he was scheduled to leave Alpha Troop that morning to become the squadron intelligence staff officer. But he had grown up in a family where service to the Nation was something you did. So, when the relatively new Alpha Troop commander asked him if he would take the place of the medevaced platoon leader (the platoon sergeant was also out of action that day), he didn't give it a second thought. Besides it was, in his own words, "a piece of cake" mission.

The mission for 2nd platoon's 28 troopers and six ACAVs on 11 January was to conduct a route clearance of Highway 13, followed by providing security for the convoy due later in the day. Just by coincidence, an M163 'Vulcan' track—in Vietnam for field testing—was at Thunder III and tagged along with 2nd Platoon.[1] The plan was for 3rd Platoon, per SOP, to head south along Highway 13 to meet the northbound convoy at Lai Khe, while Fritz and the 2nd Platoon would move north to clear the road. Reaching An Loc without incident, Fritz radioed the all clear. The ACAVs of the 3rd Platoon integrated themselves into the wheeled vehicle convoy at Lai Khe and headed north, destination Quan Loi. In accordance with SOP, the 2nd Platoon turned around and headed back south to a point where they would laager off the road (between An Loc and Thunder III), serving as a reaction force in case of ambush. They had received some rifle fire near that location on the trip north, so Fritz hoped to "snatch up this little NVA that had been sniping at us." He told the platoon that he was "probably an NVA that got a new AK47 rifle for Christmas and he was trying it out and he wasn't very good with it yet." That "little NVA" was in fact part of a dug-in and well-camouflaged NVA force that lay in ambush.

The enemy commander from the 141st Regiment, 7th (NVA) Division, had selected his ambush position exceptionally well. He split his approximately 200-man force into two sections. The soldiers on the west side of the 20-foot wide road were dug into individual and crew positions and were very well camouflaged. The element on the east side of the slightly elevated roadway (the larger of the two elements) was sited in a depression that had once been a railway (built by the French to haul rubber from the huge plantations south to Saigon). Unused for the previous 15 years, the rail bed was overgrown with vegetation, providing excellent concealment for the ambushers. The depression also meant that they were slightly below the line of fire from their comrades on the west side of the highway. The NVA commander didn't have any mortars with him, so he instructed some of his RPG gunners to fire their anti-tank weapons in an indirect fire mode. As Hal Fritz said afterwards: "[T]he NVA that had us in a very effective crossfire … an effective crossfire without getting themselves caught in the middle of it. And they were, you know, they were very close."

The company probably moved into these positions before daylight on the 11th. They must have watched—undetected—as the 2nd Platoon drove north. The NVA commander may have decided that his luck was eventually going to run out; or, maybe he thought that the ACAVs were the leading elements of the wheeled convoy that local VC told him was due that morning. Or, more probably, he thought he had been discovered when the lead ACAV opened fire with his .50-cal. As it turns out, the ambushers had not yet been detected. The TC was merely 'test-firing' his machine gun at a hapless wild boar running across Highway 13.

Regardless of the reason, the NVA company commander gave the order to fire when all the armored vehicles were in the killing zone. It was 10:15 AM, Saturday, 11 January 1969. The 2nd Platoon vehicles were trapped in a deadly crossfire the entire length of the 300-meter long ambush. The RPG gunners could hardly miss from just three to five meters away. The front and rear vehicles blocked the road in both directions. As SSG Dennis Hutchinson, an FO from A-3/197 Artillery, said later: "They were well concealed and heavily armed and caught us by complete surprise."

The fight quickly degenerated into seven individual firefights. The enemy riflemen, machine gunners, and RPG teams focused their fire on the tracked vehicle immediately to their front. The Blackhorse crews defended themselves from fire that seemed to come from every direction.

The most memorable actions of the day belong to Hal Fritz, the senior ranking man in the ambush killing zone. Initially, he tried to control the action from atop his ACAV, but the hail of RPGs—focused on his vehicle with two antennas—took out his .50-cal. machine gun, destroyed both radios, and killed his side gunners (SP4 Thomas Bullard and SP4 Charles Day). So Hal—despite severe wounds of his own—jumped down to the bullet-beaten ground and headed for the Vulcan with, as he recalled thirty years later, "the rockets whizzing by." The NVA didn't know about this 'secret' weapon, but Hal had received the briefing and seen a firepower demonstration. He understood that this weapon could make the difference between life and death for himself and the 27 Alpha Troopers and Vulcan crewmen under his command.

The Vulcan carried a basic load of 1,100 rounds for its six-barreled, 20 mm Gatling gun. At the maximum rate of fire, the crew could shoot their entire basic load in about 20 seconds.

The NVA who ambushed the column weren't aware of just how much firepower the Vulcan could put out, but they were about to find out. The Vulcan pulled onto the shoulder of the road, traversed its turret, and aimed at the dug-in enemy soldiers in the sunken railroad on the east side of Highway 13. The gunner loosed a 30-round burst down the depression that ran parallel to the roadway.

It was almost as if the gods of war had called a time out—a momentary silence descended over that little piece of Thunder Road as both the Alpha troopers and the NVA tried to grasp what had just happened.

The silence was only temporary. The "brrrrrrrp" of the six-barreled Gatling gun shook the shock out of the rest of the column. Troopers dismounted the M60s from their burning tracks and engaged the enemy. The NVA, recognizing the threat coming from the funny-looking M113, returned fire.

Meanwhile, Fritz continued on foot towards the tail end of the column. He saw that his Alpha troopers and the NVA soldiers were going at each other "eyeball-to-eyeball." He was worried that the 60-vehicle convoy might arrive at any moment. Driving a 5,000 gallon tanker filled with aviation gas into that cauldron of fire would not be a good thing. He had to do something.

The enemy had recovered from the initial shock caused by the Vulcan, and their overwhelming numbers and firepower were beginning to tell. They outnumbered 2nd Platoon by about ten to one. With RPGs, recoilless rifles, .51-caliber and 7.62 mm machine guns, and AK47s, all dug in, the NVA held all the advantages. Hal Fritz briefly thought they were all goners. "I saw my childhood and my adulthood right there, just in a flash." But he quickly realized that this was for real and that their only chance of survival was to consolidate as much firepower as he could muster to counter the ambushing NVA. If he could do that, and if his radio transmissions had been heard—and those were two *very* big ifs—then maybe, maybe they would survive. He saw bullets "that seemed to be floating by in slow motion"; he heard the sound of his own voice and saw himself in action, but it seemed like he was another person. He snapped back to reality. He would just have to make up for the lack of maneuver, firepower, and communications with personal example. SGT Don Larson saw it all. He recalled:

> After we established our initial defensive fire, Lieutenant Fritz dismounted his vehicle and began moving along our positions directing our fire, pointing out enemy concentrations, aiding in the removal of wounded and repositioning men in order to counteract each enemy concentration. All this time, Lieutenant Fritz was in an open and completely exposed position … It was at this time that a force of 30 to 40 NVA soldiers launched a ground assault from both flanks

in an attempt to overrun our position. We immediately engaged them with every weapon we had. Lieutenant Fritz grabbed an M60 and from an exposed position, began directing intense fire on the attacking NVA elements.

For 30 minutes, Hal Fritz kept his battered platoon together. He was everywhere at once, seeming to divine somehow where the next crisis point would come. He led, he fought, and he prayed. Finally, he heard the welcome sounds of the relief column approaching.

The relief force, however, stopped short of the ambush site. The dust and smoke from the battle, as well as the cloud of dust generated by the approaching armored column itself, made it hard to see. Even worse was the fact that all of the combatants—NVA and Blackhorse troopers alike—were on the ground and covered in red dirt. From a distance, the relief column could not tell who was friend and who was foe. Hal Fritz made his final courageous dash through the sheets of enemy fire toward the lead tank. As he was approaching, he saw the 90 mm cannon turn in his direction and—unbelievably—fire a round. An RPG had also spotted the relief column and had followed Fritz up the road. Fritz accomplished his mission; the NVA did not.

Despite his wounds, Hal Fritz stayed on the battlefield until all of his men had been evacuated.[2]

George Patton's observation adds a simple elegance to what Hal Fritz did: "He simply could not be defeated." For his part, Hal was a bit more philosophical. He later told a reporter: "people sometimes fail to realize that recipients of the Medal are just ordinary people who happened to be at the right place at the wrong time, so to speak."

Sources

Research for this book involved over 50 books and hundreds of unit reports. In addition, the author interviewed over 500 Blackhorse veterans in person, by telephone or e-mail. These veterans were the heart and soul of the Regiment in Vietnam, and their words are the heart and soul of this history. Many of these troopers graciously shared scrapbooks, unpublished memoirs, letters, photos, and other memorabilia, providing poignant insights into who we were. Numerous family members, including parents, spouses, siblings, and children also contributed their memories to this narrative. The *Armor in Vietnam* monograph series, published by the US Army Armor School in 1973–74, the Office of the Chief of Military History Vietnam Interview Tapes, and the Library of Congress Veterans' History Project were great sources for interviews with veterans of the Blackhorse and those that worked with the Regiment in Vietnam. After-action reports (especially Combat After Action Reports, Operations Report—Lessons Learned, Senior Officer Debriefing Reports, and Annual Historical Summaries), unit and individual award packages, evaluation reports from the Regiment, 1st Cavalry Division, 9th Infantry Division, and II Field Force Vietnam, provided substantial input on operations, specific combat actions, and organizational data. Many of the unit reports and records have been digitized and can be found online. Original copies of these reports—some including maps and photographs—can be found at the National Archives at College Park, MD. Articles in *Armor, Infantry, Military Review, U.S. Army Aviation Digest, Hurricane* (II Field Force), and other Department of Defense periodicals proved excellent sources for contemporary accounts of Blackhorse operations. The online *Newspapers.com* is an invaluable resource for a wide variety of newspapers from the Vietnam era. The following is a list of the most significant sources used while preparing this history.

Books

Bahnsen, John and Wess Roberts, *American Warrior: A Combat Memoir of Vietnam*, Kensington Publishing Corporation, NY, 2007

Carland, John, *United States Army in Vietnam, Combat Operations: Stemming the Tide, May 1965 to October 1966*, Center of Military History, US Army, Washington, DC, 2000

Cash, John, John Albright and Allan Sandstrum, *Seven Firefights in Vietnam*, Office of the Chief of Military History, Department of the Army, Washington, DC, 1970

Chamberlain, Ernest, *The 33rd Regiment—North Vietnamese Army: Their Story*, Point Lonsdale, Victoria, Australia, 2014; *The Viet Cong D440 Battalion: Their Story*, Point Lonsdale, Victoria, Australia, 2013; *The Viet Cong D445 Battalion: Their Story*, Point Lonsdale, Victoria, Australia, 2011

Clancy, Tom and Frederick Franks, Jr., *Into the Storm: A Study in Command*, Berkley Books, NY, 1998

Clarke, Jeffrey, *United States Army in Vietnam, Advice and Support: The Final Years, 1965–1973*, Center of Military History, US Army, Washington, DC, 1988

Coleman, J.D., *Incursion*, St. Martin Press, NY, 1991

Cosmas, Graham, *United States Army in Vietnam, MACV The Joint Command in the Years of Escalation, 1962–1967*, Center of Military History, US Army, Washington, DC, 2006; *United States Army in Vietnam, MACV The Joint Command in the Years of Withdrawal, 1968–1973*, Center of Military History, US Army, Washington, DC, 2006

Creighton, Neal, *A Different Path: The Story of an Army Family*, Xlibris Corporation, September 5, 2008

Haworth, Larry, *Tales of Thunder Road*, ACW Press, Eugene, OR, 2004

MacGarrigle, George, *United States Army in Vietnam, Combat Operations: Taking the Offensive, October 1966 to October 1967*, Center of Military History, US Army, Washington, DC, 1998

Menzel, Sewell, *Battle Captain*, Author House, Bloomington, IN, 2007

Nolan, Keith, *Into Cambodia*, Presidio, Novato, CA, 1990

Ott, MG David, *Vietnam Studies: Field Artillery, 1954–1973*, Department of the Army, Washington, DC, 1975

Poindexter, John and the Veterans of Alpha Troop, *The Anonymous Battle*, self-published, December 2004

Rogers, LTG Bernard, *Vietnam Studies, Cedar Falls- Junction City: A Turning Point*, Department of the Army, Washington, DC, 1989

Schumacher, John, *A Soldier of God Remembers*, Eagle Commission c/o Grace Brethren Investment Foundation, Inc., Winona Lake, IN, 2000

Sinsigalli, Richard, *Chopper Pilot: Not All of Us Were Heroes*, Turner Publishing Co., Paducah, KY, 2002

Sorley, Lewis, *A Better War*, Harcourt Brace & Company, NY, 1999; *Press On! Selected Works of General Donn A. Starry, Volume II*, Combat Studies Institute Press, US Army Combined Arms Center, Ft. Leavenworth, KS, 2009

Squires, Bill, *Find the Bastards… Then Pile On*, Turner Publishing Co., Paducah, KY, 1997

Starry, MG Donn, *Vietnam Studies: Mounted Combat in Vietnam*, Office of the Chief of Military History, Department of the Army, Washington, DC, 1989

Stoddard, Jack and Edward Cook, *Patton's Boys*, Berea Printing Company, Berea, OH, 2015

Stokes, William, III and Douglas Kibbey, *2d Squadron, 11th Armored Cavalry Regiment, Vietnam, April 1971—March 1972*, Mariner Publishing, Buena Vista, CA, 2009

Walter, Pete (Ed.), *The Blackhorse Regiment in Vietnam, 1966–1972*, 11th Armored Cavalry Veterans of Vietnam and Cambodia, Kendall/Hunt Publishing Company, Dubuque, IA, 1997

Willbanks, James, *The Tet Offensive: A Concise History*, Columbia University Press, NY, 2006

Department of Defense Publications

Armor in Vietnam: Combat Notes, Headquarters, US Army Vietnam, 22 November 1969

Armor Organization for Counterinsurgency Operations in Vietnam, Army Concepts Team in Vietnam (ACTIV), 9 February 1966

Blackhorse Newspaper, 1968–1971

Evaluation of US Army Combat Operations in Vietnam (ARCOV), ARCOV Evaluation Team, US Army, Vietnam, 25 April 1966

Field Manual (FM) 17-1, Armor Operations, Headquarters, Department of the Army, Washington, DC, 1963 and 1966

FM 17-35, Armored Cavalry Platoon, Troop and Squadron, Headquarters, Department of the Army, Washington, DC, 1960

FM 17-95, The Armored Cavalry Regiment, Headquarters, Department of the Army, Washington, DC, 1960 and 1966

FM 31-16, Counterguerrilla Operations, Headquarters, Department of the Army, Washington, DC, March 1967

Handbook for US Forces in Vietnam, Headquarters, US Military Assistance Command, Vietnam, April 1967

History and Role of Armor, US Army Armor School, April 1974

Mechanized and Armor Combat Operations in Vietnam (MACOV), MACOV Study Group, Headquarters, Department of the Army, 28 March 1967 (seven volumes)

The Blackhorse Magazine, volumes 1–4

The Role of Armored Cavalry in Counterinsurgent Operations, US Army Armor Center Combat Developments Agency, Ft. Knox, KY, 1962

The Shield and the Hammer; The 1st Cavalry Division (Airmobile) in War Zone C and Western III Corps, Headquarters, 1st Cavalry Division (Airmobile), undated [1969]

Endnotes

Introduction

1 In the Cavalry, soldiers have traditionally been known as "troopers."

2 In the United States Cavalry, traditionally, company-sized units (typically between 100 and 200 troopers) are called "troops," battalion-sized units "squadrons" (typically 800–1,000 troopers), and brigade-sized units "regiments" (typically 2,500–4,000 troopers). The company-sized artillery units in an armored cavalry regiment are called "batteries," while the tank companies retain their name as "companies." Cavalrymen are a generally ornery, but tradition-loving lot and these designations are still used today.

3 Motto of the Regiment in Vietnam.

4 GM 100 was not really an armored force as it contained only ten light tanks; the rest of its equipment was mostly trucks. Nonetheless, GM 100's fate was—and still is today—held up as an example of the failure of 'armored' forces in a counterinsurgency environment.

5 1st Squadron, 4th Cavalry; 3rd Squadron, 4th Cavalry; 1st Squadron, 9th Cavalry (Air) and 1st Battalion, 69th Armor.

6 Respectively referred to as the Quarterhorse and Three-Quarterhorse.

Chapter 1: Preparing for War: Southeast Germany to Southeast United States to Southeast Asia, 1964 to 1966

1 The "lead scout" who remarked on the "damfine fight" was First Sergeant Chicken, an Apache Scout.

2 The fight at Ojos Azules was remarkable as it was the last horse-mounted charge in the history of the US Cavalry. It was also one of the first fights in which the Colt M1911 .45-caliber pistol was used in combat. Eleventh Cavalry officers spoke glowingly after the battle about the effectiveness of the weapon. Fifty-three years later, Lieutenant Hal Fritz used virtually the same pistol during the ambush for which he was awarded the Medal of Honor. He said afterwards: "[T]hat was a good weapon; it certainly saved me that day."

3 Led by Major General Hamilton Howze, son of Major Robert Howze who led the last mounted charge at Ojos Azules in 1916.

4 None of the dozens of officers and NCOs interviewed for this history had ever heard of the 1962 study. All of them had either served on the faculty of or been a student at the Armor School in the mid- to late-1960s.

5 In the US Army, the commander is typically called "6." His vehicle is numbered 6 and his radio call sign is 6. Traditionally, the commander of the 11th Cavalry is known as "Blackhorse 6."

6 The military phonetic alphabet is used to ensure similar-sounding letters are not confused; thus, "m" is "Mike" and "n" is "November."

7   For the bulk of its training, for example, 3/11 had only one-quarter of its authorized NCOs and the bulk of its junior officers were on their first active duty assignments. One after-action report stated: "The late arrival (20 May) of many key NCOs and specialists, i.e. tank commanders, gunners, squad leaders, section chiefs (artillery), detracted from the effectiveness of training." About half of the troopers who would be going to war with the 11th Cavalry—a large proportion of whom were mid-grade and junior NCOs—were not even assigned to the Regiment until about 60 days before they deployed to South Vietnam.

8   LTC Tiger Howell, the 1/11 commander, later wrote: "Counter-ambush drills were practiced and perfected in the United States before deployment and when properly applied [in Vietnam] were uniformly effective."

9   A "track" is any armored vehicle with tracks as opposed to wheels. Thus the leader in a track was a "track commander."

10   The addition of a fifth trooper to the crew—armed with a grenade launcher—ensured protection to the rear in the jungle and during road convoys.

11   Because of the demands for aircraft and qualified crews in Vietnam, the Army recognized in late spring 1966 that Air Cav Troop would not be able to deploy at the same time as the rest of the Regiment. According to a MACV report: "By end FY [Fiscal Year] 66, the Army will have a requirement for approximately 14,300 aviators vs. a projected strength of approximately 9,700." The plan was to have the troop arrive in December or early January 1967.

12   Carol Doda was one of the first topless go-go dancers to improve her bust via "better living through chemistry." She grew from a natural 34 to a silicone-enhanced 44. She performed her 'topless swim' act 12 times nightly at the Condor Club at the corner of Broadway and Columbus in North Beach.

Chapter 2: The Blackhorse Enters Combat: September 1966 to May 1967

1   South Vietnam was divided into four corps tactical zones—I CTZ just south of the Demilitarized Zone (DMZ), II CTZ in the Central Highlands, III CTZ around Saigon, and IV CTZ in the Mekong Delta. In 1970, the four corps were renamed to 'military regions' but the boundaries did not change.

2   Throughout this text, enemy units are distinguished between Viet Cong (VC) and North Vietnamese Army (NVA). Similarly, Army of the Republic of Vietnam are identified by (ARVN). Units without these identifiers are American.

3   GIs found the war and environment in Vietnam so different from anything in their lives up to that point, that they called everything outside of Vietnam 'The World'.

4   India Troop's Rick Organ has always remembered that date. "September 11, 1966, the [3rd Squadron] 11th Armored Cavalry Regiment lands in Vietnam! From September 11, 1966 thru September 11, 2001, I always remembered the day we landed in Vung Tau, Vietnam. Now, every American remembers 9/11!"

5   John Albright vividly recalls that horse: "There was a Vietnamese girl standing with a horse; a black horse. It was the sorriest damn looking horse I ever saw."

6   Typically, military units move in three groups. The "advanced party" arrives first to coordinate the logistical and administrative details of a unit's arrival. The "main body" includes the bulk of the unit, while the "rear party" is the last to arrive after clearing the area from where the unit came.

7   When the Regiment deployed to Vietnam, armored cavalry regiments were not authorized their own shoulder patch. Troopers were expected to wear the patch of the Corps or Army to which

they were assigned. After the personal intervention of the Chief of Staff of the Army (who visited the Blackhorse in Vietnam at Christmas), the Army approved the Blackhorse patch for the 11th Cavalry in the spring of 1967 (see Appendix 1).

8   There never was a serious ground assault against the camp until April 1975, when the South Vietnamese 18th Infantry Division made a determined last stand in the defense of Saigon.

9   The tail end of the convoy—two Charlie Troop ACAVs and 17 trucks—was short of the killing zone when the ambush was sprung. They stopped on the highway and were not damaged.

10   Each tactical military vehicle has a unique 'bumper number' stenciled on it, front and back, identifying the unit and the number of that vehicle within the unit.

11   At least four rounds aimed at C-16 during its multiple runs missed because the VC gunners misjudged its speed.

12   The body of a Chinese soldier was found during the sweep of the battlefield on 22 November.

13   Neil Keltner received his Distinguished Service Cross in almost record time. General Harold Johnson, Chief of Staff of the Army, presented it to him in an awards ceremony at the base camp on Christmas Eve, just 33 days after the 21 November ambush.

14   The squadron closed on the new base camp on the afternoon of the 22nd. Two days later, the mess halls were brimming with the smells of turkey, stuffing, and cranberry jelly—it was Thanksgiving Day. As Raye Ashe recalls: "To many, who had been in the ambush ... it was perhaps the most thankful Thanksgiving Day of their lives."

15   Attleboro marked the first time B-52s were used in direct support of ground forces. It would not be the last.

16   As Westmoreland's operations officer, DePuy was the driving force behind removing tanks from the Blackhorse recon troops. Despite this early skepticism about the viability of armor, DePuy became not only a convert but an influential voice in armor's valuable role, both during and after Vietnam.

17   Larry Gunderman recalls: "We were out, probably on a typical search and destroy ... We were east of Xuan Loc when we got the change in mission from Regiment ... We did it on the fly. It was a typical armor mounted warfare thing. We got the change of mission order: "Move to and secure Lai Khe." And that's what we did. Everybody [troop commanders] got orders on the fly ... Ten and a half hours later—without dropping a track—we closed and secured Lai Khe. And then nothing happened."

18   At the beginning of February 1967, about 400,000 US (264,000+ Army) troops were in country. Another 15,000+ were added during the month.

19   A situation where the track on an armored vehicle comes off the road wheels, stopping the vehicle in place.

20   When Air Cav Troop arrived in country in December 1966, it included an Aero Rifle Platoon (ARP)—as per the Table of Organization and Equipment (TO&E). However, in March 1967, just two months after becoming operational, the ARP was converted into a Long Range Reconnaissance Patrol platoon (LRRP). In August 1968, under guidance from Colonel George Patton, the platoon was reestablished in accordance with the TO&E.

21   Named TF Oregon as it was the home state of the MACV Chief of Staff, Major General William Rosson, the initial TF commander. It consisted of the 1st Brigade, 101st Airborne; the 3rd Brigade, 25th Infantry Division and the 196th Light Infantry Brigade.

22   Fox Troop's Specialist 4 (SP4) Tom Thornburg admires them to this day, especially the ones he encountered in the battle on 24 September. "These were Recon Scout "Killers" and they were really good ... These were professionals who fought the Japanese, the French and now the Americans ... without ever taking a break." But, Tom concludes, "Losing to them was never even a consideration."

Chapter 3: The Fight Intensifies: May to July 1967

1 General Nguyen Chi Thanh, also known as Truong Son, was the military commander of the VC from 1964 to 1967 and a member of the Communist Party Politburo in Hanoi. He was considered to be one of the NVA's leading strategic thinkers. He designed the Tet '68 military offensive, but died on 7 July 1967 (either from a heart attack or a B-52 strike) before the plan was executed.

2 In a Hurst Performance Products initiative, each of the 33 race car drivers wore the insignia of an Army, Marine, Navy, or Air Force unit then serving in Vietnam.

3 A full-color picture of Kerry Nelson in his gunner's seat (taken by Co Rentmeester from the bottom of the turret) appeared in *Life* magazine, which hit the newsstand less than two weeks after the 21 May ambush. That picture won Rentmeester World Press Photo of the Year honors.

4 Two years later, while on his second tour with Mike Company, David Wright met one of the VC who had fired at his tank that day. The enemy soldier had surrendered after the ambush. He volunteered and was trained as a Kit Carson Scout. Assigned to 3/11, he informed the squadron commander (LTC Dave Doyle, who was the Squadron operations officer at the time of the ambush) that he had been one of the RPG gunners on 21 May 1967. In fact, he said he was the one who fired the first shot at M-34. He told his former target that Wright's return fire had killed his comrades and wounded him. After discussing the battle (through an interpreter), the former VC rose. "In very broken English, he apologized for his actions during the ambush. He then offered his hand in friendship." Wright recalls his emotions at that point. "What was I to do? Here I was with a loaded weapon on my hip and a former enemy soldier, who had tried to kill me, was asking for my forgiveness. The question still remains, could I have shot him right there in the TOC?"

5 Vehicles turn 45 degrees from the direction of travel, alternating left and right from the first to last vehicle in the column.

6 Although he is assumed to have been killed on 21 May 1967, because his body was burned beyond recognition, Walter Simpson was declared missing in action. One year and a day later (22 May 1968), he was declared killed due to hostile action, body not recovered.

7 Puglisi distinctly remembers a badly wounded Vietnamese woman lying next to the woodpile as well.

8 The MACV history for 1968 discusses the enemy's use of increased radio chatter to pinpoint operational information: "Through his monitoring capability, the enemy was able to gain early warning of impending Allied operations. At times, intercept allowed him to gauge the size and intent of the operation. A PW [prisoner of war] indicated there was a noticeable increase in communications, beginning with FACs, when an operation was about to occur. The broadcasts were correlated with US maps, and this allowed the enemy the option of either engaging the Allies by ambush or avoiding them entirely."

9 Even before the Regiment learned of *Dai Uy* Trang's treachery, Blackhorse Troopers suspected there had been a leak. A post-mortem of the ambush by the regimental intelligence officer concluded: "[T]he Viet Cong were probably aware of the intended operation on Route 20 and had sufficient time to coordinate with the D800 Dong Nai Battalion for reinforcements." *Dai Uy* Trang was turned over to South Vietnamese authorities, interrogated, and executed.

10 About ten kilometers further along Highway 20 from the 21 July 1967 ambush site.

11 Despite their wounds, the crew of L-33 reorganized in the roadside ditch, and, along with some other Lima troopers, later returned to the moat and cleared it of VC with grenades and rifles.

12 The absence of any tanks in the second Lima Troop march segment, due primarily to the road condition rather than tactical considerations, made it difficult for them to gain fire superiority until Kilo Troop's arrival. As a result, a disproportionate number of the casualties came from within this element.

13 All three died that day.

14 An M79 round will not explode until at least 30 meters after being fired from its launcher.

Chapter 4: The Blackhorse Makes Its Reputation: Late 1967 to Late 1968

1 By the end of 1967, General Westmoreland and his staff considered 60 percent of the roads in South Vietnam as 'secure' (i.e., "those that could be traveled during daylight hours without an armored escort"), compared to only 30 percent at the beginning of the year. The MACV *Command History* for 1967 noted: "Rome Plows of US Land Clearing Teams cleared 100 to 300 meter wide strips along many RVN highways. The resulting open areas lessened VC capability to mount ambushes and reduced the effectiveness of those which occurred. During the month following land clearing activities along Route 20, 1, and 2 there were no ambushes of the 11th ACR; previously many ambushes had occurred." The Viet Cong never again held sway in the area, and it was only the overwhelming tide of North Vietnamese power that reversed that trend—and not until 1975.

2 The official US Army history says: "According to a later Communist account, some 31,700 personnel entered South Vietnam during 1967, more than twice the number that infiltrated during the previous year ..."

3 As part of its pre-Tet offensive deception plan, Hanoi mounted a major operation against the Marine outpost at Khe Sanh, just miles from the Laotian and North Vietnamese borders. Fearing that defeat at Khe Sanh would be equivalent to the French defeat at Dien Bien Phu in 1954, Westmoreland—with strong encouragement from President Johnson—became fixated on the battle there, to the detriment of being prepared elsewhere.

4 In the end, the three 11th Cavalry squadrons, the 25th Division's 3/4th Cavalry, and troop-sized elements of the 1/4th Cavalry and 3/5th Cavalry, all contributed to countering the Communists' offensive against the Saigon-Bien Hoa-Long Binh complex. The armored cavalry's ability to move, shoot, and communicate under even the most difficult conditions saved the day. It wasn't airmobile infantry, or special forces, or masses of air strikes that threw back and soundly defeated the attacking VC forces; it was the cavalry. And once the ring of steel—consisting of over 500 armored vehicles, reinforced with helicopter gunships and self-propelled mortars and artillery—was in place, battalions' worth of battle-hardened VC guerrillas and NVA regulars could not penetrate it.

5 Even though designed for radio-research missions, the 409th's M113s all had side-mounted machine guns and protective armor shields. From the outside, they looked just like ACAVs.

6 In the face of overwhelming intelligence evidence, MACV and the South Vietnamese Joint General Staff cancelled the cease fire that had been agreed to by both sides for the Tet holidays.

7 Vietnamese sweep meant "if there were any mines, run over them" and keep going.

8 There was a direct correlation between the serious losses on 29 January and the assumption of command of 1st Squadron by a new commander the next day. Specialist 5 Jim Traner recalls: "I remember an order came down to make sure we had our names in our boots. Why? So the morgue guys could match up the limbs with the correct bodies. Talk about a morale booster. I still remember the body bags on the LZ [landing zone] in the evening because it was too risky for the dust-offs to come in to that small clearing in the dark."

9 Under normal circumstances, map sheets were covered in clear acetate and operations order graphics were printed on the acetate using a grease pencil (a crayon-like writing instrument designed specifically for this purpose). When a new operations order was prepared, the old graphics could

be erased and the new graphics placed on the same acetate, allowing the map sheets to be used repeatedly. On 31 January, there wasn't time for such niceties.

10 Military vehicles are equipped with head and tail lights that can be switched by the driver from 'normal' (for use in peacetime) to blackout drive. The blackout drive feature is a small white light in the front and two 'cat's eyes' red lights on the back. These lights are sufficient for trained drivers to move at slow speeds (15 mph) and still see the ground, as well as the vehicles in front of them. Delta Company's Pat Andrews was so used to driving his tank without lights that he was stopped one night shortly after returning home from Vietnam. The New Jersey policeman asked him if the car's lights worked; they did, but Pat was "driving by moonlight" as he had done for the previous year. The policeman let him go.

11 Repercussions from the destruction caused by the Regiment's firepower began almost immediately. Within 24 hours, Blackhorse 6 had been directed to not fire tank main gun rounds in any built-up area without the explicit permission of LTG Weyand. Several months later, 1st Squadron was working for the Capital Military Assistance Command (CMAC) in Bien Hoa. CPT Bill Hansen recalls: "You needed a general officer's permission to lock and load a .50-caliber."

12 It was this "wall-to-wall" talent that convinced Tom White to make a career in the Army, a career that culminated with his serving as the 18th Secretary of the Army in 2001–2003.

13 Communist leaders determined that the secrecy surrounding the February attacks had caused many units to not get the word in a timely manner, resulting in their late or even non-arrival on the battlefield. Orders for the Mini-Tet offensive were distributed widely and well in advance of the attack, but some of the orders were captured. As a result, numerous units were interdicted well short of their objectives.

14 Terry Wallace returned to Cam My in 1973. He was serving as the senior militia advisor for Gia Dinh Province. Cam My was in his area, so he landed there one day. "The orphanage was gone and the locals said Father John had been killed and the nuns driven off. Never been sure of the truth as the folks were pretty frightened of the chopper and me. I had a great interpreter so the questions were clear. The orphanage was gone though."

15 This turned out to be a double-edged sword. The improved defenses enabled the militia to hold off the VC assault much longer than during the 9 March battle. However, once overrun, the VC then used these same bunkers to defend against the follow-on 2/11 assault.

16 Instead of the expected airmobile force, they were attacked by armored vehicles. As the D445 (VC) Battalion history says: "The situation was extremely dangerous. Our troops had to fight against the enemy tanks—while setting up a battle position to fire on the counter-attacking enemy aircraft."

17 An agent later reported that, at the same time as the attack on Cam My, three well-armed enemy battalions crossed Highway 1 headed south. This was, apparently, a regiment of the 5th (VC) Division moving into the May Tao Secret Zone under cover of the attack on Cam My.

18 One Hotel Company tank and no ACAVs were considered combat losses as a result of this battle; four Blackhorse troopers were killed at Cam My on 5 May.

19 Captured enemy documents revealed that this same notion was current among a number of enemy units. Communist documents captured and translated after the start of the Paris peace talks noted that the negotiations "have done much to encourage 'peace illusions' and the 'fear of the last shot.'"

20 One of the unique aspects of 3/11's campaign in Hau Nghia was the prominent role played by Mike Company's M48 tanks. Since mobility across the dry rice paddies was never an issue, they had unlimited access to and on the battlefield. The thick armor could withstand the anti-tank fire better than the ACAVs, and the 90mm cannon was much more effective against the hedgerow bunkers. Whereas canister was used most frequently in the jungles, during March and April 1968, the combination of high explosive (HE) and canister was found to be golden.

21 In early 1998, Neal Creighton (3/11 commander in 1968) and his former operations officer, John Getgood, returned to Hau Nghia Province and toured many of the battlefields they fought on in 1968. One of their escorts was the former commander of the 9th (VC) Division, Colonel Kham, whose 271st Regiment opposed them in March. Much of this section is taken from Creighton's recollections of that visit. Additional information about Le Cong Lam is derived from the *Washington Post*, 18 March 1968.

22 BG Nguyen Xuan Thinh had been relieved of command of the 22nd (ARVN) Infantry Division. He then replaced an even more incompetent leader of the 25th Division in December. He was an artillery officer by training and a 1964 graduate of the US Army Command and General Staff College at Fort Leavenworth. He was awarded a US Silver Star for battlefield bravery during Mini-Tet. Second Squadron and Air Cavalry Troop would later work for him in 1971 when he led South Vietnamese operations in Cambodia. By that time and because of his leadership, the 25th (ARVN) Infantry Division was rated as one of the three *best* in all of the South Vietnamese Army.

23 By using this term, LTG Weyand avoided the thorny issue of who was in command. He also used a term that artilleryman Thinh could easily understand. The end result was an unqualified success, in no small part due to the personalities and abilities of the commanders involved.

24 Kilo Troop was under the operational control of various infantry units starting on 12 March and, therefore, not available in Hau Nghia Province.

25 When recon troops and tank companies cross-reinforce each other with platoons, they are known as "teams."

26 An agent reported through ARVN channels on 11 March that there were at least 500 VC in the area of Bao Canh Na. That report reached 3rd Squadron on the 14th—two days *after* this operation.

27 The official report says that two of the prisoners were shot by the militiamen while attempting to escape; some eyewitnesses didn't remember seeing them trying to escape.

28 After-action assessments of the course of the battle indicate that the captives' actions may have been part of a well-conceived ambush. As the command historian wrote: "The interrogated prisoner's claim that there was a food and weapons cache at Objective 3 [Hamlet 3]—when looked at in retrospect—has the odious smell of a trap."

29 Interviewed shortly after the engagement, Creighton said it was a "much larger force than I originally thought." The Duc Hoa Subsector commander, who was on the ground with his soldiers, told his radio operator to listen in on the VC radio net during the fight. The intercepted transmissions indicated that two companies were initially in Bao Canh Na. The enemy commander on the ground called for reinforcements and two VC battalions responded.

30 Don Robison was replaced as the Mike Company commander by CPT Stanley Nelka, who was badly wounded in the same tank in his first firefight. He was replaced by CPT Bob Wilson, who was killed in action on 6 May. Mike Company had four company commanders in less than two months. Neal Creighton believes that this was no accident. "They [VC/NVA] went for the tanks. They turned everything on the tanks … They were a greater danger to them. That's what they feared …" They also knew the tanks with two antennas were commanders' tanks.

31 The American advisor with the militia platoon, an Armor captain named Hempstead, mounted M-66 after Robison was killed. He jumped on the back deck and helped pull Robison's body out of the turret, then climbed in. Although the tank could not shoot, the radios still worked. He became an impromptu radio relay, serving as a vital communications link between Creighton and the rest of Mike Company.

32 The four hamlets were spread over an area about one kilometer wide and two kilometers deep.

33 Elements of the 49th (ARVN) Infantry made contact with a group of about 200 VC/NVA to the northwest of Bao Canh Na on the morning of 13 March, while a Lima Troop ambush patrol made contact on the night of the 12th to the southeast of the village.

34 Other reports put the total enemy killed at between 135 and 145. There had been ten prisoners, but two of them were shot by the militia.

35 Deusebio was scheduled to meet his wife on R&R in Hawaii the following day. She was notified of his death while waiting for him in Hawaii.

36 According to Bill Hansen, the squadron intelligence officer at the time, Jack Nielsen was "a World War II veteran, crusty, a little bandy rooster, good fighter."

37 The Regiment's Intelligence Summary (INTSUM) described the rains as "torrential," preventing, on at least one occasion, aerial reinforcement during a night attack outside Tay Ninh City. Almost three inches of rain fell on the morning of 14 May, for example—with the temperature climbing to 97° by mid-afternoon.

38 The M113s of the mechanized infantry from the 25th Infantry Division that usually operated in the area were not configured as ACAVs; they did not have armor around the TC's position.

Chapter 5: The Bloodiest Year: 1969

1 Vietnamization, pacification, diplomatic isolation, peace negotiations, and gradual withdrawal.

2 On 12 April, MACV announced it would no longer use the term "search and destroy operations" because it was "over-used and misunderstood."

3 One indication of how meaningless the body count was appears in the MACV Command History for 1968: "An interrogation of a former NVA doctor, chief of a regimental medical section, produced the following information on the VC/NVA front line medical program: There were normally four VC wounded for each KIA." WIAs have different, but almost as significant effects on military forces as do KIAs. WIAs must be evacuated, cared for, rehabilitated, and then either returned to duty or transferred to a less-demanding job or location; all these things require resources, including manpower and medicine. Under these parameters, the body count (which, in some units, included estimates of probable KIAs), by itself, told only part of the story, especially considering the willingness of the Hanoi Government to sacrifice the lives of its citizens for a political victory.

4 Air interdiction of the Ho Chi Minh Trail, primarily in Laos, was another critical element in Abrams' integrated strategy; with the cessation of bombing in North Vietnam, air assets that had previously been dedicated to that mission became available to employ against the Ho Chi Minh Trail and the Cambodian sanctuaries. There were almost 300 B-52 sorties in the area around Saigon between November 1968 and January 1969 and 500 the next three months.

5 In late 1968 and early 1969, the Communists shifted seven infantry regiments from the Central Highlands into the area around Saigon and the Mekong Delta—just to make up for the losses between February and August 1968.

6 The 33rd (NVA) Regiment, attached to the 5th (VC) Division for the post-Tet offensive, had orders to reinforce the 274th Regiment. They were taken under fire by artillery and gunships well east of Long Binh and never entered the battle. The 275th Regiment was supposed to attack Bien Hoa at the same time, but two of the three battalions got lost en route to their attack positions and failed to accomplish their missions.

7 NVA Private Tran Van Thiel, captured after the fight, said that he and his comrades "were very happy" with this news; some even brought along can openers in anticipation of finally getting a decent meal.

8 Chain link fence sections that caused the shaped-charge warhead of an RPG to detonate early.

9 Named for the 1/11 Executive Officer (XO), Major (MAJ) William Privette.

10 Pacific Architects and Engineers, the ubiquitous civilian contractor located on almost every American base in South Vietnam.

11　The 152mm gun on the Sheridan fired a so-called flechette anti-personnel round filled with almost 9,000 metal arrows about 2 inches long. The 90mm cannon on the M48 tank fired a canister round filled with over 1,200 steel ball bearings.

12　Donald Kelly was also awarded a Distinguished Service Cross for his gallantry on 19 April 1969.

13　When engaging a target with the main gun, the tank gunner says "on the way" to alert the rest of the crew that he is about to pull the trigger.

14　Everybody understood just how sensitive an area the plantation was, so special permission had to be obtained from higher headquarters to return fire a day before the operation officially kicked off. The area was so politically sensitive that MACV representatives did not initially use the name Michelin Rubber Plantation when discussing Operation *Atlas Wedge* with members of the media.

15　George Red Elk was awarded a Silver Star for his actions on the 18th.

16　LTC John McEnery was awarded a Distinguished Service Cross (DSC) for his actions on 20 March. ARP SGT Frank Saracino, Jr., was posthumously awarded a DSC for his gallantry in this same fight. Lima Troop's PSG Donald Biggin was awarded a DSC for his heroism on 18 March.

17　Many thought that some of the areas were inaccessible to armor. The after-action report said otherwise: "Operation *Montana Raider* proved that 'There are no untankable areas.'"

18　Command and control within the Blackhorse was really stressed during Operation *Montana Raider* by changes of command. Leach assumed command on 6 April, a week before the operation kicked off. LTC Merritte Ireland, the 1/11 commander, was medically evacuated with a high fever of unknown origin on the day before the start of Phase I; his XO (MAJ Privette) followed with similar symptoms the following day. Ireland was replaced by the Air Cav Troop commander, MAJ John "Doc" Bahnsen. Five days into *Montana Raider*, LTC Jim Aarestad became the 2/11 commander, assuming leadership from Lee Duke in a scheduled change of command. Fortunately, the Regiment was blessed with exceptionally competent staffs and subordinate commanders, so these changes did not have any adverse effects on mission accomplishment. But there was little time for the formalities of changes of command and smooth transitions. As Jimmy Leach said: "We were not loafing."

19　A tactical formation used when contact is expected, but the exact location of the enemy is unknown. Two platoons move in column on parallel paths, and the third platoon moves on line in between them, forming a box-like formation.

20　M48 tanks have a 7.62 mm machine gun coaxially mounted next to the main gun—commonly called the "coax."

21　Pongratz' Distinguished Service Cross cites his actions on both 13 and 18 April 1969.

22　About one-third of the normal daily ration for a VC guerrilla.

23　3rd Squadron, 11th Cavalry was at Blackhorse Base Camp drawing Sheridans.

24　As an example of how the plan was executed, during the hectic night of 11–12 August, TF 1/16 Infantry—with two organic mechanized infantry companies and an airmobile infantry company from 5/7th Cavalry—was alerted to be prepared to execute up to four of the counterattack options. In each case, however, the defenders of the four affected FSBs were able to fend off the enemy themselves. TF 1/16 executed a fifth counterattack option after daylight on the 12th. They were able to do so because of the comprehensive plan developed before the battle started.

25　Ashbee Tyree was awarded a Silver Star for his leadership and coolness under fire that night.

26　The CEV was a modified M60 tank, designed with engineer-specific changes, including a dozer blade, a bunker-busting 165 mm cannon, and a lifting boom. This may have been the first-ever combat action by CEVs in US Army history.

27　That base defense officer later said that Duprey's decision "probably saved the day for us."

28　The left arm is the one used to charge the .50-cal. whenever you change boxes of ammo or have a misfire.

29　The former plantation manager's villa, complete with swimming pool.

30 Probably from a 409th Radio Research Detachment radio intercept.

31 By contrast, at FSB Aspen, "Before the first sergeant of H Company, 1SG Russell Crowley could yell incoming, the entire perimeter opened up. Two NVA appeared on the top of the berm, but the instant response killed them [after-action report]." This action preempted a battalion-sized attack on the FSB. The next day, ABC News reporter Don Baker flew with Thunderhorse 6 to Sidewinder. They talked with two US advisors. MAJ Bradin asked Baker if he wanted to do a story of Sidewinder, and Baker told him he'd been told that ABC didn't want "anymore war stories."

32 John Sexton was captured by the VC after the 12 August fight. He spent the next two-plus years in jungle cages, dodging B-52 strikes and enduring repeated interrogations. He was released by the VC in October 1971. Jim Bradin recalls the sense of loss and gloom in the Regiment the night of 12 August. Four decades later, he reminded Jimmy Leach: "That was not our finest hour. I remember you stood up at the TOC that night and said it was the darkest day in the history of the Regiment."

33 According to South Vietnamese sources, 47,000 enemy personnel rallied to Saigon's side during 1969—more than double the 1968 figure of 23,000.

Chapter 6: Expanding the War: 1970 to Early 1971

1 These claims are almost ten times the number of tanks and armored vehicles *assigned* to all Army, Marine Corps, and ARVN units in all of South Vietnam

2 As part of the Vietnamization program, on 1 July 1970 the four corps tactical zones in Vietnam were renamed military regions (MR). The boundaries did not change and they retained their previous numerical designations—III CTZ became MR III.

3 The 11th Cavalry knew this last report was only half the story. While operating along the border, scouts watched the truck convoys in Cambodia "with their lights on" hauling in material. Aero scouts and the regimental intelligence officer flew the border every night. They developed a very accurate picture of where the major cache sites were north of the border. Colonel Donn Starry, who assumed command of the Blackhorse in December 1969, recalled later: "If you kept everything quiet up there, you could hear them unloading the trucks and what not. In some cases, they were just across the border ... I was pissed off at the intel system [for claiming most of the stuff was coming down the Ho Chi Minh Trail]." Once inside Cambodia, Colonel Starry directed scouts to look inside the shipping crates for bills of lading. Most had the name of a freighter on them, dates of sailing, etc. Starry later talked with a colonel who was the head of the Cambodian Army transportation corps. "In his notebook, he had what they had carried in his trucks ... He had all the cache sites numbered." The Blackhorse staff matched it with the bills of lading, then reported it to higher headquarters. Their response? "That's impossible."

4 Bill Paris relates: "So I go over to his side of the aircraft and I holler his name as I kind of come around the bubble. He screams at me. He was trapped under the wreckage ... The transmission of the aircraft has fallen on him and has him now pinned. So, as I say, he's burning ... "You've got to try and get out." He's saying, "I can't! I can't! I'm on fire! Help me! Help!" You reach a point real quickly where things boil down to what's important. At that particular moment in time I only had two choices here. I can walk away and let him finish burning to death or I can do something about this ... I'm faced with the basic question: are you willing to watch your co-pilot burn alive? Are you willing to watch another human being suffer, what I consider one of the ultimate, worst forms of death? ... I did what I thought I had to do. I took out my .45, which was the only damn thing that stuck with me, and I shot him."

5 Marshall's son, 1LT Jay Marshall, served with 3/11 in Kuwait and Germany 22 years later.

6   In the middle of the fight, the artillery was running low on ammo. The squadron requested an emergency resupply, and the 1st Cav came through, airlifting a full basic load into FSB Ruth in record time.

7   Third Squadron remained in the vicinity of Loc Ninh, just in case the 7th (NVA) Division got any ideas about crossing the border again.

8   Both Blackhorse squadrons on *Fresh Start* had an engineer land clearing company (equipped with 30 Rome Plows each) working with it. A company could clear 100–200 acres of jungle a day.

9   As a major general, Nash commanded the 1st Armored Division in Bosnia in 1995.

10   The Regiment came across a covered but above-ground bicycle factory while inside Cambodia. Starry said: "The bicycles were shipped in parts. Handlebars, wheels, and so forth. And they'd set up a Henry Ford-type assembly thing is this factory and they were putting the bicycles together. Thousands of them. Thousands of them!"

11   Communications intercepts—a so-called "density plot"—served as the primary source for putting the circles on the map where the main headquarters (COSVN) and its subordinate headquarters were thought to be. As noted below, however, COSVN had some warning before the attack and was able to move before the first GIs crossed the border. Four months after the operation started, Lieutenant General (LTG) Michael Davison, acknowledged: "We knew where the COSVN head-quarters was located … Unfortunately, they started moving out the afternoon before we went in there … there is evidence that they had figured out through their own intelligence sources that we were coming, because they moved in a helluva hurry."

12   In his after-action report, the II Field Force intelligence officer concluded that enemy "forces were apparently surprised by the speed of the allied operations across the border."

13   1/11 was initially tasked with protecting the supply line inside South Vietnam supporting the attack.

14   A line drawn on a map—usually on a recognizable terrain feature—used to control the start of an attack.

15   Starry recalled: "Miles Sisson, the tank company commander, great young soldier. He was wounded about the tenth day. That company was fearless … What a great guy. Boy, he was a fearsome company commander."

16   Myllin Henrich was killed in action on 23 June 1970.

17   Donn Starry vividly remembers linking up with the colonel in command of the 3rd (ARVN) Airborne Brigade that went into Fishhook ahead of the 11th Cavalry. In a pre-operation coordi-nation meeting, he told BG Shoemaker, "General I will be on the first lift, first ship." Shoemaker asked if that wasn't a little far forward for the brigade commander. He replied: "General, where I lead, they will follow." Starry met the colonel next in Cambodia. "I met him out in the middle of the jungle. He actually had a bottle of champagne I shared with him to celebrate our link-up. Quite a guy! A good, good unit … He was right on time, right on schedule."

18   MACV estimated that between the several emergency relocations and the loss of 29 tons of captured commo gear, the enemy did not reestablish complete command and control until after September 1970.

19   In its official history, the Corps of Engineers proudly states that "the bridge was completed eight hours after the first engineer troops had arrived by helicopter." These were eight hours that the Blackhorse could not afford to spend waiting on the wrong side of the river.

20   The airstrip was big enough to land C-130 transport aircraft.

21   Monsieur De Bort was the cousin of General Jean Delaunay, an Indochina veteran and later Chief of Staff of the French Army. De Bort and his family left the plantation the following day; he'd had enough 'liberations' for one lifetime. He told a reporter: "I have been liberated four times—first by the Viet Cong, then by the Cambodians, then by the Viet Cong again, and now

by the Americans … There is nothing left for us here." Before he left, however, he cleaned out his pantry. LT Jay Ward recalls: "The next day he sent over a cardboard box loaded with French canned goods and a bottle of Champagne. Brookshire had the goods distributed to the fighting men in the line troops. I never learned what happened to the Champagne but I'm certain someone was very grateful for de Bort's thoughtfulness."

22 1SGT Vernon Nevil "cringed" when he heard Nixon announce that all Americans would be out of Cambodia by the end of June. "It was a blunder to make the announcement to all the world, including the enemy, that on a given day, we would pull back and not attack again … The enemy knew we were leaving and they were still there."

23 Pulitzer Prize winning (1973) *Chicago Tribune* reporter Bill Currie, who accompanied the Regiment into Cambodia, spoke with one tank commander who "was thrilled to see his armored vehicles charging in line thru a rubber plantation guns blazing; bearing down on a retreating enemy. "I expected to see someone waving a saber and blowing a bugle … " For this reporter, himself a combat veteran, the operation—especially around Snuol—"brought back old memories" of World War II."

24 Although the doctors wanted to evacuate Donn Starry to Japan to treat his wounds, he went AWOL from the hospital and returned within days to reassume command of the Regiment. He was replaced in June by Colonel John Gerrity.

25 LTC Jim Reed, the 1/11 commander, compared the experience of entering these caches to "going into a deserted department store."

26 In fact, it took two years—until the so-called Easter Offensive in April 1972—for Hanoi to recoup its losses and mount another offensive. By then, most American ground troops—including the 11th Cavalry—had gone home.

27 Soldiers wear the patch of the unit they served with in combat on the right shoulder of their uniforms.

Chapter 7: Mission Accomplished: November 1970 to March 1972

1 Lieutenant Colonel (LTC) Bill Stokes, the last 2/11 commander in Vietnam, recalls that between 1,500 and 2,000 troopers were assigned to the squadron during its last year in country—well above the authorized strength. Many of the excess personnel were short-timers assigned from units going home. "The additional strength supported base security requirements," according to Stokes—including the squadron rear at Phu Loi, squadron forward at Cu Chi, a fire support base, and one or two night defensive positions.

2 The brigade task force consisted of: 2/5th Cav, 1/7th Cav, 2/8th Cav, 1/12th Cav, 1/21st Artillery; F Battery, 79th Aerial Rocket Artillery; F Troop, 1/9th Cav; D Company, 229th Assault Helicopter Battalion; 501st Engineer Company, 215th Support Battalion, 525th Signal Company, and Headquarters Company, 3rd Brigade.

3 Named for the acting 2/11 Command Sergeant Major, Robert Bolan, killed in action on 28 July 1970.

4 The 60th Land Clearing Company had been operating in Hau Nghia Province for almost two weeks, but was routinely being attacked by company-size units that inflicted heavy casualties and damage to the Rome Plows. The company was hitting an average of 20 mines a day. The company commander and a platoon leader were among the four engineers killed in those two weeks; another 71 were wounded, some more than once.

5 The guns were part of Alpha Battery, 2nd Battalion, 32nd Artillery. As Ballantyne recalls, "for all intents and practical purposes, they belonged to the squadron," providing direct support on call.

6   Second Squadron's border camp along the East-West German border was named for Lee on Memorial Day, 1976.

7   Mike Aguilar was killed in a helicopter crash on 10 May 1972. He had transferred to the 1st Cav Division after 2/11 left country. 'Doc' Balas wears his KIA bracelet to this day.

8   Eighty enemy fighting positions averaging 2'×3'×8' in size were discovered in the triangular complex. The bunkers were connected by underground tunnels that ran five to six feet in length, allowing the defenders to move to whichever side of the triangle that was the most threatened without being seen. Anti-tank mines were strategically placed around the area to impede the advance of any attacking force. In the course of their search, troopers found two large caches containing a dozen RPG rounds, 200 grenades, and 1,000 pounds of rice.

9   The battle around Krek took place at the same time as one other significant event involving the Blackhorse. On 13 October, SSG John Sexton, the only Blackhorse Trooper held as a prisoner of war by the Viet Cong, was released.

10   In 1999, BG Terry Tucker, the 56th Colonel of the Regiment, told the Blackhorse veterans that Forame and Skiles had been located. "For the past 2 years, I have been privileged to command Joint Task Force "Full Accounting" … In January 1998, we investigated the site of a 19 December 1971 OH-6 helicopter crash in central Cambodia. In March 1999, we excavated that crash site. The recovery team did not find remains of the crew. However, they did find several items of personal effects. Found were a military identification card and part of another card with an unidentified sticker on it. The recovery team could clearly identify the photograph and name on the Identification Card, but could not identify the sticker on the second card. Upon my arrival, several possible explanations were offered as to what the sticker might be. After listening to their speculation, I opened my wallet, removed my Blackhorse Association Membership Card, and showed them the exact symbol they were trying to figure out. It was a Blackhorse patch. The crew of that OH-6 was 1LT Peter Forame and WO1 Thomas Skiles, Air Cavalry Troop, 11 ACR, two of the last Blackhorse troopers to die in Southeast Asia … Although we may never recover their remains, we can never forget their sacrifice."

11   Named for SGT Willis Andrews, killed in action on 17 April 1971.

Epilogue: Blackhorse Forever: The Legacy

1   Combined with the 11th Cavalry's two previous tours along the East German and Czech borders in 1946–48 and 1957–64, the Regiment served 31 years as part of America's Border Legion.

2   Motto of the 11th Armored Cavalry Veterans of Vietnam and Cambodia.

3   The members of the 11th ACVVC have donated more than a million dollars in scholarships to the spouses, children, and grandchildren of troopers who served in the Blackhorse in Vietnam.

4   Co-hosted by the BHA.

Appendix 1: History and Patch of the 11th United States Cavalry Regiment

1   First Squadron remained at Ft. Des Moines for a year, then moved to Ft. Ethan Allen.

2   Reserve Officer Training Corps and Citizen's Military Training Corps.

3   The author remembers such signs at Camp Carson, CO, when his father was the Regimental Adjutant in the early 1950s.

4   The members of the Advanced Planning Group were: MAJ Norman, an S-3, Liaison Officer, the S-4, the First and Third Squadron S-2s, the Second Squadron S-3 Air, three Squadron supply

NCOs, and one NCO from HHT, Regiment. If MAJ Kelly's memory is accurate, one or more of these individuals is responsible for coming up with the initial Blackhorse patch design.

5   Regimental guidons at that time were the traditional armor (vice cavalry) colors, yellow with green lettering.

6   Grady Cowan recalls that Casterman showed two drawings to him and his fellow platoon sergeants in June or July 1966. On one, the rearing black horse was set against a yellow background (*a la* the 1st Cav Division), and a red-over-white background on the other. The three experienced Cavalry NCOs all voted for red-over-white: "we don't want no patch with yellow in it."

7   The vehicles probably belonged to Third Squadron's India Troop, crossed-attached with tanks from Mike Company, which was OPCON to the 3rd Brigade, 101st Airborne Division in late January 1968.

8   Bob Kickenweitz has his own story about the Blackhorse patch. "One day my wife and I were out Christmas shopping. I had my 11th Cav hat on, a guy two aisles over spotted my hat and pointed to the hat and said '11th Armored Cavalry?' I said 'yes, were you in the cav?' He said 'no, when I was in Fort Carson we had to study you guys'. I said 'really?' He then said 'you guys were the best'. I said 'thanks,' then turned to my wife and said 'they had to study us, God do I feel old'. She laughed … I'm proud that I was a part of something bigger than myself. I'm proud to be part of the legend, I'm proud I went to Vietnam, and I'm proud to be an American."

9   Troopers who had the good fortune to serve in the Regiment in combat and again in Germany or Ft. Irwin, wore the Blackhorse patch on both sleeves, making them "Blackhorse sandwiches." A new generation of Blackhorse veterans quickly adopted the same "unauthorized" combat patch. As with the original locally-procured Blackhorse patches from Vietnam, HQDA felt obliged to remind Iraq and Afghanistan veterans that such patches were unauthorized. "What are they gonna do, send me to Afghanistan?"

Appendix 3: Blackhorse Medal of Honor Recipients

1   The Vulcan was originally designed as an air defense system. But the success of the twin-forty Dusters and .50-cal. gun trucks in base camp defense and convoy security in Vietnam convinced the Vulcan project manager that his new weapon might play a role in ground defense as well. The vehicles were so new that in lieu of the standard USA numbers on the side, these M163s were simply numbered 1 through 6.

2   Hal returned to the scene of the ambush late on the 11th. Amongst the detritus of that hellacious battle, he found the engraved cigarette lighter that his wife Mary had given him as he went off to war. The lighter was somewhat worse for the wear—carried in the left top pocket of his jungle fatigues, it had deflected an enemy rifle bullet. That bullet had Hal's name on it, but it was apparently misspelled.

Index